Corrective Readi

MW01492111

Thinking Basics

Comprehension A

Siegfried Engelmann • Phyllis Haddox • Susan Hanner • Jean Osborn

**SRA
McGraw-Hill**

Columbus, Ohio

A Division of The **McGraw·Hill** *Companies*

PHOTO CREDITS
Cover Photo: ©David Madison Photography

SRA/McGraw-Hill

A Division of The **McGraw·Hill** *Companies*

2002 Imprint
Copyright © 1999 by SRA/McGraw-Hill.

Send all inquiries to:
SRA/McGraw-Hill
8787 Orion Place
Columbus, OH 43240-4027

Printed in the United States of America.

ISBN 0-02-674797-9

8 9 10 11 12 BCM 08 07 06 05 04

Table of Contents

Please read the **Comprehension A Teacher's Guide** before presenting this program.

Note: Blue bullets (●) indicate the introduction of a new skill or new procedure.

Introduction

Today we're starting a comprehension program. The program will help you understand better what people say and what you read. Each lesson has at least six tasks. You can earn 1 point for each task. Here's how you earn those points:
1. Answer questions out loud with the group.
2. Follow my signals.
3. Answer questions when I call on you.
   If you work extra hard, you can earn bonus points also.

EXERCISE 1

● **SOME, ALL, NONE**
1. My turn to hold up **all** the fingers on one hand. (Hold up all five fingers on one hand.) My turn to hold up **some** of the fingers on one hand. (Hold up two fingers.) My turn to hold up **some** of the fingers on one hand. (Hold up three fingers.) My turn to hold up **none** of the fingers on one hand. (Hold up a fist, no fingers.)
2. Your turn. Hold up **some** of the fingers on one hand. (Signal.) ✔ Hold up **none** of the fingers on one hand. (Signal.) ✔ Hold up **all** the fingers on one hand. (Signal.) ✔ (Repeat step 2 until firm.)
3. Watch me. You'll tell me if I'm holding up **all** of the fingers, **some** of the fingers, or **none** of the fingers on my hand.
   (Hold up a fist, no fingers.) Everybody, am I holding up **all, some,** or **none?** (Signal.) *None.*
   (Hold up two fingers.) Am I holding up **all, some,** or **none?** (Signal.) *Some.*
   (Hold up all five fingers on one hand.) Am I holding up **all, some,** or **none?** (Signal.) *All.*

(Hold up four fingers.) Am I holding up **all, some,** or **none?** (Signal.) *Some.*
(Repeat step 3 until firm.)

Points
(Pass out the Workbooks. Make sure that each student has a pencil.)
Everybody, open your Workbook to Lesson A. ✔

You're going to record your points for the task we just did. Remember, you earn 1 point for each task by answering the questions out loud with the group, following my signals, and answering questions when I call on you.
Here are the names of the students who earned 1 point for this task. (List the names of students who earned 1 point.)
If I didn't say your name, you didn't earn a point for this task, but you can still earn points for the rest of the tasks in the lesson. Record your points in Box 1 at the top of your Workbook page. (Check and correct.)

EXERCISE 2

● **DEDUCTIONS**
1. Everybody, touch the blue A in your Workbook. ✔

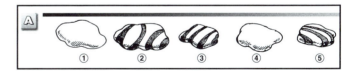

Here's a rule about the things in the picture. Listen. **All the striped things are glerps.** Everybody, say that rule. (Signal.) *All the striped things are glerps.* (Repeat the rule until firm.)
That rule tells you about some of the objects in part A.
2. Everybody, look at the numbers under the objects. Touch object 1. ✔ Does the rule tell about that object? (Signal.) *No.* (Call on a student.) Why not? Idea: Because it's not striped.

3. Everybody, touch object 2. ✔ Does the rule tell about that object? (Signal.) *Yes.* (Call on a student.) How do you know? Idea: Because it's striped.

4. Everybody, touch object 3. ✔ Does the rule tell about that object? (Signal.) *Yes.* (Call on a student.) How do you know? Idea: Because it's striped.

5. Listen. **All the striped things are glerps.** Everybody, say that rule again. (Signal.) *All the striped things are glerps.*

6. Your turn. **Circle** all the things the rule tells about. (Wait.)

7. (Call on a student.) Read the number of each object you circled. *2, 3, 5.* Everybody, mark your answer with an X if it's wrong. (Wait.)

Points

Everybody, you're going to record your points for the task we just did. Here are the names of the students who earned 1 point for this task. (List the names of students who earned 1 point.)

Record your points in Box 1 at the top of your Workbook page. (Check and correct.)

=========== EXERCISE 3 ===========

● **MAKING UP STATEMENTS**

1. Everybody, touch the green B in your Workbook. ✔

One dog in the picture is black, one dog is white, and one dog is spotted. You're going to make up statements about the dogs.

2. Everybody, touch the black dog. ✔ What is the black dog carrying? (Signal.) *A book.* My turn to say the statement about (pause) the black dog. **The black dog is carrying a book.** Everybody, say that statement. (Signal.) *The black dog is carrying a book.* (Repeat the statement until firm.)

3. Everybody, touch the white dog. ✔ What is the white dog carrying? (Signal.) *A shoe.* Say the statement about (pause) **the white dog.** (Pause.) Get ready. (Signal.) *The white dog is carrying a shoe.* (Repeat the statement until firm.)

4. Everybody, touch the spotted dog. ✔ What is the spotted dog carrying? (Signal.) *A doll.* Say the statement about (pause) **the spotted dog.** (Pause.) Get ready. (Signal.) *The spotted dog is carrying a doll.* (Repeat the statement until firm.)

5. Let's do those statements once more. Everybody, say the statement about (pause) **the black dog.** (Pause.) Get ready. (Signal.) *The black dog is carrying a book.* Say the statement about (pause) **the white dog.** (Pause.) Get ready. (Signal.) *The white dog is carrying a shoe.* Say the statement about (pause) **the spotted dog.** (Pause.) Get ready. (Signal.) *The spotted dog is carrying a doll.* (Repeat step 5 until firm.)

Individual test

Call on individual students to do one of the tasks in step 5.

Points

Everybody, you're going to record your points for the task we just did. Here are the names of the students who earned 1 point for this task. (List the names of students who earned 1 point.)

Record your points in Box 1 at the top of your Workbook page. (Check and correct.)

══════ EXERCISE 4 ══════

- **SAME/DIFFERENT**
1. Everybody, touch the orange C in your Workbook. ✔

  Touch object 1 and object 2. ✔ Keep touching them. Those objects are the same in some way. My turn. How are they the same? They are triangles.
2. Your turn. How are objects 1 and 2 the same? (Signal.) *They are triangles.*
3. Touch object 1 and object 3. 1 and 3. ✔ Keep touching them. Those objects are the same in some way. Everybody, how are objects 1 and 3 the same? (Signal.) *They are striped.*
   To correct students who say *They are both striped:*
   a. They **are** striped.
   b. How are objects 1 and 3 the same? (Signal.) *They are striped.*
4. Touch object 2 and object 4. ✔ Keep touching them. Those objects are the same in some way. Everybody, how are objects 2 and 4 the same? (Signal.) *They are black.*
5. Touch object 3 and object 4. ✔ Keep touching them. Those objects are the same in some way. Everybody, how are objects 3 and 4 the same? (Signal.) *They are circles.*
6. (Repeat steps 2–5 until firm.)

7. Everybody, touch object 2. ✔ (Call on a student.) Name an object that is the same as object 2. Responses: Object 1, object 4. Everybody, tell how those objects are the same. (Pause.) Get ready. (Signal.) *They are ____.*
8. (Call on a student.) Name another object that is the same as object 2. Response. Everybody, tell how those objects are the same. (Pause.) Get ready. (Signal.) *They are ____.*
9. Everybody, touch object 3. ✔ (Call on a student.) Name an object that is the same as object 3. Responses: Object 1, object 4. Everybody, tell how those objects are the same. (Pause.) Get ready. (Signal.) *They are ____.*
10. (Call on a student.) Name another object that is the same as object 3. Response. Everybody, tell how those objects are the same. (Pause.) Get ready. (Signal.) *They are ____.*

Points

Everybody, you're going to record your points for the task we just did. Here are the names of the students who earned 1 point for this task. (List the names of students who earned 1 point.)
Record your points in Box 1 at the top of your Workbook page. (Check and correct.)

━━━━━━━━━ **EXERCISE 5** ━━━━━━━━━

● **DEDUCTIONS**

1. Everybody, touch the red D in your Workbook. ✔ You're going to learn how to make a deduction about those pictures. You'll say three statements, one statement for each picture.

2. Touch picture 1. ✔ I'll say the statement for that picture. Listen. **All dogs bark.** Say it. (Signal.) *All dogs bark.* (Repeat the statement until firm.)

3. Touch picture 2. ✔ Here's the statement. **Fido is a dog.** Say it. (Signal.) *Fido is a dog.* (Repeat the statement until firm.)

4. Touch picture 3. ✔ Here's the statement. **So, Fido barks.** Say it. (Signal.) *So, Fido barks.* (Repeat the statement until firm.)

5. I'll say all three statements. You touch the pictures, starting with picture 1. **All dogs bark.** ✔ **Fido is a dog.** ✔ **So, Fido barks.** ✔

6. Your turn. Touch picture 1 and say the statement. (Signal.) *All dogs bark.*
   Picture 2. (Signal.) *Fido is a dog.*
   Picture 3. (Signal.) *So, Fido barks.*
   (Repeat step 6 until firm.)

7. I'm going to start with the statement about **all dogs** and say the statements without looking at the pictures and then you'll say them. Listen. **All dogs bark. Fido is a dog. So, Fido barks.** Listen again. **All dogs bark. Fido is a dog. So, Fido barks.** Your turn. Say the statements. (Signal.) *All dogs bark. Fido is a dog. So, Fido barks.* (Repeat the statements until firm.)

> **Individual test**
> (Call on individual students.)
> Say the statements.

Points

Everybody, you're going to record your points for the task we just did. Here are the names of the students who earned 1 point for this task. (List the names of students who earned 1 point.)

Record your points in Box 1 at the top of your Workbook page. (Check and correct.)

━━━━━━━━━ **EXERCISE 6** ━━━━━━━━━

MAKING UP STATEMENTS

1. Everybody, touch the purple E in your Workbook. ✔

One boy in the picture is on the porch, one boy is on the stairs, and one boy is on the sidewalk. You're going to make up statements about the boys.

2. Everybody, touch the boy who's on the stairs. ✔
   Touch the boy who's on the porch. ✔ What is the boy on the porch doing? (Signal.) *Watching TV.*
   My turn to say the statement about (pause) the boy on the porch. **The boy on the porch is watching TV.** Everybody, say that statement. (Signal.) *The boy on the porch is watching TV.* (Repeat the statement until firm.)

3. Everybody, touch the boy on the stairs. ✔ What is the boy on the stairs doing? (Signal.) *Reading a book.*
   Say the statement about (pause) **the boy on the stairs.** (Pause.) Get ready. (Signal.) *The boy on the stairs is reading a book.* (Repeat until firm.)

4. Everybody, touch the boy who's on the sidewalk. ✔ What is the boy on the sidewalk doing? (Signal.) *Eating a sandwich.*
Say the statement about (pause) **the boy on the sidewalk.** (Pause.) Get ready. (Signal.) *The boy on the sidewalk is eating a sandwich.* (Repeat until firm.)

5. Let's do those statements once more. Everybody, say the statement about (pause) **the boy on the porch.** (Pause.) Get ready. (Signal.) *The boy on the porch is watching TV.*
Say the statement about (pause) **the boy on the stairs.** (Pause.) Get ready. (Signal.) *The boy on the stairs is reading a book.*
Say the statement about (pause) **the boy on the sidewalk.** (Pause.) Get ready. (Signal.) *The boy on the sidewalk is eating a sandwich.*
(Repeat step 5 until firm.)

> ***Individual test***
> Call on individual students to do one of the tasks in step 5.

Points

Everybody, you're going to record your points for the task we just did. Here are the names of the students who earned 1 point for this task. (List the names of students who earned 1 point.)
Record your points in Box 1 at the top of your Workbook page. (Check and correct.)

(Award a maximum of 3 bonus points to students who worked extra hard during the lesson.) Record your bonus points in Box 2 at the top of your Workbook page. (Check and correct.)

Everybody, add up your points for the whole lesson. Write the total in the total box. (Check and correct.)

Point Summary Chart

Now look at the inside front cover of your Workbook. You will enter your total points for each lesson on this chart. Write your total points for Lesson A in the box marked Lesson A. (Check and correct.)

Point Schedule for Lesson A

Box	Maximum Points
1. [maximum = 1 point for each exercise, Exercises 1–6]	6
2. [maximum = 3 bonus points]	(3)

END OF LESSON A

Introduction

Remember, you can earn 1 point for each task. Here's how you earn those points:

1. Answer questions out loud with the group.
2. Follow my signals.
3. Answer questions when I call on you. If you work extra hard, you can earn bonus points also.

EXERCISE 1

- **SOME, ALL, NONE**

1. Your turn. Hold up **none** of the fingers on one hand. (Signal.) ✔ Hold up **all** of the fingers on one hand. (Signal.) ✔ Hold up **some** of the fingers on one hand. (Signal.) ✔ (Repeat step 1 until firm.)

2. Watch me. You'll tell me if I'm holding up **all** of the fingers, **some** of the fingers, or **none** of the fingers on my hand. (Hold up two fingers.) Everybody, am I holding up **all, some,** or **none?** (Signal.) *Some.*
(Hold up a fist, no fingers.) Am I holding up **all, some,** or **none?** (Signal.) *None.*
(Hold up all five fingers on one hand.) Am I holding up **all, some,** or **none?** (Signal.) *All.*
(Hold up three fingers.) Am I holding up **all, some,** or **none?** (Signal.) *Some.*
(Repeat step 2 until firm.)

Points

(Pass out the Workbooks. Make sure that each student has a pencil.)

Everybody, open your Workbook to Lesson B. ✔ You're going to record your points for the task we just did. Remember, you earn 1 point for each task by answering the questions out loud with the group, following my signals, and answering questions when I call on you.

Here are the names of the students who earned 1 point for this task. (List the names of students who earned 1 point.)

If I didn't say your name, you didn't earn a point for this task, but you can still earn points for the rest of the tasks in the lesson. Record your points in Box 1 at the top of your Workbook page. (Check and correct.)

EXERCISE 2

MAKING UP STATEMENTS

1. Everybody, touch part A in your Workbook. ✔

One box in the picture is striped, one box is black, and one box is spotted. You're going to make up statements about the boxes.

2. Everybody, touch the box that is striped. ✔ What does the striped box have in it? (Signal.) *A monkey.*
My turn to say the statement about (pause) the striped box. **The striped box has a monkey in it.** Everybody, say that statement. (Signal.) *The striped box has a monkey in it.* (Repeat until firm.)

3. Everybody, touch the black box. ✔ What does the black box have in it? (Signal.) *A dog.*
Say the statement about (pause) **the black box.** (Pause.) Get ready. (Signal.) *The black box has a dog in it.* (Repeat until firm.)

4. Everybody, touch the spotted box. ✔ What does the spotted box have in it? (Signal.) *A cat.*
Say the statement about (pause) **the spotted box.** (Pause.) Get ready. (Signal.) *The spotted box has a cat in it.* (Repeat until firm.)

5. Let's do those statements once more. Everybody, say the statement about (pause) **the striped box.** (Pause.) Get ready. (Signal.) *The striped box has a monkey in it.*
Say the statement about (pause) **the black box.** (Pause.) Get ready. (Signal.) *The black box has a dog in it.*
Say the statement about (pause) **the spotted box.** (Pause.) Get ready. (Signal.) *The spotted box has a cat in it.*
(Repeat step 5 until firm.)

> **Individual test**
> Call on individual students to do one of the tasks in step 5.

Points

Everybody, you're going to record your points for the task we just did. Here are the names of the students who earned 1 point for this task. (List the names of students who earned 1 point.)

Record your points in Box 1 at the top of your Workbook page. (Check and correct.)

EXERCISE 3

DEDUCTIONS

1. Everybody, touch part B. ✔

 Here's a rule about the things in the picture. Listen. **All the small birds fly.** Everybody, say that rule. (Signal.) *All the small birds fly.* (Repeat until firm.)
 That rule tells about some of the objects in part B.
2. Everybody, touch object 1. ✔ Does the rule tell about that object? (Signal.) *Yes.* (Call on a student.) How do you know? Idea: Because it's small.
3. Everybody, touch object 2. ✔ Does the rule tell about that object? (Signal.) *No.* (Call on a student.) Why not? Idea: Because it's not small.
4. Everybody, touch object 3. ✔ Does the rule tell about that object? (Signal.) *No.* (Call on a student.) Why not? Idea: Because it's not small.
5. Listen. **All the small birds fly.** Everybody, say that rule again. (Signal.) *All the small birds fly.*

6. Your turn. **Underline** all the things the rule tells about. (Wait.)
7. (Call on a student.) Read the number of each object you underlined. *1, 4, 5.*
 Everybody, mark your answer with an **X** if it's wrong. (Wait.)

Points

Everybody, you're going to record your points for the task we just did. Here are the names of the students who earned 1 point for this task. (List the names of students who earned 1 point.)

Record your points in Box 1 at the top of your Workbook page. (Check and correct.)

EXERCISE 4

DEDUCTIONS

1. Everybody, touch part C. ✔ You're going to learn how to make a deduction about those pictures. You'll say three statements, one statement for each picture.

2. Touch picture 1. ✔ I'll say the statement for that picture. Listen. **All dogs bark.** Say it. (Signal.) *All dogs bark.* (Repeat until firm.)
3. Touch picture 2. ✔ Here's the statement. **Fido is a dog.** Say it. (Signal.) *Fido is a dog.* (Repeat until firm.)
4. Touch picture 3. ✔ Here's the statement. **So, Fido barks.** Say it. (Signal.) *So, Fido barks.* (Repeat until firm.)
5. I'll say all three statements. You touch the pictures, starting with picture 1. **All dogs bark.** ✔ **Fido is a dog.** ✔ **So, Fido barks.** ✔
6. Your turn. Touch picture 1 and say the statement. (Signal.) *All dogs bark.*
 Picture 2. (Signal.) *Fido is a dog.*
 Picture 3. (Signal.) *So, Fido barks.*
 (Repeat step 6 until firm.)

7. I'm going to start with the statement about **all dogs** and say the statements without looking at the pictures, and then you'll say them. Listen. **All dogs bark. Fido is a dog. So, Fido barks.** Listen again. **All dogs bark. Fido is a dog. So, Fido barks.** Your turn. Say the statements. (Signal.) *All dogs bark. Fido is a dog. So, Fido barks.* (Repeat until firm.)

> **Individual test**
> (Call on individual students.)
> Say the statements.

Points

Everybody, you're going to record your points for the task we just did. Here are the names of the students who earned 1 point for this task. (List the names of students who earned 1 point.) Record your points in Box 1 at the top of your Workbook page. (Check and correct.)

EXERCISE 5

SAME/DIFFERENT

1. Everybody, touch part D. Touch object 1 and object 3. ✔ Keep touching them. Those objects are the same in some way. My turn. How are they the same? They are squares.

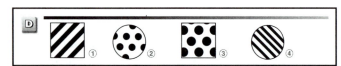

2. Your turn. How are objects 1 and 3 the same? (Signal.) *They are squares.*
3. Touch object 1 and object 4. 1 and 4. ✔ Keep touching them. Those objects are the same in some way. Everybody, how are objects 1 and 4 the same? (Signal.) *They are striped.*

   To correct students who say *They are both striped:*
   a. They **are** striped.
   b. How are objects 1 and 4 the same? (Signal.) *They are striped.*

4. Touch object 2 and object 4. ✔ Keep touching them. Those objects are the same in some way. Everybody, how are objects 2 and 4 the same? (Signal.) *They are circles.*
5. Touch object 2 and object 3. ✔ Keep touching them. Those objects are the same in some way. Everybody, how are objects 2 and 3 the same? (Signal.) *They are spotted.*
6. (Repeat steps 2–5 until firm.)
7. Everybody, touch object 3. ✔ (Call on a student.) Name an object that is the same as object 3. Responses: Object 1, object 2. Everybody, tell how those objects are the same. (Pause.) Get ready. (Signal.) *They are*

   ____.

8. (Call on a student.) Name another object that is the same as object 3. Response. Everybody, tell how those objects are the same. (Pause.) Get ready. (Signal.) *They are* ____.
9. Everybody, touch object 4. ✔ (Call on a student.) Name an object that is the same as object 4. Responses: Object 1, object 2. Everybody, tell how those objects are the same. (Pause.) Get ready. (Signal.) *They are* ____.
10. (Call on a student.) Name another object that is the same as object 4. Response. Everybody, tell how those objects are the same. (Pause.) Get ready. (Signal.) *They are* ____.

Points

Everybody, you're going to record your points for the task we just did. Here are the names of the students who earned 1 point for this task. (List the names of students who earned 1 point.) Record your points in Box 1 at the top of your Workbook page. (Check and correct.)

EXERCISE 6

DEDUCTIONS

1. Everybody, touch part E. ✔ You're going to make a deduction about those pictures. You'll say three statements, one statement for each picture.

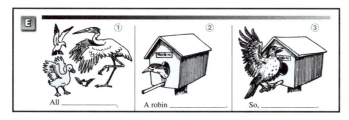

2. Touch picture 1. ✔ I'll say the statement for that picture. Listen. **All birds have wings. Say it.** (Signal.) *All birds have wings.* (Repeat until firm.)

3. Touch picture 2. ✔ Here's the statement. **A robin is a bird. Say it.** (Signal.) *A robin is a bird.* (Repeat until firm.)

4. Touch picture 3. ✔ Here's the statement. **So, a robin has wings. Say it.** (Signal.) *So, a robin has wings.* (Repeat until firm.)

5. I'll say all three statements. You touch the pictures, starting with picture 1. **All birds have wings. ✔ A robin is a bird. ✔ So, a robin has wings. ✔**

6. Your turn. Touch picture 1 and say the statement. (Signal.) *All birds have wings.* Picture 2. (Signal.) *A robin is a bird.* Picture 3. (Signal.) *So, a robin has wings.* (Repeat step 6 until firm.)

7. I'm going to start with the statement about **all birds** and say the statements without looking at the pictures, and then you'll say them. Listen. **All birds have wings. A robin is a bird. So, a robin has wings.** Listen again. **All birds have wings. A robin is a bird. So, a robin has wings.** Your turn. Say the statements. (Signal.) *All birds have wings. A robin is a bird. So, a robin has wings.* (Repeat until firm.)

Individual test
(Call on individual students.)
Say the statements.

Points

Everybody, you're going to record your points for the task we just did. Here are the names of the students who earned 1 point for this task. (List the names of students who earned 1 point)
Record your points in Box 1 at the top of your Workbook page. (Check and correct.)

EXERCISE 7

MAKING UP STATEMENTS

1. Everybody, touch part F. ✔ One boat in the picture has a sail, one boat has a motor, and one boat has oars. You're going to make up statements about the boats.

2. Everybody, touch the boat that has oars. ✔ Touch the boat that has a sail. ✔ What does the boat with a sail have in it? (Signal.) *A dog.* My turn to say the statement about (pause) the boat with a sail. **The boat with a sail has a dog in it.** Everybody, say that statement. (Signal.) *The boat with a sail has a dog in it.* (Repeat until firm.)

3. Everybody, touch the boat that has a motor. ✔ What does the boat with a motor have in it? (Signal.) *A bear.*
Say the statement about (pause) **the boat with a motor.** (Pause.) Get ready. (Signal.) *The boat with a motor has a bear in it.* (Repeat until firm.)

4. Everybody, touch the boat that has oars. ✔ What does the boat with oars have in it? (Signal.) *A tree.*
Say the statement about (pause) **the boat with oars.** (Pause.) Get ready. (Signal.) *The boat with oars has a tree in it.* (Repeat until firm.)

5. Let's do those statements once more.
Everybody, say the statement about (pause)
the boat with a sail. (Pause.) Get ready.
(Signal.) *The boat with a sail has a dog in it.*
Say the statement about (pause) **the boat
with a motor.** (Pause.) Get ready. (Signal.)
The boat with a motor has a bear in it.
Say the statement about (pause) **the boat
with oars.** (Pause.) Get ready. (Signal.) *The
boat with oars has a tree in it.*
(Repeat step 5 until firm.)

Individual test
Call on individual students to do one of the
tasks in step 5.

Points

Everybody, you're going to record your points
for the task we just did. Here are the names of
the students who earned 1 point for this task.
(List the names of students who earned
1 point.)
Record your points in Box 1 at the top of your
Workbook page. (Check and correct.)

========= **EXERCISE 8** =========

● **DEDUCTIONS**
1. I'll say a deduction you've done before. Then
you'll say it.
2. Listen. **All birds have wings. A robin is a
bird. So, a robin has wings.**
3. Your turn. Say the whole deduction. (Signal.)
*All birds have wings. A robin is a bird. So, a
robin has wings.* (Repeat until firm.)

Individual test
(Call on individual students.)
Say the whole deduction.

Points

Everybody, you're going to record your points
for the task we just did. Here are the names of
the students who earned 1 point for this task.
(List the names of students who earned
1 point.)

Record your points in Box 1 at the top of your
Workbook page. (Check and correct.)

(Award a maximum of 3 bonus points to
students who worked extra hard during the
lesson.) Record your bonus points in Box 2 at
the top of your Workbook page. (Check and
correct.)

Everybody, add up your points for the whole
lesson. Write the total in the total box. (Check
and correct.)

Point Summary Chart

Now look at the inside front cover of your
Workbook. You will enter your total points for
each lesson on this chart. Write your total points
for Lesson B in the box marked Lesson B.
(Check and correct.)

Point Schedule for Lesson B

Box	Maximum Points
1. [maximum = 1 point for each exercise, Exercises 1–8]	8
2. [maximum = 3 bonus points]	(3)

END OF LESSON B

Introduction

Remember, you can earn 1 point for each task. Here's how you earn those points:

1. Answer questions out loud with the group.
2. Follow my signals.
3. Answer questions when I call on you. If you work extra hard, you can earn bonus points also.

━━━ EXERCISE 1 ━━━

DEDUCTIONS

1. I'll say a deduction you've done before. Then you'll say it.
2. Listen. **All dogs bark. Fido is a dog. So, Fido barks.**
3. Your turn. Say the whole deduction. (Signal.) *All dogs bark. Fido is a dog. So, Fido barks.* (Repeat until firm.)

> ***Individual test***
> (Call on individual students.)
> Say the whole deduction.

Points

(Pass out the Workbooks. Make sure that each student has a pencil.)

Everybody, open your Workbook to Lesson C. You're going to record your points for the task we just did. Here are the names of the students who earned 1 point for this task.

(List the names of students who earned 1 point.)

Record your points in Box 1 at the top of your Workbook page. (Check and correct.)

━━━ EXERCISE 2 ━━━

SOME, ALL, NONE

1. Your turn. Hold up **some** of the fingers on one hand. (Signal.) ✔ Hold up **all** of the fingers on one hand. (Signal.) ✔ Hold up **none** of the fingers on one hand. (Signal.) ✔ (Repeat step 1 until firm.)
2. Watch me. You'll tell me if I'm holding up **all** of the fingers, **some** of the fingers, or **none** of the fingers on my hand. (Hold up all five fingers on one hand.) Everybody, am I holding up **all, some,** or **none?** (Signal.) *All.* (Hold up a fist, no fingers.) Am I holding up **all, some,** or **none?** (Signal.) *None.* (Hold up three fingers.) Am I holding up **all, some,** or **none?** (Signal.) *Some.* (Hold up four fingers.) Am I holding up **all, some,** or **none?** (Signal.) *Some.* (Repeat step 2 until firm.)

Points

Everybody, you're going to record your points for the task we just did. Here are the names of the students who earned 1 point for this task.

(List the names of students who earned 1 point.)

Record your points in Box 1 at the top of your Workbook page. (Check and correct.)

━━━ EXERCISE 3 ━━━

DEDUCTIONS

1. I'll say a deduction you've done before. Then you'll say it.
2. Listen. **All birds have wings. A robin is a bird. So, a robin has wings.**
3. Your turn. Say the whole deduction. (Signal.) *All birds have wings. A robin is a bird. So, a robin has wings.* (Repeat until firm.)

> ***Individual test***
> (Call on individual students.)
> Say the whole deduction.

Points

Everybody, you're going to record your points for the task we just did. Here are the names of the students who earned 1 point for this task.

(List the names of students who earned 1 point.)

Record your points in Box 1 at the top of your Workbook page. (Check and correct.)

LESSON C

═══ EXERCISE 4 ═══

MAKING UP STATEMENTS

1. Everybody, touch part A in your Workbook. ✔ One dog in the picture is spotted, one dog is black, and one dog is white. You're going to make up statements about the dogs.

2. Everybody, touch the spotted dog. ✔ What is the spotted dog doing? (Signal.) *Running.* My turn to say the statement about (pause) the spotted dog. **The spotted dog is running.** Everybody, say that statement. (Signal.) *The spotted dog is running.* (Repeat until firm.)

3. Everybody, touch the black dog. ✔ What is the black dog doing? (Signal.) *Sitting.* Say the statement about (pause) **the black dog.** (Pause.) Get ready. (Signal.) *The black dog is sitting.* (Repeat until firm.)

4. Everybody, touch the white dog. ✔ What is the white dog doing? (Signal.) *Jumping.* Say the statement about (pause) **the white dog.** (Pause.) Get ready. (Signal.) *The white dog is jumping.* (Repeat until firm.)

5. Let's do those statements again. Say the statement about (pause) **the spotted dog.** (Pause.) Get ready. (Signal.) *The spotted dog is running.* Say the statement about (pause) **the black dog.** (Pause.) Get ready. (Signal.) *The black dog is sitting.* Say the statement about (pause) **the white dog.** (Pause.) Get ready. (Signal.) *The white dog is jumping.* (Repeat step 5 until firm.)

> **Individual test**
> Call on individual students to do one of the tasks in step 5.

Points

Everybody, you're going to record your points for the task we just did. Here are the names of the students who earned 1 point for this task.

(List the names of students who earned 1 point.)

Record your points in Box 1 at the top of your Workbook page. (Check and correct.)

═══ EXERCISE 5 ═══

DEDUCTIONS

1. Everybody, touch part B. ✔ Here's a rule about the things in the picture. Listen. **All the cats have long tails.** Everybody, say that rule. (Signal.) *All the cats have long tails.* (Repeat until firm.)
   That rule tells about some of the objects in part B.

2. Everybody, touch object 1. ✔ Does the rule tell about that object? (Signal.) *Yes.* (Call on a student.) How do you know? Idea: Because it's a cat.

3. Everybody, touch object 2. ✔ Does the rule tell about that object? (Signal.) *No.* (Call on a student.) Why not? Idea: Because it's not a cat.

4. Everybody, touch object 3. ✔ Does the rule tell about that object? (Signal.) *Yes.* (Call on a student.) How do you know? Idea: Because it's a cat.

5. Listen. **All the cats have long tails.** Everybody, say that rule again. (Signal.) *All the cats have long tails.*

6. Your turn. **Make a box around** all the things the rule tells about. (Wait.)

7. (Call on a student.) Read the number of each object you made a box around. *1, 3, 4.* Everybody, mark your answer with an **X** if it's wrong. (Wait.)

Points

Everybody, you're going to record your points for the task we just did. Here are the names of the students who earned 1 point for this task.

(List the names of students who earned 1 point.)

Record your points in Box 1 at the top of your Workbook page. (Check and correct.)

EXERCISE 6

● **SAME/DIFFERENT**

1. Everybody, touch part C. ✔

2. Touch object 3 and object 4. ✔ Those objects are the same in some way. Everybody, how are they the same? (Signal.) *They are cats.*

3. Touch object 1 and object 3. 1 and 3. ✔ Those objects are the same in some way. Everybody, how are objects 1 and 3 the same? (Signal.) *They are black.*

4. Touch object 2 and object 4. ✔ Those objects are the same in some way. Everybody, how are objects 2 and 4 the same? (Signal.) *They are spotted.*

5. Touch object 1 and object 2. ✔ Those objects are the same in some way. Everybody, how are objects 1 and 2 the same? (Signal.) *They are dogs.*

6. (Repeat steps 2–5 until firm.)

7. Everybody, touch object 1. ✔ (Call on a student.) Name an object that is the same as object 1. Responses: Object 2, object 3. Everybody, tell how those objects are the same. (Pause.) Get ready. (Signal.) *They are ____.*

8. (Call on a student.) Name another object that is the same as object 1. Response. Everybody, tell how those objects are the same. (Pause.) Get ready. (Signal.) *They are ____.*

9. Everybody, touch object 3. ✔ (Call on a student.) Name an object that is the same as object 3. Responses: Object 1, object 4. Everybody, tell how those objects are the same. (Pause.) Get ready. (Signal.) *They are ____.*

10. (Call on a student.) Name another object that is the same as object 3. Response. Everybody, tell how those objects are the same. (Pause.) Get ready. (Signal.) *They are ____.*

Points

Everybody, you're going to record your points for the task we just did. Here are the names of the students who earned 1 point for this task. (List the names of students who earned 1 point.)

Record your points in Box 1 at the top of your Workbook page. (Check and correct.)

EXERCISE 7

DEDUCTIONS

1. Everybody, touch part D. ✔ You're going to make a deduction about those pictures. You'll say three statements, one statement for each picture.

2. Touch picture 1. ✔ I'll say the statement for that picture. Listen. **All cats have teeth.** Say it. (Signal.) *All cats have teeth.* (Repeat until firm.)

3. Touch picture 2. ✔ Here's the statement. **Tom is a cat.** Say it. (Signal.) *Tom is a cat.* (Repeat until firm.)

4. Touch picture 3. ✔ Here's the statement. **So, Tom has teeth.** Say it. (Signal.) *So, Tom has teeth.* (Repeat until firm.)

5. I'll say all three statements. You touch the pictures, starting with picture 1. **All cats have teeth.** ✔ **Tom is a cat.** ✔ **So, Tom has teeth.** ✔

6. Your turn. Touch picture 1 and say the statement. (Signal.) *All cats have teeth.*
Picture 2. (Signal.) *Tom is a cat.*
Picture 3. (Signal.) *So, Tom has teeth.*
(Repeat step 6 until firm.)

7. I'm going to start with the statement about **all cats** and say the statements without looking at the pictures, and then you'll say them. Listen. **All cats have teeth. Tom is a cat. So, Tom has teeth.** Listen again. **All cats have teeth. Tom is a cat. So, Tom has teeth.** Your turn. Say the statements. (Signal.) *All cats have teeth. Tom is a cat. So, Tom has teeth.* (Repeat until firm.)

Individual test
(Call on individual students.)
Say the statements.

Points

Everybody, you're going to record your points for the task we just did. Here are the names of the students who earned 1 point for this task. (List the names of students who earned 1 point.)

Record your points in Box 1 at the top of your Workbook page. (Check and correct.)

━━━━━━━ EXERCISE 8 ━━━━━━━

MAKING UP STATEMENTS

1. Everybody, touch part E. ✔ One boy in the picture is wearing a striped shirt, one boy is wearing a spotted shirt, and one boy is wearing a black shirt. You're going to make up statements about the boys.

2. Everybody, touch the boy wearing a striped shirt. ✔ What is the boy wearing a striped shirt holding? (Signal.) *A ball.*
My turn to say the statement about (pause) the boy wearing a striped shirt. **The boy wearing a striped shirt is holding a ball.**
Everybody, say that statement. (Signal.) *The boy wearing a striped shirt is holding a ball.* (Repeat until firm.)

3. Everybody, touch the boy wearing a spotted shirt. ✔ What is the boy wearing a spotted shirt holding? (Signal.) *A radio.*
Say the statement about (pause) **the boy wearing a spotted shirt.** (Pause.) Get ready. (Signal.) *The boy wearing a spotted shirt is holding a radio.* (Repeat until firm.)

4. Everybody, touch the boy wearing a black shirt. ✔ What is the boy wearing a black shirt holding? (Signal.) *A dog.*
Say the statement about (pause) **the boy wearing a black shirt.** (Pause.) Get ready. (Signal.) *The boy wearing a black shirt is holding a dog.* (Repeat until firm.)

5. Let's do those statements once more. Everybody, say the statement about (pause) **the boy wearing a striped shirt.** (Pause.) Get ready. (Signal.) *The boy wearing a striped shirt is holding a ball.*
Say the statement about (pause) **the boy wearing a spotted shirt.** (Pause.) Get ready. (Signal.) *The boy wearing a spotted shirt is holding a radio.*
Say the statement about (pause) **the boy wearing a black shirt.** (Pause.) Get ready. (Signal.) *The boy wearing a black shirt is holding a dog.*
(Repeat step 5 until firm.)

Individual test
Call on individual students to do one of the tasks in step 5.

Points

Everybody, you're going to record your points for the task we just did. Here are the names of the students who earned 1 point for this task. (List the names of students who earned 1 point.)

Record your points in Box 1 at the top of your Workbook page. (Check and correct.)

EXERCISE 9

- **DEDUCTIONS**

1. Everybody, touch part F. ✔ I'll say rules. Some of the rules do not tell about all the pictures in part F.

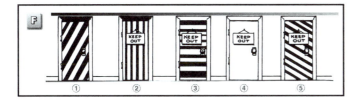

2. Listen. **All the doors have handles.** Everybody, say that rule. (Signal.) *All the doors have handles.* (Repeat until firm.) That rule does not tell about all the pictures because door 2 does not have a handle. Everybody, touch that door. ✔

3. Listen. **All the doors have handles.** Say that rule. (Signal.) *All the doors have handles.* (Call on a student.) Why doesn't that rule tell about all the pictures? Idea: Because door 2 does not have a handle.

4. New rule. Listen. **All the doors have stripes.** Everybody, say that rule. (Signal.) *All the doors have stripes.* (Repeat until firm.) Does that rule tell about all the pictures? (Signal.) *No.* Everybody, touch the door that doesn't follow the rule. ✔

5. Listen. All the doors have stripes. (Call on a student.) Why doesn't that rule tell about all the pictures? Idea: Because door 4 does not have stripes.

6. New rule. Listen. **All the doors are closed.** Everybody, say that rule. (Signal.) *All the doors are closed.* (Repeat until firm.) Does that rule tell about all the pictures? (Signal.) *Yes.* Everybody, say the rule that tells about all the doors. (Signal.) *All the doors are closed.*

7. New rule. Listen. **All the doors have signs.** Everybody, say that rule. (Signal.) *All the doors have signs.* (Repeat until firm.) Does that rule tell about all the pictures? (Signal.) *No.* Everybody, touch the door that doesn't follow the rule. ✔

8. Listen. All the doors have signs. (Call on a student.) Why doesn't that rule tell about all the pictures? Idea: Because door 1 doesn't have a sign.

> ***Individual test***
> (Call on individual students.)
> Say a rule that tells about all the doors.

Points

Everybody, you're going to record your points for the task we just did. Here are the names of the students who earned 1 point for this task. (List the names of students who earned 1 point.)

Record your points in Box 1 at the top of your Workbook page. (Check and correct.)

(Award a maximum of 3 bonus points to students who worked extra hard during the lesson.) Record your bonus points in Box 2 at the top of your Workbook page. (Check and correct.)

Everybody, add up your points for the whole lesson. Write the total in the total box. (Check and correct.)

Point Summary Chart

Now look at the inside front cover of your Workbook. You will enter your total points for each lesson on this chart. Write your total points for Lesson C in the box marked Lesson C. (Check and correct.)

Point Schedule for Lesson C

Box	Maximum Points
1. [maximum = 1 point for each exercise, Exercises 1–9]	9
2. [maximum = 3 bonus points]	(3)

END OF LESSON C

EXERCISE 1

DEDUCTIONS

1. I'll say a deduction you've done before. Then you'll say it.
2. Listen. **All cats have teeth. Tom is a cat. So, Tom has teeth.**
3. Your turn. Say the whole deduction. (Signal.) *All cats have teeth. Tom is a cat. So, Tom has teeth.* (Repeat until firm.)

Individual test
(Call on individual students.)
Say the whole deduction.

Points

(Pass out the Workbooks. Make sure that each student has a pencil.)
Everybody, open your Workbook to Lesson D. You're going to record your points for the task we just did. Here are the names of the students who earned 1 point for this task.
(List the names of students who earned 1 point.)
Record your points in Box 1 at the top of your Workbook page. (Check and correct.)

EXERCISE 2

● **MAKING UP STATEMENTS**

1. Everybody, touch part A in your Workbook. ✔

One girl in the picture is wearing a dress, one girl is wearing shorts, and one girl is wearing slacks. You're going to make up statements about the girls.

2. Everybody, touch the girl wearing a dress. ✔
   What is the girl wearing a dress doing? (Signal.) *Eating a hot dog.*

My turn to say the statement about the girl wearing a dress. **The girl wearing a dress is eating a hot dog.** Everybody, say that statement. (Signal.) *The girl wearing a dress is eating a hot dog.* (Repeat until firm.)

3. Everybody, touch the girl wearing shorts. ✔
   What is the girl wearing shorts doing? (Signal.) *Riding a bike.*
   Say the statement about the girl wearing shorts. (Pause.) Get ready. (Signal.) *The girl wearing shorts is riding a bike.* (Repeat until firm.)

4. Everybody, touch the girl wearing slacks. ✔
   What is the girl wearing slacks doing? (Signal.) *Climbing a ladder.*
   Say the statement about the girl wearing slacks. (Pause.) Get ready. (Signal.) *The girl wearing slacks is climbing a ladder.* (Repeat until firm.)

5. Let's do those statements once more.
   Everybody, say the statement about the girl wearing a dress. (Pause.) Get ready. (Signal.) *The girl wearing a dress is eating a hot dog.*
   Say the statement about the girl wearing shorts. (Pause.) Get ready. (Signal.) *The girl wearing shorts is riding a bike.*
   Say the statement about the girl wearing slacks. (Pause.) Get ready. (Signal.) *The girl wearing slacks is climbing a ladder.*
   (Repeat step 5 until firm.)

Individual test
Call on individual students to do one of the tasks in step 5.

Points

Everybody, you're going to record your points for the task we just did. Here are the names of the students who earned 1 point for this task.
(List the names of students who earned 1 point.)
Record your points in Box 1 at the top of your Workbook page. (Check and correct.)

EXERCISE 3

● **SOME, ALL, NONE**

1. Everybody, touch part B. ✔

2. Look at the doors that are open. Everybody, tell me how many doors are open: **all, some,** or **none.** (Pause.) Get ready. (Signal.) *All.*

3. Look at the doors that have stripes. Tell me how many doors have stripes: **all, some,** or **none.** (Pause.) Get ready. (Signal.) *Some.*

4. Look at the doors that have a cat behind them. Tell me how many doors have a cat behind them: **all, some,** or **none.** (Pause.) Get ready. (Signal.) *Some.*

5. Look at the doors that have a handle. Tell me how many doors have a handle: **all, some,** or **none.** (Pause.) Get ready. (Signal.) *All.*

6. Look at the doors that have an elephant behind them. Tell me how many doors have an elephant behind them: **all, some,** or **none.** (Pause.) Get ready. (Signal.) *None.*

7. (Repeat steps 2–6 until firm.)

Points

Everybody, you're going to record your points for the task we just did. Here are the names of the students who earned 1 point for this task. (List the names of students who earned 1 point.)

Record your points in Box 1 at the top of your Workbook page. (Check and correct.)

EXERCISE 4

SAME/DIFFERENT

1. Everybody, touch part C. ✔

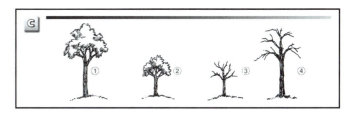

2. Touch object 3 and object 4. ✔ Those objects are the same in some way. Everybody, how are they the same? (Signal.) *They don't have leaves.*

3. Touch object 1 and object 4. 1 and 4. ✔ Those objects are the same in some way. Everybody, how are objects 1 and 4 the same? (Signal.) *They are tall.*

4. Touch object 1 and object 2. ✔ Those objects are the same in some way. Everybody, how are objects 1 and 2 the same? (Signal.) *They have leaves.*

5. Touch object 2 and object 3. ✔ Those objects are the same in some way. Everybody, how are objects 2 and 3 the same? (Signal.) *They are short.*

6. (Repeat steps 2–5 until firm.)

7. Everybody, touch object 1. ✔ (Call on a student.) Name an object that is the same as object 1. Responses: Object 2, object 4. Everybody, tell how those objects are the same. (Pause.) Get ready. (Signal.) *They are ____.*

8. (Call on a student.) Name another object that is the same as object 1. Response. Everybody, tell how those objects are the same. (Pause.) Get ready. (Signal.) *They are ____.*

9. Everybody, touch object 3. ✔ (Call on a student.) Name an object that is the same as object 3. Responses: Object 2, object 4. Everybody, tell how those objects are the same. (Pause.) Get ready. (Signal.) *They are ____.*

10. (Call on a student.) Name another object that is the same as object 3. Response. Everybody, tell how those objects are the same. (Pause.) Get ready. (Signal.) *They are ____.*

Points

Everybody, you're going to record your points for the task we just did. Here are the names of the students who earned 1 point for this task. (List students who earned 1 point.)

Record your points in Box 1 at the top of your Workbook page. (Check and correct.)

EXERCISE 5

DEDUCTIONS

1. Everybody, touch part D. ✔ You're going to make a deduction about those pictures. You'll say three statements, one statement for each picture.

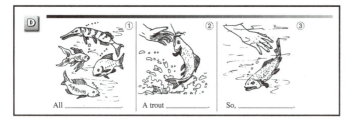

2. Touch picture 1. ✔ I'll say the statement for that picture. Listen. **All fish swim.** Say it. (Signal.) *All fish swim.* (Repeat until firm.)

3. Touch picture 2. ✔ Here's the statement. **A trout is a fish.** Say it. (Signal.) *A trout is a fish.* (Repeat until firm.)

4. Touch picture 3. ✔ Here's the statement. **So, a trout swims.** Say it. (Signal.) *So, a trout swims.* (Repeat until firm.)

5. I'll say all three statements. You touch the pictures, starting with picture 1. **All fish swim.** ✔ **A trout is a fish.** ✔ **So, a trout swims.** ✔

6. Your turn. Touch picture 1 and say the statement. (Signal.) *All fish swim.*
   Picture 2. (Signal.) *A trout is a fish.*
   Picture 3. (Signal.) *So, a trout swims.*
   (Repeat step 6 until firm.)

7. I'm going to start with the statement about **all fish** and say the statements without looking at the pictures, and then you'll say them. Listen. **All fish swim. A trout is a fish. So, a trout swims.** Listen again. **All fish swim. A trout is a fish. So, a trout swims.** Your turn. Say the statements. (Signal.) *All fish swim. A trout is a fish. So, a trout swims.* (Repeat until firm.)

Individual test
(Call on individuals.) Say the statements.

Points

Everybody, you're going to record your points for the task we just did. Here are the names of the students who earned 1 point for this task. (List students who earned 1 point.)

Record your points in Box 1 at the top of your Workbook page. (Check and correct.)

EXERCISE 6

MAKING UP STATEMENTS

1. Everybody, touch part E. ✔ One animal in the picture is swimming, and one animal is jumping. You're going to make up statements about the animals.

2. Everybody, touch the animal that is swimming. ✔ What kind of animal is that? (Signal.) *A fish.*
   My turn to say the statement about the animal that is swimming. **The animal that is swimming is a fish.** Everybody, say that statement. (Signal.) *The animal that is swimming is a fish.* (Repeat until firm.)

3. Touch the animal that is jumping. ✔ What kind of animal is that? (Signal.) *A frog.*
   Say the statement about the animal that is jumping. (Pause.) Get ready. (Signal.) *The animal that is jumping is a frog.* (Repeat until firm.)

4. Let's do those statements once more. Say the statement about the animal that is swimming. (Pause.) Get ready. (Signal.) *The animal that is swimming is a fish.*
   Say the statement about the animal that is jumping. (Pause.) Get ready. (Signal.) *The animal that is jumping is a frog.* (Repeat step 4 until firm.)

Individual test

Call on individual students to do one of the tasks in step 4.

Points

Everybody, you're going to record your points for the task we just did. Here are the names of the students who earned 1 point for this task. (List the names of students who earned 1 point.)

Record your points in Box 1 at the top of your Workbook page. (Check and correct.)

===================== EXERCISE 7 =====================

● **DEDUCTIONS**

1. Everybody, touch part F. ✔ I'll say rules. Some of the rules do not tell about all the pictures in part F.

2. Listen. **All the dogs are standing.** Everybody, say that rule. (Signal.) *All the dogs are standing.* (Repeat until firm.) Does that rule tell about all the pictures? (Signal.) *Yes.* Everybody, say the rule that tells about all the dogs. (Signal.) *All the dogs are standing.*

3. New rule. Listen. **All the dogs are spotted.** Everybody, say that rule. (Signal.) *All the dogs are spotted.* (Repeat until firm.) Does that rule tell about all the pictures? (Signal.) *No.* Everybody, touch the dog that doesn't follow the rule. ✔

4. Listen. All the dogs are spotted. (Call on a student.) Why doesn't that rule tell about all the pictures? Idea: *Because dog 3 is not spotted.*

5. New rule. Listen. **All the dogs have long tails.** Everybody, say that rule. (Signal.) *All the dogs have long tails.* (Repeat until firm.) Does that rule tell about all the pictures?

(Signal.) *Yes.* Everybody, say the rule that tells about all the dogs. (Signal.) *All the dogs have long tails.*

6. New rule. Listen. **All the dogs have collars.** Everybody, say that rule. (Signal.) *All the dogs have collars.* (Repeat until firm.) Does that rule tell about all the pictures? (Signal.) *No.* Everybody, touch the dog that doesn't follow the rule. ✔

7. Listen. All the dogs have collars. (Call on a student.) Why doesn't that rule tell about all the pictures? Idea: *Because dog 5 doesn't have a collar.*

Individual test

(Call on individual students.)

Say a rule that tells about all the dogs.

Points

Everybody, you're going to record your points for the task we just did. Here are the names of the students who earned 1 point for this task. (List the names of students who earned 1 point.)

Record your points in Box 1 at the top of your Workbook page. (Check and correct.)

===================== EXERCISE 8 =====================

● **SAME/DIFFERENT**

1. Everybody, touch part G. ✔ All the objects in part G are the same. Look at them and figure out how they are the same. Everybody, how are all the objects the same? (Signal.) *They are triangles.*

2. Touch triangles 1 and 3. ✔ Those triangles are the same in another way. Everybody, how are triangles 1 and 3 the same? (Signal.) *They are striped.*
Listen. Triangles 1 and 3 are **different** in one way. (Call on a student.) How are triangles 1 and 3 different? Idea: *One of them is upside down.*

3. Everybody, touch triangles 2 and 4. 2 and 4. ✔ Those triangles are the **same** in some way. Everybody, how are they the same? (Signal.) *They are black.* (Call on a student.) How are triangles 2 and 4 **different?** Idea: One of them is upside down.

4. Everybody, touch triangles 4 and 5. ✔ (Call on a student.) How are triangles 4 and 5 different? Idea: One is black and one is white.

5. Everybody, touch triangles 1 and 4. ✔ (Call on a student.) How are triangles 1 and 4 different? Idea: One is striped and one is black.

6. Everybody, touch triangles 1 and 2. ✔ Those triangles are different in more than one way. (Call on a student.) What's one way that triangles 1 and 2 are different? Ideas: One is striped and one is black; one of them is upside down. (Call on another student.) What's another way that triangles 1 and 2 are different? Response.

7. Everybody, touch triangles 3 and 4. ✔ Those triangles are different in more than one way. (Call on a student.) What's one way that triangles 3 and 4 are different? Ideas: One is striped and one is black; one of them is upside down. (Call on another student.) What's another way that triangles 3 and 4 are different? Response.

8. Everybody, touch triangles 2 and 5. ✔ (Call on a student.) Name two ways that those triangles are different. Ideas: One is black and one is white; one of them is upside down.

Points

Everybody, you're going to record your points for the task we just did. Here are the names of the students who earned 1 point for this task. (List the names of students who earned 1 point.)
Record your points in Box 1 at the top of your Workbook page. (Check and correct.)

EXERCISE 9

● **DEDUCTIONS**

1. Everybody, touch part H. ✔ Some of the doors are glass doors. The glass doors have the same thing behind them. Everybody, what's behind all the glass doors? (Signal.) *A dog.*

Listen to the rule about the glass doors. **All the glass doors have a dog behind them.** Everybody, say that rule. (Signal.) *All the glass doors have a dog behind them.* (Repeat until firm.)

2. Everybody, touch object 1. ✔ The rule does **not** tell about that door because it is **not** a glass door.

3. Everybody, say the rule. (Signal.) *All the glass doors have a dog behind them.* Everybody, touch object 2. ✔ The rule tells about that door because it **is** a glass door.

4. Everybody, touch object 3. ✔ Does the rule tell about that door? (Signal.) *No.* (Call on a student.) Why not? Idea: Because it's not a glass door.

5. Everybody, touch object 4. ✔ Does the rule tell about that door? (Signal.) *Yes.* (Call on a student.) How do you know? Idea: Because it's a glass door.

6. Everybody, say the rule about all the glass doors. (Signal.) *All the glass doors have a dog behind them.* (Repeat until firm.)

7. Here's the rule about the doors, not just the glass doors. **Some of the doors have a dog behind them.** Everybody, say that rule. (Signal.) *Some of the doors have a dog behind them.* (Repeat until firm.)

8. You're going to tell me **all** or **some.** Listen. Do **all** the **glass doors** or **some** of the **glass doors** have a dog behind them? (Signal.) *All.*
   Say the rule about **all the glass doors.** Get ready. (Signal.) *All the glass doors have a dog behind them.*
   Listen. Do **all** the **doors** or **some** of the **doors** have a dog behind them? (Signal.) *Some.*
   Say the rule about **some of the doors.** Get ready. (Signal.) *Some of the doors have a dog behind them.*
   (Repeat step 8 until firm.)

9. Everybody, circle all the objects this rule tells about. **All the glass doors have a dog behind them.** (Wait.)

10. Let's check your work. (Call on a student.) Read the number of each object you circled. *2, 4, 6.*
    Everybody, mark your answer with an X if it's wrong. (Wait.)

11. Everybody, cross out all the objects this rule tells about. **Some of the doors have a dog behind them.** (Wait.)

12. (Call on a student.) Read the number of each object you crossed out. *2, 4, 5, 6.*
    Everybody, mark your answer with an X if it's wrong. (Wait.)

Points

Everybody, you're going to record your points for the task we just did. Here are the names of the students who earned 1 point for this task. (List the names of students who earned 1 point.)
Record your points in Box 1 at the top of your Workbook page. (Check and correct.)

(Award a maximum of 3 bonus points and have students record them in Box 2.)
(Have students total their points and enter the total on the Point Summary Chart.)

Point Schedule for Lesson D

Box		Maximum Points
1.	[maximum = 1 point for each exercise, Exercises 1–9]	9
2.	[maximum = 3 bonus points]	(3)

END OF LESSON D

EXERCISE 1

DEDUCTIONS

1. I'll say a deduction you've done before. Then you'll say it.
2. Listen. **All cats have teeth. Tom is a cat. So, Tom has teeth.**
3. Your turn. Say the whole deduction. (Signal.) *All cats have teeth. Tom is a cat. So, Tom has teeth.* (Repeat until firm.)

> **Individual test**
> (Call on individual students.)
> Say the whole deduction.

Points

(Pass out the Workbooks. Make sure that each student has a pencil.)
Everybody, open your Workbook to Lesson E. You're going to record your points for the task we just did. Here are the names of the students who earned 1 point for this task.
(List the names of students who earned 1 point.)
Record your points in Box 1 at the top of your Workbook page. (Check and correct.)

EXERCISE 2

DEDUCTIONS

1. I'll say another deduction you've done before. Then you'll say it.
2. Listen. **All fish swim. A trout is a fish. So, a trout swims.**
3. Your turn. Say the whole deduction. (Signal.) *All fish swim. A trout is a fish. So, a trout swims.* (Repeat until firm.)

> **Individual test**
> (Call on individual students.)
> Say the whole deduction.

Points

Everybody, you're going to record your points for the task we just did. Here are the names of the students who earned 1 point for this task. (List the names of students who earned 1 point.)
Record your points in Box 1 at the top of your Workbook page. (Check and correct.)

EXERCISE 3

MAKING UP STATEMENTS

1. Everybody, touch part A in your Workbook. ✔

One man in the picture is wearing a hat, one man is wearing a jacket, and one man is wearing glasses. You're going to make up statements about the men.

2. Everybody, touch the man wearing a hat. ✔
   What is the man wearing a hat doing? (Signal.) *Sawing a board.*
   My turn to say the statement about the man wearing a hat. **The man wearing a hat is sawing a board.** Everybody, say that statement. (Signal.) *The man wearing a hat is sawing a board.* (Repeat until firm.)

3. Everybody, touch the man wearing a jacket. ✔
   What is the man wearing a jacket doing? (Signal.) *Digging a hole.*
   Say the statement about the man wearing a jacket. (Pause.) Get ready. (Signal.) *The man wearing a jacket is digging a hole.* (Repeat until firm.)

4. Everybody, touch the man wearing glasses. ✔
   What is the man wearing glasses doing? (Signal.) *Carrying a board.*
   Say the statement about the man wearing glasses. (Pause.) Get ready. (Signal.) *The man wearing glasses is carrying a board.* (Repeat until firm.)

5. Let's do those statements once more. Everybody, say the statement about the man wearing a hat. (Pause.) Get ready. (Signal.) *The man wearing a hat is sawing a board.* Say the statement about the man wearing a jacket. (Pause.) Get ready. (Signal.) *The man wearing a jacket is digging a hole.* Say the statement about the man wearing glasses. (Pause.) Get ready. (Signal.) *The man wearing glasses is carrying a board.* (Repeat step 5 until firm.)

> ### Individual test
> Call on individual students to do one of the tasks in step 5.

Points

Everybody, you're going to record your points for the task we just did. Here are the names of the students who earned 1 point for this task. (List the names of students who earned 1 point.)

Record your points in Box 1 at the top of your Workbook page. (Check and correct.)

======== EXERCISE 4 ========

SOME, ALL, NONE

1. Everybody, touch part B. ✔

2. Look at the dogs that are big. Everybody, tell me how many dogs are big: **all, some,** or **none.** (Pause.) Get ready. (Signal.) *Some.*
3. Look at the dogs that have spots. Tell me how many dogs have spots: **all, some,** or **none.** (Pause.) Get ready. (Signal.) *All.*
4. Look at the dogs that are sitting. Tell me how many dogs are sitting: **all, some,** or **none.** (Pause.) Get ready. (Signal.) *None.*
5. Look at the dogs that are wearing a collar. Tell me how many dogs are wearing a collar: **all, some,** or **none.** (Pause.) Get ready. (Signal.) *All.*

6. Look at the dogs that have a long tail. Tell me how many dogs have a long tail: **all, some,** or **none.** (Pause.) Get ready. (Signal.) *Some.*
7. (Repeat steps 2–6 until firm.)

Points

Everybody, you're going to record your points for the task we just did. Here are the names of the students who earned 1 point for this task. (List the names of students who earned 1 point.)

Record your points in Box 1 at the top of your Workbook page. (Check and correct.)

======== EXERCISE 5 ========

SAME/DIFFERENT

1. Everybody, touch part C. ✔

2. Touch object 2 and object 4. ✔ Those objects are the same in some way. Everybody, how are they the same? (Signal.) *They are girls.*
3. Touch object 1 and object 2. 1 and 2. ✔ Those objects are the same in some way. Everybody, how are objects 1 and 2 the same? (Signal.) *They are tall.*
4. Touch object 1 and object 3. ✔ Those objects are the same in some way. Everybody, how are objects 1 and 3 the same? (Signal.) *They are boys.*
5. Touch object 3 and object 4. ✔ Those objects are the same in some way. Everybody, how are objects 3 and 4 the same? (Signal.) *They are short.*
6. (Repeat steps 2–5 until firm.)

7. Everybody, touch object 2. ✔ (Call on a student.) Name an object that is the same as object 2. Responses: Object 1, object 4. Everybody, tell how those objects are the same. (Pause.) Get ready. (Signal.) *They are ____.*

8. (Call on a student.) Name another object that is the same as object 2. Response. Everybody, tell how those objects are the same. (Pause.) Get ready. (Signal.) *They are ____.*

9. Everybody, touch object 3. ✔ (Call on a student.) Name an object that is the same as object 3. Responses: Object 1, object 4. Everybody, tell how those objects are the same. (Pause.) Get ready. (Signal.) *They are ____.*

10. (Call on a student.) Name another object that is the same as object 3. Response. Everybody, tell how those objects are the same. (Pause.) Get ready. (Signal.) *They are ____.*

Points

Everybody, you're going to record your points for the task we just did. Here are the names of the students who earned 1 point for this task. (List the names of students who earned 1 point.)

Record your points in Box 1 at the top of your Workbook page. (Check and correct.)

========= **EXERCISE 6** =========

DEDUCTIONS

1. Everybody, touch part D. ✔ You're going to make a deduction about those pictures. You'll say three statements, one statement for each picture.

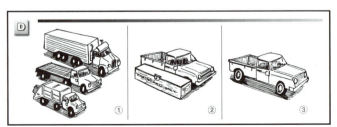

2. Touch picture 1. ✔ I'll say the statement for that picture. Listen. **All trucks have wheels.** Say it. (Signal.) *All trucks have wheels.* (Repeat until firm.)

3. Touch picture 2. ✔ Here's the statement. **A pickup is a truck.** Say it. (Signal.) *A pickup is a truck.* (Repeat until firm.)

4. Touch picture 3. ✔ Here's the statement. **So, a pickup has wheels.** Say it. (Signal.) *So, a pickup has wheels.* (Repeat until firm.)

5. I'll say all three statements. You touch the pictures, starting with picture 1. **All trucks have wheels. ✔ A pickup is a truck. ✔ So, a pickup has wheels. ✔**

6. Your turn. Touch picture 1 and say the statement. (Signal.) *All trucks have wheels.* Picture 2. (Signal.) *A pickup is a truck.* Picture 3. (Signal.) *So, a pickup has wheels.* (Repeat step 6 until firm.)

7. I'm going to start with the statement about **all trucks** and say the statements without looking at the pictures, and then you'll say them. Listen. **All trucks have wheels. A pickup is a truck. So, a pickup has wheels.** Listen again. **All trucks have wheels. A pickup is a truck. So, a pickup has wheels.** Your turn. Say the statements. (Signal.) *All trucks have wheels. A pickup is a truck. So, a pickup has wheels.* (Repeat until firm.)

Individual test
(Call on individual students.)
Say the statements.

Points

Everybody, you're going to record your points for the task we just did. Here are the names of the students who earned 1 point for this task. (List the names of students who earned 1 point.)

Record your points in Box 1 at the top of your Workbook page. (Check and correct.)

EXERCISE 7

DEDUCTIONS

1. Everybody, touch part E. ✔ I'll say rules. Some of the rules do not tell about all the pictures in part E.

2. Listen. **All the trees are tall.** Everybody, say that rule. (Signal.) *All the trees are tall.* (Repeat until firm.)
   Does that rule tell about all the pictures? (Signal.) *No.*
   Everybody, touch the tree that doesn't follow the rule. ✔

3. Listen. **All the trees are tall.** (Call on a student.) Why doesn't that rule tell about all the pictures? Idea: Because tree 4 is not tall.

4. New rule. Listen. **All the trees have leaves.** Everybody, say that rule. (Signal.) *All the trees have leaves.* (Repeat until firm.)
   Does that rule tell about all the pictures? (Signal.) *No.*
   Everybody, touch the tree that doesn't follow that rule. ✔

5. Listen. All the trees have leaves. (Call on a student.) Why doesn't that rule tell about all the pictures? Idea: Because tree 2 does not have leaves.

6. New rule. Listen. **All the trees have a broken branch.** Everybody, say that rule. (Signal.) *All the trees have a broken branch.* (Repeat until firm.)
   Does that rule tell about all the pictures? (Signal.) *Yes.* Everybody, say the rule that tells about all the trees. (Signal.) *All the trees have a broken branch.*

7. New rule. Listen. **All the trees have fruit.** Everybody, say that rule. (Signal.) *All the trees have fruit.* (Repeat until firm.)
   Does that rule tell about all the pictures? (Signal.) *No.* Everybody, touch the tree that doesn't follow the rule. ✔

8. Listen. All the trees have fruit. (Call on a student.) Why doesn't that rule tell about all the pictures? Idea: Because tree 5 doesn't have fruit.

> ***Individual test***
> (Call on individual students.)
> Say a rule that tells about all the trees.

Points

Everybody, you're going to record your points for the task we just did. Here are the names of the students who earned 1 point for this task. (List the names of students who earned 1 point.)
Record your points in Box 1 at the top of your Workbook page. (Check and correct.)

LESSON E

EXERCISE 8

SAME/DIFFERENT

1. Everybody, touch part F. ✔ All the objects in part F are the same. Look at them and figure out how they are the same. Everybody, how are all the objects the same? (Signal.) *They are circles.*

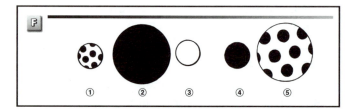

2. Touch circles 2 and 4. ✔ Those circles are the same in another way. Everybody, how are circles 2 and 4 the same? (Signal.) *They are black.*
   Listen. Circles 2 and 4 are **different** in one way. (Call on a student.) How are circles 2 and 4 different? Idea: One is big and one is small.

3. Everybody, touch circles 1 and 5. ✔ Those circles are the **same** in some way. Everybody, how are they the same? (Signal.) *They are spotted.* (Call on a student.) How are circles 1 and 5 **different?** Idea: One is big and one is small.

4. Everybody, touch circles 3 and 4. ✔ (Call on a student.) How are circles 3 and 4 different? Idea: One is black and one is white.

5. Everybody, touch circles 1 and 4. ✔ (Call on a student.) How are circles 1 and 4 different? Idea: One is spotted and one is black.

6. Everybody, touch circles 2 and 3. ✔ Those circles are different in more than one way. (Call on a student.) What's one way that circles 2 and 3 are different? Ideas: One is big and one is small; one is black and one is white.
   (Call on another student.) What's another way that circles 2 and 3 are different? Response.

7. Everybody, touch circles 4 and 5. ✔ Those circles are different in more than one way. (Call on a student.) What's one way that circles 4 and 5 are different? Ideas: One is spotted and one is black; one is small and one is big.
   (Call on another student.) What's another way that circles 4 and 5 are different? Response.

8. Everybody, touch circles 3 and 5. ✔ (Call on a student.) Name two ways that those circles are different. Ideas: One is spotted and one is white; one is small and one is big.

Points

Everybody, you're going to record your points for the task we just did. Here are the names of the students who earned 1 point for this task. (List the names of students who earned 1 point.)
Record your points in Box 1 at the top of your Workbook page. (Check and correct.)

EXERCISE 9

DEDUCTIONS

1. Everybody, touch part G. ✔ Some of the doors are glass doors. The glass doors have the same thing behind them. Everybody, what's behind all the glass doors? (Signal.) *A boy.*
   Listen to the rule about the glass doors. **All the glass doors have a boy behind them.** Everybody, say that rule. (Signal.) *All the glass doors have a boy behind them.* (Repeat until firm.)

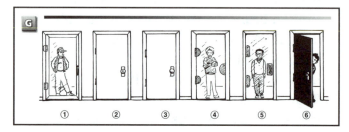

2. Everybody, touch object 1. ✔ The rule tells about that door because it **is** a glass door.

3. Everybody, say the rule. (Signal.) *All the glass doors have a boy behind them.* Everybody, touch object 2. ✔ The rule does **not** tell about that door because it is **not** a glass door.

4. Everybody, touch object 3. ✔ Does the rule tell about that door? (Signal.) *No.* (Call on a student.) Why not? Idea: Because it's not a glass door.

5. Everybody, touch object 4. ✔ Does the rule tell about that door? (Signal.) *Yes.* (Call on a student.) How do you know? Idea: Because it's a glass door.

6. Everybody, say the rule about all the glass doors. (Signal.) *All the glass doors have a boy behind them.* (Repeat until firm.)

7. Here's the rule about the doors, not just the glass doors. **Some of the doors have a boy behind them.** Everybody, say that rule. (Signal.) *Some of the doors have a boy behind them.* (Repeat until firm.)

8. You're going to tell me **all** or **some.** Listen. Do **all** the **glass doors** or **some** of the **glass doors** have a boy behind them? (Signal.) *All.*
   Say the rule about **all the glass doors.** Get ready. (Signal.) *All the glass doors have a boy behind them.*
   Listen. Do **all** the **doors** or **some** of the **doors** have a boy behind them? (Signal.) *Some.*
   Say the rule about **some of the doors.** Get ready. (Signal.) *Some of the doors have a boy behind them.* (Repeat step 8 until firm.)

9. Everybody, underline all the objects this rule tells about. **All the glass doors have a boy behind them.** (Wait.)

10. Let's check your work. (Call on a student.) Read the number of each object you underlined. *1, 4, 5.*
    Everybody, mark your answer with an X if it's wrong. (Wait.)

11. Everybody, cross out all the objects this rule tells about. **Some of the doors have a boy behind them.** (Wait.)

12. (Call on a student.) Read the number of each object you crossed out. *1, 4, 5, 6.* Everybody, mark your answer with an X if it's wrong. (Wait.)

Points

Everybody, you're going to record your points for the task we just did. Here are the names of the students who earned 1 point for this task. (List the names of students who earned 1 point.)

Record your points in Box 1 at the top of your Workbook page. (Check and correct.)

(Award bonus points and have students record them in Box 2.)

(Have students total their points and enter the total on the Point Summary Chart.)

Point Schedule for Lesson E

Box		Maximum Points
1.	[maximum = 1 point for each exercise, Exercises 1–9]	9
2.	[maximum = 3 bonus points]	(3)

END OF LESSON E

Note: After completing Lesson E, present Fact Game Lesson 1.

FACT GAME
LESSON 1

After Lesson E

> **Note:** After presenting Lesson E, present this Fact Game Lesson. For the Fact Game, students are paired. Each pair has an A member and a B member. Assign partners and indicate whether each member is an A or a B. You will need one die for the game, and each student will need a pencil and a Workbook.

━━━━━ EXERCISE 1 ━━━━━

● **FACT GAME**

1. Everybody, exchange Workbooks with your partner. (Wait.) Now open the Workbook to page 92. These are items for a Fact Game. You'll work in pairs. All A members, raise your hand. ✔ All B members, raise your hand. ✔

2. Everybody, touch the scorecard at the top of the page. ✔ Every time you get an item right, your partner will make a check on your scorecard. Each check mark stands for one point. So, if you get seven items right, you'll earn seven points.

3. For the first item, A members will tell the answer to B members. B members will make a check mark if the item is right. Here we go. (Hand the die to the first student.)
Roll the die and tell us how many dots are on top. (Wait.)
I'll read the item for that number. Follow along and don't say the answer. (Read the item that corresponds to the number.)
A members, raise your hand. ✔ Whisper the answer to your partner. (Wait.)
B members, raise your hand. ✔ The correct answer to that item is____. Raise your hand again if your partner got it right. ✔ If your partner got it right, make a check mark in Box 1 of your partner's scorecard. Box 1. (Check and correct.)

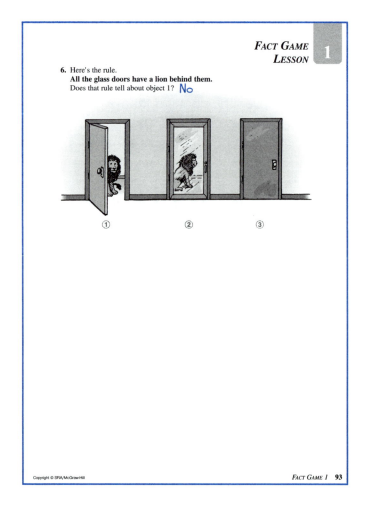

4. Now we'll switch. B members will whisper the answer. A members will mark their partner's scorecard. (Pass the die to the next student.) Roll the die and say the number. (After the student says the number:) I'll read the item for that number. Follow along, but don't say the answer. (Read the item.)
B members, whisper the answer to your partner. (Wait.)
The correct answer is ____. A members, raise your hand if your partner got it right. ✔
A members who raised your hand, make a check mark in Box 1 of your partner's scorecard. (Check and correct.)

5. Now the die goes to the next student. (Pass the die to the next student.)
Roll the die and say the number. (Wait.)
I'll read the item for that number. Follow along. (Read the item.) A members, whisper the answer to your partner. (Wait.)
The correct answer is ____. B members, raise your hand if your partner got it right. (Check and correct.) B members who raised your hand, make a check mark in Box 2 if you already made a check mark in Box 1. Make a check mark in Box 1 if you haven't made a check mark. ✔

6. (Pass the die to the next student.)
Roll the die and say the number. (Wait.)
I'll read the item for that number. Follow along. (Read the item.) B members, whisper the answer to your partner. (Wait.)
The correct answer is ____. A members, raise your hand if your partner got it right. ✔
A members who raised your hand, make a check mark in Box 2 if you already made a check mark in Box 1. Make a check mark in Box 1 if you haven't made a check mark. (Check and correct.)

7. (Pass the die to the next student.) Roll the die and say the number. (Wait.)
I'll read the item for that number. Follow along. (Read the item.) A members, whisper the answer. (Wait.)
The correct answer is ____. B members, raise your hand if your partner got it right. Then make a check mark in the next box. (Check and correct.)

8. (Play the game for 15 minutes more, following the procedures in step 7. Alternate turns for B members and A members.)

Points for Fact Game

1. At the end of the game: Raise your hand if you earned 8 or more points. If you earned 8 or more points, you get 5 bonus points.
2. Everybody, write your game points in Box 1 on your Point Chart. Write your bonus points in Box 2. ✔
3. Add up your points for the whole lesson. Write the total in the Total box. (Check and correct.)

Point Summary Chart

(Tell students to write their point total in the box labeled **FG1** on the Point Summary Chart.)

● **Six-Lesson Point Summary**
(Tell students to add the point totals for Lessons A through E and FG1 on the Point Summary Chart and to write the total for the preprogram.) [Maximum for Preprogram = 49 points, without bonus points]

END OF FACT GAME 1

PRESENT LESSON 1 NEXT

Note: Blue bullets (●) indicate the introduction of a new skills or new procedure.

Introduction

For students who have completed the preprogram: Here are facts about the rest of this program.

For students who have not completed the preprogram: Today we're starting a comprehension program. The program will help you understand better what people say and what you read.

For all students: Each lesson has three parts. The first part is Thinking Operations, the second part is Workbook Exercises, and the third part is Information. You can earn 14 points for a lesson. If you work extra hard, you can earn bonus points. Starting at Lesson 20, we will have a test every ten days. You can earn 25 points on each test day.

THINKING OPERATIONS

First we're going to do **Thinking Operations.** We will work on ways to figure out difficult problems. At first the problems will be easy, but they will get harder as we go through the program. Remember—these operations are important.

You can earn 5 points for Thinking Operations. Here's how you earn those points:

1. Answer questions out loud with the group.
2. Follow my signals.
3. Answer questions when I call on you.

═══════ **EXERCISE 1** ═══════

● **TRUE—FALSE**

The first Thinking Operation today is **True— False.**

1. I'm going to make statements about a truck. If the statement is right, say **yes.** If the statement is not right, say **no.**

2. Listen. A truck is good to eat. Is that right? (Signal.) *No.*
   Listen. A truck can carry things. Is that right? (Signal.) *Yes.*
   Listen. A truck has hands. Is that right? (Signal.) *No.*
   Listen. A truck has wheels. Is that right? (Signal.) *Yes.*
   Listen. A truck has headlights. Is that right? (Signal.) *Yes.*

3. Listen again. If I make a statement that is right, say **true.** If I make a statement that is not right, say **false.**

4. What are you going to say if I make a statement that is **right?** (Signal.) *True.*
   What are you going to say if I make a statement that is **not right?** (Signal.) *False.*
   (Repeat step 4 until firm.)

5. Listen. A truck is good to eat. Is that true or false? (Signal.) *False.*

   To correct:
   a. Is a truck good to eat? (Signal.) *No.*
   b. What do you say if I make a statement that is not right? (Signal.) *False.*
   c. (Repeat step 5.)

   Listen. A truck can carry things. Is that true or false? (Signal.) *True.*
   Listen. A truck has hands. Is that true or false? (Signal.) *False.*
   Listen. A truck has wheels. Is that true or false? (Signal.) *True.*
   Listen. A truck has headlights. Is that true or false? (Signal.) *True.*
   (Repeat step 5 until firm.)

   Individual test
   Call on individual students to do part of step 5.

EXERCISE 2

- **STATEMENT INFERENCE**

The next Thinking Operation is **Statement Inference.**

Task A

1. Listen. Big truck drivers eat a lot. Say that statement. (Signal.) *Big truck drivers eat a lot.*

   To correct students who do not repeat every word in the statement:
   a. Listen. Big truck drivers eat a lot.
   b. Everybody, say the statement with me. (Signal.) Big truck drivers eat a lot. (Repeat until firm.)
   c. Your turn. Say the statement. (Signal.) *Big truck drivers eat a lot.*
   d. (Repeat steps b and c until firm.)

2. Now you're going to answer some questions about the statement.

   To correct any wrong answers to Statement Inference questions:
   a. (Repeat the statement.)
   b. (Repeat the question the student missed, emphasizing the key words.)

3. **Who** eat a lot? (Signal.) *Big truck drivers.*
   What do big truck drivers **do?**
   (Signal.) *Eat a lot.*
   How **much** do big truck drivers eat?
   (Signal.) *A lot.*
   What **kind** of truck drivers eat a lot?
   (Signal.) *Big.*

   To correct students who say *Big truck drivers:*
   a. The answer is **big.**
   b. What **kind** of truck drivers eat a lot? (Signal.) *Big.*
   (Repeat step 3 until firm.)

   > **Individual test**
   > Ask individual students a question from step 3.

Task B

1. Listen. They sat on yellow pillows. Say that statement. (Signal.) *They sat on yellow pillows.* (Repeat until the students say every word in the statement.)

2. Now you're going to answer some questions about the statement. What did they sit on? (Signal.) *Yellow pillows.*
   What **kind** of pillows did they sit on? (Signal.) *Yellow.*
   Who sat on yellow pillows? (Signal.) *They.*
   What did they **do?** (Signal.) *Sat on yellow pillows.*
   (Repeat step 2 until firm.)

   > **Individual test**
   > Call on individual students to answer a question from step 2.

EXERCISE 3

- **SAME: Color**

The next Thinking Operation is **Same.**

1. Everybody, think of a **blue** circle and a **blue** bird.
2. How are a **blue** circle and a **blue** bird the same? (Signal.) *They are blue.*

   To correct students who say *They are both blue:*
   a. They **are** blue.
   b. How are a blue circle and a blue bird the same? (Signal.) *They are blue.*

3. Everybody, think of a **red** house and a **red** shirt.
4. How are a **red** house and a **red** shirt the same? (Signal.) *They are red.*
5. Everybody, think of a blue **circle** and a red **circle.**
6. How are a blue **circle** and a red **circle** the same? (Signal.) *They are circles.*
7. Everybody, think of a red **house** and a brown **house.**
8. How are a red **house** and a brown **house** the same? (Signal.) *They are houses.*
   You're right. They are houses.
9. (Repeat steps 1–8 until firm.)

   > **Individual test**
   > Call on different students for step 2, 4, 6, or 8.

EXERCISE 4

- **DEDUCTIONS: With Nonsense Words**

The next Thinking Operation is **Deductions.**

Task A

1. I'm going to tell you rules with made-up words.
2. Listen to this rule. **All** lums sing.
3. Everybody, say the rule. (Signal.) *All lums sing.* (Repeat until firm.)
   What sings? (Signal.) *All lums.*
   To correct students who don't say *All lums:*
   a. **All** lums. What sings? **All** lums.
   b. Everybody, what sings? (Signal.) *All lums.*
4. (Repeat steps 2 and 3 until firm.)

Task B

1. Listen to this rule. **All** glips laugh.
2. Everybody, say the rule. (Signal.) *All glips laugh.* (Repeat until firm.)
   What laughs? (Signal.) *All glips.*
   What do **all** glips do? (Signal.) *Laugh.* (Repeat step 2 until firm.)

EXERCISE 5

- **DEDUCTIONS: With *all***

1. Listen to this rule. **All** fish swim. Everybody, say that. (Signal.) *All fish swim.* (Repeat until firm.)
2. What do **all** fish do? (Signal.) *Swim.*
3. Say the rule again. (Signal.) *All fish swim.*
4. Listen. Sharks are fish. Everybody, say that. (Signal.) *Sharks are fish.*
5. Listen. **All** fish swim. Sharks are fish. So, sharks (pause; signal) *swim.*
   To correct:
   a. **All** fish swim. Sharks are fish. So, sharks (pause) **swim.**
   b. Your turn. (Repeat step 5.)
   Yes, sharks swim.
6. Listen. **All** fish swim. Sharks are fish. So (pause; signal), *sharks swim.* (Repeat step 6 until firm.)

EXERCISE 6

- **DEFINITIONS**

The next Thinking Operation is **Definitions.**

Task A

1. **Masticate** means **chew.** What does **masticate** mean? (Signal.) *Chew.* What word means **chew?** (Signal.) *Masticate.*
2. I'll say a sentence one way. Listen. Cows masticate grass. Now I'll say that sentence with a different word for **masticate.** Cows chew grass. Your turn. Cows masticate grass. Say that. (Signal.) *Cows masticate grass.* (Repeat sentence until firm.)
3. Now say that sentence with a different word for **masticate.** (Pause.) Get ready. (Signal.) *Cows chew grass.* (Repeat sentence until firm.)
   Now say that sentence with a different word for **chew.** (Pause.) Get ready. (Signal.) *Cows masticate grass.* (Repeat sentence until firm.) (Repeat step 3 until firm.)
4. Listen to this sentence. Some people masticate gum. Say that. (Signal.) *Some people masticate gum.* (Repeat until firm.)
5. Now say that sentence with a different word for **masticate.** (Pause.) Get ready. (Signal.) *Some people chew gum.* (Repeat until firm.)
   Now say that sentence with a different word for **chew.** (Pause.) Get ready. (Signal.) *Some people masticate gum.* (Repeat sentence until firm.) (Repeat step 5 until firm.)
6. Listen to this sentence. The cow is masticating. Say that. (Signal.) *The cow is masticating.* (Repeat until firm.)
7. Now say that sentence with a different word for **masticating.** (Pause.) Get ready. (Signal.) *The cow is chewing.* (Repeat until firm.)
   Now say that sentence with a different word for **chewing.** (Pause.) Get ready. (Signal.) *The cow is masticating.* (Repeat sentence until firm.) (Repeat step 7 until firm.)

Task B

1. **Obtain** means **get.** What does **obtain** mean? (Signal.) *Get.*
   What word means **get?** (Signal.) *Obtain.*
2. I'll say a sentence one way. Listen. She is going to obtain some food. Now I'll say that sentence with a different word for **obtain.** She is going to get some food. Your turn. She is going to obtain some food. Say that. (Signal.) *She is going to obtain some food.* (Repeat until firm.)
3. Now say that sentence with a different word for **obtain.** (Pause.) Get ready. (Signal.) *She is going to get some food.* (Repeat until firm.)
   Now say that sentence with a different word for **get.** (Pause.) Get ready. (Signal.) *She is going to obtain some food.* (Repeat until firm.)
   (Repeat step 3 until firm.)
4. Listen to this sentence. Sid wanted to obtain a car. Say that. (Signal.) *Sid wanted to obtain a car.* (Repeat until firm.)
5. Now say that sentence with a different word for **obtain.** (Pause.) Get ready. (Signal.) *Sid wanted to get a car.* (Repeat until firm.)
   Now say that sentence with a different word for **get.** (Pause.) Get ready. (Signal.) *Sid wanted to obtain a car.* (Repeat until firm.)
   (Repeat step 5 until firm.)
6. Listen to this sentence. He gets a lot of marbles. Say that. (Signal.) *He gets a lot of marbles.* (Repeat until firm.)
7. Now say that sentence with a different word for **gets.** (Pause.) Get ready. (Signal.) *He obtains a lot of marbles.* (Repeat until firm.)
   Now say that sentence with a different word for **obtains.** (Pause.) Get ready. (Signal.) *He gets a lot of marbles.* (Repeat until firm.)
   (Repeat step 7 until firm.)

EXERCISE 7

- **DESCRIPTION**

The next Thinking Operation is **Description.**

1. I'm going to tell you about an object you know. But I'm going to call it a funny name. See if you can figure out what object I'm talking about. Wait until I ask you for the answer.
2. (Hold up one finger.) A slup is an animal. (Hold up two fingers.) A slup says moo.
3. Everybody, let's say the things you know about a slup. (Respond with the students.) (Hold up one finger.) *A slup is an animal.* (Hold up two fingers.) *A slup says moo.* (Repeat step 3 until the students are responding with you.)
4. You say the two things you know about a slup. (Hold up one finger.) *A slup is an animal.* (Hold up two fingers.) *A slup says moo.* (Repeat until the students say the statements in order.)
5. Everybody, tell me the kind of animal I am calling a slup. (Signal.) *A cow.* Yes, it's really a cow.

EXERCISE 8

- **CLASSIFICATION**

The next Thinking Operation is **Classification.**

1. We're going to do some class names. I'm going to name some objects. You're going to tell me a class the objects are in.
2. Listen. Apple, egg, bread, meat, pie. Everybody, what class? (Signal.) *Food.* Yes, food. If you can eat it, it's food.
3. Listen. Dog, rabbit, cat, bird, elephant. Everybody, what class? (Signal.) *Animals.* Yes, animals.
4. Listen. Car, truck, bus, plane, bicycle. Everybody, what class? (Signal.) *Vehicles.* Yes, vehicles. If it's **made** to take things places, it's a vehicle.
   To correct:
   a. Listen. A car, a truck, a bus, a plane, and a bicycle are in the class of **vehicles.**
   b. What class? (Signal.) *Vehicles.*
   c. (Repeat step 4.)
5. (Repeat steps 2–4 until firm.)

6. Listen. Cup, glass, box, bag, bottle. Everybody, what class? (Signal.) *Containers.* Yes, containers. If it's **made** to put things in, it's a container.

7. Listen. Saw, hammer, pliers, scissors. Everybody, what class? (Signal.) *Tools.* Yes, tools. If it helps you do a job, it's a tool.

8. (Repeat steps 6 and 7 until firm.)

Individual test

1. I'll name a class. See how many objects you can name in that class. Listen. **Vehicles.** (Call on one student.)

2. (Repeat step 1 for **containers, animals, food,** and **tools.**)

Points for Thinking Operations

Everybody, you're going to record your points for Thinking Operations. Remember, you earn 5 points for this part of the lesson by answering the questions out loud with the group, following my signals, and answering questions when I call on you.

Here are the names of the students who earned points today. (List the names of students who performed well and how many points they earned. Award bonus points to students who worked extra hard.

(Tell students who earned no points:) If I didn't say your name, you didn't earn any points for Thinking Operations, but you can still earn points for the next two parts of the lesson.

(Pass out the Workbooks.) Everybody, open your Workbook to Lesson 1. ✔

Record your points for Thinking Operations in Box 1 at the top of your Workbook page. Record your bonus points in Box 4. (Check and correct.) [Maximum = 5 points]

Record your bonus points in Box 4. (Check and correct.) [Maximum = 3 points per lesson]

WORKBOOK EXERCISES

Now we are going to do Workbook problems. Some of the problems are like Thinking Operations you have just done. Remember to follow my instructions carefully when we do the Workbook problems. You earn 5 points if you make no mistakes, 3 points if you make only one or two mistakes, and 0 points if you make three or more mistakes.

EXERCISE 9

● **DESCRIPTION**

1. Everybody, touch part A in your Workbook. ✔ I'm going to describe one of the objects. You have to figure out which object I describe. I'll call one object a reep. Listen. A reep is a container. You find a reep in the kitchen. A reep has a handle. You use a reep on the stove. **Draw a line under** the object I'm calling a reep. (Wait.)

2. I'm going to call another object a flam. Listen. A flam is an animal. Some people have pet flams. A flam can climb trees. **Circle** the object I'm calling a flam. (Wait.)

3. Last problem. Listen. A bup is an appliance. A bup is made of metal. You put clothes in a bup. **Make a box around** the object I'm calling a bup. (Wait.)

4. Everybody, get ready to check your work. Make an X next to any item that is wrong. Here's what I said about a reep. It's a container, you find it in the kitchen, it has a handle, and you use it on the stove. Everybody, what's the real name of that object? (Signal.) *A pot.* Yes, a pot. How did you mark the pot? (Signal.) *Made a line under it.* Yes, a line under the pot. Make an X next to the pot if you didn't make a line under it.

5. Here's what I said about a flam. It's an animal that some people have for a pet. It can climb trees. Everybody, what's the real name of that object? (Signal.) *A cat.* Yes, a cat. How did you mark the cat? (Signal.)

Circled it. Yes, a circle around the cat. Make an X next to the cat if you didn't make a circle around it.

6. Here's what I said about a bup. It's an appliance, it's made of metal, and you put clothes in it. Everybody, what's the real name of that object? (Signal.) *A washing machine.* Yes, a washing machine. How did you mark the washing machine? (Signal.) *Made a box around it.* Yes, made a box around it. Make an X next to the washing machine if you didn't make a box around it.

7. Raise your hand if you got all the items right. (Praise the students who raise their hands.)

EXERCISE 10

● **TRUE—FALSE**

1. Everybody, touch part B in your Workbook. ✔ I'll say statements about the picture. Some of these statements are true and some are false.

2. Everybody, look at item 1. Touch the word **true** for item 1. ✔ Everybody, touch the word **false** for item 1. ✔
   (Repeat step 2 for items 2, 3, and 4.)

3. Look at the picture and get ready to circle **true** or **false** for item 1. Here's the statement. **All** the cups have broken handles. If that statement is true, circle the word **true.** If that statement is false, circle the word **false.** Everybody, circle **true** or **false** for item 1. (Wait.)

4. Here's the statement for item 2. **All** the cups are full. Circle **true** or **false** for item 2. (Wait.)

5. Here's the statement for item 3. **All** the cups are empty. Circle **true** or **false** for item 3. (Wait.)

6. Here's the statement for item 4. **All** the cups have good handles. Circle **true** or **false** for item 4. (Wait.)

7. Let's check item 1. **All** the cups have broken handles. (Call on a student.) Is that statement true or false? (Signal.) *False.* Everybody, mark your answer with an X if it is wrong.

8. Item two. **All** the cups are full. (Call on a student.) Is that statement true or false? (Signal.) *False.* Everybody, mark your answer with an X if it is wrong.

9. Item three. **All** the cups are empty. (Call on a student.) Is that statement true or false? (Signal.) *False.* Everybody, mark your answer with an X if it is wrong.

10. Item four. **All** the cups have good handles. (Call on a student.) Is that statement true or false? (Signal.) *True.* Everybody, mark your answer with an X if it is wrong.

11. Raise your hand if you got all the answers right. (Praise students who got all the answers correct.)

EXERCISE 11

- **CLASSIFICATION**

1. Pencils down. Don't write anything yet. Everybody, touch the instructions for part C in your Workbook. ✔ I'll read the first instruction. Listen. Circle the tools.
2. What are you going to do to every tool in the picture? (Signal.) *Circle it.*
3. I'll read the next instruction. Cross out the vehicles. What are you going to do to every vehicle? (Signal.) *Cross it out.* Everybody, do it. Circle the tools and cross out the vehicles. (Wait.)
4. Get ready to mark your papers. Put an X by any object you got wrong.
5. What class is a **boat** in? (Signal.) *Vehicles.* How did you mark the **boat?** (Signal.) *Crossed it out.*
6. (Repeat step 5 for **hammer, wrench, bus, screwdriver, airplane, bicycle, shovel,** and **truck.**)

Points for Workbook

Write the number of mistakes at the top of your Workbook page. ✔

Raise your hand if you made zero, one, or two mistakes on the Workbook page. If you made no mistakes, you earned 5 points for Workbooks. If you made one or two mistakes, you earned 3 points. If you made three or more mistakes, you earned 0 points for Workbook today. Record your points in Box 2 at the top of your Workbook page. (Check and correct.)

INFORMATION

Now we're going to work on Information. We will start with some facts and later we will do some poems. Learn all the facts and the poems that we work on, because you will be tested on the information after you have learned it. You can earn 4 points for Information. Here's how you earn points.
1. Answer the questions out loud with the group.
2. Follow my signals.
3. Answer questions when I call on you.

EXERCISE 12

- **CALENDAR: Months in a Year**

Task A
1. Raise your hand if you know how many months are in a year and can name the months in a year.
2. (Call on each student whose hand is raised.) How many months are in a year? *Twelve.* Name the months in a year. *January, February, March, April, May, June, July, August, September, October, November, December.*

Note: Only students who do not respond correctly to step 2 above are to work on tasks B–F.

Task B
1. There are twelve months in a year. How many months are in a year? (Signal.) *Twelve.*
2. Tell me the fact about how many months are in a year. (Signal.) *There are twelve months in a year.* (Repeat until firm.)

Note: Do not work on tasks C–F for more than four minutes. Stop wherever you are in the exercise after four minutes. The exercise will be repeated in the next lesson.

Task C
1. I'll name the first three months. Listen. January, February, March. Your turn. Name the first three months. (Signal.) *January, February, March.* (Repeat until firm.)
2. You named some of the months. Everybody, tell me the fact about how many months are in a year. (Pause.) Get ready. (Signal.) *There are twelve months in a year.* (Repeat until firm.)

Individual test
(Call on individual students to do one of the following tasks:)
   a. Name the first three months.
   b. Tell me the fact about how many months are in a year.

Task D

1. Here are the next three months. Listen. April, May, June. Your turn. Name those months. (Signal.) *April, May, June.* (Repeat until firm.)

2. Now I'll name the first six months. Listen. January, February, March, April, May, June. Your turn. Name the first six months. (Signal.) *January, February, March, April, May, June.* (Repeat until firm.)

> **Individual test**
> (Call on individual students to do one of the following tasks:)
>   a. Name the first six months.
>   b. Tell me the fact about how many months are in a year.

Task E

1. Here are the next three months. Listen. July, August, September. Your turn. Name those months. (Signal.) *July, August, September.* (Repeat until firm.)

2. Now I'll name the first nine months. Listen. January, February, March, April, May, June, July, August, September. Your turn. Name the first nine months. (Signal.) *January, February, March, April, May, June, July, August, September.* (Repeat until firm.)

> **Individual test**
> (Call on individual students to do one of the following tasks:)
>   a. Name the first nine months.
>   b. Tell me the fact about how many months are in a year.

Task F

1. Here are the last three months. Listen. October, November, December. Your turn. Name those months. (Signal.) *October, November, December.* (Repeat until firm.)

2. Now I'll name all twelve months. Listen. January, February, March, April, May, June, July, August, September, October, November, December. Your turn. Name all twelve months. (Signal.) *January, February, March, April, May, June, July, August, September, October, November, December.* (Repeat until firm.)

> **Individual test**
> (Call on individual students to do one of the following tasks:)
>   a. Name all twelve months in a year.
>   b. Tell me the fact about how many months are in a year.

● **Points for Information**

Everybody, you're going to record your points for Information.

(List the names of the students who performed well and how many points each one earned for Information. Award 0 to 4 points.)

(Award bonus points to students who worked extra hard.)
[Maximum bonus points not to exceed 3 per lesson.]

Record your points for Information in Box 3 at the top of your Workbook page. Record your bonus points in Box 4. (Check and correct.)

(Tell students who didn't earn any points:)
If I didn't say your name, you didn't earn any points for Information, but you can earn points in the next lesson.

Add up your points for Lesson 1 and write the total in the Total box. (Check and correct.)

Point Summary Chart
Now look at the inside front cover of your Workbook. You will enter your total points for Lesson 1 in the box marked Lesson 1. (Check and correct.)

Point Schedule

Box		Maximum Points
1	Thinking Operations	5
2	Workbook	5
3	Information	4
4	Bonus points	(3)

END OF LESSON 1

THINKING OPERATIONS

First we're going to do Thinking Operations. We will work on ways to figure out difficult problems. At first the problems will be easy, but they will get harder as we go through the program.

Remember—these operations are important. You can earn 5 points for Thinking Operations. Here's how you earn those points:

1. Answer questions out loud with the group.
2. Follow my signals.
3. Answer questions when I call on you.

EXERCISE 1

DEDUCTIONS: With Nonsense Words

The first Thinking Operation today is **Deductions.**

Task A

1. I'm going to tell you rules with made-up words.
2. Listen to this rule. **All** trees slup.
3. Everybody, say the rule. (Signal.) *All trees slup.* (Repeat until firm.)
   What slups? (Signal.) *All trees.*
   To correct students who don't say *All trees:*
   a. **All** trees. What slups? **All** trees.
   b. Everybody, what slups? (Signal.) *All trees.*
4. (Repeat steps 2 and 3 until firm.)

Task B

1. Listen to this rule. **All** flams breathe.
2. Everybody, say the rule. (Signal.) *All flams breathe.* (Repeat until firm.)
   What breathes? (Signal.) *All flams.*
   What do **all** flams do? (Signal.) *Breathe.* (Repeat step 2 until firm.)

EXERCISE 2

DEDUCTIONS: With *all*

1. Listen to this rule. **All** birds have feathers. Everybody, say that. (Signal.) *All birds have feathers.* (Repeat until firm.)
2. What do **all** birds have? (Signal.) *Feathers.*
3. Say the rule again. (Signal.) *All birds have feathers.*

4. Listen. Robins are birds. Everybody, say that. (Signal.) *Robins are birds.*
5. Listen. **All** birds have feathers. Robins are birds. So, robins (pause; signal) *have feathers.*
   To correct:
   a. **All** birds have feathers. Robins are birds. So, robins (pause) **have feathers.**
   b. Your turn. (Repeat step 5.)
   Yes, robins have feathers.
6. Listen. **All** birds have feathers. Robins are birds. So (pause; signal), *robins have feathers.* (Repeat step 6 until firm.)

EXERCISE 3

SAME: Color

The next Thinking Operation is **Same.**

1. Everybody, think of a **black** car and a **black** pen.
2. How are a **black** car and a **black** pen the same? (Signal.) *They are black.*
   To correct students who say *They are both black:*
   a. They **are** black.
   b. How are a **black** car and a **black** pen the same? (Signal.) *They are black.*
3. Everybody, think of a black **car** and a red **car.**
4. How are a black **car** and a red **car** the same? (Signal.) *They are cars.*
5. Everybody, think of a **yellow** pencil and a **yellow** wall.
6. How are a **yellow** pencil and a **yellow** wall the same? (Signal.) *They are yellow.*
7. Everybody, think of a yellow **pencil** and a red **pencil.**
8. How are a yellow **pencil** and a red **pencil** the same? (Signal.) *They are pencils.*
9. Everybody, think of a yellow **wall** and a blue **wall.**
10. How are a yellow **wall** and a blue **wall** the same? (Signal.) *They are walls.*
11. (Repeat steps 1–10 until firm.)

Individual test
Call on individual students to do step 2, 4, 6, 8, or 10.

========== EXERCISE 4 ==========

DEFINITIONS

The next Thinking Operation is **Definitions.**

Task A

1. **Obtain** means **get.** What does **obtain** mean? (Signal.) *Get.*
   What word means **get?** (Signal.) *Obtain.*

2. I'll say a sentence one way. Listen. Jim knew where to get frogs. Now I'll say that sentence with a different word for **get.** Jim knew where to obtain frogs. Your turn. Jim knew where to get frogs. Say that. (Signal.) *Jim knew where to get frogs.* (Repeat until firm.)

3. Now say that sentence with a different word for **get.** (Pause.) Get ready. (Signal.) *Jim knew where to obtain frogs.* (Repeat until firm.)
   Now say that sentence with a different word for **obtain.** (Pause.) Get ready. (Signal.) *Jim knew where to get frogs.* (Repeat until firm.)
   (Repeat step 3 until firm.)

4. Listen to this sentence. Sally obtained a new shirt. Say that. (Signal.) *Sally obtained a new shirt.* (Repeat until firm.)

5. Now say that sentence with a different word for **obtained.** (Pause.) Get ready. (Signal.) *Sally got a new shirt.* (Repeat until firm.)
   Now say that sentence with a different word for **got.** (Pause.) Get ready. (Signal.) *Sally obtained a new shirt.* (Repeat until firm.)
   (Repeat step 5 until firm.)

6. Listen to this sentence. They will get a newspaper. Say that. (Signal.) *They will get a newspaper.* (Repeat until firm.)

7. Now say that sentence with a different word for **get.** (Pause.) Get ready. (Signal.) *They will obtain a newspaper.* (Repeat until firm.)
   Now say that sentence with a different word for **obtain.** (Pause.) Get ready. (Signal.) *They will get a newspaper.* (Repeat until firm.)
   (Repeat step 7 until firm.)

Task B

1. **Masticate** means **chew.** What does **masticate** mean? (Signal.) *Chew.*
   What word means **chew?** (Signal.) *Masticate.*

2. I'll say a sentence one way. Listen. The man is masticating gum. Now I'll say that sentence with a different word for **masticating.** The man is chewing gum. Your turn. The man is masticating gum. Say that. (Signal.) *The man is masticating gum.* (Repeat until firm.)

3. Now say that sentence with a different word for **masticating.** (Pause.) Get ready. (Signal.) *The man is chewing gum.* (Repeat until firm.)
   Now say that sentence with a different word for **chewing.** (Pause.) Get ready. (Signal.) *The man is masticating gum.* (Repeat until firm.)
   (Repeat step 3 until firm.)

4. Listen to this sentence. We chew with our teeth. Say that. (Signal.) *We chew with our teeth.* (Repeat until firm.)

5. Now say that sentence with a different word for **chew.** (Pause.) Get ready. (Signal.) *We masticate with our teeth.* (Repeat until firm.)
   Now say that sentence with a different word for **masticate.** (Pause.) Get ready. (Signal.) *We chew with our teeth.* (Repeat until firm.)
   (Repeat step 5 until firm.)

6. Listen to this sentence. The pig will masticate corn. Say that. (Signal.) *The pig will masticate corn.* (Repeat until firm.)

7. Now say that sentence with a different word for **masticate.** (Pause.) Get ready. (Signal.) *The pig will chew corn.* (Repeat until firm.)
   Now say that sentence with a different word for **chew.** (Pause.) Get ready. (Signal.) *The pig will masticate corn.* (Repeat until firm.)
   (Repeat step 7 until firm.)

========== EXERCISE 5 ==========

TRUE—FALSE

The next Thinking Operation is **True—False.**

1. I'm going to make statements about a dog. If the statement is right, say **yes.** If the statement is not right, say **no.**

2. Listen. A dog has a tail. Is that right? (Signal.) *Yes.*
   Listen. A dog lives underwater. Is that right? (Signal.) *No.*
   Listen. A dog can drive a car. Is that right? (Signal.) *No.*

Listen. A dog barks. Is that right?
(Signal.) *Yes.*
Listen. A dog goes to sleep. Is that right?
(Signal.) *Yes.*
3. Listen again. If I make a statement that is right, say **true.** If I make a statement that is not right, say **false.**
4. What are you going to say if I make a statement that is **right?** (Signal.) *True.* What are you going to say if I make a statement that is **not right?** (Signal.) *False.* (Repeat step 4 until firm.)
5. Listen. A dog has a tail. Is that true or false? (Signal.) *True.*

   To correct:
   a. Does a dog have a tail? (Signal.) *Yes.*
   b. What do you say if I make a statement that is right? (Signal.) *True.*
   c. (Repeat step 5.)
   Listen. A dog lives underwater. Is that true or false? (Signal.) *False.*
   Listen. A dog can drive a car. Is that true or false? (Signal.) *False.*
   Listen. A dog barks. Is that true or false? (Signal.) *True.*
   Listen. A dog goes to sleep. Is that true or false? (Signal.) *True.*
   (Repeat step 5 until firm.)

> **Individual test**
> Call on individuals to do part of step 5.

═══════════ **EXERCISE 6** ═══════════

STATEMENT INFERENCE

The next Thinking Operation is **Statement Inference.**

Task A

1. Listen. Jean wore thick glasses. Say that statement. (Signal.) *Jean wore thick glasses.*
   To correct students who do not repeat every word in the statement:
   a. Listen. Jean wore thick glasses.
   b. Everybody, say the statement with me. (Signal. Respond with the students.) *Jean wore thick glasses.* (Repeat until firm.)
   c. Your turn. Say the statement. (Signal.) *Jean wore thick glasses.*
   d. (Repeat steps b and c until firm.)

2. Now you're going to answer some questions about the statement.
   To correct any wrong answers to Statement Inference questions:
   a. (Repeat the statement.)
   b. (Repeat the question the student missed, emphasizing the key words.)
3. What **kind** of glasses did Jean wear? (Signal.) *Thick.*
   To correct students who say *Thick glasses:*
   a. The answer is **thick.**
   b. What **kind** of glasses did Jean wear? (Signal.) *Thick.* (Repeat until firm.)
   Who wore thick glasses? (Signal.) *Jean.*
   What did Jean **do?** (Signal.) *Wore thick glasses.*
   What did Jean **wear?** (Signal.) *Thick glasses.*

> **Individual test**
> Ask individual students a question from step 3.

Task B

1. Listen. A large truck brought the cement. Say that statement. (Signal.) *A large truck brought the cement.* (Repeat until the students say every word in the statement.)
2. Now you're going to answer some questions about the statement. What did a large truck **do?** (Signal.) *Brought the cement.*
   What **kind** of truck brought the cement? (Signal.) *Large.*
   What did a large truck **bring?** (Signal.) *The cement.*
   What brought the cement? (Signal.) *A large truck.*
   How many trucks brought the cement? (Signal.) *One.*

> **Individual test**
> Ask individual students a question from step 2.

EXERCISE 7

DESCRIPTION

The next Thinking Operation is **Description.**

1. I'm going to tell you about an object you know. But I'm going to call it a funny name. See if you can figure out what object I'm talking about. Wait until I ask you for the answer.

2. (Hold up one finger.) A tunk is a tool. (Hold up two fingers.) A tunk is used to pound nails.

3. Everybody, let's say the things you know about a tunk. (Respond with the students.) (Hold up one finger.) *A tunk is a tool.* (Hold up two fingers.) *A tunk is used to pound nails.* (Repeat until firm.)

4. You say the two things you know about a tunk. (Hold up one finger.) *A tunk is a tool.* (Hold up two fingers.) *A tunk is used to pound nails.* (Repeat until the students say the statements in order.)

5. Everybody, tell me the kind of tool I am calling a tunk. (Signal.) *A hammer.* Yes, it's really a hammer.

EXERCISE 8

CLASSIFICATION

The next Thinking Operation is **Classification.**

1. We're going to do some class names. I'm going to name some objects. You're going to tell me a class the objects are in.

2. Listen. Bag, box, bottle, purse, jar. Everybody, what class? (Signal.) *Containers.* Yes, containers. If it's **made** to hold things, it's a container.

   To correct:
   a. Listen. A bag, a box, a bottle, a purse, and a jar are in the class of containers.
   b. What class? (Signal.) *Containers.*
   c. (Repeat step 2.)

3. Listen. Tiger, lion, elephant, mouse, rabbit. Everybody, what class? (Signal.) *Animals.* Yes, animals.

4. Listen. Tables, chairs, cabinets, beds. Everybody, what class? (Signal.) *Furniture.* Yes, furniture.

5. (Repeat steps 2–4 until firm.)

6. Listen. Movie theater, church, school, house. Everybody, what class? (Signal.) *Buildings.* Yes, buildings.

7. Listen. Car, bicycle, truck, motorcycle. Everybody, what class? (Signal.) *Vehicles.* Yes, vehicles. If it's **made** to take things places, it's a vehicle.

8. (Repeat steps 6 and 7 until firm.)

Individual test

1. I'll name a class. See how many objects you can name in that class. Listen. **Containers.** (Call on one student.)

2. (Repeat step 1 for **animals, furniture, buildings,** and **vehicles.**)

Points for Thinking Operations

Everybody, you're going to record your points for Thinking Operations. Remember, you earn 5 points for this part of the lesson by answering questions out loud with the group, following my signals, and answering questions when I call on you.

Here are the names of the students who earned points today.

(List the names of students who performed well and how many points they earned. Award bonus points to students who worked extra hard.

(Tell students who earned no points:) If I didn't say your name, you didn't earn any points for Thinking Operations, but you can still earn points for the next two parts of the lesson.

(Pass out the Workbooks.) Everybody, open your Workbook to Lesson 2. Record your points for Thinking Operations in Box 1 at the top of your Workbook page. Record your bonus points in Box 4. (Check and correct.)

WORKBOOK EXERCISES

Now we are going to do Workbook problems. Some of the problems are like Thinking Operations you have just done. Remember to follow my instructions carefully when we do the Workbook problems. You earn 5 points if you make no mistakes, 3 points if you make only one or two mistakes, and 0 points if you make three or more mistakes.

EXERCISE 9

DESCRIPTION

1. Everybody, touch part A in your Workbook. ✔ I'm going to describe one of the objects. You have to figure out which object I describe. I'll call one object a gim. Listen. A gim is furniture. A gim is usually made of wood. A gim has a seat, a back, and legs. **Make a 1 on** the object I'm calling a gim. (Wait.)

2. I'm going to call another object a lerm. Listen. A lerm is made of paper. You read a lerm. A lerm has a cover and pages. **Draw a line under** the object I'm calling a lerm. (Wait.)

3. Last problem. Listen. A zoop is a tool. A zoop has a handle and a blade. You cut your food with a zoop. **Make a box around** the object I'm calling a zoop. (Wait.)

4. Everybody, get ready to check your work. Make an X next to any item that is wrong. Here's what I said about a gim. It's furniture. It is usually made of wood. It has a seat, a back, and legs.
   Everybody, what's the real name of that object? (Signal.) *A chair.* Yes, a chair. How did you mark the chair? (Signal.) *Made a 1 on it.* Yes, made a 1 on it. Make an X next to the chair if you didn't make a 1 on it.

5. Here's what I said about a lerm. It is made of paper. You read it. It has a cover and pages. Everybody, what's the real name of that object? (Signal.) *A book.* Yes, a book. How did you mark the book? (Signal.) *Drew a line under it.* Yes, drew a line under it. Make an X next to the book if you didn't draw a line under it.

6. Here's what I said about a zoop. It is a tool. It has a handle and a blade. You cut your food with it. Everybody, what's the real name of that object? (Signal.) *A knife.* Yes, a knife. How did you mark the knife? (Signal.) *Made a box around it.* Yes, made a box around it. Make an X next to the knife if you didn't make a box around it.

7. Raise your hand if you got all the items right. (Praise the students who raise their hands.)

EXERCISE 10

TRUE—FALSE

Task A

1. Everybody, touch part B in your Workbook. ✔ I'll say statements about the picture. Some of these statements are true and some are false.

2. Everybody, look at item 1. Touch the word **true** for item 1. ✔ Everybody, touch the word **false** for item 1. ✔
   (Repeat step 2 for items 2, 3, and 4.)

3. Look at the picture and get ready to circle **true** or **false** for item 1. Here's the statement: **All** the vehicles have wheels. If that statement is true, circle the word **true.** If that statement is false, circle the word **false.** Everybody, circle **true** or **false** for item 1. (Wait.)

4. Here's the statement for item 2. **All** the vehicles can take you places. Circle **true** or **false** for item 2. (Wait.)

5. Here's the statement for item 3. **All** the vehicles are cars. Circle **true** or **false** for item 3. (Wait.)

6. Here's the statement for item 4. **All** the vehicles are black. Circle **true** or **false** for item 4. (Wait.)

7. Let's check item 1. **All** the vehicles have wheels. (Call on a student.) Is that statement true or false? (Signal.) *True.* Mark your answer with an X if it is wrong.

8. Item 2. **All** the vehicles can take you places. (Call on a student.) Is that statement true or false? (Signal.) *True.* Mark your answer with an X if it is wrong.

9. Item 3. **All** the vehicles are cars. (Call on a student.) Is that statement true or false? (Signal.) *True.*
   Mark your answer with an X if it is wrong.
10. Item 4. **All** the vehicles are black. (Call on a student.) Is that statement true or false? (Signal.) *False.*
   Mark your answer with an X if it is wrong.
11. Raise your hand if you got all the answers right. (Praise the students who raise their hands.)

Task B

1. Everybody, touch part C in your Workbook. ✔ I'll say statements about the picture. Some of these statements are true and some are false.
2. Everybody, look at item 1. Touch the word **true** for item 1. ✔ Everybody, touch the word **false** for item 1. ✔
   (Repeat step 2 for items 2, 3, and 4.)
3. Look at the picture and get ready to circle **true** or **false** for item 1. Here's the statement. **All** the people are happy. If that statement is **true,** circle the word **true.** If that statement is false, circle the word **false.** Everybody, circle **true** or **false** for item 1. (Wait.)
4. Here's the statement for item 2. **All** the people are sad. Circle **true** or **false** for item 2. (Wait.)
5. Here's the statement for item 3. **All** the people are wearing glasses. Circle **true** or **false** for item 3. (Wait.)
6. Here's the statement for item 4. **All** the people have dark hair. Circle **true** or **false** for item 4. (Wait.)
7. Let's check item 1. **All** the people are happy. (Call on a student.) Is that statement true or false? (Signal.) *False.*
   Mark your answer with an X if it is wrong.
8. Item 2. **All** the people are sad. (Call on a student.) Is that statement true or false? (Signal.) *False.*
   Mark your answer with an X if it is wrong.
9. Item 3. **All** the people are wearing glasses. (Call on a student.) Is that statement true or false? (Signal.) *True.*
   Mark your answer with an X if it is wrong.

10. Item 4. **All** the people have dark hair. (Call on a student.) Is that statement true or false? (Signal.) *False.*
   Mark your answer with an X if it is wrong.
11. Raise your hand if you got all the answers right. (Praise the students who raise their hands.)

━━━━━━━━━━ **EXERCISE 11** ━━━━━━━━━━

CLASSIFICATION

1. Pencils down. Don't write anything yet. Everybody, touch the instructions for part D in your Workbook. I'll read the first instruction. Listen. Underline the containers.
2. What are you going to do to every container in the picture? (Signal.) *Underline it.*
3. I'll read the next instruction. Circle the animals. What are you going to do to every animal in the picture? (Signal.) *Circle it.* Everybody, do it. Underline the containers and circle the animals. (Wait.)

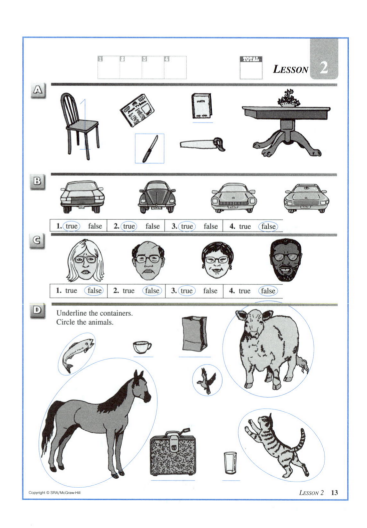

4. Get ready to mark your papers. Put an X by any object you got wrong.
5. What class is a **cup** in? (Signal.) *Containers.* How did you mark the **cup?** (Signal.) *Underlined it.*
6. (Repeat step 5 for **fish, glass, cow, bag, horse, suitcase, cat,** and **bird.**)

Points for Workbook

Write the number of mistakes at the top of your Workbook page. ✔

Raise your hand if you made zero, one, or two mistakes on the Workbook page. If you made no mistakes, you earned 5 points for Workbooks. If you made one or two mistakes, you earned 3 points. If you made three or more mistakes, you earned 0 points for Workbooks today. Record your points in Box 2 at the top of your Workbook page. (Check and correct.)

INFORMATION

Now we're going to work on Information. We will start with some facts and later we will do some poems. Learn all the facts and the poems that we work on, because you will be tested on the information after you have learned it. You can earn 4 points for Information. Here's how you earn points.
1. Answer the questions out loud with the group.
2. Follow my signals.
3. Answer questions when I call on you.

EXERCISE 12

CALENDAR: Months in a Year

Task A
1. Raise your hand if you know how many months are in a year and can name the months in a year.
2. (Call on each student whose hand is raised.) How many months are in a year? *Twelve.* Name the months in a year. *January, February, March, April, May, June, July, August, September, October, November, December.*

Note: Only students who do not respond correctly to step 2 above are to work on tasks B–F.

Task B
1. There are twelve months in a year. How many months are in a year? (Signal.) *Twelve.*
2. Tell me the fact about how many months are in a year. (Signal.) *There are twelve months in a year.* (Repeat until firm.)

Note: Do not work on tasks C–F for more than four minutes. Stop wherever you are in the exercise after four minutes. The exercise will be repeated in the next lesson.

Task C
1. I'll name the first three months. Listen. January, February, March. Your turn. Name the first three months. (Signal.) *January, February, March.* (Repeat until firm.)
2. You named some of the months. Everybody, tell me the fact about how many months are in a year. (Pause.) Get ready. (Signal.) *There are twelve months in a year.* (Repeat until firm.)

> ***Individual test***
> (Call on individual students to do one of the following tasks:)
>   a. Name the first three months.
>   b. Tell me the fact about how many months are in a year.

Task D

1. Here are the next three months. Listen. April, May, June. Your turn. Name those months. (Signal.) *April, May, June.* (Repeat until firm.)

2. Now I'll name the first six months. Listen. January, February, March, April, May, June. Your turn. Name the first six months. (Signal.) *January, February, March, April, May, June.* (Repeat until firm.)

> **Individual test**
>
> (Call on individual students to do one of the following tasks:)
>
>   a. Name the first six months.
>   b. Tell me the fact about how many months are in a year.

Task E

1. Here are the next three months. Listen. July, August, September. Your turn. Name those months. (Signal.) *July, August, September.* (Repeat until firm.)

2. Now I'll name the first nine months. Listen. January, February, March, April, May, June, July, August, September. Your turn. Name the first nine months. (Signal.) *January, February, March, April, May, June, July, August, September.* (Repeat until firm.)

> **Individual test**
>
> (Call on individual students to do one of the following tasks:)
>
>   a. Name the first nine months.
>   b. Tell me the fact about how many months are in a year.

Task F

1. Here are the last three months. Listen. October, November, December. Your turn. Name those months. (Signal.) *October, November, December.* (Repeat until firm.)

2. Now I'll name all twelve months. Listen. January, February, March, April, May, June, July, August, September, October, November, December. Your turn. Name all twelve months. (Signal.) *January, February, March, April, May, June, July, August, September, October, November, December.* (Repeat until firm.)

> **Individual test**
>
> (Call on individual students to do one of the following tasks:)
>
>   a. Name all twelve months in a year.
>   b. Tell me the fact about how many months are in a year.

Points for Information

Everybody, you're going to record your points for Information.

(List the names of the students who performed well and how many points each one earned for Information. Award 0 to 4 points.)

(Award bonus points to students who worked extra hard.)
[Maximum bonus points not to exceed 3 per lesson.]

Record your points for Information in Box 3 at the top of your Workbook page. Record your bonus points in Box 4. (Check and correct.)

(Tell students who didn't earn any points:)
If I didn't say your name, you didn't earn any points for Information, but you can earn points in the next lesson.
Add up your points for Lesson 2 and write the total in the Total box. (Check and correct.)

Point Summary Chart

Now look at the inside front cover of your Workbook. You will enter your total points for Lesson 2 in the box marked Lesson 2. (Check and correct.)

Point Schedule

Box		Maximum Points
1	Thinking Operations	5
2	Workbook	5
3	Information	4
4	Bonus points	(3)

END OF LESSON 2

THINKING OPERATIONS

First we're going to do Thinking Operations. We will work on ways to figure out difficult problems. At first the problems will be easy, but they will get harder as you go through the program. Remember—these operations are important.

You can earn 5 points for Thinking Operations. Here's how you earn those points:
1. Answer questions out loud with the group.
2. Follow my signals.
3. Answer questions when I call on you.

EXERCISE 1

STATEMENT INFERENCE

The first Thinking Operation today is **Statement Inference.**

Task A

1. Listen. Blue sharks get very big. Say that statement. (Signal.) *Blue sharks get very big.*

   To correct the students who do not repeat every word in the statement:
   a. Listen. Blue sharks get very big.
   b. Everybody, say the statement with me. (Signal. Respond with the students.) Blue sharks get very big. (Repeat until firm.)
   c. Your turn. Say the statement. *Blue sharks get very big.*
   d. (Repeat steps b and c until firm.)

2. Now you're going to answer some questions about the statement.

   To correct any wrong answers to Statement Inference questions:
   a. (Repeat the statement.)
   b. (Repeat the question the student missed, emphasizing the key words.)

3. **What** get very big? (Signal.) *Blue sharks.*
   What **kind** of sharks get very big? (Signal.) *Blue.*

   To correct students who say *Blue sharks:*
   a. The answer is blue.
   b. What kind of sharks get very big? (Signal.) *Blue.*
   (Repeat step 3 until firm.)
   What do blue sharks **do?** (Signal.) *Get very big.*

Individual test
Call on individual students to answer a question from step 3.

Task B

1. Listen. The old women were waiting for a bus. Say that statement. (Signal.) *The old women were waiting for a bus.* (Repeat until the students say every word in the statement.)

2. Now you're going to answer some questions about the statement. What were the old women **doing?** (Signal.) *Waiting for a bus.*
   What were the old women **waiting for?** (Signal.) *A bus.*
   Who was waiting for a bus? (Signal.) *The old women.*
   How many buses were the old women waiting for? (Signal.) *One.*
   What **kind** of women were waiting for a bus? (Signal.) *Old.*

Individual test
Call on individual students to answer a question from step 2.

EXERCISE 2

● **DEFINITIONS**

The next Thinking Operation is **Definitions.**
1. **Complete** means **finish.**
2. What does **complete** mean? (Signal.) *Finish.*
   What word means **finish?** (Signal.) *Complete.*
   (Repeat step 2 until firm.)
3. Listen. He will complete all the work. Say that. (Signal.) *He will complete all the work.* (Repeat until firm.)
   Say that sentence with a different word for **complete.** (Pause.) Get ready. (Signal.) *He will finish all the work.* (Repeat until firm.)
   (Repeat step 3 until firm.)
4. Listen. How much can you finish? Say that. (Signal.) *How much can you finish?* (Repeat until firm.)
   Say that sentence with a different word for **finish.** (Pause.) Get ready. (Signal.) *How much can you complete?* (Repeat until firm.)
   (Repeat step 4 until firm.)

5. Listen. She will complete that quickly. Say that. (Signal.) *She will complete that quickly.* (Repeat until firm.)
   Say that sentence with a different word for **complete.** (Pause.) Get ready. (Signal.) *She will finish that quickly.* (Repeat until firm.) (Repeat step 5 until firm.)

═══════ EXERCISE 3 ═══════

● **DEFINITIONS**

1. **Masticate.** (Pause.) What does **masticate** mean? (Signal.) *Chew.*
   And what word means **chew?** (Signal.) *Masticate.* (Repeat step 1 until firm.)
2. Listen. The dog will masticate a bone. Say that. (Signal.) *The dog will masticate a bone.* (Repeat until firm.)
   Now say that sentence with a different word for **masticate.** (Pause.) Get ready. (Signal.) *The dog will chew a bone.* (Repeat until firm.) (Repeat step 2 until firm.)
3. **Obtain.** (Pause.) What does **obtain** mean? (Signal.) *Get.* What word means **get?** (Signal.) *Obtain.* (Repeat step 3 until firm.)
4. Listen. Can you obtain a new pencil? Say that. (Signal.) *Can you obtain a new pencil?* (Repeat until firm.)
   Now say that sentence with a different word for **obtain.** (Pause.) Get ready. (Signal.) *Can you get a new pencil?* (Repeat until firm.) (Repeat step 4 until firm.)

═══════ EXERCISE 4 ═══════

DEDUCTIONS: With *all*
The next Thinking Operation is **Deductions.**

Task A

1. Listen to this rule. **All** shoes are clothing. Everybody, say that. (Signal.) *All shoes are clothing.* (Repeat until firm.)
2. What are **all** shoes? (Signal.) *Clothing.*
3. Say the rule again. (Signal.) *All shoes are clothing.*
4. Listen. Sneakers are shoes. Everybody, say that. (Signal.) *Sneakers are shoes.*
5. Listen. **All** shoes are clothing. Sneakers are shoes. So, sneakers (pause; signal) *are clothing.* Yes, sneakers are clothing.

6. Listen. **All** shoes are clothing. Sneakers are shoes. So (pause; signal), *sneakers are clothing.* (Repeat step 6 until firm.)

Task B

1. Listen to this rule. **All** plants grow. Everybody, say that. (Signal.) *All plants grow.* (Repeat until firm.)
2. What do all plants do? (Signal.) *Grow.*
3. Say the rule again. (Signal.) *All plants grow.*
4. Listen. Carrots are plants. Everybody, say that. (Signal.) *Carrots are plants.*
5. Listen. **All** plants grow. Carrots are plants. So, carrots (pause; signal) *grow.* Yes, carrots grow.
6. Listen. **All** plants grow. Carrots are plants. So (pause; signal), *carrots grow.* (Repeat step 6 until firm.)

═══════ EXERCISE 5 ═══════

● **SAME: Class**
The next Thinking Operation is **Same.**

Task A

1. Remember, vehicles are made to take things places. When I call on you, name some vehicles. (Call on individual students. Accept all reasonable responses.)
2. Everybody, what class are cars and bicycles and jets in? (Signal.) *Vehicles.* Yes, vehicles. So how are a car and a jet the same? (Signal.) *They are vehicles.*

   To correct students who say *They are both vehicles:*
   a. They **are** vehicles.
   b. How are a car and a jet the same? (Signal.) *They are vehicles.*
   c. (Repeat step 2.)
3. A bicycle and a wagon. (Pause.) How are they the same? (Signal.) *They are vehicles.*
4. A red bicycle and a red building. (Pause.) How are they the same? (Signal.) *They are red.*
5. A fast car and a fast cat. (Pause.) How are they the same? (Signal.) *They are fast.*
6. A car and a bicycle. (Pause.) How are they the same? (Signal.) *They are vehicles.*
7. (Repeat steps 3–6 until firm.)

Task B

1. Remember, tools are made to help people work. When I call on you, name some tools. (Call on different students. Accept all reasonable responses.)
2. Everybody, what class are screwdrivers and saws and ladders in? (Signal.) *Tools.* Yes, tools. So, how are a screwdriver and a saw the same? (Signal.) *They are tools.*
3. A tall ladder and a tall flagpole. (Pause.) How are they the same? (Signal.) *They are tall.*
4. A ladder and a hammer. (Pause.) How are they the same? (Signal.) *They are tools.*
5. A screwdriver and a wrench. (Pause.) How are they the same? (Signal.) *They are tools.*
6. A blue boat and a blue screwdriver. (Pause.) How are they the same? (Signal.) *They are blue.*
7. (Repeat steps 3–6 until firm.)

EXERCISE 6

CLASSIFICATION

The next Thinking Operation is **Classification.**

1. We're going to do some class names. I'm going to name some objects. You're going to tell me a class the objects are in.
2. Listen. Hammer, pliers, wrench, screwdriver. Everybody, what class? (Signal.) *Tools.* Yes, tools. If it helps you do a job, it's a tool.
   To correct:
   a. Listen. A hammer, pliers, a wrench, and a screwdriver are in the class of tools.
   b. What class? (Signal.) *Tools.*
   c. (Repeat step 2.)
3. Listen. Ice-cream cone, hamburger, corn, bread. Everybody, what class? (Signal.) *Food.* Yes, food. If you can eat it, it's food.
4. Listen. Refrigerator, dishwasher, dryer. Everybody, what class? (Signal.) *Appliances.* Yes, appliances. If you plug it in to use in the house, it's an appliance.
5. (Repeat steps 2–4 until firm.)
6. Listen. Grass, trees, flowers, bushes. Everybody, what class? (Signal.) *Plants.* Yes, plants.
7. Listen. Movie theaters, gas stations, houses. Everybody, what class? (Signal.) *Buildings.* Yes, buildings.

8. (Repeat steps 6 and 7 until firm.)

Individual test

1. I'll name a class. See how many objects you can name in that class. Listen. **Appliances.** (Call on one student.)
2. (Repeat step 1 for **tools, food, plants,** and **buildings.**)

EXERCISE 7

DESCRIPTION

The next Thinking Operation is **Description.**

1. I'm going to tell you about an object you know. But I'm going to call it a funny name. See if you can figure out what object I'm talking about. Wait until I ask you for the answer.
2. (Hold up one finger.) A bamp is a building. (Hold up two fingers.) A bamp has teachers and classrooms in it.
3. Everybody, let's say the things you know about a bamp. (Respond with the students.) (Hold up one finger.) *A bamp is a building.* (Hold up two fingers.) *A bamp has teachers and classrooms in it.* (Repeat until firm.)
4. You say the two things you know about a bamp. (Hold up one finger.) *A bamp is a building.*
   (Hold up two fingers.) *A bamp has teachers and classrooms in it.* (Repeat until the students say the statements in order.)
5. Everybody, tell me the kind of building I am calling a bamp. (Signal.) *A school.* Yes, it's really a school.

EXERCISE 8

● DESCRIPTION

1. Here's the rule. **Flim** is a funny word that we'll use for window. What word are we using for window? (Signal.) *Flim.* And what does **flim** mean? (Signal.) *Window.*
2. Listen to this sentence. A flim is made of glass. Everybody, say it. (Signal.) *A flim is made of glass.*
   What does flim mean? (Signal.) *Window.*
   A flim is made of glass. Is that statement true or false? (Signal.) *True.*

To correct:

a. What does flim mean? (Signal.) *Window.*

b. A window is made of glass. Is that statement true or false? (Signal.) *True.* Yes, it's true. So this statement is also true: A flim is made of glass.

c. (Repeat step 2 until firm.)

3. Next sentence. A flim can fly. Everybody, say it. (Signal.) *A flim can fly.*
What does flim mean? (Signal.) *Window.*
Listen. A flim can fly. Is that statement true or false? (Signal.) *False.*

4. Next sentence. A rock can break a flim. Everybody, say it. (Signal.) *A rock can break a flim.* Is that statement true or false? (Signal.) *True.*

5. Next sentence. A flim eats breakfast. Everybody, say it. (Signal.) *A flim eats breakfast.* Is that statement true or false? (Signal.) *False.*

6. Next sentence. You can see light through a flim. Everybody, say it. (Signal.) *You can see light through a flim.* Is that statement true or false? (Signal.) *True.*

Points for Thinking Operations

Everybody, you're going to record your points for Thinking Operations. Remember, you earn 5 points for this part of the lesson by answering questions out loud with the group, following my signals, and answering questions when I call on you.

Here are the names of the students who earned points. (List the names of students who performed well and how many points they earned. Award bonus points to students who worked extra hard.)

(Tell students who didn't earn any points:) If I didn't say your name, you didn't earn any points for Thinking Operations, but you can still earn points for the next two parts of the lesson.

(Pass out the Workbooks.) Open your Workbook to Lesson 3. Record your points for Thinking Operations in Box 1 at the top of your Workbook page. Record your bonus points in Box 4. (Check and correct.)

WORKBOOK EXERCISES

Now we are going to do Workbook problems. Some of the problems are like Thinking Operations you have just done. Remember to follow my instructions carefully when we do the Workbook problems. You earn 5 points if you make no mistakes, 3 points if you make only one or two mistakes, and 0 points if you make three or more mistakes.

EXERCISE 9

● **SAME**

1. Everybody, touch part A in your Workbook. ✔ Now touch box 1. Don't write anything until I tell you to. Some of the objects in box 1 are usually the same color. You're going to **make a line under** all the objects that are usually the same color. What are you going to do to all the objects that are usually the same color? (Signal.) *Make a line under them.* Do it. ✔

2. Touch box 2. Some of the objects in that box are in the same class. You're going to **circle** each object that is in the same class. What are you going to do to each object that is in the same class? (Signal.) *Circle it.* Do it. ✔

3. Touch box 3. Some of the objects in that box are the same shape. You're going to **make a box around** each object that is the same shape. What are you going to do to each object that is the same shape? (Signal.) *Make a box around it.* Do it. ✔

4. Get ready to mark your papers. Put an X above any object you get wrong. In box 1 you made a line under all the objects that are usually the same color. Name the objects you underlined. (Call on one student.) *A carrot and an orange.*
Everybody, what color are those objects? (Signal.) *Orange.*
Mark the items you missed.

5. In box 2, you circled the objects that are in the same class. Name the objects you circled. (Call on one student.) *A horse and a chicken.*

Everybody, what class are those objects in? (Signal.) *Animals.*

6. In box 3, you made a box around the objects that are the same shape. Name the objects you made a box around. (Call on one student.) *A baseball, an orange, and an apple.*

Everybody, what shape are those objects? (Signal.) *Round.*

EXERCISE 10

DESCRIPTION

1. Everybody, touch part B in your Workbook. ✔ I'm going to describe one of the objects. You have to figure out which object I describe. I'll call one object a miz. Listen. A miz is clothing. A miz can be made of cloth or leather. A miz is worn on your hand. **Make a 2 on** the object I'm calling a miz. (Wait.)

2. I'm going to call another object a sab. Listen. A sab is a container. A sab is made of glass. A sab has a lid.
Draw a line under the object I'm calling a sab. (Wait.)

3. Last problem. Listen. A lang is found in the kitchen. A lang is an appliance. A lang is used to keep food cold. **Circle** the object I'm calling a lang. (Wait.)

4. Everybody, get ready to check your work. Make an X next to any item that is wrong. Here's what I said about a miz. It is clothing. It can be made of cloth or leather. It is worn on your hand. Everybody, what's the real name of that object? (Signal.) *A glove.* Yes, a glove. How did you mark the glove? (Signal.) *Made a 2 on it.* Yes, made a 2 on the glove. Make an X next to the glove if you didn't make a 2 on it.

5. Here's what I said about a sab. A sab is a container. A sab is made of glass. A sab has a lid. Everybody, what's the real name of that object? (Signal.) *A jar.* Yes, a jar. How did you mark the jar? (Signal.) *Drew a line under it.* Yes, drew a line under the jar. Make an X next to the jar if you didn't draw a line under it.

6. Here's what I said about a lang. It is found in the kitchen. It is an appliance. It is used to keep food cold. Everybody, what's the real name of that object? (Signal.) *A refrigerator.* Yes, a refrigerator. How did you mark the refrigerator? (Signal.) *Circled it.* Yes, circled the refrigerator. Make an X next to the refrigerator if you didn't circle it.

7. Raise your hand if you got all the items right. (Praise the students who raise their hands.)

EXERCISE 11

TRUE—FALSE

1. Everybody, touch part C in your Workbook. ✔ I'll say statements about the picture. Some of these statements are true and some are false.

2. Everybody, look at item 1. Touch the word **true** for item 1. ✔ Everybody, touch the word **false** for item 1. ✔ (Repeat for items 2, 3, 4, and 5.)

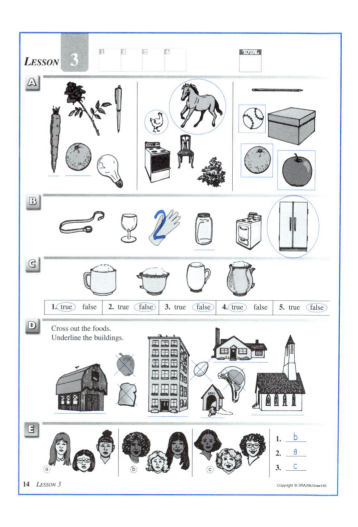

3. Look at the picture and get ready to circle **true** or **false** for item 1. Here's the statement.
   Some of the cups have broken handles. Everybody, circle **true** or **false** for item 1. (Wait.)

4. Here's the statement for item 2. **All** the cups have broken handles. Circle **true** or **false** for item 2. (Wait.)

5. Here's the statement for item 3. **Only some** of the cups are full. Circle **true** or **false** for item 3. (Wait.)

6. Here's the statement for item 4. **All** the cups are full. Circle **true** or **false** for item 4. (Wait.)

7. Here's the statement for item 5. **Some** of the cups are empty. Circle **true** or **false** for item 5. (Wait.)

8. Let's check item 1. **Some** of the cups have broken handles. (Call on a student.) Is that statement true or false? (Signal.) *True.*
   Mark your answer with an X if it is wrong.

9. Item 2. **All** the cups have broken handles. (Call on a student.) Is that statement true or false? (Signal.) *False.*
   Mark your answer with an X if it is wrong.

10. Item 3. **Only some** of the cups are full. (Call on a student.) Is that statement true or false? (Signal.) *False.*
    Mark your answer with an X if it is wrong.

11. Item 4. **All** the cups are full. (Call on a student.) Is that statement true or false? (Signal.) *True.*
    Mark your answer with an X if it is wrong.

12. Item 5. **Some** of the cups are empty. (Call on a student.) Is that statement true or false? (Signal.) *False.*
    Mark your answer with an X if it is wrong.

13. Raise your hand if you got all the answers right. (Praise the students who raise their hands.)

═══════════ EXERCISE 12 ═══════════

CLASSIFICATION

1. Pencils down. Don't write anything yet. Everybody, touch the instructions for part D in your Workbook. I'll read the first instruction. Listen. Cross out the food.

2. What are you going to do to every food in the picture? (Signal.) *Cross it out.*

3. I'll read the next instruction. Underline the buildings. What are you going to do to every building? (Signal.) *Underline it.* Everybody, do it. Cross out the food and underline the buildings. (Wait.)

4. Get ready to mark your papers. Put an X by any object you got wrong.

5. What class is an **apple** in? (Signal.) *Food.* How did you mark the **apple**? (Signal.) *Crossed it out.*

6. (Repeat step 5 for **steak, house, doghouse, barn, apartment building, bread, church,** and **egg.**)

═══════════ EXERCISE 13 ═══════════

● **TRUE—FALSE**

1. Everybody, touch part E in your Workbook. ✔ I'll say statements that are true of one of the pictures.

2. Listen: **Only some** of the girls are smiling. Touch the right picture. (Signal.) ✔ (Repeat step 2 until firm.)

3. Listen: **None** of the girls are smiling. Touch the right picture. (Signal.) (Repeat step 3 until firm.)

4. Listen: **All** of the girls are smiling. Touch the right picture. (Signal.) (Repeat step 4 until firm.)

5. (Repeat steps 2–4 until firm.)

6. Let's do it again. This time, you'll write the letter of each picture I describe. Here's item 1: **Only some** of the girls are smiling. Touch the right picture. (Signal.) What letter is under that picture? (Signal.) *B.* Write the letter **B** on line 1. (Wait.)

7. Here's item 2: **None** of the girls are smiling. Touch the right picture. (Signal.) What letter is under that picture? (Signal.) *A.* Write the letter **A** on line 2. (Wait.)

8. Here's item 3: **All** the girls are smiling. Touch the right picture. (Signal.) Write the letter of that picture on line 3. (Wait.)

9. Let's check your answer. Item 3. **All** the girls are smiling. What's the letter of that picture? (Signal.) *C.* Yes, the answer to item 3 is C.

Points for Workbook

Write the number of mistakes at the top of your Workbook page. ✔

Raise your hand if you made zero, one, or two mistakes on the Workbook page. If you made no mistakes, you earned 5 points for Workbooks. If you made one or two mistakes, you earned 3 points. If you made three or more mistakes, you earned 0 points for Workbooks today. Record your points in Box 2 at the top of your Workbook page. (Check and correct.)

INFORMATION

Now we're going to work on Information. We will start with some facts and later we will do some poems. Learn all the facts and the poems that we work on, because you will be tested on the information after you have learned it.

You can earn 4 points for Information.

Here's how you earn points.

1. Answer the questions out loud with the group.
2. Follow my signals.
3. Answer questions when I call on you.

═══ **EXERCISE 14** ═══

CALENDAR: Months in a Year

Task A

1. Raise your hand if you know how many months are in a year and can name the months in a year.
2. (Call on each student whose hand is raised.) How many months are in a year? *Twelve.* Name the months in a year. *January, February, March, April, May, June, July, August, September, October, November, December.*

> **Note:** Only students who do not respond correctly to step 2 above are to work on tasks B–F.

Task B

1. There are twelve months in a year. How many months are in a year? (Signal.) *Twelve.*
2. Tell me the fact about how many months are in a year. (Signal.) *There are twelve months in a year.* (Repeat until firm.)

> **Note:** Do not work on tasks C–F for more than four minutes. Stop wherever you are in the exercise after four minutes. The exercise will be repeated in the next lesson.

Task C

1. I'll name the first three months. Listen. January, February, March. Your turn. Name the first three months. (Signal.) *January, February, March.* (Repeat until firm.)
2. You named some of the months. Everybody, tell me the fact about how many months are in a year. (Pause.) Get ready. (Signal.) *There are twelve months in a year.* (Repeat until firm.)

> *Individual test*
> (Call on individual students to do one of the following tasks:)
> a. Name the first three months.
> b. Tell me the fact about how many months are in a year.

Task D

1. Here are the next three months. Listen. April, May, June. Your turn. Name those months. (Signal.) *April, May, June.* (Repeat until firm.)

2. Now I'll name the first six months. Listen. January, February, March, April, May, June. Your turn. Name the first six months. (Signal.) *January, February, March, April, May, June.* (Repeat until firm.)

Individual test

(Call on individual students to do one of the following tasks:)

    a. Name the first six months.
    b. Tell me the fact about how many months are in a year.

Task E

1. Here are the next three months. Listen. July, August, September. Your turn. Name those months. (Signal.) *July, August, September.* (Repeat until firm.)

2. Now I'll name the first nine months. Listen. January, February, March, April, May, June, July, August, September. Your turn. Name the first nine months. (Signal.) *January, February, March, April, May, June, July, August, September.* (Repeat until firm.)

Individual test

(Call on individual students to do one of the following tasks:)

    a. Name the first nine months.
    b. Tell me the fact about how many months are in a year.

Task F

1. Here are the last three months. Listen. October, November, December. Your turn. Name those months. (Signal.) *October, November, December.* (Repeat until firm.)

2. Now I'll name all twelve months. Listen. January, February, March, April, May, June, July, August, September, October, November, December. Your turn. Name all twelve months. (Signal.) *January, February, March, April, May, June, July, August, September, October, November, December.* (Repeat until firm.)

Individual test

(Call on individual students to do one of the following tasks:)

    a. Name all twelve months in a year.
    b. Tell me the fact about how many months are in a year.

Points for Information

Everybody, you're going to record your points for Information.

(List the names of the students who performed well and how many points each one earned for Information. Award 0 to 4 points.)

(Award bonus points to students who worked extra hard.)
[Maximum bonus points not to exceed 3 per lesson.]

Record your points for Information in Box 3 at the top of your Workbook page. Record your bonus points in Box 4. (Check and correct.)

(Tell students who didn't earn any points:)
If I didn't say your name, you didn't earn any points for Information, but you can earn points in the next lesson.

Add up your points for Lesson 3 and write the total in the Total box. (Check and correct.)

Point Summary Chart

Now look at the inside front cover of your Workbook. You will enter your total points for Lesson 3 in the box marked Lesson 3. (Check and correct.)

Point Schedule

Box		Maximum Points
1	Thinking Operations	5
2	Workbook	5
3	Information	4
4	Bonus points	(3)

END OF LESSON 3

THINKING OPERATIONS

━━━━━━━━━ **EXERCISE 1** ━━━━━━━━━

SAME: Class

The first Thinking Operation today is **Same.**

Task A

1. Remember, containers are made to put things in. When I call on you, name some containers. (Call on individual students. Accept all reasonable responses.)

2. Everybody, what class are bottles, cups, and pans in? (Signal.) *Containers. Yes, containers.* So, how are a bottle and a pan the same? (Signal.) *They are containers.*

3. A bottle and a cup. (Pause.) How are they the same? (Signal.) *They are containers.*

4. A red pan and a red apple. (Pause.) How are they the same? (Signal.) *They are red.*

5. A pan and a bowl. (Pause.) How are they the same? (Signal.) *They are containers.*

6. A small dog and a small cup. (Pause.) How are they the same? (Signal.) *They are small.*

7. A bottle and a pan. (Pause.) How are they the same? (Signal.) *They are containers.*

8. (Repeat steps 3–7 until firm.)

Task B

1. Remember, tools are made to help people work. When I call on you, name some tools. (Call on different students. Accept all reasonable responses.)

2. Everybody, what class are toothbrushes, paintbrushes, and shovels in? (Signal.) *Tools.* Yes, tools. So, how are a toothbrush and a shovel the same? (Signal.) *They are tools.*

3. A toothbrush and a paintbrush. (Pause.) How are they the same? (Signal.) *They are tools.*

4. A big cup and a big toothbrush. (Pause.) How are they the same? (Signal.) *They are big.*

5. A shovel and a hammer. (Pause.) How are they the same? (Signal.) *They are tools.*

6. A wet toothbrush and a wet cup. (Pause.) How are they the same? (Signal.) *They are wet.*

7. A toothbrush and a shovel. (Pause.) How are they the same? (Signal.) *They are tools.*

8. (Repeat steps 3–7 until firm.)

━━━━━━━━━ **EXERCISE 2** ━━━━━━━━━

● **STATEMENT INFERENCE**

The next Thinking Operation is **Statement Inference.**

Task A

1. Listen. Six containers were filled with milk. Say that statement. (Signal.) *Six containers were filled with milk.* (Repeat until firm.)

> **Individual test**
> Call on individuals to say the statement.

2. Everybody, listen. Six containers were filled with milk. What was filled with milk? (Signal.) *Six containers.*
   How many containers were filled with milk? (Signal.) *Six.* What were six containers filled with? (Signal.) *Milk.*
   (Repeat step 2 until firm.)

> **Individual test**
> Call on individual students to answer a question from step 2.

Task B

1. Listen. Full-grown frogs do not have tails. Say that statement. (Signal.) *Full-grown frogs do not have tails.* (Repeat until firm.)

> **Individual test**
> Call on individuals to say the statement.

2. Everybody, listen. Full-grown frogs do not have tails. What kind of frogs do not have tails? (Signal.) *Full-grown.*
   What don't full-grown frogs have? (Signal.) *Tails.* What do not have tails? (Signal.) *Full-grown frogs.*
   (Repeat step 2 until firm.)

> **Individual test**
> Call on individual students to answer a question from step 2.

━━━━━━━━ **EXERCISE 3** ━━━━━━━━

● **DESCRIPTION**

The next Thinking Operation is **Description.**

1. I'm going to tell you about an object you know. But I'm going to call it a funny name. See if you can figure out what object I'm talking about.
2. (Hold up one finger.) A zork is an insect. (Hold up two fingers.) A zork makes honey.
3. Everybody, say the two things you know about a zork. (Hold up one finger.) *A zork is an insect.* (Hold up two fingers.) *A zork makes honey.* (Repeat until the students say the statements in order.)
4. Everybody, tell me the kind of insect I am calling a zork. (Signal.) *A bee.*

━━━━━━━━ **EXERCISE 4** ━━━━━━━━

DESCRIPTION

1. Here's the rule. **Norg** is a funny word that we'll use for horse. What word are we using for horse? (Signal.) *Norg.*
   And what does **norg** mean? (Signal.) *Horse.*
2. Listen to this sentence. A norg has four legs. Everybody, say it. (Signal.) *A norg has four legs.*
   What does norg mean? (Signal.) *Horse.*
   A norg has four legs. Is that statement true or false? (Signal.) *True.*

   To correct:
   a. What does norg mean? (Signal.) *Horse.*
   b. A horse has four legs. Is that statement true or false? (Signal.) *True.* Yes, it's true. So this statement is also true: A norg has four legs.
   c. (Repeat step 2.)
3. Next sentence. Norgs live underwater. Everybody, say it. (Signal.) *Norgs live underwater.*
   What does norg mean? (Signal.) *Horse.*
   Listen. Norgs live underwater. Is that statement true or false? (Signal.) *False.*

4. Next sentence. A norg is alive. Everybody, say it. (Signal.) *A norg is alive.* Is that statement true or false? (Signal.) *True.*
5. Next sentence. A norg can run. Everybody, say it. (Signal.) *A norg can run.* Is that statement true or false? (Signal.) *True.*
6. Next sentence. You can put a saddle on a norg. Everybody, say it. (Signal.) *You can put a saddle on a norg.* Is that statement true or false? (Signal.) *True.*

━━━━━━━━ **EXERCISE 5** ━━━━━━━━

CLASSIFICATION

The next Thinking Operation is **Classification.**

1. We're going to do some class names. I'm going to name some objects. You're going to tell me a class the objects are in.
2. Listen. Couches, desks, bookcases, chairs. Everybody, what class? (Signal.) *Furniture.* Yes, furniture.
3. Listen. Blender, freezer, stove, refrigerator. Everybody, what class? (Signal.) *Appliances.* Yes, appliances. If you plug it in to use in the house, it's an appliance.
4. Listen. Trees, bushes, grass, flowers. Everybody, what class? (Signal.) *Plants.* Yes, plants.
5. (Repeat steps 2–4 until firm.)
6. Listen. Bananas, apples, carrots, pork chops. Everybody, what class? (Signal.) *Food.* Yes, food.
7. Listen. Trains, rowboats, canoes, airplanes. Everybody, what class? (Signal.) *Vehicles.* Yes, vehicles. If it's made to take things places, it's a vehicle.
8. (Repeat steps 6 and 7 until firm.)

┌────────────────────────────────────┐
│ *Individual test* │
│ 1. I'll name a class. See how many objects you can name in that class. Listen. **Plants.** (Call on one student.) │
│ 2. (Repeat step 1 for **furniture, appliances, food,** and **vehicles.**) │
└────────────────────────────────────┘

EXERCISE 6

DEFINITIONS

1. **Complete** means **finish**.
2. What does **complete** mean? (Signal.) *Finish.* What word means **finish?** (Signal.) *Complete.* (Repeat step 2 until firm.)
3. Listen. Can I help you complete your work? Say that. (Signal.) *Can I help you complete your work?* (Repeat until firm.)
   Now say that sentence with a different word for **complete.** (Pause.) Get ready. (Signal.) *Can I help you finish your work?* (Repeat until firm.)
   (Repeat step 3 until firm.)
4. Listen. I hope I completed it on time. Say that. (Signal.) *I hope I completed it on time.* (Repeat until firm.)
   Now say that sentence with a different word for **completed.** (Pause.) Get ready. (Signal.) *I hope I finished it on time.* (Repeat until firm.)
   (Repeat step 4 until firm.)
5. Listen. They finished the job this morning. Say that. (Signal.) *They finished the job this morning.* (Repeat until firm.)
   Now say that sentence with a different word for **finished.** (Pause.) Get ready. (Signal.) *They completed the job this morning.* (Repeat until firm.)
   (Repeat step 5 until firm.)

EXERCISE 7

DEFINITIONS

1. **Masticate.** (Pause.) What does **masticate** mean? (Signal.) *Chew.* And what word means **chew?** (Signal.) *Masticate.* (Repeat step 1 until firm.)
2. Listen. You should masticate your food carefully. Say that. (Signal.) *You should masticate your food carefully.* (Repeat until firm.)
   Now say that sentence with a different word for **masticate.** (Pause.) Get ready. (Signal.) *You should chew your food carefully.* (Repeat until firm.)
   (Repeat step 2 until firm.)

3. **Obtain.** (Pause.) What does **obtain** mean? (Signal.) *Get.* What word means **get?** (Signal.) *Obtain.* (Repeat step 3 until firm.)
4. Listen. I can obtain a good job. Say that. (Signal.) *I can obtain a good job.* (Repeat until firm.)
   Now say that sentence with a different word for **obtain.** (Pause.) Get ready. (Signal.) *I can get a good job.* (Repeat until firm.)
   (Repeat step 4 until firm.)

EXERCISE 8

- **DEDUCTIONS: With *all***

The next Thinking Operation is **Deductions.**

Task A

1. Listen to this rule. **All** snakes crawl. Everybody, say that. (Signal.) *All snakes crawl.* (Repeat until firm.)
2. Rattlers are snakes. Say that. (Signal.) *Rattlers are snakes.*
3. Listen. **All** snakes crawl. Rattlers are snakes. So, rattlers (pause; signal) *crawl.*
   Again. **All** snakes crawl. Rattlers are snakes. So (pause; signal), *rattlers crawl.*
   (Repeat step 3 until firm.)
4. You know that rattlers crawl because **all** snakes crawl. How do you know that rattlers crawl? (Signal.) *Because all snakes crawl.* (Repeat step 4 until firm.)
   To correct the failure to say *because:*
   a. **Because** all snakes crawl.
   b. How do you know that rattlers crawl? (Signal.) *Because all snakes crawl.*

Task B

1. Listen to this rule. **All** vehicles move. Everybody, say that. (Signal.) *All vehicles move.* (Repeat until firm.)
2. Trucks are vehicles. Say that. (Signal.) *Trucks are vehicles.*
3. Listen. **All** vehicles move. Trucks are vehicles. So, trucks (pause; signal) *move.*
   Again. **All** vehicles move. Trucks are vehicles. So (pause; signal), *trucks move.*
   (Repeat step 3 until firm.)

4. You know that trucks move because **all** vehicles move. How do you know that trucks move? (Signal.) *Because all vehicles move.* (Repeat step 4 until firm.)

Task C

1. Listen to this rule. **All** dogs have teeth. Everybody, say that. (Signal.) *All dogs have teeth.* (Repeat until firm.)

2. Spaniels are dogs. Say that. (Signal.) *Spaniels are dogs.*

3. Listen. **All** dogs have teeth. Spaniels are dogs. So, spaniels (pause; signal) *have teeth.* Again. **All** dogs have teeth. Spaniels are dogs. So (pause; signal), *spaniels have teeth.* (Repeat step 3 until firm.)

4. You know that spaniels have teeth because **all** dogs have teeth. How do you know that spaniels have teeth? (Signal.) *Because all dogs have teeth.* (Repeat step 4 until firm.)

● **Points**

(Pass out the Workbooks.
Award points for Thinking Operations.)

WORKBOOK EXERCISES

We're going to do Workbooks now. Remember to follow my instructions very carefully.

━━━━ EXERCISE 9 ━━━━

SAME

1. Everybody, touch part A in your Workbook. ✔ Now touch box 1. Don't write anything until I tell you to. Some of the objects in box 1 are in the same class. You're going to **make a C** on each object that is in the same class. What are you going to do to each object that is in the same class? (Signal.) *Make a C on it.* Do it. ✔

2. Touch box 2. Some of the objects in that box are the same shape. You're going to **make a line under** each object that is the same shape. What are you going to do to each object that is the same shape? (Signal.) *Make a line under it.* Do it. ✔

3. Touch box 3. Some of the objects in that box are usually the same color. You're going to **circle** each object that is usually the same color. What are you going to do to each object that is usually the same color? (Signal.) *Circle it.* Do it. ✔

4. Get ready to mark your papers. Put an X above any object you got wrong. In box 1 you made a C on some objects that are in the same class. Name the objects you made a C on. (Call on one student.) *A rowboat, a bus, and a taxi.*
Everybody, what class are those objects in? (Signal.) *Vehicles.* Mark the items you missed.

5. In box 2 you made a line under the objects that are the same shape. Name the objects you underlined. (Call on one student.) *A window and a picture.*
Everybody, what shape are those objects? (Signal.) *Square.*

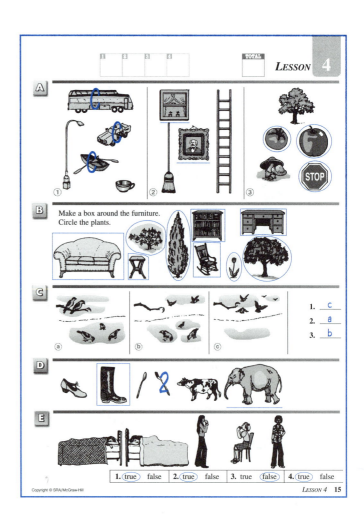

6. In box 3 you circled the objects that are usually the same color. Name the objects you circled. (Call on one student.) *An apple, a tomato, and a stop sign.*
Everybody, what color are those objects? (Signal.) *Red.*

========== EXERCISE 10 ==========

CLASSIFICATION

1. Pencils down. Don't write anything yet. Everybody, touch the instructions for part B in your Workbook. ✔ I'll read the first instruction. Listen. Make a box around the furniture.
2. What are you going to do to every piece of furniture? (Signal.) *Make a box around it.*
3. I'll read the next instruction. Circle the plants. What are you going to do to every plant? (Signal.) *Circle it.*
Everybody, do it. Make a box around the furniture and circle the plants. (Wait.)
4. Get ready to mark your papers. Put an X by any object you got wrong.
5. What class is a **couch** in? (Signal.) *Furniture.* How did you mark the **couch?** (Signal.) *Made a box around it.*
6. (Repeat step 5 for **tree, bookcase, desk, bush, table, rocker, tulip,** and **orange tree.**)

========== EXERCISE 11 ==========

TRUE—FALSE

1. Everybody, touch part C in your Workbook. I'll say statements that are true of one of the pictures.
2. Listen: **All** the birds are flying. Touch the right picture. (Signal. Repeat step 2 until firm.)
3. Listen: **None** of the birds are flying. Touch the right picture. (Signal. Repeat step 3 until firm.)
4. Listen: **Only some** of the birds are flying. Touch the right picture. (Signal. Repeat step 4 until firm.)
5. (Repeat steps 2–4 until firm.)

6. Let's do it again. This time, you'll write the letter of each picture I describe. Here's item 1: **All** the birds are flying. Touch the right picture. (Signal.) What letter is under that picture? (Signal.) *C.*
Write the letter **C** on line 1. (Wait.)
7. Here's item 2: **None** of the birds are flying. Touch the right picture. (Signal.) What letter is under that picture? (Signal.) *A.*
Write the letter **A** on line 2. (Wait.)
8. Here's item 3: **Only some** of the birds are flying. Touch the right picture. (Signal.) Write the letter of that picture on line 3. (Wait.)
9. Let's check your answer. Item 3. **Only some** of the birds are flying. What's the letter of that picture? (Signal.) *B.* Yes, the answer to item 3 is **B.**

========== EXERCISE 12 ==========

● **DESCRIPTION**

1. Everybody, touch part D in your Workbook. Figure out which object I describe. Listen. A holo is made of metal. You eat with a holo. A holo has a handle and prongs. **Make a 2 on** the object I'm calling a holo. (Wait.)
2. Listen. A carn is an animal. A carn has a tail and four legs. A carn has a trunk. **Underline** the object I'm calling a carn. (Wait.)
3. Listen. An ula is a piece of clothing. You wear an ula on your foot. An ula is made of rubber. **Make a box around** the object I'm calling an ula.
4. Everybody, get ready to check your work. Tell me the real name for the object that is made of metal, that you eat with, and that has a handle and prongs. Get ready. (Signal.) *A fork.* And how did you mark the fork? (Signal.) *Made a 2 on it.*
5. Tell me the real name for the object that is an animal, that has a tail and four legs, and has a trunk. Get ready. (Signal.) *An elephant.* And how did you mark the elephant? (Signal.) *Underlined it.*
6. Tell me the real name for the object that is a piece of clothing, that you wear on your foot, and that is made of rubber. Get ready. (Signal.) *A boot.* And how did you mark the boot? (Signal.) *Made a box around it.*

EXERCISE 13

- **TRUE—FALSE**

1. Everybody, touch part E in your Workbook. I'll say statements about the picture. Some of these statements are true and some are false.

2. Item 1. Listen. **Some** of the girls are **sleeping.** Circle **true** or **false** for item 1. (Wait.)

3. Item 2. Listen. **Some** of the girls are **eating.** Circle **true** or **false** for item 2. (Wait.)

4. Item 3. Listen. **Some** of the girls are **jumping.** Circle **true** or **false** for item 3. (Wait.)

5. Item 4. Listen. **Some** of the girls are **standing.** Circle **true** or **false** for item 4. (Wait.)

6. Let's check your answers. Mark any item you miss with an X. Everybody, tell me **true** or **false.**

7. Item 1. **Some** of the girls are **sleeping.** (Signal.) *True.*
   Item 2. **Some** of the girls are **eating.** (Signal.) *True.*
   Item 3. **Some** of the girls are **jumping.** (Signal.) *False.*
   Item 4. **Some** of the girls are **standing.** (Signal.) *True.*

- **Points**

(Award points for Workbooks.)

INFORMATION

We're going to work on Information now.

EXERCISE 14

CALENDAR: Months in a Year

Task A

1. Raise your hand if you know how many months are in a year and can name the months in a year.

2. (Call on each student whose hand is raised.) How many months are in a year? *Twelve.* Name the months in a year. *January, February, March, April, May, June, July, August, September, October, November, December.*

Note: Only students who do not respond correctly to step 2 above are to work on tasks B–F.

Task B

1. There are twelve months in a year. How many months are in a year? (Signal.) *Twelve.*

2. Tell me the fact about how many months are in a year. (Signal.) *There are twelve months in a year.* (Repeat until firm.)

Note: Do not work on tasks C–F for more than four minutes. Stop wherever you are in the exercise after four minutes. The exercise will be repeated in the next lesson.

Task C

1. I'll name the first three months. Listen. January, February, March. Your turn. Name the first three months. (Signal.) *January, February, March.* (Repeat until firm.)

2. You named some of the months. Everybody, tell me the fact about how many months are in a year. (Pause.) Get ready. (Signal.) *There are twelve months in a year.* (Repeat until firm.)

> *Individual test*
> (Call on individual students to do one of the following tasks:)
> a. Name the first three months.
> b. Tell me the fact about how many months are in a year.

Task D

1. Here are the next three months. Listen. April, May, June. Your turn. Name those months. (Signal.) *April, May, June.* (Repeat until firm.)
2. Now I'll name the first six months. Listen. January, February, March, April, May, June. Your turn. Name the first six months. (Signal.) *January, February, March, April, May, June.* (Repeat until firm.)

Individual test

(Call on individual students to do one of the following tasks:)

    a. Name the first six months.
    b. Tell me the fact about how many months are in a year.

Task E

1. Here are the next three months. Listen. July, August, September. Your turn. Name those months. (Signal.) *July, August, September.* (Repeat until firm.)
2. Now I'll name the first nine months. Listen. January, February, March, April, May, June, July, August, September. Your turn. Name the first nine months. (Signal.) *January, February, March, April, May, June, July, August, September.* (Repeat until firm.)

Individual test

(Call on individual students to do one of the following tasks:)

    a. Name the first nine months.
    b. Tell me the fact about how many months are in a year.

Task F

1. Here are the last three months. Listen. October, November, December. Your turn. Name those months. (Signal.) *October, November, December.* (Repeat until firm.)
2. Now I'll name all twelve months. Listen. January, February, March, April, May, June, July, August, September, October, November, December. Your turn. Name all twelve months. (Signal.) *January, February, March, April, May, June, July, August, September, October, November, December.* (Repeat until firm.)

Individual test

(Call on individual students to do one of the following tasks:)

    a. Name all twelve months in a year.
    b. Tell me the fact about how many months are in a year.

● **Points**

(Award points for Information.
Have the students add up their daily total.)

Point Schedule

Box		Maximum Points
1	Thinking Operations	5
2	Workbook	5
3	Information	4
4	Bonus points	(3)

END OF LESSON 4

LESSON 5

THINKING OPERATIONS

EXERCISE 1

- **DEFINITIONS**

The first Thinking Operation today is **Definitions.**

Task A

1. A **synonym** is a word that has the same meaning as another word. What's a synonym? (Signal.) *A word that has the same meaning as another word.* (Repeat until the students are responding with you.)
2. By yourselves. What's a **synonym?** (Signal.) *A word that has the same meaning as another word.* (Repeat until firm.)
3. **Masticate.** (Pause.) What does **masticate** mean? (Signal.) *Chew.*
   So what's a synonym for **masticate?** (Signal.) *Chew.* And what's a synonym for **chew?** (Signal.) *Masticate.*
4. **Complete.** (Pause.) What's a synonym for **complete?** (Signal.) *Finish.* And what's a synonym for **finish?** (Signal.) *Complete.*
5. **Obtain.** (Pause.) What's a synonym for **obtain?** (Signal.) *Get.* And what's a synonym for **get?** (Signal.) *Obtain.*
6. (Repeat steps 3–5 until firm.)

Task B

1. Listen to this sentence. George wanted to obtain a hat. Say that. (Signal.) *George wanted to obtain a hat.* (Repeat until firm.)
   Now say that sentence with a synonym for **obtain.** (Pause.) Get ready. (Signal.) *George wanted to get a hat.* (Repeat until firm.)
   (Repeat step 1 until firm.)
2. Listen to this sentence. He got a book. Say that. (Signal.) *He got a book.* (Repeat until firm.)
   Now say that sentence with a synonym for **got.** (Pause.) Get ready. (Signal.) *He obtained a book.* (Repeat until firm.)
   (Repeat step 2 until firm.)
3. **Complete.** What's a synonym for **complete?** (Signal.) *Finish.*

4. Listen to this sentence. I can complete this test. Say that. (Signal.) *I can complete this test.* (Repeat until firm.)
   Now say that sentence with a synonym for **complete.** (Pause.) Get ready. (Signal.) *I can finish this test.* (Repeat until firm.)
   (Repeat step 4 until firm.)
5. Listen to this sentence. He must complete his work before he goes home. Say that. (Signal.) *He must complete his work before he goes home.* (Repeat until firm.)
   Now say that sentence with a synonym for **complete.** (Pause.) Get ready. (Signal.) *He must finish his work before he goes home.* (Repeat until firm.)
   (Repeat step 5 until firm.)
6. **Masticate.** What's a synonym for **masticate?** (Signal.) *Chew.*
7. Listen to this sentence. I masticate my food. Say that. (Signal.) *I masticate my food.* (Repeat until firm.)
   Now say that sentence with a synonym for **masticate.** (Pause.) Get ready. (Signal.) *I chew my food.* (Repeat until firm.)
   (Repeat step 7 until firm.)
8. Listen to this sentence. Goats like to **chew.** Say that. (Signal.) *Goats like to chew.* (Repeat until firm.)
   Now say that sentence with a synonym for **chew.** (Pause.) Get ready. (Signal.) *Goats like to masticate.* (Repeat until firm.)
   (Repeat step 8 until firm.)

EXERCISE 2

- **SAME: Review**

The next Thinking Operation is **Same.**

1. Remember, vehicles are made to take things places. Tools are made to help people work. Containers are made to put things in.
2. Get ready to tell me how things are the same.
3. A bike, a motorcycle, and a boat. (Pause.) How are they the same? (Signal.) *They are vehicles.*
4. A red truck, a red cup, and a red building. (Pause.) How are they the same? (Signal.) *They are red.*

5. A yellow cup and a red basket. (Pause.) How are they the same? (Signal.) *They are containers.*

6. A screwdriver, a ladder, and a hammer. (Pause.) How are they the same? (Signal.) *They are tools.*

7. A black hammer and a black car. (Pause.) How are they the same? (Signal.) *They are black.*

8. A black wrench and a silver saw. (Pause.) How are they the same? (Signal.) *They are tools.*

9. (Repeat steps 3–8 until firm.)

EXERCISE 3

● **DESCRIPTION**

The next Thinking Operation is **Description.**

1. I'm going to tell you about an object you know. But I'm going to call it a funny name. See if you can figure out what object I'm talking about.

2. (Hold up one finger.) A gorp is a tool.
(Hold up two fingers.) A gorp is made of wood.
(Hold up three fingers.) You write with a gorp.

3. Let's say the three things we know about a gorp. (Respond with the students.)
(Hold up one finger.) *A gorp is a tool.*
(Hold up two fingers.) *A gorp is made of wood.*
(Hold up three fingers.) *You write with a gorp.* (Repeat until students are responding with you.)

4. You say the three things you know about a gorp. (Hold up one finger.) *A gorp is a tool.*
(Hold up two fingers.) *A gorp is made of wood.*
(Hold up three fingers.) *You write with a gorp.* (Repeat until the students say the statements in order.)

5. Everybody, tell me the kind of tool I am calling a gorp. (Signal.) *A pencil.* Yes, it's a pencil.

6. Think of a pencil. Is a pencil a tool? (Signal.) *Yes.* Yes, a tool is something that helps you work. Say that. (Signal.) *A tool is something that helps you work.*

EXERCISE 4

● **DESCRIPTION**

1. Here's the rule. **Zork** is a funny word that we'll use for car. What word are we using for car? (Signal.) *Zork.*
And what does **zork** mean? (Signal.) *Car.*

2. Listen to this sentence. A zork eats cake. Is that statement true or false? (Signal.) *False.*

3. Next sentence. A zork can take you places. Is that statement true or false? (Signal.) *True.*

4. Next sentence. You sit in a zork. Is that statement true or false? (Signal.) *True.*

5. Next sentence. Zorks can talk. Is that statement true or false? (Signal.) *False.*

6. Next sentence. Zorks have wheels. Is that statement true or false? (Signal.) *True.*

EXERCISE 5

CLASSIFICATION

The next Thinking Operation is **Classification.**

1. We're going to do some class names. I'm going to name some objects. You're going to tell me a class these objects are in.

2. Listen. Washing machine, blender, stove. Everybody, what class? (Signal.) *Appliances.* Yes, appliances. If you plug it in to use in the house, it's an appliance.

3. Listen. Factories, schools, stores, houses. Everybody, what class? (Signal.) *Buildings.* Yes, buildings.

4. Listen. Shovel, rake, pencil, pliers, scissors. Everybody, what class? (Signal.) *Tools.* Yes, tools. If it helps you do a job, it's a tool.

5. (Repeat steps 2–4 until firm.)

6. Listen. Box, can, purse, basket, bottle. Everybody, what class? (Signal.) *Containers.* Yes, containers. If it's **made** to put things in, it's a container.

7. Listen. Roses, lilies, trees, grass. Everybody, what class? (Signal.) *Plants.* Yes, plants.

8. (Repeat steps 6 and 7 until firm.)

Individual test
1. I'll name a class. See how many objects you can name in that class. Listen. Tools. (Call on one student.)
2. (Repeat step 1 for **appliances, buildings, containers,** and **plants.**)

━━━━━━━━━━**EXERCISE 6**━━━━━━━━━━

● **STATEMENT INFERENCE**

The next Thinking Operation is **Statement Inference.**

Task A
1. Listen. Sam looked for monarch butterflies. Say that statement. (Signal.) *Sam looked for monarch butterflies.* (Repeat until firm.)

Individual test
Call on a few individuals to say the statement.

2. Everybody, listen. Sam looked for monarch butterflies. Who looked for monarch butterflies? (Signal.) *Sam.*
What kind of butterflies did Sam look for? (Signal.) *Monarch.* What did Sam do? (Signal.) *Looked for monarch butterflies.*
What did Sam look for? (Signal.) *Monarch butterflies.*
(Repeat step 2 until firm.)

Individual test
Call on individual students to answer a question from step 2.

Task B
1. Listen. Three bears were ready for a long sleep. Say that. (Signal.) *Three bears were ready for a long sleep.* (Repeat until firm.)

Individual test
Call on individuals to say the statement.

2. Listen. Three bears were ready for a long sleep. What were three bears ready for? (Signal.) *A long sleep.*
What was ready for a long sleep? (Signal.) *Three bears.*

What **kind** of sleep were those bears ready for? (Signal.) *Long.*
(Repeat step 2 until firm.)
3. Listen. Three bears were ready for a long sleep. Now here's a question you can't answer. What color were those three bears? You don't know. The statement doesn't tell you. Here's another question you can't answer. Where do those three bears live? You don't know. So, what do you say? (Signal.) *I don't know.* That's right. The statement doesn't tell you.
4. Listen. Three bears were ready for a long sleep. Why were three bears ready for a long sleep? (Signal.) *I don't know.* Yes, the statement doesn't tell you. Did three bears finally go to sleep? (Signal.) *I don't know.* Yes, the statement doesn't tell you. What were three bears ready for? (Signal.) *A long sleep.*

To correct students who say *I don't know.*
a. Yes, you **do** know.
b. Listen to the statement. Three bears were ready for a long sleep.
c. What were three bears ready for? (Signal.) *A long sleep.*
(Repeat step 4 until firm.)

Individual test
Call on individual students to answer a question from step 2 or step 4.

━━━━━━━━━━**EXERCISE 7**━━━━━━━━━━

DEDUCTIONS: With *all*

The next Thinking Operation is **Deductions.**

Task A
1. Listen to this rule. **All** plants grow. Everybody, say that. (Signal.) *All plants grow.* (Repeat until firm.)
2. Flowers are plants. Say that. (Signal.) *Flowers are plants.*
3. Listen. **All** plants grow. Flowers are plants. So, flowers (pause; signal) *grow.* Again. **All** plants grow. Flowers are plants. So (pause; signal), *flowers grow.*
(Repeat step 3 until firm.)

4. You know that flowers grow because **all** plants grow. How do you know that flowers grow? (Signal.) *Because all plants grow.* (Repeat step 4 until firm.)

To correct the failure to say *because:*
a. **Because** all plants grow.
b. How do you know that flowers grow? (Signal.) *Because all plants grow.*

Task B

1. Listen to this rule. **All** appliances have motors. Everybody, say that. (Signal.) *All appliances have motors.* (Repeat until firm.)

2. Refrigerators are appliances. Say that. (Signal.) *Refrigerators are appliances.*

3. Listen. **All** appliances have motors. Refrigerators are appliances. So, refrigerators (pause; signal) *have motors.* Again. **All** appliances have motors. Refrigerators are appliances. So (pause; signal), *refrigerators have motors.* (Repeat step 3 until firm.)

4. You know that refrigerators have motors because **all** appliances have motors. How do you know that refrigerators have motors? (Signal.) *Because all appliances have motors.* (Repeat step 4 until firm.)

Task C

1. Listen to this rule. **All** buildings have doors. Everybody, say that. (Signal.) *All buildings have doors.* (Repeat until firm.)

2. Stores are buildings. Say that. (Signal.) *Stores are buildings.*

3. Listen. **All** buildings have doors. Stores are buildings. So, stores (pause; signal) *have doors.*
Again. All buildings have doors. Stores are buildings. So (pause; signal), *stores have doors.*
(Repeat step 3 until firm.)

4. You know that stores have doors because **all** buildings have doors. How do you know that stores have doors? (Signal.) *Because all buildings have doors.* (Repeat step 4 until firm.)

Points

(Pass out the Workbooks. Award points for Thinking Operations.)

WORKBOOK EXERCISES

We're going to do Workbooks now. Remember to follow my instructions very carefully.

EXERCISE 8

● **SAME**

1. Everybody, touch part A in your Workbook. ✔ Some of the objects in Box 1 are in the same class. **Make a line over** the objects that are in the same class. Do it. (Wait.)

2. Some of the objects in Box 2 are usually the same color. **Make an X under** the objects that are usually the same color. Do it. (Wait.)

3. Some of the objects in Box 3 are in the same class. **Make a box around** the objects that are in the same class. Do it. (Wait.)

4. Everybody, get ready to check part A. Name the class of the objects you marked in Box 1. (Pause.) Get ready. (Signal.) *Food.*
Name the color of the objects you marked in Box 2. (Pause.) Get ready. (Signal.) *Yellow.*
Name the class of the objects you marked in Box 3. (Pause.) Get ready. (Signal.) *Furniture.*

5. Which objects did you mark in Box 1? (Call on one student.) *Fried egg, hot dog, cake.* What is the same about those objects? (Call on one student.) *They are food.* How did you mark each of those objects? (Call on one student.) *Made a line over them.*

6. (Repeat step 5 for Boxes 2 and 3.)

Answer key **2.** *Banana, bus; they are yellow; made an X under them.* **3.** *Bench, bookcase, bed; they are furniture; made a box around them.*

EXERCISE 9

TRUE—FALSE

1. Everybody, touch part B in your Workbook. ✔ I'll say statements about the picture. Some of these statements are true and some are false.

2. Item 1. Listen. **Some** of the objects are **trees.** Circle **true** or **false** for item 1. (Wait.)

3. Item 2. Listen. **All** of the objects are **tall.** Circle **true** or **false** for item 2. (Wait.)

4. Item 3. Listen. **Some** of the objects are **vehicles.** Circle **true** or **false** for item 3. (Wait.)
5. Item 4. Listen. **All** of the objects have **leaves.** Circle **true** or **false** for item 4. (Wait.)
6. Let's check your answers. Mark any item you missed with an X. Everybody, tell me true or false.
7. Item 1. **Some** of the objects are **trees.** (Signal.) *True.*
   Item 2. **All** of the objects are **tall.** (Signal.) *False.*
   Item 3. **Some** of the objects are **vehicles.** (Signal.) *False.*
   Item 4. **All** of the objects have leaves. (Signal.) *False.*

EXERCISE 10

CLASSIFICATION

1. Pencils down. Don't write anything yet. Everybody, touch the instructions for part C in your Workbook. ✔ I'll read the first instruction. Listen. Underline the containers.
2. What are you going to do to every container? (Signal.) *Underline it.*
3. I'll read the next instruction. Cross out the appliances. What are you going to do to every appliance? (Signal.) *Cross it out.* Everybody, do it. Underline the containers and cross out the appliances. (Wait.)
4. Get ready to mark your papers. Put an X by any object you get wrong.
5. What class is a **bottle** in? (Signal.) *Containers.* How did you mark the **bottle?** (Signal.) *Underlined it.*
6. (Repeat step 5 for **mixer, box, pot, television, iron, purse, jar,** and **hair dryer.**)

EXERCISE 11

TRUE—FALSE

1. Everybody, touch part D in your Workbook. I'll say statements that are true of one of the pictures.
2. Listen: **None** of the pencils are long. Touch the right picture. (Signal.)
   (Repeat step 2 until firm.)

3. Listen: **All** the pencils are long. Touch the right picture. (Signal.)
   (Repeat step 3 until firm.)
4. Listen: **Only some** of the pencils are long. Touch the right picture. (Signal.)
   (Repeat step 4 until firm.)
5. (Repeat steps 2–4 until firm.)
6. Let's do it again. This time, you'll write the letter of each picture I describe. Here's item 1: **None** of the pencils are long. Touch the right picture. (Signal.) What letter is under that picture? (Signal.) *C.* Write the letter **C** on line 1. (Wait.)
7. Here's item 2: **All** the pencils are long. Touch the right picture. (Signal.) What letter is under that picture? (Signal.) *A.* Write the letter **A** on line 2. (Wait.)
8. Here's item 3: **Only some** of the pencils are long. Touch the right picture. (Signal.) Write the letter of that picture on line 3. (Wait.)
9. Let's check your answer. Item 3. **Only some** of the pencils are long. What's the letter of that picture? (Signal.) *B.* Yes, the answer to item 3 is **B.**

EXERCISE 12

DESCRIPTION

1. Everybody, touch part E in your Workbook. Figure out which object I describe. Listen. A frib is a piece of clothing. A frib keeps you warm. A frib is worn on your head. **Make a 2 on** the object I'm calling a frib. (Wait.)
2. Listen. A trible is a vehicle. A girl can ride in a trible. A trible has four wheels and a handle. **Make a 4 on** the object I'm calling a trible. (Wait.)
3. Listen. A dorn is a tool. A dorn is made of wood. You use a dorn to write with. **Make a 3 on** the object I'm calling a dorn. (Wait.)
4. Everybody, get ready to check your work. Tell me the real name for the object that is a piece of clothing, that keeps you warm, and that is worn on your head. Get ready. (Signal.) *A hat.* And how did you mark the hat? (Signal.) *Made a 2 on it.*

5. Tell me the real name for the object that is a vehicle, that a girl can ride in, and that has four wheels and a handle. Get ready. (Signal.) *A wagon.* And how did you mark the wagon? (Signal.) *Made a 4 on it.*

6. Tell me the real name for the object that is a tool, that is made of wood, and that you use to write with. Get ready. (Signal.) *A pencil.* And how did you mark the pencil? (Signal.) *Made a 3 on it.*

Points

(Award points for Workbooks.)

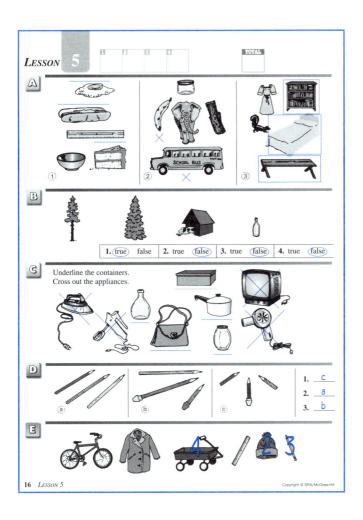

INFORMATION

We're going to work on Information now.

━━━━━ EXERCISE 13 ━━━━━

● **INFORMATION: Animals**

1. You're going to learn about animals that have a backbone. What kind of animals? (Signal.) *Animals that have a backbone.*
   There are five classes of animals that have a backbone. How many classes? (Signal.) *Five.*

2. The first class you'll learn about is **mammals.** What class? (Signal.) *Mammals.* Here are some mammals: dogs, cats, monkeys, human beings. Name some other mammals. (Call on individual students. Accept the names of any warm-blooded animals with hair, such as whales, bats, and elephants.)

3. Here's the first fact about **all mammals.** Listen. All mammals have hair. Say that fact. (Signal.) *All mammals have hair.* (Repeat until firm.)

4. All mammals have hair. Dogs, cats, monkeys, and lions are mammals. So, they have (pause; signal) *hair.* (Repeat step 4 until firm.)

5. All mammals have hair. Whales and porpoises are mammals. So, whales and porpoises have (pause; signal) *hair.* (Repeat step 5 until firm.)

Individual test
(Call on individual students to do one of the following tasks:)
   a. What's the first fact about mammals?
   b. Name some mammals.

━━━ **EXERCISE 14** ━━━

CALENDAR: Months in a Year

Task A

1. Raise your hand if you know how many months are in a year and can name the months in a year.
2. (Call on each student whose hand is raised.) How many months are in a year? *Twelve.* Name the months in a year. *January, February, March, April, May, June, July, August, September, October, November, December.*

> **Note:** Only students who do not respond correctly to step 2 above are to work on tasks B–F.

Task B

1. There are twelve months in a year. How many months are in a year? (Signal.) *Twelve.*
2. Tell me the fact about how many months are in a year. (Signal.) *There are twelve months in a year.* (Repeat until firm.)

> **Note:** Do not work on tasks C–F for more than four minutes. Stop wherever you are in the exercise after four minutes. The exercise will be repeated in the next lesson.

Task C

1. I'll name the first three months. Listen. January, February, March. Your turn. Name the first three months. (Signal.) *January, February, March.* (Repeat until firm.)
2. You named some of the months. Everybody, tell me the fact about how many months are in a year. (Pause.) Get ready. (Signal.) *There are twelve months in a year.* (Repeat until firm.)

> *Individual test*
> (Call on individual students to do one of the following tasks:)
> a. Name the first three months.
> b. Tell me the fact about how many months are in a year.

Task D

1. Here are the next three months. Listen. April, May, June. Your turn. Name those months. (Signal.) *April, May, June.* (Repeat until firm.)
2. Now I'll name the first six months. Listen. January, February, March, April, May, June. Your turn. Name the first six months. (Signal.) *January, February, March, April, May, June.* (Repeat until firm.)

> *Individual test*
> (Call on individual students to do one of the following tasks:)
> a. Name the first six months.
> b. Tell me the fact about how many months are in a year.

Task E

1. Here are the next three months. Listen. July, August, September. Your turn. Name those months. (Signal.) *July, August, September.* (Repeat until firm.)
2. Now I'll name the first nine months. Listen. January, February, March, April, May, June, July, August, September. Your turn. Name the first nine months. (Signal.) *January, February, March, April, May, June, July, August, September.* (Repeat until firm.)

> *Individual test*
> (Call on individual students to do one of the following tasks:)
> a. Name the first nine months.
> b. Tell me the fact about how many months are in a year.

Task F

1. Here are the last three months. Listen. October, November, December. Your turn. Name those months. (Signal.) *October, November, December.* (Repeat until firm.)

2. Now I'll name all twelve months. Listen. January, February, March, April, May, June, July, August, September, October, November, December. Your turn. Name all twelve months. (Signal.) *January, February, March, April, May, June, July, August, September, October, November, December.* (Repeat until firm.)

Individual test

(Call on individual students to do one of the following tasks:)

    a. Name all twelve months in a year.

    b. Tell me the fact about how many months are in a year.

Points

(Award points for Information.
Have the students add up their daily total.)

Point Schedule

Box		Maximum Points
1	Thinking Operations	5
2	Workbook	5
3	Information	4
4	Bonus points	(3)

Note: Before beginning Lesson 6, present Fact Game Lesson 2, which appears at the end of this book.

END OF LESSON 5

THINKING OPERATIONS

---EXERCISE 1---

DEDUCTIONS: With *all*

The first Thinking Operation today is **Deductions.**

Task A

1. Listen to this rule. **All** mammals have hair. Everybody, say that. (Signal.) *All mammals have hair.* (Repeat until firm.)
2. Whales are mammals. Say that. (Signal.) *Whales are mammals.*
3. Listen. **All** mammals have hair. Whales are mammals. So, whales (pause; signal) *have hair.*
   Again. **All** mammals have hair. Whales are mammals. So (pause; signal), *whales have hair.*
   (Repeat step 3 until firm.)
4. You know that whales have hair because **all** mammals have hair. How do you know that whales have hair? (Signal.) *Because all mammals have hair.*
   (Repeat step 4 until firm.)

   To correct the failure to say *because:*
   a. **Because** all mammals have hair.
   b. How do you know that whales have hair? (Signal.) *Because all mammals have hair.*

Task B

1. Listen to this rule. **All** mammals have hair. Everybody, say that. (Signal.) *All mammals have hair.* (Repeat until firm.)
2. Dogs are mammals. Say that. (Signal.) *Dogs are mammals.*
3. Listen. **All** mammals have hair. Dogs are mammals. So, dogs (pause; signal) *have hair.* Again. **All** mammals have hair. Dogs are mammals. So (pause; signal), *dogs have hair.*
   (Repeat step 3 until firm.)
4. You know that dogs have hair because **all** mammals have hair. How do you know that dogs have hair? (Signal.) *Because all mammals have hair.*
   (Repeat step 4 until firm.)

Task C

1. Listen to this rule. **All** containers can hold things. Everybody, say that. (Signal.) *All containers can hold things.*
2. Pitchers are containers. Say that. (Signal.) *Pitchers are containers.*
3. Listen. **All** containers can hold things. Pitchers are containers. So, pitchers (pause; signal) *can hold things.*
   Again. **All** containers can hold things. Pitchers are containers. So (pause; signal), *pitchers can hold things.*
   (Repeat step 3 until firm.)
4. You know that pitchers can hold things because **all** containers can hold things. How do you know that pitchers can hold things? (Signal.) *Because all containers can hold things.*
   (Repeat step 4 until firm.)

---EXERCISE 2---

● **DEDUCTIONS: With** *don't*

1. Listen to this rule. Cows **don't** fly. Everybody, say that.
   (Signal.) *Cows don't fly.*
2. What does the rule tell about cows? (Call on a student.) *They don't fly.*
3. Everybody, say the rule again. (Signal.) *Cows don't fly.* Guernseys are cows. So (pause; signal), *Guernseys don't fly.*
4. You know that Guernseys don't fly because cows don't fly. How do you know that Guernseys don't fly? (Signal.) *Because cows don't fly.*
5. (Repeat steps 3 and 4 until firm.)
6. Listen. Cows **don't** fly. Holsteins are cows. So (pause; signal), *Holsteins don't fly.*
7. You know that Holsteins don't fly because cows don't fly. How do you know that Holsteins don't fly? (Signal.) *Because cows don't fly.*
8. (Repeat steps 6 and 7 until firm.)
9. Listen. Cows **don't** fly. Herefords are cows. So (pause; signal), *Herefords don't fly.*
10. How do you know that Herefords don't fly? (Signal.) *Because cows don't fly.*
11. (Repeat steps 9 and 10 until firm.)

EXERCISE 3

STATEMENT INFERENCE

The next Thinking Operation is **Statement Inference.**

Task A

1. Listen. Jerry poured the gasoline carefully. Say that statement. (Signal.) *Jerry poured the gasoline carefully.* (Repeat until firm.)

> **Individual test**
> Call on a few individual students to say the statement.

2. Everybody, listen. Jerry poured the gasoline carefully. How did Jerry pour the gasoline? (Signal.) *Carefully.*
   Who poured the gasoline carefully? (Signal.) *Jerry.*
   What did Jerry pour carefully? (Signal.) *Gasoline.*
   What did Jerry do? (Signal.) *Poured the gasoline carefully.*
   How much gasoline did Jerry pour carefully? (Signal.) *I don't know.* That's right; the statement doesn't say.
   (Repeat step 2 until firm.)

> **Individual test**
> Call on individual students to answer a question from step 2.

Task B

1. Listen. Cottonwood trees grow rapidly. Say that statement. (Signal.) *Cottonwood trees grow rapidly.* (Repeat until firm.)

> **Individual test**
> Call on a few individual students to say the statement.

2. Everybody, listen. Cottonwood trees grow rapidly. What grows rapidly? (Signal.) *Cottonwood trees.*
   What do cottonwood trees do? (Signal.) *Grow rapidly.*

Where do cottonwood trees grow rapidly? (Signal.) *I don't know.* That's right; the statement doesn't say. What kind of trees grow rapidly? (Signal.) *Cottonwood.* How do cottonwood trees grow? (Signal.) *Rapidly.* (Repeat step 2 until firm.)

> **Individual test**
> Call on individual students to answer a question from step 2.

EXERCISE 4

DEFINITIONS

The next Thinking Operation is **Definitions.**

1. **Complete.** (Pause.) What does **complete** mean? (Signal.) *Finish.* And what word means **finish?** (Signal.) *Complete.* (Repeat step 1 until firm.)
2. Listen. Please complete your reading. Say that. (Signal.) *Please complete your reading.* (Repeat until firm.)
   Now say that sentence with a different word for **complete.** (Pause.) Get ready. (Signal.) *Please finish your reading.* (Repeat until firm.) (Repeat step 2 until firm.)

EXERCISE 5

DEFINITIONS

1. **Canine** means **dog.**
2. What does **canine** mean? (Signal.) *Dog.* What word means **dog?** (Signal.) *Canine.* (Repeat step 2 until firm.)
3. Listen. That canine is a poodle. Say that. (Signal.) *That canine is a poodle.* (Repeat until firm.)
   Now say that sentence with a different word for **canine.** (Pause.) Get ready. (Signal.) *That dog is a poodle.* (Repeat until firm.) (Repeat step 3 until firm.)
4. Listen. Do you have a dog? Say that. (Signal.) *Do you have a dog?* (Repeat until firm.)
   Now say that sentence with a different word for **dog.** (Pause.) Get ready. (Signal.) *Do you have a canine?* (Repeat until firm.) (Repeat step 4 until firm.)

5. Listen. Collies are canines. Say that. (Signal.) *Collies are canines.* (Repeat until firm.) Now say that sentence with a different word for **canines.** (Pause.) Get ready. (Signal.) *Collies are dogs.* (Repeat until firm.) (Repeat step 5 until firm.)

━━━━━━ **EXERCISE 6** ━━━━━━

DEFINITIONS

Task A

1. A **synonym** is a word that has the same meaning as another word. What's a synonym? (Signal.) A word that has the same meaning as another word. (Repeat until the students are responding with you.)

2. By yourselves. What's a **synonym?** (Signal.) *A word that has the same meaning as another word.* (Repeat until firm.)

3. **Obtain.** (Pause.) What does **obtain** mean? (Signal.) *Get.*
   So, what's a synonym for **obtain?** (Signal.) *Get.*
   And what's a synonym for **get?** (Signal.) *Obtain.*

4. **Complete.** (Pause.) What's a synonym for **complete?** (Signal.) *Finish.*
   And what's a synonym for **finish?** (Signal.) *Complete.*

5. **Masticate.** (Pause.) What's a synonym for **masticate?** (Signal.) *Chew.*
   And what's a synonym for **chew?** (Signal.) *Masticate.*

6. (Repeat steps 3–5 until firm.)

Task B

1. Listen to this sentence. You masticate bread. Say that. (Signal.) *You masticate bread.* (Repeat until firm.)
   Now say that sentence with a synonym for **masticate.** (Pause.) Get ready. (Signal.) *You chew bread.* (Repeat until firm.)
   (Repeat step 1 until firm.)

2. Listen to this sentence. She never chews her food enough. Say that. (Signal.) *She never chews her food enough. (Repeat until firm.)*
   Now say that sentence with a synonym for **chews.** (Pause.) Get ready. (Signal.) *She never masticates her food enough.* (Repeat until firm.)
   (Repeat step 2 until firm.)

3. **Obtain.** What's a synonym for **obtain?** (Signal.) *Get.*

4. Listen to this sentence. They will obtain some ice cream. Say that. (Signal.) *They will obtain some ice cream.* (Repeat until firm.)
   Now say that sentence with a synonym for **obtain.** (Pause.) Get ready. (Signal.) *They will get some ice cream.* (Repeat until firm.)
   (Repeat step 4 until firm.)

5. Listen to this sentence. They will get the books at the store. Say that. (Signal.) *They will get the books at the store.* (Repeat until firm.)
   Now say that sentence with a synonym for **get.** (Pause.) Get ready. (Signal.) *They will obtain the books at the store.* (Repeat until firm.)
   (Repeat step 5 until firm.)

6. **Complete.** What's a synonym for **complete?** (Signal.) *Finish.*

7. Listen to this sentence. He will complete the painting tomorrow. Say that. (Signal.) *He will complete the painting tomorrow.* (Repeat until firm.)
   Now say that sentence with a synonym for **complete.** (Pause.) Get ready. (Signal.) *He will finish the painting tomorrow.* (Repeat until firm.)
   (Repeat step 7 until firm.)

8. Listen to this sentence. Can you finish that drawing quickly? Say that. (Signal.) *Can you finish that drawing quickly?* (Repeat until firm.)
   Now say that sentence with a synonym for **finish.** (Pause.) Get ready. (Signal.) *Can you complete that drawing quickly?* (Repeat until firm.)
   (Repeat step 8 until firm.)

EXERCISE 7

SAME: Review

The next Thinking Operation is **Same.**

1. Remember, food is something people can eat. Appliances are plugged in to use in the house. Tools are made to help people work.
2. Get ready to tell me how things are the same.
3. A yellow banana and a yellow car. (Pause.) How are they the same? (Signal.) *They are yellow.*
4. Candy, oranges, and bread. (Pause.) How are they the same? (Signal.) *They are food.*
5. A green refrigerator and green lettuce. (Pause.) How are they the same? (Signal.) *They are green.*
6. Cold milk and a cold day. (Pause.) How are they the same? (Signal.) *They are cold.*
7. A white stove and a silver iron. (Pause.) How are they the same? (Signal.) *They are appliances.*
8. A shovel, an ax, and a knife. (Pause.) How are they the same? (Signal.) *They are tools.*
9. (Repeat steps 3–8 until firm.)

EXERCISE 8

SAME: Material

1. Wooden chairs and wooden fences are made of the same material. What material? (Signal.) *Wood.* Yes, they are made of wood. How are they the same? (Signal.) *They are made of wood.*
2. How are a wooden shelf and a wooden pencil the same? (Signal.) *They are made of wood.*
3. How are a wooden table and a wooden house the same? (Signal.) *They are made of wood.*
4. (Repeat steps 1–3 until firm.)

EXERCISE 9

DESCRIPTION

The next Thinking Operation is **Description.**

1. I'm going to tell you about an object you know. But I'm going to call it a funny name. See if you can figure out what object I'm talking about.
2. (Hold up one finger.) A snab is a building. (Hold up two fingers.) A snab has lots of seats in it. (Hold up three fingers.) You watch movies in a snab.
3. Let's say the three things we know about a snab. (Respond with students.) (Hold up one finger.) *A snab is a building.* (Hold up two fingers.) *A snab has lots of seats in it.* (Hold up three fingers.) *You watch movies in a snab.* (Repeat until the students are responding with you.)
4. You say the three things you know about a snab. (Hold up one finger.) *A snab is a building.* (Hold up two fingers.) *A snab has lots of seats in it.* (Hold up three fingers.) *You watch movies in a snab.* (Repeat until the students say the statements in order.)
5. Everybody, tell me the kind of building I am calling a snab. (Signal.) *A movie theater.* Yes, it's a movie theater.

Points

(Pass out the Workbooks.
Award points for Thinking Operations.)

We're going to do Workbooks now. Remember to follow my instructions very carefully.

EXERCISE 10

● **DESCRIPTION**

1. Everybody, touch part A in your Workbook. ✔ Now touch line 1. (Wait.)
   You're going to write a letter on that line. That letter stands for the tree that I'm going to describe.

2. Listen. This tree is big. This tree has a heart carved on the trunk. This tree has a broken branch. Listen again. (Repeat the description.) Write the letter of the tree I described on line 1. (Wait.)

3. Find line 2. You're going to write a letter of a different tree on that line. Listen. This tree has a heart carved on the trunk. This tree has a bird in it. This tree has a broken branch. Listen again. (Repeat the description.) Write the letter of the tree I described on line 2. (Wait.)

4. Find line 3. You're going to write a letter of a different tree on that line. Listen. This tree has a heart carved on the trunk. This tree is little. This tree does not have a broken branch. Listen again. (Repeat the description.) Write the letter of the tree I described on line 3. (Wait.)

5. Let's check your answers. Mark any item you miss with an X. Item 1. This tree is big, has a broken branch, and has a heart carved on the trunk. (Pause.) What's the letter of that tree? (Signal.) *B.* Yes, the answer to item 1 is **B.**

6. Item 2. This tree has a heart carved on the trunk, a bird in it, and a broken branch. (Pause.) What's the letter of that tree? (Signal.) *C.* Yes, the answer to item 2 is **C.**

7. Item 3. This tree has a heart carved on the trunk, it is little, and it does not have a broken branch. What's the letter of that tree? (Signal.) *D.* Yes, the answer to item 3 is **D.**

8. Who got all the items right? (Praise the students who got all the items right.)

=========== EXERCISE 11 ===========

TRUE—FALSE

1. Everybody, touch part B in your Workbook. I'll say statements that are true of one of the pictures.

2. Listen: **Only some** of the cats are running. Touch the right picture. (Signal.) (Repeat step 2 until firm.)

3. Listen: **Only some** of the cats are sitting. Touch the right picture. (Signal.) (Repeat step 3 until firm.)

4. Listen: **All** the cats are sleeping. Touch the right picture. (Signal.) (Repeat step 4 until firm.)

5. (Repeat steps 2–4 until firm.)

6. Let's do it again. This time, you'll write the letter of each picture I describe. Here's item 1: **Only some** of the cats are running. Touch the right picture. (Signal.) What letter is under that picture? (Signal.) *B.* Write the letter **B** on line 1. (Wait.)

7. Here's item 2: **Only some** of the cats are sitting. Touch the right picture. (Signal.) What letter is under that picture? (Signal.) *A.* Write the letter **A** on line 2. (Wait.)

8. Here's item 3: **All** the cats are sleeping. Touch the right picture. (Signal.) Write the letter of that picture on line 3. (Wait.)

9. Let's check your answer. Item 3. **All** the cats are sleeping. What's the letter of that picture? (Signal.) *C.* Yes, the answer to item 3 is **C.**

=========== EXERCISE 12 ===========

CLASSIFICATION

1. Pencils down. Don't write anything yet. Everybody, touch the instructions for part C in your Workbook. ✔ I'll read the first instruction. Listen. Circle the tools.

2. What are you going to do to every tool? (Signal.) *Circle it.*

3. I'll read the next instruction. Underline the animals. What are you going to do to every animal? (Signal.) *Underline it.* Everybody, do it. Circle the tools and underline the animals. (Wait.)

4. Get ready to mark your papers. Put an X by any object you get wrong.

5. What class is a pair of **pliers** in? (Signal.) *Tools.* How did you mark the **pliers?** (Signal.) *Circled it.*

6. (Repeat step 5 for **dog, snake, giraffe, scissors, rake, elephant, fork,** and **pig.**)

EXERCISE 13

TRUE—FALSE

1. Everybody, touch part D in your Workbook. I'll say statements about the picture. Some of the statements are true and some are false.
2. Item 1. Listen. **Some** of the shoes have **high heels.** Circle **true** or **false** for item 1. (Wait.)
3. Item 2. Listen. **All** the shoes are **black.** Circle **true** or **false** for item 2. (Wait.)
4. Item 3. Listen. **All** the shoes have **laces.** Circle **true** or **false** for item 3. (Wait.)
5. Item 4. Listen. **Some** of the shoes have **laces.** Circle **true** or **false** for item 4. (Wait.)
6. Let's check your answers. Mark any item you miss with an X. Everybody, tell me **true** or **false**.
7. Item 1. **Some** of the shoes have **high heels.** (Signal.) *True.*
   Item 2. **All** the shoes are **black.** (Signal.) *True.*
   Item 3. **All** the shoes have **laces.** (Signal.) *False.*
   Item 4. **Some** of the shoes have **laces.** (Signal.) *True.*

EXERCISE 14

SAME

1. Everybody, touch part E in your Workbook. Some of the objects in Box 1 are usually made of the same material. **Make a 3 on** the objects that are usually made of the same material. Do it. (Wait.)
2. Some of the objects in Box 2 are in the same class. **Make a 4 on** the objects that are in the same class. Do it. (Wait.)
3. Some of the objects in Box 3 are in the same class. **Draw a line under** the objects that are in the same class. Do it. (Wait.)

4. Everybody, get ready to check part E. Name the material of the objects you marked in Box 1. (Pause.) Get ready. (Signal.) *Wood.* Name the class of the objects you marked in Box 2. (Pause.) Get ready. (Signal.) *Tools.* Name the class of the objects you marked in Box 3. (Pause.) Get ready. (Signal.) *Containers.*
5. Which objects did you mark in Box 1? (Call on one student.) *Chair, desk, log.*
   What is the same about those objects? (Call on one student.) *They are made of wood.*
   How did you mark each of those objects? (Call on one student.) *Made a 3 on them.*
6. (Repeat step 5 for Boxes 2 and 3.)

Points
(Award points for Workbooks.)

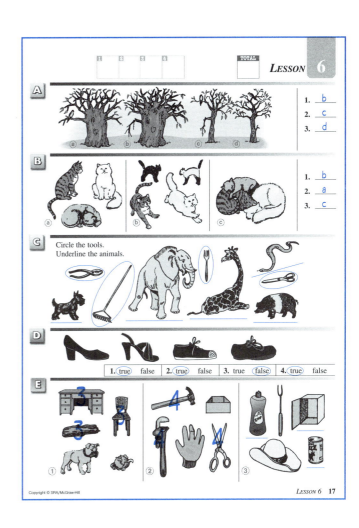

INFORMATION

We're going to work on Information now.

===== **EXERCISE 15** =====

- **INFORMATION: Animals**

1. We're going to talk about animals that have a backbone. There are five classes of animals that have a backbone. How many classes? (Signal.) *Five.*

2. Last time, you learned the name of one class of animal that has a backbone. Everybody, what's the name of that class? (Signal.) *Mammals.*

3. Name a mammal. (Call on individual students. The group is to name at least five mammals.)
   You learned a fact about **all mammals.** Everybody, say the fact about **all mammals.** (Pause.) Get ready. (Signal.) *All mammals have hair.* (Repeat until firm.)

4. Here's another fact about **all mammals.** Listen. All mammals are warm-blooded. Say that fact. (Signal.) *All mammals are warm-blooded.* (Repeat until firm.)

5. Here's what warm-blooded means. No matter how hot or cold it gets outside, the body temperature of a warm-blooded animal stays the **same.** The body temperature stays the **same.** What do you know about the body temperature of a warm-blooded animal? (Signal.) *The body temperature stays the same.* (Repeat until firm.)

6. You are a warm-blooded animal. Your body temperature is 37 degrees. So, what is your body temperature when it is 5 degrees outside? (Signal.) *37 degrees.*
   What is your body temperature when it is 40 degrees outside? (Signal.) *37 degrees.*
   Yes, the body temperature of warm-blooded animals **always** stays the same.

7. Here's that fact again. All mammals are warm-blooded. Say that fact. (Signal.) *All mammals are warm-blooded.*
   Lions are mammals. So, lions are (pause; signal) *warm-blooded.*
   (Repeat step 7 until firm.)

8. Here's that fact again. All mammals are warm-blooded. Human beings are mammals. So, human beings are (pause; signal) *warm-blooded.*
   (Repeat step 8 until firm.)

9. Here are the two facts you know about all mammals. (Hold up one finger.) First fact. All mammals have hair.
   (Hold up two fingers.) Second fact. All mammals are warm-blooded.
   Tell me the two facts you know about all mammals.
   (Hold up one finger.) First fact. *All mammals have hair.*
   (Hold up two fingers.) Second fact. *All mammals are warm-blooded.* (Repeat until the students say the facts in order.)

Individual test
(Call on individual students to do one of the following tasks:)
   a. What does warm-blooded mean?
   b. What's the first fact about all mammals?
   c. What's the second fact about all mammals?

EXERCISE 16

● **CALENDAR: Months in a Year**

1. Everybody, how many months are in a year? (Signal.) *Twelve.* You're going to name the months in a year. What are you going to name? (Signal.) *The months in a year.*

2. Name the months in a year. (Pause.) Get ready. (Signal.) *January, February, March, April, May, June, July, August, September, October, November, December.*

3. You named the (pause; signal) *months in a year.*

Individual test

Call on individual students to name the months in a year.

Points

(Award points for Information.
Have the students add up their daily total.)

Point Schedule

Box		Maximum Points
1	Thinking Operations	5
2	Workbook	5
3	Information	4
4	Bonus points	(3)

END OF LESSON 6

THINKING OPERATIONS

EXERCISE 1

- **SAME: Review**

The first Thinking Operation today is **Same.**

1. Get ready to tell me how things are the same.
2. Dogs, cows, and tigers. (Pause.) How are they the same? (Signal.) *They are animals.*
3. A yellow school and a red fire station. (Pause.) How are they the same? (Signal.) *They are buildings.*
4. A spotted couch and a spotted dog. (Pause.) How are they the same? (Signal.) *They are spotted.*
5. A chair, a dresser, and a bed. (Pause.) How are they the same? (Signal.) *They are furniture.*
6. A church, a store, and a garage. (Pause.) How are they the same? (Signal.) *They are buildings.*
7. A brown horse, a black cat, and a gray mouse. (Pause.) How are they the same? (Signal.) *They are animals.*
8. (Repeat steps 2–7 until firm.)

EXERCISE 2

SAME: Material

1. A metal car and a metal garbage can are made of the same material. What material? (Signal.) *Metal.* Yes, they are made of metal. How are they the same? (Signal.) *They are made of metal.*
2. How are a metal spoon and a metal car the same? (Signal.) *They are made of metal.*
3. How are a metal garbage can and a metal lamp the same? (Signal.) *They are made of metal.*
4. (Repeat steps 1–3 until firm.)

EXERCISE 3

DEFINITIONS

1. **Canine** means **dog.**
2. What does **canine** mean? (Signal.) *Dog.* What word means **dog?** (Signal.) *Canine.* (Repeat step 2 until firm.)

3. Listen. Why is that dog barking? Say that. (Signal.) *Why is that dog barking?* (Repeat until firm.)
   Now say that sentence with a different word for **dog.** (Pause.) Get ready. (Signal.) *Why is that canine barking?* (Repeat until firm.) (Repeat step 3 until firm.)
4. Listen. Those dogs are fighting. Say that. (Signal.) *Those dogs are fighting.* (Repeat until firm.)
   Now say that sentence with a different word for **dogs.** (Pause.) Get ready. (Signal.) *Those canines are fighting.* (Repeat until firm.) (Repeat step 4 until firm.)
5. Listen. That canine has fleas. Say that. (Signal.) *That canine has fleas.* (Repeat until firm.)
   Now say that sentence with a different word for **canine.** (Pause.) Get ready. (Signal.) *That dog has fleas.* (Repeat until firm.) (Repeat step 5 until firm.)

EXERCISE 4

DEFINITIONS

The next Thinking Operation is **Definitions.**

Task A

1. A **synonym** is a word that has the same meaning as another word. What's a **synonym?** (Signal.) A word that has the same meaning as another word. (Repeat until the students are responding with you.)
2. By yourselves. What's a synonym? (Signal.) *A word that has the same meaning as another word.* (Repeat until firm.)
3. **Canine.** (Pause.) What does **canine** mean? (Signal.) *Dog.* So, what's a synonym for **canine?** (Signal.) *Dog.* And what's a synonym for **dog?** (Signal.) *Canine.*
4. **Obtain.** (Pause.) What's a synonym for **obtain?** (Signal.) *Get.* And what's a synonym for **get?** (Signal.) *Obtain.*
5. **Finish.** (Pause.) What's a synonym for **finish?** (Signal.) *Complete.* And what's a synonym for **complete?** (Signal.) *Finish.*
6. (Repeat steps 3–5 until firm.)

Task B

1. Listen to this sentence. I will finish this job alone. Say that. (Signal.) *I will finish this job alone.* (Repeat until firm.)

   Now say that sentence with a synonym for **finish.** (Pause.) Get ready. (Signal.) *I will complete this job alone.* (Repeat until firm.) (Repeat step 1 until firm.)

2. Listen to this sentence. They completed the house in two months. Say that. (Signal.) *They completed the house in two months.* (Repeat until firm.)

   Now say that sentence with a synonym for **completed.** (Pause.) Get ready. (Signal.) *They finished the house in two months.* (Repeat until firm.) (Repeat step 2 until firm.)

3. **Canine.** What's a synonym for **canine?** (Signal.) *Dog.*

4. Listen to this sentence. The canine barked at the mail carrier. Say that. (Signal.) *The canine barked at the mail carrier.* (Repeat until firm.)

   Now say that sentence with a synonym for **canine.** (Pause.) Get ready. (Signal.) *The dog barked at the mail carrier.* (Repeat until firm.) (Repeat step 4 until firm.)

5. Listen to this sentence. Dogs chase their tails. Say that. (Signal.) *Dogs chase their tails.* (Repeat until firm.)

   Now say that sentence with a synonym for **dogs.** (Pause.) Get ready. (Signal.) *Canines chase their tails.* (Repeat until firm.) (Repeat step 5 until firm.)

6. **Obtain.** What's a synonym for **obtain?** (Signal.) *Get.*

7. Listen to this sentence. I obtained a prize. Say that. (Signal.) *I obtained a prize.* (Repeat until firm.)

   Now say that sentence with a synonym for **obtained.** (Pause.) Get ready. (Signal.) *I got a prize.* (Repeat until firm.) (Repeat step 7 until firm.)

8. Listen to this sentence. He obtained a ticket for me. Say that. (Signal.) *He obtained a ticket for me.* (Repeat until firm.)

   Now say that sentence with a synonym for **obtained.** (Pause.) Get ready. (Signal.) *He got a ticket for me.* (Repeat until firm.) (Repeat step 8 until firm.)

================= EXERCISE 5 =================

DEFINITIONS

1. **Masticate.** (Pause.) What does **masticate** mean? (Signal.) *Chew.*

   And what word means **chew?** (Signal.) *Masticate.* (Repeat step 1 until firm.)

2. Listen. This meat is hard to masticate. Say that. (Signal.) *This meat is hard to masticate.* (Repeat until firm.)

   Now say that sentence with a different word for **masticate.** (Pause.) Get ready. (Signal.) *This meat is hard to chew.* (Repeat until firm.) (Repeat step 2 until firm.)

================= EXERCISE 6 =================

DESCRIPTION

The next Thinking Operation is **Description.**

1. I'm going to tell you about an object you know. But I'm going to call it a funny name. See if you can figure out what object I'm talking about.

2. (Hold up one finger.) A bem is a vehicle. (Hold up two fingers.) A bem has three wheels.

   (Hold up three fingers.) You pedal a bem.

3. Let's say the three things we know about a bem. (Respond with students. Hold up one finger.) *A bem is a vehicle.*

   (Hold up two fingers.) *A bem has three wheels.*

   (Hold up three fingers.) *You pedal a bem.* (Repeat until the students are responding with you.)

4. You say the three things you know about a bem. (Hold up one finger.) *A bem is a vehicle.*

   (Hold up two fingers.) *A bem has three wheels.*

   (Hold up three fingers.) *You pedal a bem.* (Repeat until the students say the statements in order.)

LESSON 7

5. Everybody, tell me the kind of vehicle I am calling a bem. (Signal.) *Tricycle.* Yes, it's really a tricycle.
6. Think of a tricycle. Is a tricycle a vehicle? (Signal.) *Yes.* Yes, a vehicle is something that takes things places. Say that. (Signal.) *A vehicle is something that takes things places.*

EXERCISE 7

• **DEDUCTIONS: With *all***

The next Thinking Operation is **Deductions.**

Task A

1. Listen to this rule. **All** trees are plants. Everybody, say that. (Signal.) *All trees are plants.* (Repeat until firm.)
2. Oaks are trees. Say that. (Signal.) *Oaks are trees.*
3. Listen. **All** trees are plants. Oaks are trees. So, oaks (pause; signal) *are plants.* Again. **All** trees are plants. Oaks are trees. So (pause; signal), *oaks are plants.* (Repeat step 3 until firm.)
4. How do you know that oaks are plants? (Signal.) *Because all trees are plants.* (Repeat step 4 until firm.)

Task B

1. Listen to this rule. **All** mammals have hair. Everybody, say that. (Signal.) *All mammals have hair.*
2. Seals are mammals. Say that. (Signal.) *Seals are mammals.*
3. Listen. **All** mammals have hair. Seals are mammals. So, seals (pause; signal) *have hair.* Again. **All** mammals have hair. Seals are mammals. So (pause; signal), *seals have hair.* (Repeat step 3 until firm.)
4. How do you know that seals have hair? (Signal.) *Because all mammals have hair.* (Repeat step 4 until firm.)

EXERCISE 8

DEDUCTIONS: With *don't*

1. Listen to this rule. Insects **don't** have bones. Everybody, say that. (Signal.) *Insects don't have bones.*
2. What does the rule tell about insects? (Call on a student.) *They don't have bones.*
3. Everybody, say the rule again. (Signal.) *Insects don't have bones.* Ladybugs are insects. So (pause; signal), *ladybugs don't have bones.*
4. You know that ladybugs **don't** have bones because insects **don't** have bones. How do you know that ladybugs **don't** have bones? (Signal.) *Because insects don't have bones.*
5. (Repeat steps 3 and 4 until firm.)
6. Listen. Insects **don't** have bones. Grasshoppers are insects. So (pause; signal), *grasshoppers don't have bones.*
7. You know that grasshoppers **don't** have bones because insects **don't** have bones. How do you know that grasshoppers **don't** have bones? (Signal.) *Because insects don't have bones.*
8. (Repeat steps 6 and 7 until firm.)
9. Listen. Insects **don't** have bones. Dragonflies are insects. So (pause; signal), *dragonflies don't have bones.*
10. How do you know that dragonflies **don't** have bones? (Signal.) *Because insects don't have bones.*
11. (Repeat steps 9 and 10 until firm.)

EXERCISE 9

STATEMENT INFERENCE

The next Thinking Operation is **Statement Inference.**

Task A

1. Listen. Those papers were completed very easily. Say that statement. (Signal.) *Those papers were completed very easily.* (Repeat until firm.)

> *Individual test*
> Call on a few individual students to say the statement.

2. Everybody, listen. Those papers were completed very easily. How were those papers completed? (Signal.) *Very easily.*
What was completed very easily? (Signal.) *Those papers.*
How many papers were completed very easily? (Signal.) *I don't know.* That's right; the statement doesn't say.
(Repeat step 2 until firm.)

> **Individual test**
> Call on individual students to answer a question from step 2.

Task B

1. Listen. A large iceberg began to melt slowly. Say that statement. (Signal.) *A large iceberg began to melt slowly.* (Repeat until firm.)

> **Individual test**
> Call on individuals to say the statement.

2. Everybody, listen. A large iceberg began to melt slowly. What began to melt slowly? (Signal.) *A large iceberg.*
What kind of iceberg began to melt slowly? (Signal.) *Large.*
What did a large iceberg do? (Signal.) *Began to melt slowly.*
How did a large iceberg begin to melt? (Signal.) *Slowly.*
When did a large iceberg begin to melt slowly? (Signal.) *I don't know.* That's right; the statement doesn't say. How many icebergs began to melt slowly? (Signal.) *One.*
(Repeat step 2 until firm.)

> **Individual test**
> Call on individual students to answer a question from step 2.

Points

(Pass out the Workbooks.
Award points for Thinking Operations.)

WORKBOOK EXERCISES

We're going to do Workbooks now. Remember to follow my instructions carefully.

━━━━━ **EXERCISE 10** ━━━━━

DESCRIPTION

1. Everybody, touch part A in your Workbook. ✔ Now touch line 1. (Wait.) You're going to write a letter on that line. That letter stands for the hat that I'm going to describe.

2. Listen. This hat has a band with dots on it. This hat does not have a feather. This hat has a tall top. Listen again. (Repeat the description.) Write the letter of the hat I described on line 1. (Wait.)

3. Find line 2. You're going to write the letter of a different hat on that line. Listen. This hat is flat. This hat has a feather. This hat has a striped band. Listen again. (Repeat the description.) Write the letter of the hat I described on line 2. (Wait.)

4. Find line 3. You're going to write the letter of a different hat on that line. Listen. This hat has a band with dots. This hat is flat. This hat is wide. Listen again. (Repeat the description.) Write the letter of the hat I described on line 3. (Wait.)

5. Let's check your answers. Mark any item you miss with an X. Item 1. This hat has a band with dots on it, it does not have a feather, and it has a tall top. (Pause.) What's the letter of that hat? (Signal.) *A.* Yes, the answer to item 1 is **A.**

6. Item 2. This hat is flat, it has a feather, and it has a striped band. (Pause.) What's the letter of that hat? (Signal.) *C.* Yes, the answer to item 2 is **C.**

7. Item 3. This hat has a band with dots and it is flat and wide. What's the letter of that hat? (Signal.) *D.* Yes, the answer to item 3 is **D.**

8. Who got all the items right? (Praise the students who got all the items right.)

EXERCISE 11

SAME

1. Everybody, touch part B in your Workbook. ✔ Some of the objects in Box 1 are used for cutting. **Make an X over** the objects that are used for cutting. Do it. (Wait.)
2. Some of the objects in Box 2 are usually made of the same material. **Make a box around** the objects that are usually made of the same material. Do it. (Wait.)
3. Some of the objects in Box 3 are in the same class. **Make a 3 on** the objects that are in the same class. Do it. (Wait.)
4. Everybody, get ready to check part B. Name the class of the objects you marked in Box 1. (Pause.) Get ready. (Signal.) *Cutting tools.* Name the material of the objects you marked in Box 2. (Pause.) Get ready. (Signal.) *Metal.* Name the class of the objects you marked in Box 3. (Pause.) Get ready. (Signal.) *Appliances.*
5. Which objects did you mark in Box 1? (Call on one student.) *Ax, knife, saw.* What is the same about those objects? (Call on one student.) *They are cutting tools.* How did you mark each of those objects? (Call on one student.) *Made an X over them.*
6. (Repeat step 5 for Boxes 2 and 3.)

EXERCISE 12

• **TRUE—FALSE**

1. Everybody, touch part C in your Workbook. ✔ I'll say statements that are true of one of the pictures. You write the letter of the right picture. Don't get fooled, because I might say statements about the same picture twice.
2. Item 1. **All** the shirts are striped. Write the letter of the picture on line 1. (Wait.)
3. Item 2. **Only some** of the shirts are white. Write the letter of the picture on line 2. (Wait.)
4. Item 3. **None** of the shirts are striped. Write the letter of the picture on line 3. (Wait.)
5. Item 4. **All** the shirts are white. Write the letter of the picture on line 4. (Wait.)

6. Let's check your answers. Mark any items you missed with an X. Tell me the letter of the right picture.
7. Item 1. **All** the shirts are striped. (Signal.) *B.*
8. (Repeat step 7 for items 2–4.)

EXERCISE 13

TRUE—FALSE

1. Everybody, touch part D in your Workbook. I'll say statements about the picture. Some of these statements are true and some are false.
2. Item 1. Listen. **One** of the dogs is **sleeping.** Circle **true** or **false** for item 1.
3. Item 2. Listen. **None** of the dogs are **standing.** Circle **true** or **false** for item 2.
4. Item 3. Listen. **None** of the dogs are **eating.** Circle **true** or **false** for item 3.
5. Item 4. Listen. **Some** of the dogs are **eating.** Circle **true** or **false** for item 4.
6. Item 5. Listen. **All** of the dogs are **eating.** Circle **true** or **false** for item 5.
7. Let's check your answers. Mark any item you missed with an X. Everybody, tell me **true** or **false.**
8. Item 1. **One** of the dogs is **sleeping.** (Signal.) *True.*
   Item 2. **None** of the dogs are **standing.** (Signal.) *False.*
   Item 3. **None** of the dogs are **eating.** (Signal.) *True.*
   Item 4. **Some** of the dogs are **eating.** (Signal.) *False.*
   Item 5. **All** of the dogs are **eating.** (Signal.) *False.*

EXERCISE 14

CLASSIFICATION

1. Pencils down. Don't write anything yet. Everybody, touch the instructions for part E in your Workbook. ✔ I'll read the first instruction. Listen. Make a box around the foods.
2. What are you going to do to every food? (Signal.) *Make a box around it.*

3. I'll read the next instruction. Cross out the vehicles. What are you going to do to every vehicle? (Signal.) *Cross it out.*
   Everybody, do it. Make a box around the foods and cross out the vehicles. (Wait.)
4. Get ready to mark your papers. Put an X by any object you got wrong.
5. What class is a **van** in? (Signal.) *Vehicles.* How did you mark the **van?** (Signal.) *Crossed it out.*
6. (Repeat step 5 for **carrot, racing car, lettuce, helicopter, train, bicycle,** and **hot dog.**)

Points
(Award points for Workbooks.)

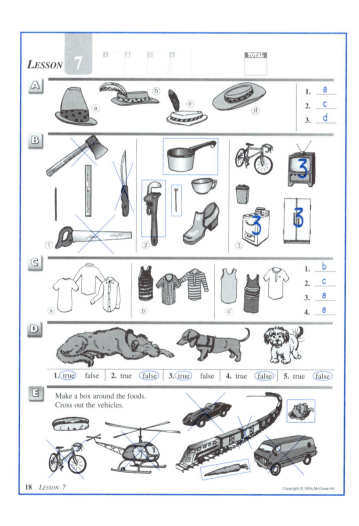

INFORMATION

We're going to work on Information now.

EXERCISE 15

CALENDAR: Months in a Year
1. Everybody, how many months are in a year? (Signal.) *Twelve.*
   You're going to name the months in a year. What are you going to name? (Signal.) *The months in a year.*
2. Name the months in a year. (Pause.) Get ready. (Signal.) *January, February, March, April, May, June, July, August, September, October, November, December.* (Repeat until firm.)
3. You named the (pause; signal) *months in a year.*

> *Individual test*
> Call on individual students to name the months in a year.

EXERCISE 16

● **INFORMATION: Animals**

Task A
1. We're going to talk about animals that have a backbone. There are five classes of animals that have a backbone. How many classes of those animals are there? (Signal.) *Five.* Yes, there are five classes of animals that have a backbone.
2. Which class have you learned facts about? (Signal.) *Mammals.*
   Tell me the two facts you've learned about **all mammals.** (Hold up one finger.) First fact. *All mammals have hair.* (Hold up two fingers.) Second fact. *All mammals are warm-blooded.* (Repeat until the students say the facts in order.)
   What does **warm-blooded** mean? (Call on one student.) The answer should contain the idea that the body temperature stays the same.

3. Squirrels are mammals. Tell me the two facts you know about **squirrels.** (Hold up one finger.) First fact. *Squirrels have hair.*
   To correct students who say *All mammals have hair* **or** *They have hair:*
   a. Tell me about **squirrels.**
   b. (Repeat step 3.)
   (Hold up two fingers.) Second fact. *Squirrels are warm-blooded.* (Repeat until the students say the facts in order.)

4. Whales are mammals. Tell me the two facts you know about **whales.** (Hold up one finger.) First fact. *Whales have hair.* (Hold up two fingers.) Second fact. *Whales are warm-blooded.* (Repeat until the students say the facts in order.)

Task B

1. You're learning about animals that have a backbone. How many classes of those animals are there? (Signal.) *Five.*
   Which class have you been learning about? (Signal.) *Mammals.*

2. The next class you're going to learn about is **reptiles.** Which class? (Signal.) *Reptiles.* Snakes, crocodiles, lizards, and turtles are reptiles. Here's the first fact about **all reptiles.** Listen. All reptiles are cold-blooded. Say that fact. (Signal.) *All reptiles are cold-blooded.* (Repeat until firm.)

3. Here's what cold-blooded means. The body temperature of a cold-blooded animal does **not** stay the same. When it's warm outside, the body temperature gets warm. When it's cold outside, the body temperature gets cold. The body temperature does **not** stay the same. What do you know about the body temperature of a cold-blooded animal? (Signal.) *The body temperature does not stay the same.*

4. A crocodile is cold-blooded. If it's **cold** outside, the body temperature of a crocodile gets (pause; signal) *cold.* If it's hot outside, the body temperature of a crocodile gets (pause; signal) *hot.*

5. Here's that fact again. All reptiles are cold-blooded. Say that fact. (Signal.) *All reptiles are cold-blooded.*
   Alligators are reptiles. So, alligators are (pause; signal) *cold-blooded.*

6. Here's that fact again. All reptiles are cold-blooded. Lizards are reptiles. So, lizards are (pause; signal) cold-blooded.
   (Repeat step 6 until firm.)

Individual test
(Call on individual students to do one of the following tasks:)
   a. Name two classes of animals that have a backbone.
   b. What does cold-blooded mean?
   c. Name some reptiles.
   d. What's the first fact about reptiles?

Points
(Award points for Information.
Have the students add up their daily total.)

END OF LESSON 7

THINKING OPERATIONS

━━━━━ **EXERCISE 1** ━━━━━

SAME: Review

The first Thinking Operation today is **Same.**

1. Get ready to tell me how things are the same.
2. A large cow and a large car. (Pause.) How are they the same? (Signal.) *They are large.*
3. A tall tree and a tall giraffe. (Pause.) How are they the same? (Signal.) *They are tall.*
4. A toaster, an iron, and a radio. (Pause.) How are they the same? (Signal.) *They are appliances.*
5. A gray pig, a white dog, and a red bird. (Pause.) How are they the same? (Signal.) *They are animals.*
6. A bush, grass, a flower, and a tree. (Pause.) How are they the same? (Signal.) *They are plants.*
7. A blue airplane and an orange car. (Pause.) How are they the same? (Signal.) *They are vehicles.*
8. (Repeat steps 2–7 until firm.)

━━━━━ **EXERCISE 2** ━━━━━

● **SAME: Place**

1. A truck and a car can be found in some of the same places. You can find a truck and a car in a garage.
2. Name another place you can find a truck and a car. (Call on individual students. Praise reasonable responses; for example, a road, a street, a parking lot.)
   A truck and a car are the same because you find them in some of the same places.

━━━━━ **EXERCISE 3** ━━━━━

● **SAME: Actions**

1. We're going to talk about frogs and birds. Frogs and birds are the same because they **do some of the same things.** My turn to name some of those things. Frogs and birds see. Frogs and birds breathe. Frogs and birds move.
2. Frogs and birds **do** some of the same things. See if you can name three of the same things that frogs and birds do. (Call on three or four individual students. Each student may repeat actions already mentioned, but should also say one new action. Praise reasonable responses.)
3. Frogs and birds are the same because they **do** some things that are the same. Frogs and birds are also the same because they are in the same class. Everybody, tell me that class. (Signal.) *Animals.* Yes, they are animals. How are they the same? (Signal.) *They are animals.*

━━━━━ **EXERCISE 4** ━━━━━

STATEMENT INFERENCE

The next Thinking Operation is **Statement Inference.**

Task A

1. Listen. The hungry canines were getting nervous. Say that statement. (Signal.) *The hungry canines were getting nervous.* (Repeat until firm.)

┌─────────────────────────────────────┐
│ **Individual test** │
│ Call on a few individual students to say the statement. │
└─────────────────────────────────────┘

2. Everybody, listen. The hungry canines were getting nervous. What kind of canines were getting nervous? (Signal.) *Hungry.*
   What was getting nervous? (Signal.) *The hungry canines.*
   How many hungry canines were getting nervous? (Signal.) *I don't know.*
   What were the hungry canines doing? (Signal.) *Getting nervous.*
   How were those hungry canines getting? (Signal.) *Nervous.*
   (Repeat step 2 until firm.)

┌─────────────────────────────────────┐
│ **Individual test** │
│ Call on individual students to answer a question from step 2. │
└─────────────────────────────────────┘

Task B

1. Listen. A wounded zebra fell down heavily. Say that statement. (Signal.) *A wounded zebra fell down heavily.* (Repeat until firm.)

Individual test
Call on a few individual students to say the statement.

---

2. Everybody, listen. A wounded zebra fell down heavily. What did a wounded zebra do? (Signal.) *Fell down heavily.*
   What fell down heavily?
   (Signal.) *A wounded zebra.*
   How did a wounded zebra fall?
   (Signal.) *Heavily.*
   What kind of zebra fell down heavily?
   (Signal.) *Wounded.*
   Where did a wounded zebra fall down?
   (Signal.) *I don't know.* That's right. The statement doesn't say.
   (Repeat step 2 until firm.)

Individual test
Call on individual students to answer a question from step 2.

=========== **EXERCISE 5** ===========

DEFINITIONS

The next Thinking Operation is **Definitions**.

1. **Indolent** means **lazy.**
2. What does **indolent** mean? (Signal.) *Lazy.*
   What word means **lazy?** (Signal.) *Indolent.*
   (Repeat step 2 until firm.)
3. Listen. Some dogs are indolent. Say that. (Signal.) *Some dogs are indolent.* (Repeat until firm.)
   Now say that sentence with a different word for **indolent.** (Pause.) Get ready. (Signal.) *Some dogs are lazy.* (Repeat until firm.)
   (Repeat step 3 until firm.)
4. Listen. They are lazy. Say that. (Signal.) *They are lazy.* (Repeat until firm.)
   Now say that sentence with a different word for **lazy.** (Pause.) Get ready. (Signal.) *They are indolent.* (Repeat until firm.)
   (Repeat step 4 until firm.)

5. Listen. He is too indolent to go to the store. Say that. (Signal.) *He is too indolent to go to the store.* (Repeat until firm.)
   Now say that sentence with a different word for **indolent.** (Pause.) Get ready. (Signal.) *He is too lazy to go to the store.* (Repeat until firm.)
   (Repeat step 5 until firm.)

=========== **EXERCISE 6** ===========

DEFINITIONS

1. **Canine.** (Pause.) What's a synonym for **canine?** (Signal.) *Dog.* And what's a synonym for **dog?** (Signal.) *Canine.* (Repeat step 1 until firm.)
2. Listen. What kind of canine do you like? Say that. (Signal.) *What kind of canine do you like?* (Repeat until firm.)
   Now say that sentence with a synonym for **canine.** (Pause.) Get ready. (Signal.) *What kind of dog do you like?* (Repeat until firm.)
   (Repeat step 2 until firm.)
3. **Complete.** (Pause.) What's a synonym for **complete?** (Signal.) *Finish.* And what's a synonym for **finish?** (Signal.) *Complete.* (Repeat step 3 until firm.)
4. Listen. Will you finish that drawing? Say that. (Signal.) *Will you finish that drawing?* (Repeat until firm.)
   Now say that sentence with a synonym for **finish.** (Pause.) Get ready. (Signal.) *Will you complete that drawing?* (Repeat until firm.)
   (Repeat step 4 until firm.)
5. **Obtain.** (Pause.) What's a synonym for **obtain?** (Signal.) *Get.* And what's a synonym for **get?** (Signal.) *Obtain.* (Repeat step 5 until firm.)
6. Listen. Where did you get that hat? Say that. (Signal.) *Where did you get that hat?* (Repeat until firm.)
   Now say that sentence with a synonym for **get.** (Pause.) Get ready. (Signal.) *Where did you obtain that hat?* (Repeat until firm.)
   (Repeat step 6 until firm.)

================== EXERCISE 7 ==================

DEDUCTIONS: With *all*

The next Thinking Operation is **Deductions.**

1. Listen to this rule. **All** birds are warm-blooded. Everybody, say that. (Signal.) *All birds are warm-blooded.*
(Repeat step 1 until firm.)

2. Eagles are birds. Say that. (Signal.) *Eagles are birds.*

3. Listen. **All** birds are warm-blooded. Eagles are birds. So, eagles (pause; signal) *are warm-blooded.*
Again. **All** birds are warm-blooded. Eagles are birds. So (pause; signal), *eagles are warm-blooded.*
(Repeat step 3 until firm.)

4. How do you know that eagles are warm-blooded? (Signal.) *Because all birds are warm-blooded.*
(Repeat step 4 until firm.)

================== EXERCISE 8 ==================

• **DEDUCTIONS: With *don't***

Task A

1. Listen to this rule. Snakes **don't** have ears. Everybody, say that. (Signal.) *Snakes don't have ears.*

2. What does the rule tell about snakes? (Call on one student.) *They don't have ears.*

3. Everybody, say the rule again. (Signal.) *Snakes don't have ears.* Rattlers are snakes. So (pause; signal), *rattlers don't have ears.*

4. How do you know that rattlers **don't** have ears? (Signal.) *Because snakes don't have ears.*

5. (Repeat steps 3 and 4 until firm.)

6. Listen. Snakes don't have ears. Pythons are snakes. So (pause; signal), *pythons don't have ears.*

7. How do you know that pythons **don't** have ears? (Signal.) *Because snakes don't have ears.*

8. (Repeat steps 6 and 7 until firm.)

9. Listen. Snakes **don't** have ears. King snakes are snakes. So (pause; signal), *king snakes don't have ears.*

10. How do you know that king snakes **don't** have ears? (Signal.) *Because snakes don't have ears.*

11. (Repeat steps 9 and 10 until firm.)

Task B

1. Listen to this rule. Whales **don't** lay eggs. Everybody, say that. (Signal.) *Whales don't lay eggs.*

2. What does the rule tell about whales? (Call on one student.) *They don't lay eggs.*

3. Everybody, say the rule again. (Signal.) *Whales don't lay eggs.*
Blue whales are whales. So (pause; signal), *blue whales don't lay eggs.*

4. How do you know that blue whales **don't** lay eggs? (Signal.) *Because whales don't lay eggs.*

5. (Repeat steps 3 and 4 until firm.)

6. Listen. Whales **don't** lay eggs. Finback whales are whales. So (pause; signal), *finback whales don't lay eggs.*

7. How do you know that finback whales **don't** lay eggs? (Signal.) *Because whales don't lay eggs.*

8. (Repeat steps 6 and 7 until firm.)

9. Listen. Whales **don't** lay eggs. Humpback whales are whales. So (pause; signal), *humpback whales don't lay eggs.*

10. How do you know that humpback whales **don't** lay eggs? (Signal.) *Because whales don't lay eggs.*

11. (Repeat steps 9 and 10 until firm.)

================== EXERCISE 9 ==================

DESCRIPTION

The next Thinking Operation is **Description.**

1. I'm going to tell you about an object you know. But I'm going to call it a funny name. See if you can figure out what object I'm talking about.

2. (Hold up one finger.) A sull is an animal. (Hold up two fingers.) A sull lives on a farm. (Hold up three fingers.) A sull lays eggs.

3. Let's say the three things we know about a sull. (Respond with students. Hold up one finger.) *A sull is an animal.*
(Hold up two fingers.) *A sull lives on a farm.*
(Hold up three fingers.) *A sull lays eggs.*
(Repeat until students are responding with you.)

4. You say the three things you know about a sull. (Hold up one finger.) *A sull is an animal.*
(Hold up two fingers.) *A sull lives on a farm.*
(Hold up three fingers.) *A sull lays eggs.*
(Repeat until the students say the statements in order.)

5. Everybody, tell me the kind of animal I am calling a sull. (Signal.) *Chicken.* Yes, it's really a chicken.

6. Think of a chicken. Is a chicken an animal? (Signal.) *Yes.*
Is a chicken food? (Signal.) *Yes.* Yes, food is something you can eat. Say that. (Signal.) *Food is something you can eat.*

Points

(Pass out the Workbooks.
Award points for Thinking Operations.)

WORKBOOK EXERCISES

We're going to do Workbooks now. Remember to follow my instructions very carefully.

=== **EXERCISE 10** ===

SAME

1. Everybody, touch part A in your Workbook. ✔ Some of the objects in box 1 are made of the same material. **Cross out** the objects that are made of the same material. Do it. (Wait.)

2. Some of the objects in box 2 are in the same class and found in the same place. **Circle** the objects that are in the same class and found in the same place. Do it. (Wait.)

3. Some of the objects in box 3 are in the same class. **Make a line under** the objects that are in the same class. Do it. (Wait.)

4. Everybody, get ready to check part A. Name the material of the objects you marked in box 1. (Pause.) Get ready. (Signal.) *Wood.* Name the place and class of the objects you marked in box 2. (Pause.) Get ready. (Signal.) *Bedroom furniture.*
Name the class of the objects you marked in box 3. (Pause.) Get ready. (Signal.) *Buildings.*

5. Which objects did you mark in Box 1? (Call on one student.) *Fence, table, board.*
What is the same about those objects? (Call on one student.) *They are made of wood.*
How did you mark each of those objects? (Call on one student.) *Crossed them out.*

6. (Repeat step 5 for Boxes 2 and 3.)

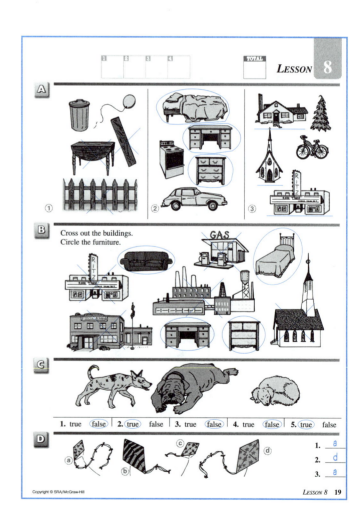

8. Item 1. **None** of the dogs are **sleeping.**
   (Signal.) *False.*
   Item 2. **Some** of the dogs are **sleeping.**
   (Signal.) *True.*
   Item 3. **All** of the dogs are **sleeping.**
   (Signal.) *False.*
   Item 4. **Some** of the dogs are **eating.**
   (Signal.) *False.*
   Item 5. **None** of the dogs are **eating.**
   (Signal.) *True.*

EXERCISE 11

CLASSIFICATION

1. Pencils down. Don't write anything yet. Everybody, touch the instructions for part B in your Workbook. ✔ I'll read the first instruction. Listen. Cross out the buildings.
2. What are you going to do to every building? (Signal.) *Cross it out.*
3. I'll read the next instruction. Circle the furniture. What are you going to do to every piece of furniture? (Signal.) *Circle it.* Everybody, do it. Cross out the buildings and circle the furniture. (Wait.)
4. Get ready to mark your papers. Put an X by any object you got wrong.
5. What class is a **school** in? (Signal.) *Buildings.* How did you mark the **school?** (Signal.) *Crossed it out.*
6. (Repeat step 5 for **gas station, bed, theater, dresser, factory, couch, desk,** and **church.**)

EXERCISE 12

TRUE—FALSE

1. Everybody, touch part C in your Workbook. ✔ I'll say statements about the picture. Some of these statements are true and some are false.
2. Item 1. Listen. **None** of the dogs are **sleeping.** Circle **true** or **false** for item 1.
3. Item 2. Listen. **Some** of the dogs are **sleeping.** Circle **true** or **false** for item 2.
4. Item 3. Listen. **All** of the dogs are **sleeping.** Circle **true** or **false** for item 3.
5. Item 4. Listen. **Some** of the dogs are **eating.** Circle **true** or **false** for item 4.
6. Item 5. Listen. **None** of the dogs are **eating.** Circle **true** or **false** for item 5.
7. Let's check your answers. Mark any item you missed with an X. Everybody, tell me **true** or **false.**

EXERCISE 13

● **DESCRIPTION**

1. Everybody, touch part D in your Workbook. ✔ The kites are lettered. Get ready to write the letter of each kite I describe. Don't get fooled, because I may describe the same kite twice.
2. Item 1. This kite is covered with stars. This kite is little. This kite has a long tail. Listen again. (Repeat the description.) Write the letter of the right kite on line 1.
3. Item 2. This kite has a long tail. This kite is big. This kite is covered with stars. Listen again. (Repeat the description.) Write the letter of the right kite on line 2.
4. Item 3. This kite is little. This kite is covered with stars. This kite has a long tail. Listen again. (Repeat the description.) Write the letter of the right kite on line 3.
5. Let's check your answers. Mark any item you miss with an X.
6. Item 1. This kite is covered with stars. This kite is little. This kite has a long tail. Everybody, what letter? (Signal.) *A.*
7. (Repeat step 6 for items 2 and 3.)

Points
(Award points for Workbooks.)

INFORMATION

We're going to work on Information now.

EXERCISE 14

● **INFORMATION: Animals**

1. You're learning about animals that have a backbone. How many classes of those animals are there? (Signal.) *Five.*
   You've learned facts about two of those classes. Which classes? (Signal.) *Mammals and reptiles.* (Repeat until firm.)

2. Name a mammal. (Call on individual students.) The group is to name at least five mammals.
   You learned two facts about **all mammals.** Everybody, tell me those two facts. (Hold up one finger.) First fact. *All mammals have hair.* (Hold up two fingers.) Second fact. *All mammals are warm-blooded.* Repeat until students say the facts in order.

3. Name a reptile. (Call on individual students.) The group is to name at least four reptiles.
   You learned one fact about **all reptiles.** Everybody, tell me that fact. (Signal.) *All reptiles are cold-blooded.* (Repeat until firm.)

4. What class are turtles in? (Signal.) *Reptiles.* So, tell me a fact you know about **turtles.** (Signal.) *Turtles are cold-blooded.*
   To correct students who say *All reptiles are cold-blooded* **or** *They are cold-blooded:*
   a. Tell me about **turtles.**
   b. (Repeat step 4.)
   (Repeat until firm.)

5. What class are dogs in? (Signal.) *Mammals.* So, tell me the two facts you know about **dogs.** (Hold up one finger.) First fact. *Dogs have hair.*
   (Hold up two fingers.) Second fact. *Dogs are warm-blooded.* (Repeat until the students say the facts in order.)

Individual test
Call on individual students to do step 4 or 5.

EXERCISE 15

CALENDAR: Months in a Year

1. Everybody, how many months are in a year? (Signal.) *Twelve.* You're going to name the months in a year. What are you going to name? (Signal.) *The months in a year.*

2. Name the months in a year. (Pause.) Get ready. (Signal.) *January, February, March, April, May, June, July, August, September, October, November, December.* (Repeat until firm.)

3. You named the (pause; signal) *months in a year.*

Individual test
Call on individual students to name the months in a year.

Points

(Award points for Information.
Have the students add up their daily total.)

END OF LESSON 8

THINKING OPERATIONS

================= EXERCISE 1 =================

DESCRIPTION

The first Thinking Operation is **Description.**

1. I'm going to tell you about an object you know. But I'm going to call it a funny name. See if you can figure out what object I'm talking about.
2. (Hold up one finger.) A gant is an animal. (Hold up two fingers.) Some gants live in Africa. (Hold up three fingers.) A gant has a trunk.
3. Let's say the three things we know about a gant. (Respond with students. Hold up one finger.) *A gant is an animal.* (Hold up two fingers.) *Some gants live in Africa.* (Hold up three fingers.) *A gant has a trunk.* (Repeat until students are responding with you.)
4. You say the three things you know about a gant. (Hold up one finger.) *A gant is an animal.* (Hold up two fingers.) *Some gants live in Africa.* (Hold up three fingers.) *A gant has a trunk.* (Repeat until the students say the statements in order.)
5. Everybody, tell me the kind of animal I'm calling a gant. (Signal.) *An elephant.* Yes, it's an elephant.

================= EXERCISE 2 =================

DEFINITIONS

The next Thinking Operation is **Definitions.**

1. **Indolent** means **lazy.**
2. What does **indolent** mean? (Signal.) *Lazy.* What word means **lazy?** (Signal.) *Indolent.* (Repeat step 2 until firm.)

3. Listen. The indolent donkey would not walk. Say that. (Signal.) *The indolent donkey would not walk.* (Repeat until firm.) Now say that sentence with a different word for **indolent.** (Pause.) Get ready. (Signal.) *The lazy donkey would not walk.* (Repeat until firm.) (Repeat step 3 until firm.)
4. Listen. Sometimes I feel lazy. Say that. (Signal.) *Sometimes I feel lazy.* (Repeat until firm.) Now say that sentence with a different word for **lazy.** (Pause.) Get ready. (Signal.) *Sometimes I feel indolent.* (Repeat until firm.) (Repeat step 4 until firm.)
5. Listen. When I feel indolent, I take a walk. Say that. (Signal.) *When I feel indolent, I take a walk.* (Repeat until firm.) Now say that sentence with a different word for **indolent.** (Pause.) Get ready. (Signal.) *When I feel lazy, I take a walk.* (Repeat until firm.) (Repeat step 5 until firm.)

================= EXERCISE 3 =================

DEFINITIONS

1. **Masticate.** (Pause.) What's a synonym for **masticate?** (Signal.) *Chew.* And what's a synonym for **chew?** (Signal.) *Masticate.* (Repeat step 1 until firm.)
2. Listen. The lion masticated some meat. Say that. (Signal.) *The lion masticated some meat.* (Repeat until firm.) Now say that sentence with a synonym for **masticate.** (Pause.) Get ready. (Signal.) *The lion chewed some meat.* (Repeat until firm.) (Repeat step 2 until firm.)
3. **Canine.** (Pause.) What's a synonym for **canine?** (Signal.) *Dog.* And what's a synonym for **dog?** (Signal.) *Canine.* (Repeat step 3 until firm.)

4. Listen. Some canines sleep all day. Say that. (Signal.) *Some canines sleep all day.* (Repeat until firm.)

   Now say that sentence with a synonym for **canines.** (Pause.) Get ready. (Signal.) *Some dogs sleep all day.* (Repeat until firm.) (Repeat step 4 until firm.)

5. **Complete.** (Pause.) What's a synonym for **complete?** (Signal.) *Finish.* And what's a synonym for **finish?** (Signal.) *Complete.* (Repeat step 5 until firm.)

6. Listen. We'll eat after you finish your homework. Say that. (Signal.) *We'll eat after you finish your homework.* (Repeat until firm.) Now say that sentence with a synonym for **finish.** (Pause.) Get ready. (Signal.) *We'll eat after you complete your homework.* (Repeat step 6 until firm.)

═══════ EXERCISE 4 ═══════

● **DEDUCTIONS: With *all* and *every***
The next Thinking Operation is **Deductions.**

Task A

1. I'll say a rule one way with the word **all.** Then I'll say it another way with the word **every.** What two words am I going to use? (Hold up one finger.) *All.* (Hold up two fingers.) *Every.* (Repeat until firm.)

2. Listen. **All** alligators eat. Say that. (Signal.) *All alligators eat.*

   Now I'll say the same rule with **every. Every** alligator eats. Say that. (Signal.) *Every alligator eats.*

Task B

1. What are the two words we're using? (Hold up one finger.) *All.* (Hold up two fingers.) *Every.*

2. Here's a new rule. **Every** girl eats. Say that. (Signal.) *Every girl eats.*

   Now I'll say the same rule with **all. All** girls eat. Say that. (Signal.) *All girls eat.* Now you say it with **every.** (Pause.) Get ready. (Signal.) *Every girl eats.*

   Now say it with **all.** (Pause.) Get ready. (Signal.) *All girls eat.*

Task C

1. Here's a new rule. **All** cows give milk. Say that. (Signal.) *All cows give milk.*

   Now say it with **every.** (Pause.) Get ready. (Signal.) *Every cow gives milk.*

   Now say it with **all.** (Pause.) Get ready. (Signal.) *All cows give milk.* (Repeat step 1 until firm.)

2. Here's a new rule. **Every** car is a vehicle. Say that. (Signal.) *Every car is a vehicle.*

   Now say it with **all.** (Pause.) Get ready. (Signal.) *All cars are vehicles.*

   Now say it with **every.** (Pause.) Get ready. (Signal.) *Every car is a vehicle.* (Repeat step 2 until firm.)

┌─────────────────────────────────────┐
Individual test
Call on individual students to do one step in Task C.
└─────────────────────────────────────┘

═══════ EXERCISE 5 ═══════

● **DEDUCTIONS: With *all***

1. Listen to this rule. **All** trees have roots. Everybody, say that. (Signal.) *All trees have roots.*

2. Elms are trees. So (pause; signal), *elms have roots.* How do you know that elms have roots? (Signal.) *Because all trees have roots.*

   To correct students who say *All trees have roots:*
   a. **Because** all trees have roots.
   b. How do you know that elms have roots? (Signal.) *Because all trees have roots.*
   c. (Repeat step 2.)
   (Repeat step 2 until firm.)

3. Listen. **All** trees have roots. Oaks are trees. So (pause; signal), *oaks have roots.* How do you know that oaks have roots? (Signal.) *Because all trees have roots.* (Repeat step 3 until firm.)

4. Listen. **All** trees have roots. Poplars are trees. So (pause; signal), *poplars have roots.* How do you know that poplars have roots? (Signal.) *Because all trees have roots.* (Repeat step 4 until firm.)

EXERCISE 6

STATEMENT INFERENCE

The next Thinking Operation is **Statement Inference.**

Task A

1. Listen. She looked at him coolly. Say that statement. (Signal.) *She looked at him coolly.* (Repeat until firm.)

> **Individual test**
> Call on a few individual students to say the statement.

2. Everybody, listen. Whom did she look at coolly? (Signal.) *Him.*
   Why did she look at him coolly? (Signal.) *I don't know.* That's right; the statement doesn't say. What did she do? (Signal.) *Looked at him coolly.*
   How did she look at him? (Signal.) *Coolly.* (Repeat step 2 until firm.)

> **Individual test**
> Call on individual students to answer a question from step 2.

Task B

1. Listen. The noisy jets flew over the airport. Say that statement. (Signal.) *The noisy jets flew over the airport.* (Repeat until firm.)

> **Individual test**
> Call on a few individual students to say the statement.

2. Everybody, listen. The noisy jets flew over the airport. What did the noisy jets do? (Signal.) *Flew over the airport.* What kind of jets flew over the airport? (Signal.) *Noisy.*
   Where did the noisy jets fly? (Signal.) *Over the airport.* What did the noisy jets fly over? (Signal.) *The airport.*
   What flew over the airport? (Signal.) *The noisy jets.*

How many noisy jets flew over the airport? (Signal.) *I don't know.* That's right, the statement doesn't say.
(Repeat step 2 until firm.)

> **Individual test**
> Call on individual students to answer a question from step 2.

EXERCISE 7

SAME: Review

The next Thinking Operation is **Same.**

1. Get ready to tell me how things are the same.
2. An old theater, a large house, and a gray barn. (Pause.) How are they the same? (Signal.) *They are buildings.*
3. A tall tree and a short bush. (Pause.) How are they the same? (Signal.) *They are plants.*
4. A blue whale and a blue house. (Pause.) How are they the same? (Signal.) *They are blue.*
5. A paper bag and a plastic cup. (Pause.) How are they the same? (Signal.) *They are containers.*
6. A cold day and cold milk. (Pause.) How are they the same? (Signal.) *They are cold.*
7. A long box and a long carrot. (Pause.) How are they the same? (Signal.) *They are long.*
8. (Repeat steps 2–7 until firm.)

EXERCISE 8

SAME: Place

1. A bird and a butterfly can be found in some of the same places. You can find a bird and a butterfly in a tree.
2. Name another place you can find a bird and a butterfly. (Call on individual students. Praise reasonable responses, for example, in the sky, in a meadow, in the country.)
   A bird and a butterfly are the same because you find them in some of the same places.

EXERCISE 9

SAME: Actions

1. We're going to talk about cows and tigers. Cows and tigers are the same because they **do some things** that are the same. My turn to name some of those things. Cows and tigers sleep. Cows and tigers breathe. Cows and tigers hear.

2. Cows and tigers **do** some of the same things. See if you can name three of the same things that cows and tigers do. (Call on three or four individual students. Each student may repeat actions already mentioned, but should also say one new action. Praise reasonable responses.)

3. Cows and tigers are the same because they do some of the same things. Cows and tigers are also the same because they are in the same class. Everybody, tell me that class. (Signal.) *Animals.* Yes, they are animals. How are they the same? (Signal.) *They are animals.*

Individual test

(Call on individual students. Present one of the following tasks:)

a. Cows and tigers are the same because they do some of the same things. Name three of the same things they do.

b. Cows and tigers are the same because they are in the same class. Name that same class.

Points

(Pass out the Workbooks.
Award points for Thinking Operations.)

WORKBOOK EXERCISES

We're going to do Workbooks now. Remember to follow my instructions very carefully.

EXERCISE 10

CLASSIFICATION

1. Pencils down. Don't write anything yet. Everybody, touch the instructions for Part A in your Workbook. ✔ I'll read the first instruction. Listen. Make a box around the plants.

2. What are you going to do to every plant? (Signal.) *Make a box around it.*

3. I'll read the next instruction. Underline the appliances. What are you going to do to every appliance? (Signal.) *Underline it.* Everybody, do it. Make a box around the plants and underline the appliances. (Wait.)

4. Get ready to mark your papers. Put an X by any object you got wrong.

5. What class is a **tulip** in? (Signal.) *Plants.* How did you mark the **tulip?** (Signal.) *Made a box around it.*

6. (Repeat step 5 for **evergreen tree, freezer, dishwasher, dryer, bush, mixer, toaster,** and **potted plant.**)

EXERCISE 11

DESCRIPTION

1. Everybody, touch part B in your Workbook. The glasses are lettered. Get ready to write the letter of each glass I describe. Don't get fooled, because I may describe the same glass twice.

2. Item 1. This glass is tall. This glass is not full. This glass has a straw in it. Listen again. (Repeat the description.) Write the letter of the right glass on line 1.

3. Item 2. This glass is full. This glass has a straw in it. This glass is not tall. Listen again. (Repeat the description.) Write the letter of the right glass on line 2.

4. Item 3. This glass is full. This glass has a straw in it. This glass is short. Listen again.

(Repeat the description.) Write the letter of the right glass on line 3.

5. Let's check your answers. Mark any items you missed with an X.

6. Item 1. This glass is tall. This glass is empty. This glass has a straw in it. Everybody, what letter? (Signal.) *B.*

7. (Repeat step 6 for items 2 and 3.)

━━━━━━━━━ **EXERCISE 12** ━━━━━━━━━

SAME

1. Everybody, touch part C in your Workbook. Some of the objects in box 1 are in the same class. **Make a line over** the objects that are in the same class. Do it. (Wait.)

2. Some of the objects in box 2 are found in the same place. **Make a box around** the objects that are found in the same place. Do it. (Wait.)

3. Some of the objects in box 3 are usually the same color. **Make a 3 on** the objects that are usually the same color. Do it. (Wait.)

4. Everybody, get ready to check part C. Name the class of the objects you marked in box 1. (Pause.) Get ready. (Signal.) *Animals.*
Name the place of the objects you marked in box 2. (Pause.) Get ready. (Signal.) *Bathroom.*
Name the color of the objects you marked in box 2. (Pause.) Get ready. (Signal.) *Green.*

5. Which objects did you mark in box 1? (Call on one student.) *Deer, bear, bird.*
What is the same about those objects? (Call on one student.) *They are animals.* How did you mark each of those objects? (Call on one student.) *Made a line over them.*

6. (Repeat step 5 for boxes 2 and 3.)

━━━━━━━━━ **EXERCISE 13** ━━━━━━━━━

TRUE—FALSE

1. Everybody, touch part D in your Workbook. ✔ I'll say statements about the picture. Some of these statements are true and some are false.

2. Item 1. Listen. **All** of the pencils are **long.** Circle **true** or **false** for item 1.

3. Item 2. Listen. **None** of the pencils are **long.** Circle **true** or **false** for item 2.

4. Item 3. Listen. **Some** of the pencils are **long.** Circle **true** or **false** for item 3.

5. Item 4. Listen. **None** of the pencils are **broken.** Circle **true** or **false** for item 4.

6. Item 5. Listen. **All** of the pencils are **broken.** Circle **true** or **false** for item 5.

7. Let's check your answers. Mark any item you missed with an X. Everybody, tell me **true** or **false.**

8. Item 1. **All** of the pencils are **long.** (Signal.) *False.*
Item 2. **None** of the pencils are **long.** (Signal.) *True.*
Item 3. **Some** of the pencils are **long.** (Signal.) *False.*
Item 4. **None** of the pencils are **broken.** (Signal.) *True.*
Item 5. **All** of the pencils are **broken.** (Signal.) *False.*

Points

(Award points for Workbooks.)

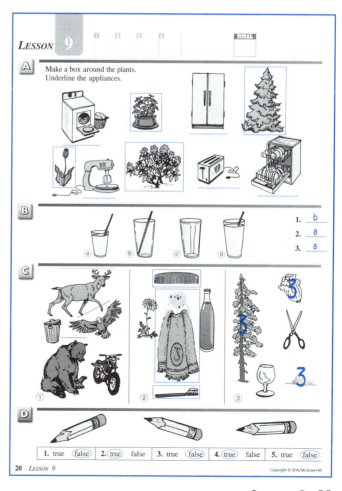

INFORMATION

We're going to work on Information now.

EXERCISE 14

● **INFORMATION: Animals**

1. You're learning about animals that have a backbone. How many classes of those animals are there? (Signal.) *Five.*
   You've learned facts about two of those classes. Which classes? (Signal.) *Mammals and reptiles.* (Repeat until firm.)

2. Name a mammal. (Call on individual students. The group is to name at least five mammals.)
   You learned two facts about **all mammals.** Everybody, tell me those two facts. (Hold up one finger.) First fact. *All mammals have hair.* (Hold up two fingers.) Second fact. *All mammals are warm-blooded.* (Repeat until the students say the facts in order.)

3. Name a reptile. (Call on individual students.) The group is to name at least four reptiles.
   You learned one fact about **all reptiles.** Tell me that fact. (Signal.) *All reptiles are cold-blooded.* (Repeat until firm.)
   What does cold-blooded mean? (Call on one student. The answer should contain the idea that the body temperature does not stay the same.)

4. Here's another fact about **all reptiles.** Listen. All reptiles are born on land. Say that fact. (Signal.) *All reptiles are born on land.* (Repeat until firm.)

5. Turtles, snakes, lizards, and alligators are born from eggs. Those eggs are laid on land. Where do reptiles lay their eggs? (Signal.) *On land.*

6. Here are the two facts you've learned about **all reptiles.** (Hold up one finger.) First fact. All reptiles are cold-blooded. (Hold up two fingers.) Second fact. All reptiles are born on land. Tell me the two facts about **all reptiles.**
   (Hold up one finger.) First fact. *All reptiles are cold-blooded.*
   (Hold up two fingers.) Second fact. *All reptiles are born on land.* (Repeat until students say the facts in order.)

7. What class are lizards in? (Signal.) *Reptiles.*
   So tell me the two facts you know about **lizards.** (Hold up one finger.) First fact. *Lizards are cold-blooded.*
   (Hold up two fingers.) Second fact. *Lizards are born on land.* (Repeat until the students say the facts in order.)

8. What class are rattlesnakes in? (Signal.) *Reptiles.*
   So, tell me the two facts you know about **rattlesnakes.** (Hold up one finger.) First fact. *Rattlesnakes are cold-blooded.*
   (Hold up two fingers.) Second fact. *Rattlesnakes are born on land.* (Repeat until the students say the facts in order.)

Individual test
(Call on individual students to do one of the following tasks:)
a. Name some reptiles.
b. What are the two facts you know about all reptiles?

EXERCISE 15

CALENDAR: Months in a Year

1. I'll name some months of the year. When I stop, you name the rest of the months.

2. My turn. January, February, March, April (pause; signal), *May, June, July, August, September, October, November, December.* (Repeat step 2 until firm.)

3. Here's another one. My turn. January, February, March, April, May, June, July, August (pause; signal), *September, October, November, December.* (Repeat step 3 until firm.)

Individual test

(Call on individual students to do one of the following tasks:)

    a. How many months are in a year?

    b. Name the months of the year.

    c. Name the rest of the months.

       (Repeat step 2 or step 3.)

Points

(Award points for Information.

Have the students add up their daily total.)

END OF LESSON 9

THINKING OPERATIONS

---EXERCISE 1---

STATEMENT INFERENCE

The first Thinking Operation today is **Statement Inference.**

Task A

1. Listen. He promised to tell the completed story. Say that statement. (Signal.) *He promised to tell the completed story.* (Repeat until firm.)

> **Individual test**
> Call on individuals to say the statement.

2. Everybody, listen. He promised to tell the completed story. What kind of story did he promise to tell? (Signal.) *Completed.*
   What did he promise to tell? (Signal.) *The completed story.*
   What did he do? (Signal.) *Promised to tell the completed story.*
   Where did he promise to tell the completed story? (Signal.) *I don't know.*
   How many completed stories did he promise to tell? (Signal.) *One.*
   When did he promise to tell the completed story? (Signal.) *I don't know.*
   (Repeat step 2 until firm.)

> **Individual test**
> Call on individual students to answer a question from step 2.

Task B

1. Listen. The reptiles were moving slowly under the log. Say that statement. (Signal.) *The reptiles were moving slowly under the log.* (Repeat until firm.)

> **Individual test**
> Call on individuals to say the statement.

2. Everybody, listen. The reptiles were moving slowly under the log. How were the reptiles moving under the log? (Signal.) *Slowly.*
   Where were the reptiles moving slowly? (Signal.) *Under the log.*
   What was moving slowly under the log? (Signal.) *The reptiles.*
   What kind of reptiles were moving slowly under the log? (Signal.) *I don't know.*
   What were the reptiles doing? (Signal.) *Moving slowly under the log.*
   What were the reptiles moving slowly under? (Signal.) *The log.*
   (Repeat step 2 until firm.)

> **Individual test**
> Call on individual students to answer a question from step 2.

---EXERCISE 2---

DEFINITIONS

The next Thinking Operation is **Definitions.**

1. **Indolent.** (Pause.) What's a synonym for **indolent?** (Signal.) *Lazy.* And what's a synonym for **lazy?** (Signal.) *Indolent.*
   (Repeat step 1 until firm.)

2. Listen. Do you ever feel indolent? Say that. (Signal.) *Do you ever feel indolent?* (Repeat until firm.)
   Now say that sentence with a synonym for **indolent.** (Pause.) Get ready. (Signal.) *Do you ever feel lazy?* (Repeat until firm.)
   (Repeat step 2 until firm.)

3. **Complete.** (Pause.) What's a synonym for **complete?** (Signal.) *Finish.* And what's a synonym for **finish?** (Signal.) *Complete.*
   (Repeat step 3 until firm.)

4. Listen. Take time to finish that book. Say that. (Signal.) *Take time to finish that book.* (Repeat until firm.)
   Now say that sentence with a synonym for **finish.** (Pause.) Get ready. (Signal.) *Take time to complete that book.* (Repeat until firm.)
   (Repeat step 4 until firm.)

5. **Obtain.** (Pause.) What's a synonym for **obtain?** (Signal.) *Get.*
   And what's a synonym for **get?** (Signal.) *Obtain.*
   (Repeat step 5 until firm.)

6. Listen. She wants to get some popcorn. Say that. (Signal.) *She wants to get some popcorn.* (Repeat until firm.)
Now say that sentence with a synonym for **get.** (Pause.) Get ready. (Signal.) *She wants to obtain some popcorn.* (Repeat until firm.)
(Repeat step 6 until firm.)

=========== **EXERCISE 3** ===========

DEDUCTIONS: With *all* and *every*
The next Thinking Operation is **Deductions.**

Task A
1. I'll say a rule one way with the word **all.** Then I'll say it another way with the word **every.** What two words am I going to use? (Hold up one finger.) *All.* (Hold up two fingers.) *Every.* (Repeat until firm.)
2. Listen. **Every** tiger runs. Say that. (Signal.) *Every tiger runs.*
Now I'll say the same rule with **all. All** tigers run. Say that. (Signal.) *All tigers run.*

Task B
1. What are the two words we're using? (Hold up one finger.) *All.* (Hold up two fingers.) *Every.*
2. Here's a new rule. **Every** week has seven days. Say that. (Signal.) *Every week has seven days.*
Now I'll say the same rule with **all. All** weeks have seven days. Say that. (Signal.) *All weeks have seven days.*
Now you say it with **every.** (Pause.) Get ready. (Signal.) *Every week has seven days.*
Now say it with **all.** (Pause.) Get ready. (Signal.) *All weeks have seven days.*
3. Here's a new rule. **All** knives cut. Say that. (Signal.) *All knives cut.*
Now say it with **every.** (Pause.) Get ready. (Signal.) *Every knife cuts.* Now say it with **all.** (Pause.) Get ready. (Signal.) *All knives cut.* (Repeat step 3 until firm.)
4. Here's a new rule. **Every** baby eats. Say that. (Signal.) *Every baby eats.*
Now say it with **all.** (Pause.) Get ready. (Signal.) *All babies eat.* Now say it with **every.** (Pause.) Get ready. (Signal.) *Every baby eats.*
(Repeat step 4 until firm.)

Individual test
Call on individuals to do step 3 or 4.

=========== **EXERCISE 4** ===========

DEDUCTIONS: With *every*
1. Listen to this rule. **Every** mammal is warm-blooded. Everybody, say that. (Signal.) *Every mammal is warm-blooded.*
2. Horses are mammals. So (pause; signal), *horses are warm-blooded.* How do you know that horses are warm-blooded? (Signal.) *Because every mammal is warm-blooded.* (Repeat step 2 until firm.)
To correct students who say *Every mammal is warm-blooded:*
a. **Because** every mammal is warm-blooded.
b. How do you know that horses are warm-blooded? (Signal.) *Because every mammal is warm-blooded.*
c. (Repeat step 2.)
(Repeat step 2 until firm.)
3. Listen. **Every** mammal is warm-blooded. Tigers are mammals. So (pause; signal), *tigers are warm-blooded.*
How do you know tigers are warm-blooded? (Signal.) *Because every mammal is warm-blooded.*
(Repeat step 3 until firm.)
4. Listen. **Every** mammal is warm-blooded. Dogs are mammals. So (pause; signal), *dogs are warm-blooded.* How do you know that dogs are warm-blooded? (Signal.) *Because every mammal is warm-blooded.*
(Repeat step 4 until firm.)

=========== **EXERCISE 5** ===========

DESCRIPTION
The next Thinking Operation is **Description.**
1. I'm going to tell you about an object you know. But I'm going to call it a funny name. See if you can figure out what object I'm talking about.
2. (Hold up one finger.) A gaff is made of metal. (Hold up two fingers.) A gaff is a container. (Hold up three fingers.) You open a gaff with a can opener.

3. Let's say the three things we know about a gaff. (Respond with students. Hold up one finger.) *A gaff is made of metal.*
(Hold up two fingers.) *A gaff is a container.*
(Hold up three fingers.) *You open a gaff with a can opener.* (Repeat until students are responding with you.)

4. You say the three things you know about a gaff. (Hold up one finger.) *A gaff is made of metal.*
(Hold up two fingers.) *A gaff is a container.*
(Hold up three fingers.) *You open a gaff with a can opener.* (Repeat until the students say the statements in order.)

5. Everybody, tell me what I'm calling a gaff. (Signal.) *A can.* Yes, it's really a can.

━━━━━━━ **EXERCISE 6** ━━━━━━━

DESCRIPTION

1. Here's the rule. **Grib** is a funny word that we'll use for box. What word are we using for box? (Signal.) *Grib.*
And what does **grib** mean? (Signal.) *Box.*

2. Listen to this sentence. A grib can walk. Is that statement true or false? (Signal.) *False.*

3. Next sentence. A grib can hold things. Is that statement true or false? (Signal.) *True.*

4. Next sentence. A grib goes to sleep. Is that statement true or false? (Signal.) *False.*

5. Next sentence. A grib can be made of cardboard. Is that statement true or false? (Signal.) *True.*

6. Next sentence. Gribs have four sides and a bottom. Is that statement true or false? (Signal.) *True.*

━━━━━━━ **EXERCISE 7** ━━━━━━━

SAME: Actions

The next Thinking Operation is **Same.**

1. We're going to talk about knives and saws. Knives and saws are the same because you do some of the same things with them. My turn to name some of those things. You can lift knives and saws. You can hold knives and saws by the handle. You can put knives and saws away.

2. You **do** some of the same things with knives and saws. See if you can name three of the same things that you do with them. (Call on three or four individual students. Each student may repeat actions already mentioned, but should also say one new action. Praise reasonable responses.)

3. Knives and saws are the same because you **do** some of the same things with them. Knives and saws are also the same because they are in the same class.
Everybody, tell me that class. (Signal.) *Tools.*
Yes, they are tools. How are they the same? (Signal.) *They are tools.*

┌─────────────────────────────────────┐
Individual test
(Call on individual students. Present one of the following tasks:)
   a. Knives and saws are the same because you **do** some of the same things with them. Name three of those same things.
   b. Knives and saws are the same because they are in the same class. Name that same class.
└─────────────────────────────────────┘

━━━━━━━ **EXERCISE 8** ━━━━━━━

● **SAME: Review**

Task A

1. A red car and a red truck are the same because they are the same **color.** Everybody, tell me that **color.** (Signal.) *Red.*

2. Here's another way a red car and a red truck are the same. You can **do** some of the same things with them. Name at least three of the same things that you can **do** with a red car and a red truck. (Call on individual students. Praise reasonable responses; for example, steer it, wash it, turn it.)

3. Here's another way a red car and a red truck are the same. They are made of the same **material.** Everybody, tell me that **material.** (Signal.) *Metal.* Yes, they are made of metal. How are they the same? (Signal.) *They are made of metal.*

4. Here's another way a red car and a red truck are the same. They are in the same **class.** Everybody, tell me that **class.** (Signal.) *Vehicles.* Yes, they are vehicles. How are they the same? (Signal.) *They are vehicles.*

5. Here's another way a red car and a red truck are the same. You find them in some of the same **places.** Name some of those **places.** (Call on individual students. Praise reasonable responses; for example, in a garage, on a road, on a bridge.)

Task B

1. A gray bird and a gray monkey are the same because they **do** some of the same things. Get ready to name at least three things they **do** that are the same. (Call on individual students. Praise reasonable responses; for example, they breathe, they eat, they hear.)

2. Another way a gray bird and a gray monkey are the same is that they are the same **color.** Everybody, tell me that **color.** (Signal.) *Gray.* Yes, they are gray. How are they the same? (Signal.) *They are gray.*

3. Another way a gray bird and a gray monkey are the same is that you find them in some of the same **places.** Name some of those **places.** (Call on individual students. Praise reasonable responses; for example, zoo, jungle.)

4. Another way a gray bird and a gray monkey are the same is that they are in the same class. Everybody, tell me that **class.** (Signal.) *Animals.* Yes, they are animals. How are they the same? (Signal.) *They are animals.*

Individual test

(Call on individual students to do one of the following tasks:)

    a. Name three ways a red car and a red truck are the same.

    b. Name three ways a gray bird and a gray monkey are the same.

Points

(Pass out the Workbooks.
Award points for Thinking Operations.)

WORKBOOK EXERCISES

We're going to do Workbooks now. Remember to follow my instructions very carefully.

═══ **EXERCISE 9** ═══

DESCRIPTION

1. Everybody, touch part A in your Workbook. ✔ Figure out which object I describe. Listen. A snorp is powered by the wind. A snorp does not have an engine or wheels. A snorp is a vehicle. **Make a box around** the object I'm calling a snorp. (Wait.)

2. Listen. You eat a mungo. The outside of a mungo is green. The inside of a mungo is pink. **Make an X on** the object I'm calling a mungo. (Wait.)

3. Listen. A zado is an animal. A zado has four legs. A zado barks. **Circle** the object I'm calling a zado. (Wait.)

4. Everybody, get ready to check your work. Tell me the real name for the object that is powered by the wind, that does not have an engine or wheels, and that is a vehicle. Get ready. (Signal.) *A sailboat.* And how did you mark the sailboat? (Signal.) *Made a box around it.*

5. Tell me the real name for the object that you eat, that is green on the outside, and that is pink on the inside. Get ready. (Signal.) *A watermelon.* And how did you mark the watermelon? (Signal.) *Made an X on it.*

6. Tell me the real name for the object that is an animal, that has four legs, and that barks. Get ready. (Signal.) *A dog.* And how did you mark the dog? (Signal.) *Circled it.*

═══ **EXERCISE 10** ═══

SAME

1. Everybody, touch part B in your Workbook. ✔ Some of the objects in box 1 are in the same class. **Circle** the objects that are in the same class. Do it. (Wait.)

2. Some of the objects in box 2 are made of the same material. **Cross out** the objects that are made of the same material. Do it. (Wait.)
3. Some of the objects in box 3 are in the same class. **Make a line over** the objects that are in the same class. Do it. (Wait.)
4. Everybody, get ready to check part B. Name the class of the objects you marked in box 1. (Pause.) Get ready. (Signal.) *Vehicles.* Name the material of the objects you marked in box 2. (Pause.) Get ready. (Signal.) *Plastic.* Name the class of the objects you marked in box 3. (Pause.) Get ready. (Signal.) *Clothing.*
5. Which objects did you mark in box 1? (Call on one student.) *Sailboat, bus, bicycle.* What is the same about those objects? (Call on one student.) *They are vehicles.* How did you mark each of those objects? (Call on one student.) *Circled them.*
6. (Repeat step 5 for Boxes 2 and 3.)

━━━━━━━━ **EXERCISE 11** ━━━━━━━━

TRUE—FALSE

1. Everybody, touch part C in your Workbook. ✔ I'll say statements that are true of one of the pictures. You write the letter of the right picture. Don't get fooled, because I may say statements about the same picture twice.
2. Item 1. **None** of the shoes are long. Write the letter of the picture on line 1. (Wait.)
3. Item 2. **All** of the shoes are black. Write the letter of the picture on line 2. (Wait.)
4. Item 3. **Only some** of the shoes are long. Write the letter of the picture on line 3. (Wait.)
5. Item 4. **All** of the shoes are long. Write the letter of the picture on line 4. (Wait.)
6. Let's check your answers. Mark any items you missed with an X. Tell me the letter of the right picture.
7. Item 1. **None** of the shoes are long. (Signal.) *B.*
8. (Repeat step 7 for items 2–4.)

━━━━━━━━ **EXERCISE 12** ━━━━━━━━

CLASSIFICATION

1. Pencils down. Don't write anything yet. Everybody, touch the instructions for part D in your Workbook. ✔ I'll read the first instruction. Listen. Underline the vehicles.
2. What are you going to do to every vehicle? (Signal.) *Underline it.*
3. I'll read the next instruction. Cross out the tools. What are you going to do to every tool? (Signal.) *Cross it out.* Everybody, do it. Underline the vehicles and cross out the tools. (Wait.)
4. Get ready to mark your papers. Put an X by any object you got wrong.
5. What class is a **pencil** in? (Signal.) *Tools.* How did you mark the **pencil?** (Signal.) *Crossed it out.*
6. (Repeat step 5 for **toothbrush, motorcycle, wagon, ax, sailboat, knife, car, saw,** and **pickup truck.**)

━━━━━━━━ **EXERCISE 13** ━━━━━━━━

TRUE—FALSE

1. Everybody, touch part E in your Workbook. I'll say statements about the picture. Some of these statements are true and some are false.
2. Item 1. Listen. **Two** of the boys are **swimming.** Circle **true** or **false** for item 1. (Wait.)
3. Item 2. Listen. **None** of the boys are **swimming.** Circle **true** or **false** for item 2. (Wait.)
4. Item 3. Listen. **All** of the boys are **swimming.** Circle **true** or **false** for item 3. (Wait.)
5. Item 4. Listen. **Some** of the boys are **eating.** Circle **true** or **false** for item 4. (Wait.)
6. Item 5. Listen. **None** of the boys are **eating.** Circle **true** or **false** for item 5. (Wait.)
7. Let's check your answers. Mark any items you missed with an X. Everybody, tell me **true** or **false.**

8. Item 1. **Two** of the boys are **swimming.**
(Signal.) *True.*
Item 2. **None** of the boys are **swimming.**
(Signal.) *False.*
Item 3. **All** of the boys are **swimming.**
(Signal.) *False.*
Item 4. **Some** of the boys are **eating.**
(Signal.) *False.*
Item 5. **None** of the boys are **eating.**
(Signal.) *True.*

Points
(Award points for Workbooks.)

INFORMATION

We're going to work on Information now.

EXERCISE 14

CALENDAR: Months in a Year

1. I'll name some months of the year. When I stop, you name the rest of the months.
2. My turn. January, February, March, April, May, June (pause; signal), *July, August, September, October, November, December.* (Repeat step 2 until firm.)
3. Here's another one. My turn. January, February, March (pause; signal), *April, May, June, July, August, September, October, November, December.* (Repeat step 3 until firm.)

Individual test
(Call on individual students to do one of the following tasks:)
   a. How many months are in a year?
   b. Name the months of the year.
   c. Name the rest of the months. (Repeat step 2 or step 3.)

EXERCISE 15

INFORMATION: Animals

1. You're learning about animals that have a backbone. How many classes of those animals are there? (Signal.) *Five.*
You've learned facts about two of those classes. Which classes? (Signal.) *Mammals and reptiles.* (Repeat until firm.)
2. Name a mammal. (Call on individual students. The group is to name at least five mammals.)
You learned two facts about **all mammals.** Everybody, tell me those two facts. (Hold up one finger.) First fact. *All mammals have hair.* (Hold up two fingers.) Second fact. *All mammals are warm-blooded.* (Repeat until the students say the facts in order.)

3. Name a reptile. (Call on individual students.) The group is to name at least four reptiles. You learned two facts about **all reptiles.** Everybody, tell me those two facts. (Hold up one finger.) First fact. *All reptiles are cold-blooded.*
(Hold up two fingers.) Second fact. *All reptiles are born on land.* (Repeat until students say the facts in order.)

4. What class are monkeys in? (Signal.) *Mammals.* So, tell me the two facts you know about **monkeys.** (Hold up one finger.) First fact. *Monkeys have hair.*
(Hold up two fingers.) Second fact. *Monkeys are warm-blooded.* (Repeat until students say the facts in order.)

5. What class are alligators in? (Signal.) *Reptiles.* So, tell me the two facts you know about **alligators.** (Hold up one finger.) First fact. *Alligators are cold-blooded.*
(Hold up two fingers.) Second fact. *Alligators are born on land.* (Repeat until students say the facts in order.)

=== EXERCISE 16 ===

- **INFORMATION: Animals**
1. You're going to learn about another class of animals that have a backbone.
2. Eagles are not mammals or reptiles. They are birds. Name another bird. (Call on individual students. The group is to name at least four birds.)
3. Here's the first fact about **all birds.** Listen. All birds have feathers. Say that fact. (Signal.) *All birds have feathers.* (Repeat until firm.) Yes, even birds that can't fly have feathers.
4. Here's that fact again. All birds have feathers. Eagles are birds. So, eagles (pause; signal) *have feathers.*
Robins are birds. So, robins (pause; signal) *have feathers.*
Ducks are birds. So, ducks (pause; signal) *have feathers.*

5. Everybody, tell me the first fact about **all birds.** (Signal.) *All birds have feathers.* Here's the second fact about **all birds.** Listen. All birds are warm-blooded. Say that fact. (Signal.) *All birds are warm-blooded.* (Repeat until firm.)

6. Here are the two facts you've learned about **all birds.** (Hold up one finger.) First fact. All birds have feathers.
(Hold up two fingers.) Second fact. All birds are warm-blooded. Your turn. Tell me the two facts about **all birds.** (Hold up one finger.) First fact. *All birds have feathers.*
(Hold up two fingers.) Second fact. *All birds are warm-blooded.* (Repeat until students say the facts in order.)

7. Penguins are birds. So, tell me the two facts you know about **penguins.** (Hold up one finger.) First fact. *Penguins have feathers.*
(Hold up two fingers.) Second fact. *Penguins are warm-blooded.* (Repeat until students say the facts in order.)

8. Ostriches are birds. So, tell me the two facts you know about **ostriches.** (Hold up one finger.) First fact. *Ostriches have feathers.*
(Hold up two fingers.) Second fact. *Ostriches are warm-blooded.* (Repeat until students say the facts in order.)

Individual test
(Call on individual students to do one of the following tasks:)
a. Robins are birds. What two facts do you know about robins?
b. Sparrows are birds. What two facts do you know about sparrows?
c. Name three mammals.
d. Name three reptiles.
e. Name three birds.

Points
(Award points for Information.
Have the students add up their daily total.)

- **Five-Lesson Point Summary**
(Tell students to add the point totals for Lessons 6 through 10 on the Point Summary Chart and to write the total for Block 2.)

END OF LESSON 10

THINKING OPERATIONS

=====EXERCISE 1=====

• **DEDUCTIONS: With *all* and *every***

The first Thinking Operation today is **Deductions.**

1. I'll say rules with **all** or **every.** You say them the other way. What two words are we going to use? (Hold up one finger.) *All.* (Hold up two fingers.) *Every.*

2. Listen. **Every** animal breathes. Say that. (Signal.) *Every animal breathes.*
Now say it the other way. Get ready. (Signal.) *All animals breathe.*
(Repeat step 2 until firm.)

3. Here's a new rule. **All** living things must die. Say that. (Signal.) *All living things must die.*
Now say it the other way. Get ready. (Signal.) *Every living thing must die.*
(Repeat step 3 until firm.)

4. Here's a new rule. **All** wolves eat meat. Say that. (Signal.) *All wolves eat meat.*
Now say it the other way. Get ready. (Signal.) *Every wolf eats meat.*
(Repeat step 4 until firm.)

5. Here's a new rule. **All** cows eat plants. Say that. (Signal.) *All cows eat plants.*
Now say it the other way. Get ready. (Signal.) *Every cow eats plants.*
(Repeat step 5 until firm.)

=====EXERCISE 2=====

• **DEDUCTIONS: With *no* and *don't***

Task A

1. I'll say a rule one way with the word **no.** Then I'll say it another way with the word **don't.**

2. Listen. **No** snakes have legs. Say that. (Signal.) *No snakes have legs.*
Now I'll say the same rule with **don't.** Snakes **don't** have legs. Say that. (Signal.) *Snakes don't have legs.*

Task B

1. Here's a new rule. Trees **don't** fly. Say that. (Signal.) *Trees don't fly.*
Now I'll say the same rule with **no. No** trees fly. Say that. (Signal.) *No trees fly.*

2. Now say the rule that starts with **trees.** (Pause.) Get ready. (Signal.) *Trees don't fly.*
Now say the rule that starts with **no trees.** (Pause.) Get ready. (Signal.) *No trees fly.*
(Repeat step 2 until firm.)

Task C

1. Here's a new rule. **No** bottles have feet. Say that. (Signal.) *No bottles have feet.*
Now say the rule that starts with **bottles.** (Pause.) Get ready. (Signal.) *Bottles don't have feet.*
Now say the rule that starts with **no bottles.** (Pause.) Get ready. (Signal.) *No bottles have feet.*
(Repeat step 1 until firm.)

2. Here's a new rule. Chickens **don't** sing. Say that. (Signal.) *Chickens don't sing.*
Now say the rule that starts with **no chickens.** (Pause.) Get ready. (Signal.) *No chickens sing.*
Now say the rule that starts with **chickens.** (Pause.) Get ready. (Signal.) *Chickens don't sing.* (Repeat step 2 until firm.)

Individual test
Call on individual students to do one step in Task C.

=====EXERCISE 3=====

DEDUCTIONS: With *all*

1. Listen to this rule. **All** reptiles are cold-blooded. Everybody, say that. (Signal.) *All reptiles are cold-blooded.*

2. Pythons are reptiles. So (pause; signal), *pythons are cold-blooded.* How do you know that pythons are cold-blooded? (Signal.) *Because all reptiles are cold-blooded.*

To correct students who say *All reptiles are cold-blooded:*

a. **Because** all reptiles are cold-blooded.

b. How do you know that pythons are cold-blooded? (Signal.) *Because all reptiles are cold-blooded.*

c. (Repeat step 2.)

(Repeat step 2 until firm.)

3. Listen. **All** reptiles are cold-blooded. King snakes are reptiles. So (pause; signal), *king snakes are cold-blooded.* How do you know that king snakes are cold-blooded? (Signal.) *Because all reptiles are cold-blooded.* (Repeat step 3 until firm.)

4. Listen. **All** reptiles are cold-blooded. Cobras are reptiles. So (pause; signal), *cobras are cold-blooded.* How do you know that cobras are cold-blooded? (Signal.) *Because all reptiles are cold-blooded.* (Repeat step 4 until firm.)

───────────── EXERCISE 4 ─────────────

SAME: Review

The next Thinking Operation is **Same.**

Task A

1. A blue bird and a blue butterfly are the same because they are the same **color.** Everybody, tell me that **color.** (Signal.) *Blue.* Yes, they are blue. How are they the same? (Signal.) *They are blue.*

2. Here's another way a blue bird and a blue butterfly are the same. You find them in some of the same **places.** Name some of those **places.** (Call on individual students. Praise reasonable responses; for example, in trees, on the ground, in the air.)

3. Here's another way a blue bird and a blue butterfly are the same. They **do** some things that are the same. Name at least three things they **do** that are the same. (Call on individual students. Praise reasonable responses; for example, see, fly, eat.)

4. Here's another way a blue bird and a blue butterfly are the same. They are in the same **class.** Everybody, tell me that **class.** (Signal.) *Animals.* Yes, they are animals. How are they the same? (Signal.) *They are animals.*

Task B

1. A plastic toothbrush and a plastic comb are the same because they are made of the same **material.** Everybody, tell me that **material.** (Signal.) *Plastic.* Yes, they are made of plastic. How are they the same? (Signal.) *They are made of plastic.*

2. Here's another way a plastic toothbrush and a plastic comb are the same. They are in the same **class.** Everybody, tell me that **class.** (Signal.) *Tools.* Yes, they are tools. How are they the same? (Signal.) *They are tools.*

3. Here's another way a plastic toothbrush and a plastic comb are the same. You **do** some of the same things with them. Name at least three of the same things you **do** with a plastic toothbrush and a plastic comb. (Call on individual students. Praise reasonable responses; for example, hold them, move them, clean them.)

4. Here's another way a toothbrush and a comb are the same. You find them in some of the same **places.** Name some of those **places.** (Call on individual students. Praise reasonable responses; for example, bathroom, store.)

Individual test

(Call on individual students to do one of the following tasks:)

a. Name three ways that a blue bird and a blue butterfly are the same.

b. Name three ways that a plastic toothbrush and a plastic comb are the same.

───────────── EXERCISE 5 ─────────────

● **SAME: Object Rules**

1. Anything you can point to is an object. What do we call anything you can point to? (Signal.) *An object. (*Point to the objects and say:) I'll name some objects. An eraser, a book, a boy. When I call on you, name three more objects. (Call on individual students.)

2. I'll name three ways that a table and a ball are the same. (Hold up one finger.) They are objects.
   (Hold up two fingers.) They take up space. (Hold up three fingers.) You find them in some place.

3. Do it with me. Name those three ways that a table and a ball are the same. (Respond with the students. Hold up one finger.) *They are objects.*
   (Hold up two fingers.) *They take up space.* (Hold up three fingers.) *You find them in some place.* (Repeat until the students are responding with you.)

4. All by yourselves. Name those three ways that a table and a ball are the same. (Hold up one finger.) *They are objects.*
   (Hold up two fingers.) *They take up space.* (Hold up three fingers.) *You find them in some place.* (Repeat until firm.)

5. Anything you can point to is an object. Can you point to a truck and a mouse? (Signal.) *Yes.*
   So, are a truck and a mouse objects? (Signal.) *Yes.*
   So, name three ways that a truck and a mouse are the same. (Hold up one finger.) *They are objects.* (Hold up two fingers.) *They take up space.* (Hold up three fingers.) *You find them in some place.* (Repeat until firm.)

6. Anything you can point to is an object. Can you point to a boy and a tree? (Signal.) *Yes.*
   So, are a boy and a tree objects? (Signal.) *Yes.*
   So, name three ways that a boy and a tree are the same. (Hold up one finger.) *They are objects.* (Hold up two fingers.) *They take up space.* (Hold up three fingers.) *You find them in some place.* (Repeat until firm.)

EXERCISE 6

DEFINITIONS

The next Thinking Operation is **Definitions.**

1. **Amble** means **walk slowly.**

2. What does **amble** mean? (Signal.) *Walk slowly.*
   What word means **walk slowly?** (Signal.) *Amble.* (Repeat step 2 until firm.)

3. Listen. Let's walk slowly to the store. Say that. (Signal.) *Let's walk slowly to the store.* (Repeat until firm.)
   Now say that sentence with a different word for **walk slowly.** (Pause.) Get ready. (Signal.) *Let's amble to the store.* (Repeat until firm.) (Repeat step 3 until firm.)

4. Listen. The dog ambled into the street. Say that. (Signal.) *The dog ambled into the street.* (Repeat until firm.)
   Now say that sentence with different words for **ambled.** (Pause.) Get ready. (Signal.) *The dog walked slowly into the street.* (Repeat until firm.)
   (Repeat step 4 until firm.)

5. Listen. The cow ambled across the field. Say that. (Signal.) *The cow ambled across the field.* (Repeat until firm.)
   Now say that sentence with different words for **ambled.** (Pause.) Get ready. (Signal.) *The cow walked slowly across the field.* (Repeat until firm.)
   (Repeat step 5 until firm.)

EXERCISE 7

DESCRIPTION

The next Thinking Operation is **Description.**

1. I'm going to tell you about an object you know. But I'm going to call it a funny name. See if you can figure out what object I'm talking about.

2. (Hold up one finger.) A tam is an animal. (Hold up two fingers.) A tam is a pet. (Hold up three fingers.) A tam meows.

3. Let's say the three things we know about a tam. (Respond with the students. Hold up one finger.) *A tam is an animal.*
(Hold up two fingers.) *A tam is a pet.*
(Hold up three fingers.) *A tam meows.*
(Repeat until students are responding with you.)

4. You say the three things you know about a tam. (Hold up one finger.) *A tam is an animal.* (Hold up two fingers.) *A tam is a pet.* (Hold up three fingers.) *A tam meows.* (Repeat until the students say the statements in order.)

5. Everybody, tell me what kind of animal I'm calling a tam. (Signal.) *A cat.* Yes, it's really a cat.

═══════════ EXERCISE 8 ═══════════

STATEMENT INFERENCE

The next Thinking Operation is **Statement Inference.**

Task A

1. Listen. Three mammals hid under shady trees. Say that statement. (Signal.) *Three mammals hid under shady trees.* (Repeat until firm.)

Individual test Call on a few individual students to say the statement.

2. Everybody, listen. Three mammals hid under shady trees. Where did the three mammals hide? (Signal.) *Under shady trees.*
What did three mammals do? (Signal.) *Hid under shady trees.*
How many shady trees did the three mammals hide under? (Signal.) *I don't know.*
How many mammals hid under shady trees? (Signal.) *Three.*
What kind of trees did three mammals hide under? (Signal.) *Shady.*
What hid under shady trees?
(Signal.) *Three mammals.*
What did three mammals hide under?
(Signal.) *Shady trees.*
(Repeat step 2 until firm.)

Individual test Call on individual students to answer a question from step 2.

Task B

1. Listen. A small reptile ran from the big hawk. Say that statement. (Signal.) *A small reptile ran from the big hawk.* (Repeat until firm.)

Individual test Call on a few individual students to say the statement.

2. Everybody, listen. A small reptile ran from the big hawk. What ran from the big hawk? (Signal.) *A small reptile.*
What did the small reptile do?
(Signal.) *Ran from the big hawk.*
What did the small reptile run from?
(Signal.) *The big hawk.*
What kind of reptile ran from the big hawk? (Signal.) *Small.*
What kind of hawk did the small reptile run from? (Signal.) *Big.*
Where did the small reptile run? (Signal.)
I don't know.
(Repeat step 2 until firm.)

Individual test Call on individual students to answer a question from step 2.

Points
(Pass out the Workbooks.
Award points for Thinking Operations.)

WORKBOOK EXERCISES

We're going to do the Workbooks now. Remember to follow my instructions carefully.

EXERCISE 9

● TRUE—FALSE

1. Everybody, touch part A in your Workbook. ✔ I'll say statements about the picture. Some of these statements are true, some are false, and some **may be** true or **may be** false. Everybody, touch the word **maybe** for item 1. ✔ Here's a maybe statement about the picture. Some of the boys are brothers. That **may be** true or **may be** false. We don't know. Here's another maybe statement. All the boys have a sister. That **may be** true or **may be** false. We don't know.

2. Get ready to circle **true, false,** or **maybe.** Item 1. **All** of the boys are **eating.** Circle **true, false,** or **maybe** for item 1. (Wait.)

3. Item 2. **All** of the boys are **sitting.** Circle **true, false,** or **maybe** for item 2. (Wait.)

4. Item 3. **None** of the boys are **sitting.** Circle **true, false,** or **maybe** for item 3. (Wait.)

5. Item 4. **Some** of the boys are **sitting.** Circle **true, false,** or **maybe** for item 4. (Wait.)

6. Item 5. **Some** of the boys are **sleeping.** Circle **true, false,** or **maybe** for item 5. (Wait.)

7. Let's check your answers. Mark any item you missed with an X. Everybody, tell me **true, false,** or **maybe.** Item 1. **All** of the boys are eating. (Signal.) *True.*
Item 2. **All** of the boys are sitting. (Signal.) *Maybe.*
Item 3. **None** of the boys are sitting. (Signal.) *Maybe.*
Item 4. **Some** of the boys are sitting. (Signal.) *Maybe.*
Item 5. **Some** of the boys are sleeping. (Signal.) *False.*

EXERCISE 10

DESCRIPTION

1. Everybody, touch part B in your Workbook. ✔ Figure out which object I describe. Listen. A newsh is made of metal. A newsh is a vehicle. A newsh carries many people. A newsh travels on roads.
Underline the object I'm calling a newsh. (Wait.)

2. Listen. A crumber is an appliance. A crumber gets hot when you turn it on. You can pick up a crumber with one hand. **Make a 4 on** the object I'm calling a crumber. (Wait.)

3. Listen. Diz is food. Diz comes in slices. Diz is a kind of meat. **Make a box around** the object I'm calling diz. (Wait.)

4. Everybody, get ready to check your work. Tell me the real name for the object that is made of metal, that is a vehicle, that carries many people, and that travels on roads. Get ready. (Signal.) *A bus.* And how did you mark the bus? (Signal.) *Underlined it.*

5. Tell me the real name for the object that is an appliance, that gets hot when you turn it on, and that you can pick up with one hand. Get ready. (Signal.) *An iron.* And how did you mark the iron? (Signal.) *Made a 4 on it.*

6. Tell me the real name of the object that is food, that comes in slices, and that is a kind of meat. Get ready. (Signal.) *Bacon.* And how did you mark the bacon? (Signal.) *Made a box around it.*

EXERCISE 11

SAME

1. Everybody, touch part C in your Workbook. ✔ Some of the objects in Box 1 are in the same class. **Make a box around** all the objects that are in the same class. Do it. (Wait.)

2. Some of the objects in Box 2 are often made of the same material. **Cross out** all the objects that are made of the same material. Do it. (Wait.)

3. Some of the objects in Box 3 have some of the same parts. **Make a line under** all the objects that have some of the same parts. Do it. (Wait.)

4. Everybody, get ready to check part C. Name the class of the objects you marked in Box 1. (Pause.) Get ready. (Signal.) *Furniture.*
   Name the material of the objects you marked in Box 2. (Pause.) Get ready. (Signal.) *Leather.*
   Name the parts of the objects you marked in Box 3. (Pause.) Get ready. (Signal.) *Lids and handles.*
5. Which objects did you mark in Box 1? (Call on one student.) *Rocking chair, stool, table.* What is the same about those objects? (Call on one student.) *They are furniture.* How did you mark each of those objects? (Call on one student.) *Made a box around it.*
6. (Repeat step 5 for Boxes 2 and 3.)

===== **EXERCISE 12** =====

CLASSIFICATION

1. Pencils down. Don't write anything yet. Everybody, touch the instructions for part D in your Workbook. I'll read the first instruction. Listen. Circle the foods.
2. What are you going to do to every food? (Signal.) *Circle it.*
3. I'll read the next instruction. Make a box around the buildings. What are you going to do to every building? (Signal.) *Make a box around it.*
   Everybody, do it. Circle the foods and make a box around the buildings. (Wait.)
4. Get ready to mark your papers. Put an X by any object you got wrong.
5. What class is a **cake** in? (Signal.) *Food.* How did you mark the cake? (Signal.) *Circled it.*
6. (Repeat step 5 for **school, popcorn, banana, barbershop, pancakes, bank, corn, sandwich,** and **drugstore.**)

Points

(Award points for Workbooks.)

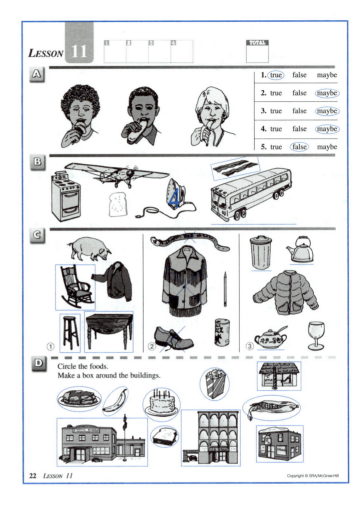

INFORMATION

We're going to work on Information now.

═══ **EXERCISE 13** ═══

- **MEMORIZATION: Poem**

Task A

1. What does a mechanic do? (Call on a student. Accept reasonable responses.) Yes, a mechanic fixes cars.
2. What does an astronomer do? (Call on a student. Accept reasonable responses.) Yes, an astronomer looks at stars.
3. Who knows how you would recognize a captain in the army? (Call on a student. Accept reasonable responses.) Yes, a captain has two bars on each shoulder.
4. Who knows what sparring is? (Call on a student. Accept reasonable responses.) Yes, sparring is light boxing. Boxers spar a lot when they are getting in shape for a fight.

Task B

1. Here's a poem that tells about the things we've talked about. Listen.
   A mechanic fixes cars,
   An astronomer looks at stars,
   A captain has two bars,
   And a boxer spars and spars.
2. Let's learn that poem. Listen. A mechanic fixes cars. Say it with me. (Signal. Respond with the students.) *A mechanic fixes cars.* Your turn. (Signal.) *A mechanic fixes cars.* (Repeat until firm.)
3. An astronomer looks at stars. Say it with me. (Signal. Respond with the students.) *An astronomer looks at stars.* Your turn. (Signal.) *An astronomer looks at stars.* (Repeat until firm.)
4. A mechanic fixes cars, an astronomer looks at stars. Say it with me. (Signal. Respond with the students.) *A mechanic fixes cars, an astronomer looks at stars.* (Repeat until the students are responding with you.) Your turn. (Signal.) *A mechanic fixes cars, an astronomer looks at stars.* (Repeat until firm.)

5. A captain has two bars. Say it. (Signal.) *A captain has two bars.* (Repeat until firm.)
6. A mechanic fixes cars, an astronomer looks at stars, a captain has two bars. Say it with me. (Signal. Respond with the students.) *A mechanic fixes cars, an astronomer looks at stars, a captain has two bars.* (Repeat until students are responding with you.)
   Your turn. (Signal.) *A mechanic fixes cars, an astronomer looks at stars, a captain has two bars.* (Repeat until firm.)
7. And a boxer spars and spars. Say it. (Signal.) *And a boxer spars and spars.* (Repeat until firm.)
8. Here's the whole poem.
   A mechanic fixes cars,
   An astronomer looks at stars,
   A captain has two bars,
   And a boxer spars and spars.
   Say it with me. (Signal. Respond with the students. Repeat until the students are responding with you.)
9. All by yourselves. Say the poem. (Signal. Students say the poem. Repeat until firm.)

═══ **EXERCISE 14** ═══

- **CALENDAR: Seasons in a Year**

1. There are four seasons in a year. How many seasons are in a year? (Signal.) *Four.*
   Tell me the fact about how many seasons are in a year. (Signal.) *There are four seasons in a year.*
2. My turn to name the seasons in a year. Winter, spring, summer, fall. Your turn. Name the seasons in a year. (Signal.) *Winter, spring, summer, fall.* (Repeat until firm.)
3. You named the four (pause; signal) *seasons in a year.*
4. How many seasons are in a year? (Signal.) *Four.*

Individual test
(Call on individual students to do one of the following tasks:)
   a. Tell me the fact about how many seasons are in a year.
   b. Name the seasons in a year.

EXERCISE 15

● **INFORMATION: Animals**

1. You're learning about animals that have a backbone. How many classes of those animals are there? (Signal.) *Five.*
   You've learned facts about three of those classes. Which classes? (Signal.) *Mammals, reptiles, and birds.* (Repeat until firm.)

2. The last class that you learned about was birds. Name a bird. (Call on individual students. The group is to name at least five birds.)
   You learned two facts about **all birds.** Everybody, tell me those two facts. (Hold up one finger.) First fact. *All birds have feathers.* (Hold up two fingers.) Second fact. *All birds are warm-blooded.* (Repeat until the students say the facts in order.)

3. Name a mammal. (Call on individual students.) The group is to name at least five mammals.
   You learned two facts about **all mammals.** Everybody, tell me those two facts. (Hold up one finger.) First fact. *All mammals have hair.* (Hold up two fingers.) Second fact. *All mammals are warm-blooded.* (Repeat until the students say the facts in order.)

4. Name a reptile. (Call on individual students.) The group is to name at least four reptiles.
   You learned two facts about **all reptiles.** Everybody, tell me those two facts. (Hold up one finger.) First fact. *All reptiles are cold-blooded.*
   (Hold up two fingers.) Second fact. *All reptiles are born on land.* (Repeat until the students say the facts in order.)

5. Tell me what class **elephants** are in. (Pause.) Get ready. (Signal.) *Mammals.*
   So, tell me the two facts you know about elephants. (Hold up one finger.) First fact. *Elephants have hair.*
   (Hold up two fingers.) Second fact. *Elephants are warm-blooded.* (Repeat until the students say the facts in order.)

6. Tell me what class **turkeys** are in. (Pause.) Get ready. (Signal.) *Birds.*
   So, tell me the two facts you know about turkeys. (Hold up one finger.) First fact. *Turkeys have feathers.*
   (Hold up two fingers.) Second fact. *Turkeys are warm-blooded.* (Repeat until the students say the facts in order.)

7. Tell me what class **crocodiles** are in. (Pause.) Get ready. (Signal.) *Reptiles.*
   So, tell me the two facts you know about crocodiles. (Hold up one finger.) First fact. *Crocodiles are cold-blooded.*
   (Hold up two fingers.) Second fact. *Crocodiles are born on land.* (Repeat until the students say the facts in order.)

Individual test
Call on individual students to do steps 5, 6, or 7.

Points
(Award points for Information.
Have the students add up their daily total.)

END OF LESSON 11

THINKING OPERATIONS

━━━━━━ EXERCISE 1 ━━━━━━

DEDUCTIONS: With *all* and *every*
The first Thinking Operation today is **Deductions.**

1. I'll say rules with **all** or **every.** You say them the other way. What two words are we going to use? (Hold up one finger.) *All.* (Hold up two fingers.) *Every.*
2. Listen. **All** people learn. Say that. (Signal.) *All people learn.*
   Now say it the other way. Get ready. (Signal.) *Every person learns.*
   (Repeat step 2 until firm.)
3. Here's a new rule. **Every** person eats. Say that. (Signal.) *Every person eats.*
   Now say it the other way. Get ready. (Signal.) *All people eat.*
   (Repeat step 3 until firm.)
4. Here's a new rule. **Every** year is fifty-two weeks long. Say that. (Signal.) *Every year is fifty-two weeks long.*
   Now say it the other way. (Signal.) *All years are fifty-two weeks long.*
   (Repeat step 4 until firm.)
5. Here's a new rule. **All** objects take up space. Say that. (Signal.) *All objects take up space.*
   Now say it the other way. (Signal.) *Every object takes up space.*
   (Repeat step 5 until firm.)

━━━━━━ EXERCISE 2 ━━━━━━

DEDUCTIONS: With *no* and *don't*

Task A

1. I'll say a rule one way with the word **no.** Then I'll say it another way with the word **don't.**
2. Listen. Babies **don't** read. Say that. (Signal.) *Babies don't read.*
   Now I'll say the same rule with **no. No** babies read. Say that. (Signal.) *No babies read.*

Task B

1. Here's a new rule. **No** trucks grow. Say that. (Signal.) *No trucks grow.*

Now I'll say the same rule with **don't.** Trucks **don't** grow. Say that. (Signal.) *Trucks don't grow.*
2. Now say the rule that starts with **no trucks.** (Pause.) Get ready. (Signal.) *No trucks grow.*
   Now say the rule that starts with **trucks.** (Pause.) Get ready. (Signal.) *Trucks don't grow.* (Repeat step 2 until firm.)

Task C

1. Here's a new rule. **No** chairs eat. Say that. (Signal.) *No chairs eat.*
   Now say the rule that starts with **chairs.** (Pause.) Get ready. (Signal.) *Chairs don't eat.*
   Now say the rule that starts with **no chairs.** (Pause.) Get ready. (Signal.) *No chairs eat.* (Repeat step 1 until firm.)
2. Here's a new rule. Trees **don't** read. Say that. (Signal.) *Trees don't read.*
   Now say the rule that starts with **no trees.** (Pause.) Get ready. (Signal.) *No trees read.*
   Now say the rule that starts with **trees.** (Pause.) Get ready. (Signal.) *Trees don't read.* (Repeat step 2 until firm.)

Individual test
Call on individuals to do one step in Task C.

━━━━━━ EXERCISE 3 ━━━━━━

● **DEDUCTIONS: With *don't***

1. Listen to this rule. Dogs **don't** have wings. Everybody, say that. (Signal.) *Dogs don't have wings.*
2. Retrievers are dogs. So (pause; signal), *retrievers don't have wings.* How do you know that retrievers don't have wings? (Signal.) *Because dogs don't have wings.*
3. Listen. Dogs **don't** have wings. Beagles are dogs. So (pause; signal), *beagles don't have wings.* How do you know that beagles don't have wings? (Signal.) *Because dogs don't have wings.*
4. Listen. Dogs **don't** have wings. Poodles are dogs. So (pause; signal), *poodles don't have wings.* How do you know that poodles don't have wings? (Signal.) *Because dogs don't have wings.*
5. (Repeat steps 2–4 until firm.)

EXERCISE 4

SAME: Objects

The next Thinking Operation is **Same.**

1. Anything you can point to is an object. What do we call anything you can point to? (Signal.) *An object.*
   I'll name some objects. A box, a flower, a rock. When I call on you, name three more objects. (Call on individual students.)

2. I'll name three ways that a banana and a rock are the same. (Hold up one finger.) They are objects.
   (Hold up two fingers.) They take up space.
   (Hold up three fingers.) You find them in some place.

3. Do it with me. Name those three ways that a banana and a rock are the same. (Respond with the students. Hold up one finger.) *They are objects.*
   (Hold up two fingers.) *They take up space.* (Hold up three fingers.) *You find them in some place.* (Repeat until the students are responding with you.)

4. All by yourselves. Name those three ways that a banana and a rock are the same. (Hold up one finger.) *They are objects.* (Hold up two fingers.) *They take up space.* (Hold up three fingers.) *You find them in some place.* (Repeat until firm.)

5. Anything you can point to is an object. Can you point to a horse and a ladder? (Signal.) *Yes.* So, are a horse and a ladder objects? (Signal.) *Yes.*
   So, name three ways that a horse and a ladder are the same. (Hold up one finger.) *They are objects.* (Hold up two fingers.) *They take up space.* (Hold up three fingers.) *You find them in some place.* (Repeat until firm.)

6. Anything you can point to is an object. Can you point to a pencil and a bird? (Signal.) *Yes.* So, are a pencil and a bird objects? (Signal.) *Yes.*
   So, name three ways that a pencil and a bird are the same. (Hold up one finger.) *They are objects.*

(Hold up two fingers.) *They take up space.*
(Hold up three fingers.) *You find them in some place.* (Repeat until firm.)

EXERCISE 5

DESCRIPTION

The next Thinking Operation is **Description.**

1. I'm going to tell you about an object you know. But I'm going to call it a funny name. See if you can figure out what object I'm talking about.

2. (Hold up one finger.) A lat is made of metal.
   (Hold up two fingers.) A lat has a point and a head.
   (Hold up three fingers.) You pound a lat with a hammer.

3. Let's say the three things we know about a lat. (Respond with the students. Hold up one finger.) *A lat is made of metal.* (Hold up two fingers.) *A lat has a point and a head.* (Hold up three fingers.) *You pound a lat with a hammer.* (Repeat until the students are responding with you.)

4. You say the three things you know about a lat. (Hold up one finger.) *A lat is made of metal.* (Hold up two fingers.) *A lat has a point and a head.* (Hold up three fingers.) *You pound a lat with a hammer.* (Repeat until the students say the statements in order.)

5. Everybody, tell me what I'm calling a lat. (Signal.) *A nail.* Yes, it's really a nail.

EXERCISE 6

DESCRIPTION

1. Here's the rule. **Yum** is a funny word that we'll use for pencil. What word are we using for pencil? (Signal.) *Yum.*

2. Listen to this sentence. A yum is used to cut meat. Is that statement true or false? (Signal.) *False.*

3. Next sentence. You can wear a yum on your foot. Is that statement true or false? (Signal.) *False.*

4. Next sentence. Most yums have a point and an eraser. Is that statement true or false? (Signal.) *True.*

5. Next sentence. You can write with a yum. Is that statement true or false? (Signal.) *True.*

6. Next sentence. A yum can walk. Is that statement true or false? (Signal.) *False.*

━━━━━━━━━━ **EXERCISE 7** ━━━━━━━━━━

STATEMENT INFERENCE

The next Thinking Operation is **Statement Inference.**

Task A

1. Listen. Most reptiles sleep during the day. Say that statement. (Signal.) *Most reptiles sleep during the day.* (Repeat until firm.)

> **Individual test**
> Call on individuals to say the statement.

2. Everybody, listen. Most reptiles sleep during the day.
   How many reptiles sleep during the day? (Signal.) *Most.*
   What do most reptiles do during the day? (Signal.) *Sleep.*
   When do most reptiles sleep? (Signal.) *During the day.*
   Where do most reptiles sleep during the day? (Signal.) *I don't know.*
   What sleeps during the day? (Signal.) *Most reptiles.*
   What kind of reptiles sleep during the day? (Signal.) *I don't know.*
   What do most reptiles do? (Signal.) *Sleep during the day.*
   (Repeat step 2 until firm.)

> **Individual test**
> Call on individual students to answer a question from step 2.

Task B

1. Listen. His sister saved money to buy hiking shoes. Say that statement. (Signal.) *His sister saved money to buy hiking shoes.* (Repeat until firm.)

> **Individual test**
> Call on individuals to say the statement.

2. Everybody, listen. His sister saved money to buy hiking shoes. What did his sister do? (Signal.) *Saved money to buy hiking shoes.*
   Why did his sister save money? (Signal.) *To buy hiking shoes.*
   What did his sister save? (Signal.) *Money.*
   How much money did his sister save? (Signal.) *I don't know.*
   What did his sister save money to buy? (Signal.) *Hiking shoes.*
   What kind of shoes did his sister save money to buy? (Signal.) *Hiking.*
   How many hiking shoes did his sister save money to buy? (Signal.) *I don't know.*
   Who saved money to buy hiking shoes? (Signal.) *His sister.*
   (Repeat step 2 until firm.)

> **Individual test**
> Call on individual students to answer a question from step 2.

━━━━━━━━━━ **EXERCISE 8** ━━━━━━━━━━

DEFINITIONS

The next Thinking Operation is **Definitions.**

1. **Amble** means **walk slowly.**

2. What does **amble** mean? (Signal.) *Walk slowly.* What word means **walk slowly?** (Signal.) *Amble.*
   (Repeat step 2 until firm.)

3. Listen. Ambling is fun. Say that. (Signal.) *Ambling is fun.* (Repeat until firm.)
   Now say that sentence with different words for **ambling.** (Pause.) Get ready. (Signal.) *Walking slowly is fun.* (Repeat until firm.)
   (Repeat step 3 until firm.)

4. Listen. The pig ambled next to the fence. Say that. (Signal.) *The pig ambled next to the fence.* (Repeat until firm.)
   Now say that sentence with different words for **ambled.** (Pause.) Get ready. (Signal.) *The pig walked slowly next to the fence.* (Repeat until firm.)
   (Repeat step 4 until firm.)

5. Listen. We walked slowly home. Say that. (Signal.) *We walked slowly home.* (Repeat until firm.)

   Now say that sentence with a different word for **walked slowly.** (Pause.) Get ready. (Signal.) *We ambled home.* (Repeat until firm.)

   (Repeat step 5 until firm.)

===================== EXERCISE 9 =====================

DEFINITIONS

1. **Indolent.** (Pause.) What's a synonym for **indolent?** (Signal.) *Lazy.* And what's a synonym for **lazy?** (Signal.) *Indolent.* (Repeat step 1 until firm.)

2. Listen. When it is sunny, I feel lazy. Say that. (Signal.) *When it is sunny, I feel lazy.* (Repeat until firm.)

   Now say that sentence with a synonym for **lazy.** (Pause.) Get ready. (Signal.) *When it is sunny, I feel indolent.* (Repeat until firm.)
   (Repeat step 2 until firm.)

3. **Canine.** (Pause.) What's a synonym for **canine?** (Signal.) *Dog.* And what's a synonym for **dog?** (Signal.) *Canine.* (Repeat step 3 until firm.)

4. Listen. His canine has a wet nose. Say that. (Signal.) *His canine has a wet nose.* (Repeat until firm.)

   Now say that sentence with a synonym for **canine.** (Pause.) Get ready. (Signal.) *His dog has a wet nose.* (Repeat until firm.)
   (Repeat step 4 until firm.)

5. **Complete.** (Pause.) What's a synonym for **complete?** (Signal.) *Finish.* And what's a synonym for **finish?** (Signal.) *Complete.* (Repeat step 5 until firm.)

6. Listen. I can't finish this work. Say that. (Signal.) *I can't finish this work.* (Repeat until firm.)

   Now say that sentence with a synonym for **finish.** (Pause.) Get ready. (Signal.) *I can't complete this work.* (Repeat until firm.)
   (Repeat step 6 until firm.)

Points

(Pass out the Workbooks.
Award points for Thinking Operations.)

120   *LESSON 12*

[WORKBOOK EXERCISES]

We're going to do the Workbooks now. Remember to follow my instructions carefully.

===================== EXERCISE 10 =====================

● **TRUE—FALSE**

1. Everybody, touch part A in your Workbook. ✔ I'll say statements about the picture. Some of these statements are true, some are false, and some **may be** true or **may be** false. Here's a maybe statement about the picture. Some of the trees are five years old. That **may be** true or **may be** false. We don't know. Here's another maybe statement. All the trees belong to Mr. Jones. That **may be** true or **may be** false. We don't know.

2. Get ready to circle **true, false,** or **maybe.** Item 1. **None** of the trees are peach trees. Circle **true, false,** or **maybe** for item 1. (Wait.)

3. Item 2. **All** of the trees are peach trees. Circle **true, false,** or **maybe** for item 2. (Wait.)

4. Item 3. **Some** of the trees have leaves. Circle **true, false,** or **maybe** for item 3. (Wait.)

5. Item 4. **All** of the trees have leaves. Circle **true, false,** or **maybe** for item 4. (Wait.)

6. Let's check your answers. Mark any item you missed with an X. Everybody, tell me **true, false,** or **maybe.** Item 1. **None** of the trees are peach trees. (Signal.) *Maybe.*
   Item 2. **All** of the trees are peach trees. (Signal.) *Maybe.*
   Item 3. **Some** of the trees have leaves. (Signal.) *True.*
   Item 4. **All** of the trees have leaves. (Signal.) *False.*

===================== EXERCISE 11 =====================

CLASSIFICATION

1. Pencils down. Don't write anything yet. Everybody, touch the instructions for part B in your Workbook. ✔ I'll read the first instruction. Listen. Underline the furniture.

2. What are you going to do to every piece of furniture? (Signal.) *Underline it.*
3. I'll read the next instruction. Make a box around the containers. What are you going to do to every container? (Signal.) *Make a box around it.*
   Everybody, do it. Underline the furniture and make a box around the containers. (Wait.)
4. Get ready to mark your papers. Put an X by any object you got wrong.
5. What class is a **glass** in? (Signal.) *Containers.* How did you mark the **glass?** (Signal.) *Made a box around it.*
6. (Repeat step 5 for **bowl, stool, garbage can, chest of drawers, bookcase, vase, jug, easy chair,** and **table.**)

EXERCISE 12

SAME

1. Everybody, touch part C in your Workbook. ✔ Some of the objects in box 1 are made of the same material. **Circle** all the objects that are made of the same material. Do it. (Wait.)
2. Some of the objects in box 2 are usually found in the same place. **Put a 2 on** all the objects that are usually found in the same place. Do it. (Wait.)
3. Some of the objects in box 3 are in the same class. **Draw a box around** all the objects that are in the same class. Do it. (Wait.)
4. Everybody, get ready to check part C. Name the material of the objects you marked in box 1. (Pause.) Get ready. (Signal.) *Metal.*
   Name the place of the objects you marked in box 2. (Pause.) Get ready. (Signal.) *Living room.*
   Name the class of the objects you marked in box 3. (Pause.) Get ready. (Signal.) *Food.*
5. Which objects did you mark in Box 1? (Call on one student.) *Can, nail, scissors.*
   What is the same about those objects? (Call on one student.) *They are made of metal.*
   How did you mark each of those objects? (Call on one student.) *Circled it.*
6. (Repeat step 5 for boxes 2 and 3.)

EXERCISE 13

TRUE—FALSE

1. Everybody, touch part D in your Workbook. ✔ I'll say statements that are true of one of the pictures. You write the letter of the right picture. Don't get fooled, because I may say statements about the same picture twice.
2. Item 1. **Only some** of the bottles are full. Write the letter of the picture on line 1. (Wait.)
3. Item 2. **All** the bottles are empty. Write the letter of the picture on line 2. (Wait.)
4. Item 3. **Only some** of the bottles are empty. Write the letter of the picture on line 3. (Wait.)
5. Item 4. **None** of the bottles are empty. Write the letter of the picture on line 4. (Wait.)
6. Let's check your answers. Mark any items you missed with an X. Tell me the letter of the right picture.
7. Item 1. **Only some** of the bottles are full. (Signal.) *E.*
8. (Repeat step 7 for items 2–4.)

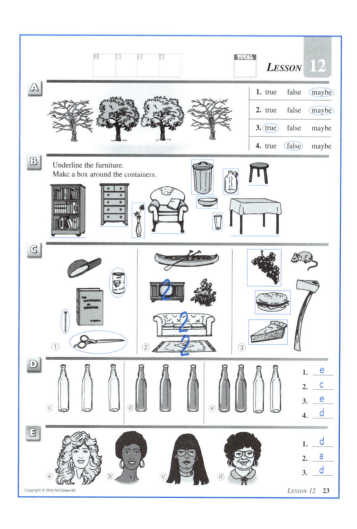

EXERCISE 14

● **DESCRIPTION**

1. Everybody, touch part E in the Workbook. ✔ Figure out which woman I describe.
2. Item 1. This woman is smiling. This woman has black hair. This woman is wearing glasses. Listen again. (Repeat the description.) Write the letter for item 1.
3. Item 2. This woman is smiling. This woman is not wearing glasses. This woman has light hair. Listen again. (Repeat the description.) Write the letter for item 2. *A.*
4. Item 3. This woman has black hair. This woman is wearing glasses. This woman is wearing earrings. Listen again. (Repeat the description.) Write the letter for item 3. *D.*
5. Let's check your answers. Mark any items you missed with an X.
6. Item 1. This woman is smiling. This woman has black hair. This woman is wearing glasses. Everybody, what letter? (Signal.) *D.*
7. (Repeat step 6 for items 2 and 3.)

Points
(Award points for Workbooks.)

INFORMATION

We're going to work on Information now.

EXERCISE 15

CALENDAR: Seasons in a Year

1. There are four seasons in a year. How many seasons are in a year? (Signal.) *Four.*
Tell me the fact about how many seasons are in a year. (Signal.) *There are four seasons in a year.*
2. My turn to name the seasons in a year. Winter, spring, summer, fall. Your turn. Name the seasons in a year. (Signal.) *Winter, spring, summer, fall.* (Repeat until firm.)
3. You named the four (pause; signal) *seasons in a year.*
4. How many seasons are in a year? (Signal.) *Four.*

Individual test
(Call on individual students to do one of the following tasks:)
   a. Tell me the fact about how many seasons are in a year.
   b. Name the seasons in a year.

EXERCISE 16

MEMORIZATION: Poem

Task A

1. What does a mechanic do? (Call on a student. Accept reasonable responses.) Yes, a mechanic fixes cars.
2. What does an astronomer do? (Call on a student. Accept reasonable responses.) Yes, an astronomer looks at stars.
3. Who knows how you would recognize a captain in the army? (Call on a student. Accept reasonable responses.) Yes, a captain has two bars on each shoulder.
4. Who knows what sparring is? (Call on a student. Accept reasonable responses.) Yes, sparring is light boxing. Boxers spar a lot when they are getting in shape for a fight.

Task B

1. Here's a poem that tells about the things we've talked about. Listen.

    A mechanic fixes cars,
    An astronomer looks at stars,
    A captain has two bars,
    And a boxer spars and spars.

2. Let's learn that poem. Listen. A mechanic fixes cars. Say it with me. (Signal. Respond with the students. Repeat until firm.) *A mechanic fixes cars.* Your turn. (Signal.) *A mechanic fixes cars.* (Repeat until firm.)

3. An astronomer looks at stars. Say it with me. (Signal. Respond with the students.) *An astronomer looks at stars.* Your turn. (Signal.) *An astronomer looks at stars.* (Repeat until firm.)

4. A mechanic fixes cars, an astronomer looks at stars. Say it with me. (Signal. Respond with the students.) *A mechanic fixes cars, an astronomer looks at stars.* (Repeat until the students are responding with you.) Your turn. (Signal.) *A mechanic fixes cars, an astronomer looks at stars.* (Repeat until firm.)

5. A captain has two bars. Say it. (Signal.) *A captain has two bars.* (Repeat until firm.)

6. A mechanic fixes cars, an astronomer looks at stars, a captain has two bars. Say it with me. (Signal. Respond with the students.) *A mechanic fixes cars, an astronomer looks at stars, a captain has two bars.* (Repeat until students are responding with you.)
    Your turn. (Signal.) *A mechanic fixes cars, an astronomer looks at stars, a captain has two bars.* (Repeat until firm.)

7. And a boxer spars and spars. Say it. (Signal.) *And a boxer spars and spars.* (Repeat until firm.)

8. Here's the whole poem.

    A mechanic fixes cars,
    An astronomer looks at stars,
    A captain has two bars,
    And a boxer spars and spars.

    Say it with me. (Signal. Respond with the students. Repeat until students respond with you.)

9. All by yourselves. Say the poem. (Signal.) The students say the poem. (Repeat until firm.)

═══ **EXERCISE 17** ═══

INFORMATION: Animals

1. You're learning about animals that have a backbone. How many classes of those animals are there? (Signal.) *Five.*
    You've learned facts about three of those classes. Which classes? (Signal.) *Mammals, reptiles, and birds.* (Repeat until firm.)

2. The last class that you learned about was birds. Name a bird. (Call on individual students. The group is to name at least five birds.)
    You learned two facts about **all birds.** Everybody, tell me those two facts. (Hold up one finger.) First fact. *All birds have feathers.* (Hold up two fingers.) Second fact. *All birds are warm-blooded.* (Repeat until the students say the facts in order.)

3. Name a mammal. (Call on individual students. The group is to name at least five mammals.)
    You learned two facts about **all mammals.** Everybody, tell me those two facts. (Hold up one finger.) First fact. *All mammals have hair.* (Hold up two fingers.) Second fact. *All mammals are warm-blooded.* (Repeat until the students say the facts in order.)

4. Name a reptile. (Call on individual students.) The group is to name at least four reptiles. You learned two facts about all reptiles. Everybody, tell me those two facts. (Hold up one finger.) First fact. *All reptiles are cold-blooded.*
    (Hold up two fingers.) Second fact. *All reptiles are born on land.* (Repeat until the students say the facts in order.)

5. Tell me what class **turtles** are in. (Pause.) Get ready. (Signal.) *Reptiles.*
    So, tell me the two facts you know about turtles. (Hold up one finger.) First fact. *Turtles are cold-blooded.*
    (Hold up two fingers.) Second fact. *Turtles are born on land.* (Repeat until the students say the facts in order.)

6. Tell me what class **dogs** are in.
   (Pause.) Get ready. (Signal.) *Mammals.*
   So, tell me the two facts you know about
   dogs.
   (Hold up one finger.) First fact. *Dogs have
   hair.* (Hold up two fingers.) Second fact.
   Dogs are warm-blooded. (Repeat until the
   students say the facts in order.)
7. Tell me what class **hawks** are in. (Pause.)
   Get ready. (Signal.) *Birds.*
   So, tell me the two facts you know about
   hawks.
   (Hold up one finger.) First fact. *Hawks have
   feathers.*
   (Hold up two fingers.) Second fact. *Hawks
   are warm-blooded.* (Repeat until the students
   say the facts in order.)

Individual test

Call on individual students to do step 5, 6,
or 7.

Points

(Award points for Information.
Have the students add up their daily total.)

END OF LESSON 12

THINKING OPERATIONS

=======EXERCISE 1=======

● **SAME: Review**

The first Thinking Operation today is **Same.**

1. We're going to name some ways that a giraffe and a goat are the same.

2. Can you point to giraffes and goats? (Signal.) *Yes.* So, are giraffes and goats objects? (Signal.) *Yes.*

3. So, name those three ways that a giraffe and a goat are the same. (Hold up one finger.) *They are objects.*
   (Hold up two fingers.) *They take up space.*
   (Hold up three fingers.) *You find them in some place.* (Repeat until firm.)

4. Listen. A giraffe and a goat also **do** some of the same things. When I call on you, name some things they **do** that are the same. (Call on individual students.)

   To correct responses that do not refer to actions:

   a. You told me another way a giraffe and a goat are the same. I asked for some things they **do** that are the same. Listen. They eat. They sleep.

   b. Name some other things that a giraffe and a goat **do** that are the same.

5. Listen. A giraffe and a goat are the same because they are in the same class. Everybody, tell me that class. (Signal.) *Animals.* Yes, they are animals. How are they the same? (Signal.) *They are animals.*

6. I'll name some ways a giraffe is the same as a goat. They are objects. They take up space. You find them in some place. They eat. They breathe. They are animals. When I call on you, see how many ways you can name that a giraffe is the same as a goat. Start with objects. (Call on individual students. Each student is to name at least seven ways a goat and a giraffe are the same.)

=======EXERCISE 2=======

● **SAME: Parts**

1. We're going to name some ways that a motorcycle and a truck are the same. Do a motorcycle and a truck have some of the same **parts?** (Signal.) *Yes.*

2. Name some of the same parts that a motorcycle and a truck have. (Call on individual students. Praise reasonable responses; for example, motor, wheels, headlights.)

   So, a motorcycle and a truck are the same because they have some of the same parts.

=======EXERCISE 3=======

DEDUCTIONS: With *all* and *every*

The next Thinking Operation is **Deductions.**

1. I'll say rules with **all** or **every.** You say them the other way. What two words are we going to use? (Hold up one finger.) *All.*
   (Hold up two fingers.) *Every.*

2. Listen. **Every** object is in some place. Say that. (Signal.) *Every object is in some place.*
   Now say it the other way. Get ready. (Signal.) *All objects are in some place.*
   (Repeat step 2 until firm.)

3. Here's a new rule. **Every** insect has six legs. Say that. (Signal.) *Every insect has six legs.*
   Now say it the other way. Get ready. (Signal.) *All insects have six legs.*
   (Repeat step 3 until firm.)

4. Here's a new rule. **Every** plant grows. Say that. (Signal.) *Every plant grows.*
   Now say it the other way. Get ready. (Signal.) *All plants grow.*
   (Repeat step 4 until firm.)

5. Here's a new rule. **All** plants have roots. Say that. (Signal.) *All plants have roots.*
   Now say it the other way. Get ready. (Signal.) *Every plant has roots.*
   (Repeat step 5 until firm.)

EXERCISE 4

• **DEDUCTIONS: With *no* and *don't***

1. I'll say rules with **no** or **don't** You say them the other way. What two words are we going to use? (Hold up one finger.) *No.* (Hold up two fingers.) *Don't.*
2. Listen. **No** worms have bones. Say that. (Signal.) *No worms have bones.*
   Now say it the other way. Get ready. (Signal.) *Worms don't have bones.*
   (Repeat step 2 until firm.)
3. Here's a new rule. Horses **don't** sing. Say that. (Signal.) *Horses don't sing.*
   Now say it the other way. Get ready. (Signal.) *No horses sing.*
   (Repeat step 3 until firm.)
4. Here's a new rule. **No** triangles have four sides. Say that. (Signal.) *No triangles have four sides.*
   Now say it the other way. Get ready. (Signal.) *Triangles don't have four sides.*
   (Repeat step 4 until firm.)
5. Here's a new rule. Squares **don't** have three sides. Say that. (Signal.) *Squares don't have three sides.*
   Now say it the other way. Get ready. (Signal.) *No squares have three sides.*
   (Repeat step 5 until firm.)

EXERCISE 5

DEDUCTIONS: With *all*

1. Listen to this rule. **All** plants grow. Everybody, say that. (Signal.) *All plants grow.*
2. Trees are plants. So (pause; signal), *trees grow.* How do you know that trees grow? (Signal.) *Because all plants grow.* (Repeat step 2 until firm.)
3. Listen. **All** plants grow. Dandelions are plants. So (pause; signal), *dandelions grow.* How do you know that dandelions grow? (Signal.) *Because all plants grow.* (Repeat step 3 until firm.)
4. Listen. **All** plants grow. Roses are plants. So (pause; signal), *roses grow.* How do you know that roses grow? (Signal.) *Because all plants grow.* (Repeat step 4 until firm.)

EXERCISE 6

DEDUCTIONS: With *no*

1. Listen to this rule. **No** cows eat meat. Everybody, say that. (Signal.) *No cows eat meat.*
2. Guernseys are cows. So (pause; signal), *no Guernseys eat meat.*
   To correct students who say *Guernseys don't eat meat:*
   a. **No** Guernseys eat meat.
   b. The rule is **no** cows eat meat.
   c. (Repeat step 2.)
   How do you know that no Guernseys eat meat? (Signal.) *Because no cows eat meat.*
3. Listen. **No** cows eat meat. Holsteins are cows. So (pause; signal), *no Holsteins eat meat.* How do you know that no Holsteins eat meat? (Signal.) *Because no cows eat meat.*
4. Listen. **No** cows eat meat. Herefords are cows. So (pause; signal), *no Herefords eat meat.* How do you know that no Herefords eat meat? (Signal.) *Because no cows eat meat.*
5. (Repeat steps 2–4 until firm.)

EXERCISE 7

DEFINITIONS
The next Thinking Operation is **Definitions.**

1. **Modify** means **change.**
2. What does **modify** mean? (Signal.) *Change.* What word means **change?** (Signal.) *Modify.* (Repeat step 2 until firm.)
3. Listen. He wants to modify his hairstyle. Say that. (Signal.) *He wants to modify his hairstyle.* (Repeat until firm.)
   Now say that sentence with a different word for **modify.** (Pause.) Get ready. (Signal.) *He wants to change his hairstyle.* (Repeat until firm.)
   (Repeat step 3 until firm.)
4. Listen. She is modifying her car. Say that. (Signal.) *She is modifying her car.* (Repeat until firm.)
   Now say that sentence with a different word for **modifying.** (Pause.) Get ready. (Signal.) *She is changing her car.* (Repeat until firm.)
   (Repeat step 4 until firm.)

5. Listen. I wish you would change your behavior. Say that. (Signal.) *I wish you would change your behavior.*
   Now say that sentence with a different word for **change.** (Pause.) Get ready. (Signal.) *I wish you would modify your behavior.*
   (Repeat until firm.)
   (Repeat step 5 until firm.)

━━━━━━━ EXERCISE 8 ━━━━━━━

STATEMENT INFERENCE

The next Thinking Operation is **Statement Inference.**

Task A

1. Listen. Linda was working hard to obtain money. Say that statement. (Signal.) *Linda was working hard to obtain money.* (Repeat until firm.)

Individual test
Call on a few individual students to say the statement.
---

2. Everybody, listen. Linda was working hard to obtain money. How was Linda working to obtain money? (Signal.) *Hard.*
   Why was Linda working hard?
   (Signal.) *To obtain money.*
   What was Linda working hard to obtain?
   (Signal.) *Money.*
   What was Linda doing to obtain money?
   (Signal.) *Working hard.*
   Who was working hard to obtain money?
   (Signal.) *Linda.*
   (Repeat step 2 until firm.)

Individual test
Call on individual students to answer a question from step 2.

Task B

1. Listen. His arm is in a cast because it is broken. Say that statement. (Signal.) *His arm is in a cast because it is broken.* (Repeat until firm.)

Individual test
Call on a few individual students to say the statement.
---

2. Everybody, listen. His arm is in a cast because it is broken. What is in a cast because it is broken? (Signal.) *His arm.*
   Why is his arm in a cast? (Signal.) *Because it is broken.*
   How did his arm get broken? (Signal.) *I don't know.*
   Where is his arm? (Signal.) *In a cast.* (Repeat step 2 until firm.)

Individual test
Call on individual students to answer a question from step 2.

━━━━━━━ EXERCISE 9 ━━━━━━━

DESCRIPTION

The next Thinking Operation is **Description.**

1. I'm going to tell you about an object you know. But I'm going to call it a funny name. See if you can figure out what object I'm talking about.
2. (Hold up one finger.) A lerm is an animal. Say that. (Signal.) *A lerm is an animal.*
   (Hold up two fingers.) A lerm is warm-blooded. Say that. (Signal.) *A lerm is warm-blooded.*
   (Hold up three fingers.) A lerm barks. Say that. (Signal.) *A lerm barks.*
3. Everybody, say the three things you know about a lerm. (Hold up one finger.) *A lerm is an animal.*
   (Hold up two fingers.) *A lerm is warm-blooded.*
   (Hold up three fingers.) *A lerm barks.*
   (Repeat until the students say the statements in order.)
4. Everybody, tell me the thing I am calling a lerm. (Signal.) *A dog.* Yes, it's really a dog.

=== EXERCISE 10 ===

DESCRIPTION

1. Here's the rule. **Drap** is a funny word that we'll use for blanket. What word are we using for blanket? (Signal.) *Drap.* And what does **drap** mean? (Signal.) *Blanket.*
2. Listen to this sentence. You find a drap on a bed. Is that statement true or false? (Signal.) *True.*
3. Next sentence. A drap keeps you warm. Is that statement true or false? (Signal.) *True.*
4. Next sentence. You keep draps in the refrigerator. Is that statement true or false? (Signal.) *False.*
5. Next sentence. A drap is made of wood. Is that statement true or false? (Signal.) *False.*
6. Next sentence. A drap grows in the ground. Is that statement true or false? (Signal.) *False.*

Points

(Pass out the Workbooks.
Award points for Thinking Operations.)

WORKBOOK EXERCISES

We're going to do Workbooks now. Remember to follow my instructions carefully.

=== EXERCISE 11 ===

CLASSIFICATION

1. Pencils down. Don't write anything yet. Everybody, touch the instructions for part A in your Workbook. ✔ I'll read the first instruction. Listen. Cross out the plants.
2. What are you going to do to every plant? (Signal.) *Cross it out.*
3. I'll read the next instruction. Underline the foods. What are you going to do to every food? (Signal.) *Underline it.* Everybody, do it. Cross out the plants and underline the foods. (Wait.)
4. Get ready to mark your papers. Put an X by any object you got wrong.
5. What class is a **hamburger** in? (Signal.) *Food.* How did you mark the **hamburger?** (Signal.) *Underlined it.*
6. (Repeat step 5 for **palm tree, grapevine, pie, eggs, tree, rose,** and **ice-cream sundae.**)

=== EXERCISE 12 ===

● **TRUE—FALSE**

1. Everybody, touch part B in your Workbook. ✔ I'll say statements about the picture.
2. Get ready to circle **true, false,** or **maybe.** Item 1. **Only one** of the girls is **smiling.** Circle **true, false,** or **maybe** for item 1. (Wait.)
3. Item 2. **Some** of the girls are **smiling.** Circle **true, false,** or **maybe.** (Wait.)
4. Item 3. **All** of the girls are **smiling.** Circle **true, false,** or **maybe.** (Wait.)
5. Item 4. **None** of the girls are **smiling.** Circle **true, false,** or **maybe.** (Wait.)
6. Item 5. **None** of the girls are **eating.** Circle **true, false,** or **maybe.** (Wait.)

7. Let's check your answers. Mark any item you missed with an X. Everybody, tell me **true, false,** or **maybe.** Item 1. **Only one** of the girls is smiling. (Signal.) *False.*
(Repeat step 7 for items 2–5.)

EXERCISE 13

DESCRIPTION

1. Everybody, touch part C in your Workbook. Figure out which house I describe.
2. Item 1. This house has a tree growing beside it. This house has a chimney. This house has a broken window. Listen again. (Repeat the description.) Write the letter for item 1. (Wait.)
3. Item 2. This house has a tree growing beside it. This house does not have broken windows. This house does not have a chimney. Listen again. (Repeat the description.) Write the letter for item 2. (Wait.)
4. Item 3. This house does not have broken windows. This house does not have a chimney. This house does have a tree growing beside it. Listen again. (Repeat the description.) Write the letter for item 3. (Wait.)
5. Let's check your answers. Mark any items you missed with an X.
6. Item 1. This house has a tree growing beside it. This house has a chimney. This house has a broken window. Everybody, what letter? (Signal.) *B.*
7. (Repeat step 6 for items 2 and 3.)

EXERCISE 14

SAME

1. Everybody, touch part D in your Workbook. Some of the objects in box 1 are found in the same place. **Underline** all the objects that are found in the same place. Do it. (Wait.)
2. Some of the objects in box 2 are tools used for measuring. **Circle** all the objects that are measuring tools. Do it. (Wait.)

3. Some of the objects in box 3 are in the same class. **Make a line over** all the objects that are in the same class. Do it. (Wait.)
4. Everybody, get ready to check part D. Name the place of the objects you marked in box 1. (Pause.) Get ready. (Signal.) *The sea.* Name the class of the objects you marked in box 2. (Pause.) Get ready. (Signal.) *Measuring tools.*
Name the class of the objects you marked in box 3. (Pause.) Get ready. (Signal.) *Tools.*
5. Which objects did you mark in box 1? (Call on one student.) *Fish, octopus, starfish.* What is the same about those objects? (Call on one student.) *They are found in the sea.* How did you mark each of those objects? (Call on one student.) *Underlined it.*
6. (Repeat step 5 for boxes 2 and 3.)

Points

(Award points for the Workbooks.)

INFORMATION

We're going to work on Information now.

EXERCISE 15

- **CALENDAR: Seasons in a Year**

1. Everybody, tell me how many seasons are in a year. (Pause.) Get ready. (Signal.) *Four.*

2. My turn to name the seasons in a year two times. Listen. Winter, spring, summer, fall, winter, spring, summer, fall. Your turn. Name the seasons in a year two times. (Signal.) *Winter, spring, summer, fall, winter, spring, summer, fall.* (Repeat until firm.)

3. Tell me what season comes after fall. (Pause 3 seconds.) Get ready. (Signal.) *Winter.*
Tell me what season comes after spring. (Pause 3 seconds.) Get ready. (Signal.) *Summer.*
Tell me what season comes after fall. (Pause 3 seconds.) Get ready. (Signal.) *Winter.*
Tell me what season comes after winter. (Pause 3 seconds.) Get ready. (Signal.) *Spring.*
Tell me what season comes after summer. (Pause 3 seconds.) Get ready. (Signal.) *Fall.*
(Repeat step 3 until firm.)

> **Individual test**
>
> (Call on individual students to do one of the following tasks:)
>   a. How many seasons are in a year?
>   b. Name the seasons in a year.
>   c. What season comes after fall?
>   d. What season comes after spring?

EXERCISE 16

- **INFORMATION: Animals**

Task A

1. See if you can figure out the class of animals I'm thinking of. I'm thinking of animals that are warm-blooded and have feathers. (Pause 3 seconds.) What class of animals am I thinking of? (Signal.) *Birds.*

2. Yes, I told you: they are warm-blooded; they have feathers. Tell me the words I said that let you know I wasn't thinking of mammals. (Pause 3 seconds.) Get ready. (Signal.) *They have feathers.*
(Repeat step 2 until firm.)

3. Name an animal in the class of birds. (Call on individual students. The group is to name at least five birds.)

4. Now I'm thinking of animals that are born on land and are cold-blooded. (Pause 3 seconds.) Everybody, what class of animals am I thinking of? (Signal.) *Reptiles.*

5. Yes, I told you: they are born on land; they are cold-blooded. Tell me the words I said that let you know I wasn't thinking of mammals. (Pause.) Get ready. (Signal.) *They are cold-blooded.*
(Repeat step 5 until firm.)

6. Name an animal in the class of reptiles. (Call on individual students. The group is to name at least four reptiles.)

Task B

1. Now I'm thinking of an animal that is warm-blooded and has hair. Tell me if I could be thinking of a sparrow. (Pause.) Get ready. (Signal.) *No.* Right.

2. I told you: it is warm-blooded; it has hair. Tell me the words I said that let you know I wasn't thinking of a sparrow. (Pause 3 seconds.) Get ready. (Signal.) *It has hair.*
(Repeat step 2 until firm.)

3. Here are the facts again. The animal is warm-blooded and has hair. Tell me if I could be thinking of a lion. (Pause.) Get ready. (Signal.) *Yes.*
What class are lions in? (Pause.) Get ready. (Signal.) *Mammals.*

4. Tell me the two facts you know about **all mammals.** (Hold up one finger.) First fact. *All mammals have hair.*
(Hold up two fingers.) Second fact. *All mammals are warm-blooded.* (Repeat until the students say the facts in order.)
So, if I'm thinking of an animal that is warm-blooded and has hair, I could be thinking of a lion.

5. Now I'm thinking of an animal that is warm-blooded and has feathers. Tell me if I could be thinking of a robin. (Pause.) Get ready. (Signal.) *Yes.*
Tell me what class robins are in. (Pause.) Get ready. (Signal.) *Birds.*

6. Tell me the two facts you know about **all birds.** (Hold up one finger.) First fact. *All birds have feathers.*
(Hold up two fingers.) Second fact. *All birds are warm-blooded.* (Repeat until the students say the facts in order.)
So, if I'm thinking of an animal that is warm-blooded and has feathers, I could be thinking of a robin.

7. Here are the facts again. The animal is warm-blooded and has feathers. Tell me if I could be thinking of an alligator. (Pause.) Get ready. (Signal.) *No.* Right.

8. I told you: it is warm-blooded; it has feathers. Tell me the words I said that let you know I wasn't thinking of an alligator. (Pause 3 seconds.) Get ready. (Signal.) *It is warm-blooded. It has feathers.*
(Repeat step 8 until firm.)

● **MEMORIZATION: Poem**
1. Here's the poem we learned.
    A mechanic fixes cars,
    An astronomer looks at stars,
    A captain has two bars,
    And a boxer spars and spars.
2. Say it with me. (Signal. Say the poem with the students. Repeat until students are responding with you.)
3. All by yourselves. Say the poem. (Signal. The students say the poem. Repeat until firm.)
   To correct:
   a. (Stop the students as soon as you hear a mistake.)
   b. (Say the line they missed.)
   c. (Have them repeat the line they missed.)
   d. (Repeat step 3.)

Individual test
Call on individual students to say the whole poem.

Points
(Award points for Information.
Have the students add up their daily total.)

END OF LESSON 13

THINKING OPERATIONS

EXERCISE 1

SAME: Review

The first Thinking Operation is **Same.**

1. We're going to name some ways that a jacket and a shoe are the same.
2. Can you point to jackets and shoes? (Signal.) *Yes.* So, are jackets and shoes objects? (Signal.) *Yes.*
3. So, name those three ways that a jacket and a shoe are the same. (Hold up one finger.) *They are objects.* (Hold up two fingers.) *They take up space.* (Hold up three fingers.) *You find them in some place.* (Repeat until firm.)
4. Listen. A jacket and a shoe are also the same because you **do** some of the same things with them. When I call on you, name some things that you **do** with them. (Call on individual students. Praise reasonable responses; for example, wear them, buy them, clean them.)
5. Listen. A jacket and a shoe are the same because they are in the same class. Everybody, tell me that class. (Signal.) *Clothing.* Yes, they are clothing. How are they the same? (Signal.) *They are clothing.*
6. I'll name some ways a jacket is the same as a shoe. They are objects. They keep you warm. They keep you dry. When I call on you, see how many ways you can name that a jacket is the same as a shoe.
   (Start with objects. Call on individual students. Each student is to name at least seven ways a jacket and a shoe are the same.)

EXERCISE 2

SAME: Parts

1. We're going to name some ways that a squirrel and a lion are the same. Do a squirrel and a lion have some of the same **body parts?** (Signal.) *Yes.*
2. Name some of the same body parts that a squirrel and a lion have. (Call on individual students. Praise reasonable responses; for example, fur, teeth, legs.)
   So, a squirrel and a lion are the same because they have some of the same body parts.

EXERCISE 3

DEFINITIONS

The next Thinking Operation is **Definitions.**

1. **Modify** means **change.**
2. What does **modify** mean? (Signal.) *Change.* What word means **change?** (Signal.) *Modify.* (Repeat step 2 until firm.)
3. Listen. Writers often change their stories. Say that. (Signal.) *Writers often change their stories.* (Repeat until firm.)
   Now say that sentence with a different word for **change.** (Pause.) Get ready. (Signal.) *Writers often modify their stories.* (Repeat until firm.)
   (Repeat step 3 until firm.)
4. Listen. That camera needs to be modified. Say that. (Signal.) *That camera needs to be modified.* (Repeat until firm.)
   Now say that sentence with a different word for **modified.** (Pause.) Get ready. (Signal.) *That camera needs to be changed.* (Repeat until firm.)
   (Repeat step 4 until firm.)
5. Listen. You should change the design. Say that. (Signal.) *You should change the design.* (Repeat until firm.)
   Now say that sentence with a different word for **change.** (Pause.) Get ready. (Signal.) *You should modify the design.* (Repeat until firm.)
   (Repeat step 5 until firm.)

━━━━━━━ EXERCISE 4 ━━━━━━━

DEFINITIONS

1. **Amble.** (Pause.) What does **amble** mean? (Signal.) *Walk slowly.* What word means **walk slowly?** (Signal.) *Amble.* (Repeat step 1 until firm.)

2. Listen. They walked slowly to school. Say that. (Signal.) *They walked slowly to school.* (Repeat until firm.)
   Now say that sentence with a different word for **walked slowly.** (Pause.) Get ready. (Signal.) *They ambled to school.* (Repeat until firm.)
   (Repeat step 2 until firm.)

3. **Lazy.** (Pause.) What's a synonym for **lazy?** (Signal.) *Indolent.* And what's a synonym for **indolent?** (Signal.) *Lazy.*
   (Repeat step 3 until firm.)

4. Listen. I am too lazy to get up early. Say that. (Signal.) *I am too lazy to get up early.* (Repeat until firm.)
   Now say that sentence with a synonym for **lazy.** (Pause.) Get ready. (Signal.) *I am too indolent to get up early.* (Repeat until firm.)
   (Repeat step 4 until firm.)

5. **Obtain.** (Pause.) What's a synonym for **obtain?** (Signal.) *Get.* And what's a synonym for **get?** (Signal.) *Obtain.*
   (Repeat step 5 until firm.)

6. Listen. It is hard to get bargains. Say that. (Signal.) *It is hard to get bargains.* (Repeat until firm.)
   Now say that sentence with a synonym for **get.** (Pause.) Get ready. (Signal.) *It is hard to obtain bargains.* (Repeat until firm.)
   (Repeat step 6 until firm.)

━━━━━━━ EXERCISE 5 ━━━━━━━

DESCRIPTION

The next Thinking Operation is **Description.**

1. I'm going to tell you about an object you know. But I'm going to call it a funny name. See if you can figure out what object I'm talking about.

2. (Hold up one finger.) A zig is an animal. Say that. *A zig is an animal.*
   (Hold up two fingers.) A zig hops. Say that. *A zig hops.*
   (Hold up three fingers.) A zig croaks. Say that. *A zig croaks.*

3. Everybody, say the three things you know about a zig. (Hold up one finger.) *A zig is an animal.* (Hold up two fingers.) *A zig hops.* (Hold up three fingers.) *A zig croaks.* (Repeat until students say the statements in order.)

4. Everybody, tell me the thing I am calling a zig. (Signal.) *A frog.* Yes, it's really a frog.

━━━━━━━ EXERCISE 6 ━━━━━━━

DEDUCTIONS: With *no* and *don't*

The next Thinking Operation is **Deductions.**

1. I'll say rules with **no** or **don't.** You say them the other way. What two words are we going to use? (Hold up one finger.) *No.*
   (Hold up two fingers.) *Don't.*

2. Listen. Fish **don't** walk. Say that. (Signal.) *Fish don't walk.*
   Now say it the other way. Get ready. (Signal.) *No fish walk.*
   (Repeat step 2 until firm.)

3. Here's a new rule. People **don't** have feathers. Say that. (Signal.) *People don't have feathers.*
   Now say it the other way. Get ready. (Signal.) *No people have feathers.*
   (Repeat step 3 until firm.)

4. Here's a new rule. **No** dogs climb trees. Say that. (Signal.) *No dogs climb trees.*
   Now say it the other way. Get ready. (Signal.) *Dogs don't climb trees.*
   (Repeat step 4 until firm.)

5. Here's a new rule. Snakes **don't** sing. Say that. (Signal.) *Snakes don't sing.*
   Now say it the other way. Get ready. (Signal.) *No snakes sing.*
   (Repeat step 5 until firm.)

LESSON **14**

EXERCISE 7

DEDUCTIONS: With *every*

1. Listen to this rule. **Every** animal breathes. Everybody, say that. (Signal.) *Every animal breathes.*
2. Antelope are animals. So (pause; signal), *antelope breathe.* How do you know that antelope breathe? (Signal.) *Because every animal breathes.*
   (Repeat step 2 until firm.)
3. Listen. **Every** animal breathes. Monkeys are animals. So (pause; signal), *monkeys breathe.* How do you know that monkeys breathe? (Signal.) *Because every animal breathes.*
   (Repeat step 3 until firm.)
4. Listen. **Every** animal breathes. Chickens are animals. So (pause; signal), *chickens breathe.* How do you know that chickens breathe? (Signal.) *Because every animal breathes.*
   (Repeat step 4 until firm.)

EXERCISE 8

DEDUCTIONS: With *don't*

1. Listen to this rule. Vehicles **don't** grow. Everybody, say that. (Signal.) *Vehicles don't grow.*
2. Cars are vehicles. So (pause; signal), *cars don't grow.* How do you know that cars **don't** grow? (Signal.) *Because vehicles don't grow.*
3. Listen. Vehicles **don't** grow. Planes are vehicles. So (pause; signal), *planes don't grow.* How do you know that planes **don't** grow? (Signal.) *Because vehicles don't grow.*
4. Listen. Vehicles don't grow. Bicycles are vehicles. So (pause; signal), *bicycles don't grow.* How do you know that bicycles don't grow? (Signal.) *Because vehicles don't grow.*
5. (Repeat steps 2–4 until firm.)

EXERCISE 9

STATEMENT INFERENCE

The next Thinking Operation is **Statement Inference.**

1. Listen. Jennifer wears glasses because she is nearsighted. Say that statement. (Signal.) *Jennifer wears glasses because she is nearsighted.* (Repeat until firm.)

Individual test
Call on a few individual students to say the statement.

---

2. Everybody, listen. Jennifer wears glasses because she is nearsighted. Who wears glasses because she is nearsighted? (Signal.) *Jennifer.*
   What does Jennifer wear because she is nearsighted? (Signal.) *Glasses.*
   What does Jennifer do?
   (Signal.) *Wears glasses.*
   Why does Jennifer wear glasses? (Signal.) *Because she is nearsighted.* (Repeat step 2 until firm.)

Individual test
Ask individual students a question from step 2.

Points
(Pass out the Workbooks.
Award points for Thinking Operations.)

134 LESSON 14

WORKBOOK
EXERCISES

We're going to do Workbooks now. Remember to follow my instructions carefully.

EXERCISE 10

DESCRIPTION

1. Everybody, touch part A in your Workbook. ✔ Figure out which object I describe. Listen. A kelt is a piece of furniture. People sit on a kelt. More than one person at a time can sit on a kelt. **Put a 7 on** the object I'm calling a kelt. (Wait.)

2. Listen. A swerp is a tool. A swerp can be made of wood. A swerp is used to measure how long things are. **Put a 2 on** the object I'm calling a swerp. (Wait.)

3. Listen. A tomo is a container. A tomo has a lid. People put their garbage in a tomo. **Put a 3 on** the object I'm calling a tomo.

4. Everybody, get ready to check your work. Tell me the real name for the object that is a piece of furniture, that people sit on, and that more than one person at a time can sit on. Get ready. (Signal.) *A couch.* And how did you mark the couch? (Signal.) *Put a 7 on it.*

5. Tell me the real name for the object that is a tool, that can be made of wood, and that is used to measure how long things are. Get ready. (Signal.) *A ruler.* And how did you mark the ruler? (Signal.) *Put a 2 on it.*

6. Tell me the real name of the object that is a container, that has a lid, and that people put their garbage in. Get ready. (Signal.) *A garbage can.* And how did you mark the garbage can? (Signal.) *Put a 3 on it.*

EXERCISE 11

TRUE—FALSE

1. Everybody touch part B in your Workbook. ✔ I'll say statements about the picture.

2. Get ready to circle **true, false,** or **maybe.** Item 1. **All** the men have hair on their heads. Circle **true, false,** or **maybe.** (Wait.)

3. Item 2. **None** of the men have long hair. Circle **true, false,** or **maybe.** (Wait.)

4. Item 3. **Some** of the men use hair spray. Circle **true, false,** or **maybe.** (Wait.)

5. Item 4. **One** man is bald. Circle **true, false,** or **maybe.** (Wait.)

6. Let's check your answers. Mark any item you missed with an X. Everybody, tell me **true, false,** or **maybe.**

7. Item 1. **All** the men have hair on their heads. (Signal.) *False.*

8. (Repeat step 7 for items 2–4.)

Answer key   2. *False*   **3.** *Maybe*   **4.** *True*

EXERCISE 12

SAME

1. Everybody, touch part C in your Workbook. ✔ Some of the objects in box 1 are in the same class of animals. **Make a box around** all the objects that are in the same class of animals. Do it. (Wait.)

2. Some of the objects in box 2 are made of the same material. **Circle** all the objects that are made of the same material. Do it. (Wait.)

3. Some of the objects in box 3 are in the same class. **Underline** all the objects that are in the same class. Do it. (Wait.)

4. Everybody, get ready to check part C. Name the animal class of the objects you marked in box 1. (Pause.) Get ready. (Signal.) *Birds.* Name the material of the objects you marked in box 2. (Pause.) Get ready. (Signal.) *Paper.* Name the class of the objects you marked in box 3. (Pause.) Get ready. (Signal.) *Vehicles.*

5. Which objects did you mark in box 1? (Call on one student.) *Owl, chicken, duck.* What is the same about those objects? (Call on one student.) *They are birds.* How did you mark each of those objects? (Call on one student.) *Made a box around it.*

6. (Repeat step 5 for boxes 2 and 3.)

Answer key   2. *Book, newspaper, bag; they are made of paper; circled it*   **3.** *Jet, train, truck; they are vehicles; underlined it.*

EXERCISE 13

CLASSIFICATION

1. Everybody, touch the instructions for part D in your Workbook. I'll read the instructions. Don't write anything. Listen. Circle the appliances. Make a box around the vehicles.
2. What are you going to do to every appliance? (Signal.) *Circle it.*
   What are you going to do to every vehicle? (Signal.) *Make a box around it.*
3. Everybody, now circle the appliances and make a box around the vehicles. (Wait.)
4. Get ready to mark your papers. Put an X by any object you got wrong.
5. What class is an **electric mixer** in? (Signal.) *Appliances.* How did you mark the **electric mixer?** (Signal.) *Circled it.*
6. (Repeat step 5 for **bicycle, wagon, stove, jeep, sailboat, TV, racing car,** and **refrigerator.**)

Points

(Award points for Workbooks.)

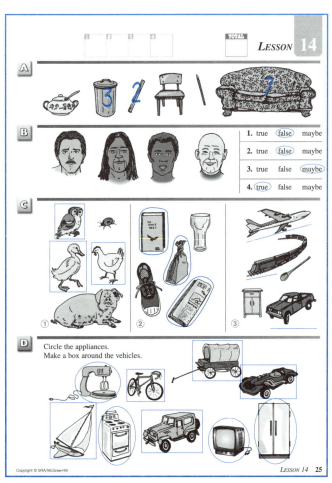

INFORMATION

We're going to work on Information now.

EXERCISE 14

MEMORIZATION: Poem

1. Here's the poem we learned.
   A mechanic fixes cars,
   An astronomer looks at stars,
   A captain has two bars,
   And a boxer spars and spars.
2. Say it with me. (Signal. Say the poem with the students. Repeat until students are responding with you.)
3. All by yourselves. Say the poem. (Signal. The students say the poem. Repeat until firm.)
   To correct:
   a. (Stop the students as soon as you hear a mistake.)
   b. (Say the line they missed.)
   c. (Have them repeat the line they missed.)
   d. (Repeat step 3.)

> *Individual test*
> Call on individuals to say the whole poem.

EXERCISE 15

- **CALENDAR: Seasons in a Year**
1. Everybody, tell me how many seasons are in a year. (Pause.) Get ready. (Signal.) *Four.*
2. Name the seasons in a year two times. (Signal.) *Winter, spring, summer, fall, winter, spring, summer, fall.* (Repeat until firm.)
3. Tell me what season comes after summer. (Pause.) Get ready. (Signal.) *Fall.*
   Tell me what season comes after fall. (Pause 3 seconds.) Get ready. (Signal.) *Winter.*
   Tell me what season comes after spring. (Pause.) Get ready. (Signal.) *Summer.*
   Tell me what season comes after fall. (Pause.) Get ready. (Signal.) *Winter.*
   Tell me what season comes after winter. (Pause 3 seconds.) Get ready. (Signal.) *Spring.* (Repeat step 3 until firm.)

Individual test

(Ask individual students to do one of the following tasks:)

    a. How many seasons are in a year?
    b. Name the seasons in a year.
    c. What season comes after winter?
    d. What season comes after fall?

EXERCISE 16

INFORMATION: Animals

Task A

1. See if you can figure out the class of animals I'm thinking of. I'm thinking of animals that are warm-blooded and have hair. (Pause 3 seconds.) What class of animals am I thinking of? (Signal.) *Mammals.*

2. Yes, I told you: they are warm-blooded; they have hair. Tell me the words I said that let you know I wasn't thinking of reptiles. (Pause 3 seconds.) Get ready. (Signal.) *They are warm-blooded. They have hair.*
   (Repeat step 2 until firm.)

3. Name an animal in the class of mammals. (Call on individual students.) The group is to name at least four mammals.

4. Now I'm thinking of animals that are born on land and are cold-blooded. (Pause 3 seconds.) Everybody, what class of animals am I thinking of? (Signal.) *Reptiles.*

5. Yes, I told you: they are born on land; they are cold-blooded. Tell me the words I said that let you know I wasn't thinking of mammals. (Pause 3 seconds.) Get ready. (Signal.) *They are cold-blooded.*
   (Repeat step 5 until firm.)

6. Name an animal in the class of reptiles. (Call on individual students.) The group is to name at least four reptiles.

Task B

1. Now I'm thinking of an animal that is warm-blooded and has feathers. Tell me if I could be thinking of a penguin. (Pause.) Get ready. (Signal.) *Yes.*
   Tell me what class penguins are in. (Pause.) Get ready. (Signal.) *Birds.*

2. Tell me the two facts you know about **all birds.** (Hold up one finger.) First fact. *All birds have feathers.* (Hold up two fingers.) Second fact. *All birds are warm-blooded.* (Repeat until the students say the facts in order.)
   So, if I'm thinking of an animal that is warm-blooded and has feathers, I could be thinking of a penguin.

3. Here are the facts again. The animal is warm-blooded and has feathers. Tell me if I could be thinking of a whale. (Pause.) Get ready. (Signal.) *No.* Right.

4. I told you: it is warm-blooded; it has feathers. Tell me the words I said that let you know I wasn't thinking of a whale. (Pause 3 seconds.) Get ready. (Signal.) *It has feathers.* (Repeat step 4 until firm.)

5. Now I'm thinking of an animal that is cold-blooded and is born on land. Tell me if I could be thinking of a porpoise. (Pause.) Get ready. (Signal.) *No.* Right.

6. I told you: it is cold-blooded; it is born on land. Tell me the words I said that let you know I wasn't thinking of a porpoise. (Pause 3 seconds.) Get ready. (Signal.) *It is cold-blooded. It is born on land.* (Repeat step 6 until firm.)

7. Here are the facts again. The animal is cold-blooded and is born on land. Tell me if I could be thinking of a lizard. (Pause 3 seconds.) Get ready. (Signal.) *Yes.*
   Tell me what class lizards are in. (Pause.) Get ready. (Signal.) *Reptiles.*

8. Tell me the two facts you know about **all reptiles.** (Hold up one finger.) First fact. *All reptiles are cold-blooded.* (Hold up two fingers.) Second fact. *All reptiles are born on land.* (Repeat until the students say the facts in order.)
   So, if I'm thinking of an animal that is cold-blooded and is born on land, I could be thinking of a lizard.

Points

(Award points for Information.
Have the students add up their daily total.)

END OF LESSON 14

THINKING OPERATIONS

EXERCISE 1

● **BASIC EVIDENCE: Using Facts**

The first Thinking Operation today is **Basic Evidence.**

1. You're going to use two facts to explain things that happened. These are the only facts you can use. (Hold up one finger.) First fact. The man was very strong. Say it. (Signal.) *The man was very strong.* (Repeat until firm.)
   (Hold up two fingers.) Second fact. The plane had a broken engine. Say it. (Signal.) *The plane had a broken engine.* (Repeat until firm.)

2. Everybody, say those facts again. (Hold up one finger.) First fact. *The man was very strong.* (Hold up two fingers.) Second fact. *The plane had a broken engine.* (Repeat until the students say the facts in order.)

3. I'll tell you what happened. Then you tell me the fact. Listen. The man could lift 200 kilograms. Tell me the fact that explains **why** the man could lift 200 kilograms. (Pause.) Get ready. (Signal.) *The man was very strong.*

4. Listen. (Hold up one finger.) First fact. The man was very strong.
   (Hold up two fingers.) Second fact. The plane had a broken engine. Here's what happened. Nobody in town wanted to fight with the man. Tell me the fact that explains **why** nobody wanted to fight with the man. (Pause.) Get ready. (Signal.) *The man was very strong.*

5. Listen. (Hold up one finger.) First fact. The man was very strong.
   (Hold up two fingers.) Second fact. The plane had a broken engine. Here's what happened. The mechanics went to work on the plane. Tell me the fact that explains **why** the mechanics went to work on the plane. (Pause.) Get ready. (Signal.) *The plane had a broken engine.*

6. Listen. (Hold up one finger.) First fact. The man was very strong.
   (Hold up two fingers.) Second fact. The plane had a broken engine. Here's what happened. The passengers were mad. Tell me the fact that explains **why** the passengers were mad. (Pause.) Get ready. (Signal.) *The plane had a broken engine.*

7. Listen. (Hold up one finger.) First fact. The man was very strong.
   (Hold up two fingers.) Second fact. The plane had a broken engine. Here's what happened. The plane did not take off on time. Tell me the fact that explains **why** the plane did not take off on time. (Pause.) Get ready. (Signal.) *The plane had a broken engine.*

8. (Repeat steps 3–7 until firm.)

EXERCISE 2

DEDUCTIONS: With *no* and *don't*

The next Thinking Operation is **Deductions.**

1. I'll say rules with **no** or **don't.** You say them the other way. What two words are we going to use? (Hold up one finger.) *No.*
   (Hold up two fingers.) *Don't.*

2. Listen. **No** reptiles fly. Say that. (Signal.) *No reptiles fly.*
   Now say it the other way. Get ready. (Signal.) *Reptiles don't fly.*
   (Repeat step 2 until firm.)

3. Here's a new rule. Appliances **don't** grow. Say that. (Signal.) *Appliances don't grow.*
   Now say it the other way. Get ready. (Signal.) *No appliances grow.*
   (Repeat step 3 until firm.)

4. Here's a new rule. **No** mammals breathe water. Say that. (Signal.) *No mammals breathe water.*
   Now say it the other way. Get ready. (Signal.) *Mammals don't breathe water.*
   (Repeat step 4 until firm.)

5. Here's a new rule. **No** girl has four legs. Say that. (Signal.) *No girl has four legs.*
   Now say it the other way. Get ready. (Signal.) *Girls don't have four legs.*
   (Repeat step 5 until firm.)

EXERCISE 3

● **DEDUCTIONS: With** *some*

Task A

1. Listen to this rule. **Some** animals fly. Everybody, say that. (Signal.) *Some animals fly.*

2. That rule doesn't tell about **all** animals. It tells about **some** animals. How many animals does it tell about? (Signal.) *Some.*

Task B

1. Listen. **Some** animals fly. Tom has an animal. So, maybe Tom's animal flies. Does Tom's animal fly? (Signal.) *Maybe.*

   To correct:
   a. Say **maybe.** The answer is **maybe.**
   b. (Repeat step 1.)

2. Listen. **Some** animals fly. Henry has an animal. Does it fly? (Signal.) *Maybe.* Right. Maybe Henry's animal flies. (Repeat step 2 until firm.)

3. Listen. **Some** animals fly. Betty has an animal. Does it fly? (Signal.) *Maybe.* Right. Maybe Betty's animal flies.

4. (Repeat steps 2 and 3 until firm.)

EXERCISE 4

DEDUCTIONS: With *every*

Task A

1. Listen to this rule. **Every** flower has petals. Everybody, say that. (Signal.) *Every flower has petals.*

2. A pansy is a flower. What does the rule let you know about a pansy? (Signal.) *A pansy has petals.* How do you know that a pansy has petals? (Signal.) *Because every flower has petals.*

   To correct students who say *All flowers have petals:*
   a. The rule is **every** flower has petals.
   b. Say the rule. (Signal.) *Every flower has petals.*
   c. (Repeat step 2.)

3. Listen. **Every** flower has petals. A daisy is a flower. What does the rule let you know about a daisy? (Signal.) *A daisy has petals.*

How do you know that a daisy has petals? (Signal.) *Because every flower has petals.*

4. (Repeat steps 2 and 3 until firm.)

Task B

1. Listen to this rule. **All** felines eat meat. Everybody, say that. (Signal.) *All felines eat meat.*

2. Leopards are felines. What does the rule let you know about leopards? (Signal.) *Leopards eat meat.* How do you know that leopards eat meat? (Signal.) *Because all felines eat meat.*

3. Listen. **All** felines eat meat. Lions are felines. What does the rule let you know about lions? (Signal.) *Lions eat meat.* How do you know that lions eat meat? (Signal.) *Because all felines eat meat.*

4. Listen. **All** felines eat meat. Jaguars are felines. What does the rule let you know about jaguars? (Signal.) *Jaguars eat meat.* How do you know that jaguars eat meat? (Signal.) *Because all felines eat meat.*

5. (Repeat steps 2–4 until firm.)

EXERCISE 5

DEDUCTIONS: With *all*

1. Listen to this rule. **All** birds have wings. Everybody, say that. (Signal.) *All birds have wings.* What do **all** birds have? (Signal.) *Wings.* What has wings? (Signal.) *All birds.*

   To correct students who don't say All birds:
   a. **All** birds. What has wings? (Signal.) *All birds.*
   b. (Repeat step 1.)

2. Say the rule again. **All** birds have wings. What does the rule let you know about **all** birds? (Signal.) *They have wings.* What does the rule let you know about **all** snakes? (Signal.) *Nothing.*

   To correct students who don't say Nothing:
   a. The answer is **nothing.**
   b. The rule tells only about birds. It tells **nothing** about snakes.
   c. (Repeat step 2.)

What does the rule let you know about **all** fish? (Signal.) *Nothing.* What does the rule let you know about **all** birds? (Signal.) *They have wings.*

3. Listen to the rule again. **All** birds have wings. Bluejays are birds. What does the rule let you know about bluejays? (Signal.) *Bluejays have wings.* How do you know that bluejays have wings? (Signal.) *Because all birds have wings.* (Repeat step 3 until firm.)

4. Listen to the rule again. **All** birds have wings. Ostriches are birds. What does the rule let you know about ostriches? (Signal.) *Ostriches have wings.* How do you know that ostriches have wings? (Signal.) *Because all birds have wings.* (Repeat step 4 until firm.)

5. Listen to the rule again. **All** birds have wings. Boa constrictors are snakes. What does the rule let you know about boa constrictors? (Signal.) *Nothing.* Yes, nothing. Because the rule tells only about birds. (Repeat step 5 until firm.)

6. Listen to the rule again. **All** birds have wings. Sharks are fish. What does the rule let you know about sharks? (Signal.) *Nothing.* Yes, nothing. Because the rule tells only about (pause; signal) *birds.*

7. Listen to the rule again. **All** birds have wings. Robins are birds. What does the rule let you know about robins? (Signal.) *Robins have wings.* How do you know that robins have wings? (Signal.) *Because all birds have wings.*

8. (Repeat steps 6 and 7 until firm.)

=========== **EXERCISE 6** ===========

- **SAME: Review**

The next Thinking Operation is **Same.**

Task A

1. Let's name some ways that a house and a store are the same. Can houses and stores be made of the same material? (Signal.) *Yes.* (Call on one student.) Name a material. (Accept a reasonable response.) Everybody, so how are they the same? (Signal.) *They can be made of* [material named].

2. Do you **do** some of the same things in a house and in a store? (Signal.) *Yes.* Name at least three of the same things that you **do** in a house and in a store. (Call on individual students. Praise reasonable responses; for example, walking, looking, talking.) So, a house and a store are the same because you **do** some of the same things in them.

3. Do a house and a store have some of the same parts? (Signal.) *Yes.* Name some of those parts. (Call on individual students. Praise reasonable responses; for example, walls, windows, doors.) So, a house and a store are the same because they have some of the same parts.

4. Can you point to a house and a store? (Signal.) *Yes.* So, name three ways a house and a store are the same. (Hold up one finger.) *They are objects.* (Hold up two fingers.) *They take up space.* (Hold up three fingers.) *You find them in some place.*

5. Do you find a house and a store in some of the same places? (Signal.) *Yes.* Name some of those places. (Call on individual students. Praise reasonable responses; for example, in the city, in the country, on corners.) So, a house and a store are the same because they are found in some of the same places.

6. Are a house and a store in the same class? (Signal.) *Yes.* What class? (Signal.) *Buildings.* So, how are they the same? (Signal.) *They are buildings.*

7. Now, when I call on you, see how many ways you can name that a house and a store are the same. (Call on individual students. Each student should name at least seven ways a house and a store are the same.)

Task B

1. Let's name some ways that a lizard and a snake are the same. Can a lizard and a snake be the same color? (Signal.) *Yes.* (Call on one student.) Name a color they can be. (Accept a reasonable response.) Everybody, so how are they the same? (Signal.) *They can be* [color named].

2. Do a lizard and a snake have some of the same body parts? (Signal.) *Yes.* Name some of those parts. (Call on individual students. Praise reasonable responses; for example, mouth, eyes, head.)
So, a lizard and a snake are the same because they have some of the same body parts.

3. Do you find a lizard and a snake in some of the same places? (Signal.) *Yes.* Name some of those places. (Call on individual students. Praise reasonable responses; for example, under trees, on the ground, behind rocks.)
So, a lizard and a snake are the same because you find them in some of the same places.

4. Do a lizard and a snake **do** some of the same things? (Signal.) *Yes.* Name at least three of the same things that they **do.** (Call on individual students. Praise all reasonable responses; for example, see, eat, sleep.)
So, a lizard and a snake are the same because they **do** some of the same things.

5. Can you point to a lizard and a snake? (Signal.) *Yes.*
So, name three ways a lizard and a snake are the same. (Hold up one finger.) *They are objects.* (Hold up two fingers.) *They take up space.* (Hold up three fingers.) *You find them in some place.*

6. Are a lizard and a snake in the same class? (Signal.) *Yes.* What class? (Signal.) *Reptiles.*
So, how are they the same? (Signal.) *They are reptiles.*

7. Now, when I call on you, see how many ways you can name that a lizard and a snake are the same. (Call on individual students. Each student should name at least seven ways a lizard and a snake are the same.)

━━━━━━━━━ **EXERCISE 7** ━━━━━━━━━

STATEMENT INFERENCE

The next Thinking Operation is **Statement Inference.**

1. Listen. Most cars have mufflers to keep them quiet. Say that statement. (Signal.) *Most cars have mufflers to keep them quiet.* (Repeat until firm.)

> **Individual test**
> Call on a few individual students to say the statement.

2. Everybody, listen. Most cars have mufflers to keep them quiet. What do most cars have to keep them quiet? (Signal.) *Mufflers.*
Why do most cars have mufflers? (Signal.) *To keep them quiet.*
What kind of mufflers do most cars have? (Signal.) *I don't know.*
How many cars have mufflers to keep them quiet? (Signal.) *Most.*
What do most cars have? (Signal.) *Mufflers.*
(Repeat step 2 until firm.)

> **Individual test**
> Call on individual students to answer a question from step 2.

=======EXERCISE 8======

DEFINITIONS

The next Thinking Operation is **Definitions.**

1. **Descend** means **go down.**
2. What does **descend** mean?
   (Signal.) *Go down.*
   What word means **go down?** (Signal.)
   Descend.
   (Repeat step 2 until firm.)
3. Listen. The plane will descend in the field.
   Say that. (Signal.) *The plane will descend in the field.* (Repeat until firm.)
   Now say that sentence with different words for **descend.** (Pause.) Get ready. (Signal.)
   The plane will go down in the field. (Repeat until firm.)
   (Repeat step 3 until firm.)
4. Listen. I cannot descend the stairs quickly.
   Say that. (Signal.) *I cannot descend the stairs quickly.* (Repeat until firm.)
   Now say that sentence with different words for **descend.** (Pause.) Get ready. (Signal.)
   I cannot go down the stairs quickly. (Repeat until firm.)
   (Repeat step 4 until firm.)
5. Listen. The firefighter went down the ladder.
   Say that. (Signal.) *The firefighter went down the ladder.* (Repeat until firm.)
   Now say that sentence with a different word for **went down.** (Pause.) Get ready. (Signal.)
   The firefighter descended the ladder. (Repeat until firm.)
   (Repeat step 5 until firm.)

=======EXERCISE 9======

DEFINITIONS

1. **Modify.** (Pause.) What's a synonym for **modify?** (Signal.) *Change.*
   And what's a synonym for **change?** (Signal.)
   Modify. (Repeat step 1 until firm.)
2. Listen. She did not want to modify her speech. Say that. (Signal.) *She did not want to modify her speech.* (Repeat until firm.)
   Now say that sentence with a synonym for **modify.** (Pause.) Get ready. (Signal.) *She did not want to change her speech.* (Repeat until firm.)
   (Repeat step 2 until firm.)

3. **Complete.** (Pause.) What's a synonym for **complete?** (Signal.) *Finish.* And what's a synonym for **finish?** (Signal.) *Complete.*
   (Repeat step 3 until firm.)
4. Listen. It took me two days to finish that book. Say that. (Signal.) *It took me two days to finish that book.* (Repeat until firm.)
   Now say that sentence with a synonym for **finish.** (Pause.) Get ready. (Signal.) *It took me two days to complete that book.* (Repeat until firm.)
   (Repeat step 4 until firm.)
5. **Amble.** (Pause.) What does **amble** mean?
   (Signal.) *Walk slowly.*
   What word means **walk slowly?** (Signal.)
   Amble. (Repeat until firm.)
6. Listen. I like to amble by the river. Say that.
   (Signal.) *I like to amble by the river.* (Repeat until firm.)
   Now say that sentence with different words for **amble.** (Pause.) Get ready. (Signal.) *I like to walk slowly by the river.* (Repeat until firm.)
   (Repeat step 6 until firm.)

=======EXERCISE 10======

● **DEFINITIONS**
1. **Canine.** What does **canine** mean? (Signal.)
   Dog.
   Chew. What does **chew** mean? (Signal.)
   Masticate. (Repeat step 1 until firm.)
2. Listen. That canine is chewing a bone. Say that sentence. (Signal.) *That canine is chewing a bone.* (Repeat until firm.)
   Now say that sentence with different words for **canine** and **chewing.** (Pause.) Get ready. (Signal.) *That dog is masticating a bone.* (Repeat until firm. Repeat step 2 until firm.)
   To correct students who do not say the new sentence:
   a. (Say the sentence correctly.)
   b. (Have the students repeat the sentence.)
   c. (Repeat step 2.)

EXERCISE 11

DESCRIPTION

The next Thinking Operation is **Description.**

1. I'm going to tell you about an object you know. But I'm going to call it a funny name. See if you can figure out what object I'm talking about.

2. (Hold up one finger.) A yed is a container. Say that. *A yed is a container.* (Hold up two fingers.) A yed is round. Say that. *A yed is round.*
   (Hold up three fingers.) You can eat cereal from a yed. Say that. *You can eat cereal from a yed.*

3. Everybody, say the three things you know about a yed. (Hold up one finger.) *A yed is a container.* (Hold up two fingers.) *A yed is round.* (Hold up three fingers.) *You can eat cereal from a yed.* (Repeat until the students say the statements in order.)

4. Everybody, tell me the thing I'm calling a yed. (Signal.) *A bowl.* Yes, it's really a bowl.

Points

(Pass out the Workbooks.
Award points for Thinking Operations.)

We're going to do Workbooks now. Remember to follow my instructions carefully.

EXERCISE 12

CLASSIFICATION

1. Everybody, touch the instructions for part A in your Workbook. ✔ I'll read the instructions. Don't write anything. Listen. Cross out the furniture. Underline the containers.

2. What are you going to do to every piece of furniture? (Signal.) *Cross it out.*

3. What are you going to do to every container? (Signal.) *Underline it.* Everybody, now cross out the furniture and underline the containers. (Wait.)

4. Get ready to mark your papers. Put an X by any object you got wrong.

5. What class is a **suitcase** in? (Signal.) *Containers.* How did you mark the **suitcase?** (Signal.) *Underlined it.*

6. (Repeat step 5 for **bucket, folding chair, kettle, vase, end table, jar,** and **bed.**)

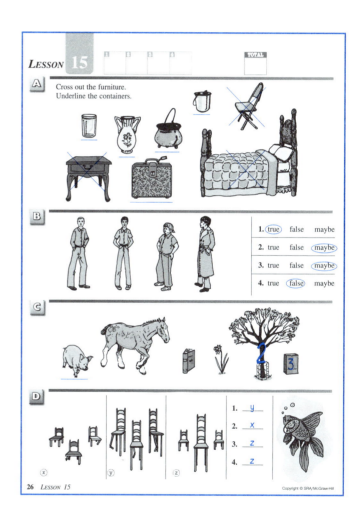

EXERCISE 13

TRUE—FALSE

1. Everybody, touch part B in your Workbook. ✔ I'll say statements about the picture.
2. Get ready to circle **true, false,** or **maybe.** Item 1. **Some** of the boys are wearing **short-sleeved** shirts. Circle **true, false,** or **maybe.** (Wait.)
3. Item 2. The boy with the coat is wearing a **long-sleeved** shirt. Circle **true, false,** or **maybe.** (Wait.)
4. Item 3. **None** of the boys have money in their pockets. Circle **true, false,** or **maybe.** (Wait.)
5. Item 4. **None** of the boys are standing up. Circle **true, false,** or **maybe.** (Wait.)
6. Let's check your answers. Mark any item you missed with an X. Everybody, tell me **true, false,** or **maybe.**
7. Item 1. **Some** of the boys are wearing **short-sleeved** shirts. (Signal.) *True.*
8. (Repeat step 7 for items 2–4.)

Answer key   2. *Maybe*   **3.** *Maybe*   **4.** *False*

EXERCISE 14

DESCRIPTION

1. Everybody, touch part C in your Workbook. ✔ Figure out which object I describe. Listen. A vum is an animal. A vum lives on a farm. Ham and bacon are made from vums. **Draw a line under** the object I'm calling a vum. (Wait.)
2. Listen. A rarp is a plant. There are many kinds of rarps. Houses can be made from rarps. **Make a 2 on** the object I'm calling a rarp. (Wait.)
3. Listen. A deez is usually made of paper. You can get a deez at a store. A deez is a container. **Make a 3 on** the object I'm calling a deez. (Wait.)
4. Everybody, get ready to check your work. Tell me the real name for the object that is an animal, that lives on a farm, and that ham and bacon are made from. Get ready. (Signal.) *A pig.* And how did you mark the pig? (Signal.) *Drew a line under it.*
5. Tell me the real name for the object that is a plant, that there are many kinds of, and that houses can be made from. Get ready. (Signal.) *A tree.* And how did you mark the tree? (Signal.) *Made a 2 on it.*
6. Tell me the real name of the object that is usually made of paper, that you can get at a store, and that is a container. Get ready. (Signal.) *A bag.* And how did you mark the bag? (Signal.) *Made a 3 on it.*

EXERCISE 15

TRUE—FALSE

1. Everybody, touch part D in your Workbook. ✔ I'll say statements that are true of one of the pictures. You write the letter of the right picture.
2. Item 1. **All** of the chairs are tall. Write the letter of the picture on line 1. (Wait.)
3. Item 2. **Only some** of the chairs are broken. Write the letter of the picture on line 2. (Wait.)
4. Item 3. **None** of the chairs are broken. Write the letter of the picture on line 3. (Wait.)
5. Item 4. **Only some** of the chairs are short. Write the letter of the picture on line 4. (Wait.)
6. Let's check your answers. Mark any items you miss with an X. Tell me the letter of the right picture.
7. Item 1. **All** of the chairs are tall. (Signal.) *Y.*
8. (Repeat step 7 for items 2–4.)

Answer key   2. *X*   **3.** *Z*   **4.** *Z*

Points

(Award points for the Workbooks.)

INFORMATION

We're going to work on Information now.
Keep your Workbook open to Lesson 15.

━━━━━━━━━ **EXERCISE 16** ━━━━━━━━━

• **INFORMATION: Animals**

1. You've learned about three classes of animals that have a backbone. Which classes? (Signal.) *Mammals, reptiles, and birds.* (Repeat until firm.)
   The next class you're going to learn about is fish. Which class? (Signal.) *Fish.*
   Name a fish. (Call on individual students. The group is to name at least four fish.)

2. Look at the picture at the bottom of your Workbook. It shows a fish. The part that is circled is called the **gill.** What's the circled part called? (Signal.) *The gill.*

3. And here's the first fact about **all fish.** Listen. All fish have gills. Say that fact. (Signal.) *All fish have gills.* (Repeat until firm.)

4. You breathe **oxygen** from the air. Fish don't have to breathe air because they have **gills.** Gills let fish breathe oxygen from the water. You can't breathe oxygen from the water because you don't have (pause; signal) *gills.* Fish can breathe oxygen from the water because fish have (pause; signal) *gills.*

5. Here's the fact again. All fish have gills. Say that fact. (Signal.) *All fish have gills.*
   Trout are fish. So, trout (pause; signal) *have gills.*
   Sharks are fish. So, sharks (pause; signal) *have gills.*

6. Everybody, tell me the first fact about **all fish.** (Signal.) *All fish have gills.*
   Here's the second fact about **all fish.** Listen. All fish are cold-blooded. Say that fact. (Signal.) *All fish are cold-blooded.* (Repeat until firm.)

7. Here are the two facts you've learned about all fish. (Hold up one finger.) First fact. *All fish have gills.* (Hold up two fingers.) Second fact. *All fish are cold-blooded.*
   Your turn. Tell me the two facts about all fish. (Hold up one finger.) First fact. *All fish have gills.* (Hold up two fingers.) Second fact. *All fish are cold-blooded.* (Repeat until the students say the facts in order.)

8. **Salmon** are fish. So, tell me the two facts you know about **salmon.** (Hold up one finger.) First fact. *Salmon have gills.* (Hold up two fingers.) Second fact. *Salmon are cold-blooded.* (Repeat until the students say the facts in order.)

9. **Tuna** are fish. So, tell me the two facts you know about **tuna.** (Hold up one finger.) First fact. *Tuna have gills.* (Hold up two fingers.) Second fact. *Tuna are cold blooded.* (Repeat until firm.)

Individual test
(Call on individual students to do one of the following tasks:)
   a. Name three fish.
   b. What are the two facts you know about fish?
   c. What does cold-blooded mean?

EXERCISE 17

CALENDAR: Seasons in a Year

1. Everybody, tell me how many seasons are in a year. (Pause.) Get ready. (Signal.) *Four.*
2. Name the seasons in a year two times. (Signal.) *Winter, spring, summer, fall, winter, spring, summer, fall.* (Repeat until firm.)
3. Tell me what season comes after winter. (Pause 3 seconds.) Get ready. (Signal.) *Spring.*
   Tell me what season comes after summer. (Pause 3 seconds.) Get ready. (Signal.) *Fall.*
   Tell me what season comes after fall. (Pause 3 seconds.) Get ready. (Signal.) *Winter.*
   Tell me what season comes after spring. (Pause 3 seconds.) Get ready. (Signal.) *Summer.*
   Tell me what season comes after fall. (Pause 3 seconds.) Get ready. (Signal.) *Winter.* (Repeat step 3 until firm.)

Individual test

(Call on individual students to do one of the following tasks:)

   a. How many seasons are in a year?
   b. Name the seasons in a year.
   c. What season comes after summer?
   d. What season comes after fall?

EXERCISE 18

MEMORIZATION: Poem

1. Here's the poem we learned.
   A mechanic fixes cars,
   An astronomer looks at stars,
   A captain has two bars,
   And a boxer spars and spars.
2. Say it with me. (Signal. Say the poem with the students. Repeat until students are responding with you.)
3. All by yourselves. Say the poem. (Signal.) The students say the poem. (Repeat until firm.)

   To correct:
   a. (Stop the students as soon as you hear a mistake.)
   b. (Say the line they missed.)
   c. (Have them repeat the line they missed.)
   d. (Repeat step 3.)

Individual test

Call on individual students to say the whole poem.

Points

(Award points for Information.
Have the students add up their daily total.)

Note: Before beginning Lesson 16, present Fact Game Lesson 3, which appears at the end of this book.

END OF LESSON 15

THINKING OPERATIONS

EXERCISE 1

● **BASIC EVIDENCE: Using Facts**

The first Thinking Operation is **Basic Evidence.**

1. You're going to use two facts to explain things that happened. These are the only facts you can use. (Hold up one finger.) First fact. She was always hungry. Say it. (Signal.) *She was always hungry.* (Repeat until firm.) (Hold up two fingers.) Second fact. She liked to read. Say it. (Signal.) *She liked to read.* (Repeat until firm.)

2. Everybody, say those facts again. (Hold up one finger.) First fact. *She was always hungry.* (Hold up two fingers.) Second fact. *She liked to read.* (Repeat until the students say the facts in order.)

3. Here's what happened. She had a reading lamp. Tell me the fact that explains **why** she had a reading lamp. (Pause.) Get ready. (Signal.) *She liked to read.*

4. Listen. (Hold up one finger.) First fact. She was always hungry.
(Hold up two fingers.) Second fact. She liked to read.

5. Here's what happened. Her refrigerator had a lot of food in it. Tell me the fact that explains **why** her refrigerator had a lot of food in it. (Pause.) Get ready. (Signal.) *She was always hungry.*

6. Here's what happened. Her room was filled with books. Tell me the fact that explains **why** her room was filled with books. (Pause.) Get ready. (Signal.) *She liked to read.*

7. Here's what happened. Her room was filled with candy bar wrappers. Tell me the fact that explains **why** her room was filled with candy bar wrappers. (Pause.) Get ready. (Signal.) *She was always hungry.*

8. Here's what happened. She ate five hamburgers. Tell me the fact that explains **why** she ate five hamburgers. (Pause.) Get ready. (Signal.) *She was always hungry.*

9. (Repeat steps 5–8 until firm.)

EXERCISE 2

SAME: Review

The next Thinking Operation is **Same.**

Task A

1. Let's name some ways that a car and a truck are the same.

2. Can you point to a car and a truck? (Signal.) *Yes.* So, name three ways that a car and a truck are the same. (Hold up one finger.) *They are objects.* (Hold up two fingers.) *They take up space.* (Hold up three fingers.) *You find them in some place.*

3. Are a car and a truck made of the same material? (Signal.) *Yes.* What material? (Signal.) *Metal.* So, how are they the same? (Signal.) *They are made of metal.*

4. Do you **do** some of the same things with a car and a truck? (Signal.) *Yes.* Name three things that you **do** with a car and a truck. (Call on individual students. Praise reasonable responses; for example, steer, drive, go from place to place.)
So, a car and a truck are the same because you **do** some of the same things with them.

5. Do a car and a truck have some of the same parts? (Signal.) *Yes.* Name some of those parts. (Call on individual students. Praise reasonable responses; for example, windows, fenders, bumpers.)
So, a car and a truck are the same because they have some of the same parts.

6. Do you find a car and a truck in some of the same places? (Signal.) *Yes.* Name some of those places. (Call on individual students. Praise reasonable responses; for example, garage, roads, driveways.)
So, a car and a truck are the same because they are found in some of the same places.

7. Are a car and a truck in the same class? (Signal.) *Yes.* What class? (Signal.) *Vehicles.* So, how are they the same? (Signal.) *They are vehicles.*

8. Now, when I call on you, see how many ways you can name that a car and a truck are the same. (Call on individual students. Each student should name at least seven ways that a car and a truck are the same.)

Task B

1. Let's name some ways that a bird and a butterfly are the same. Can a bird and a butterfly be the same color? (Signal.) *Yes.* (Call on one student.) Name a color they can be. (Accept a reasonable response.) Everybody, so how are they the same? (Signal.) *They are [color named].*

2. Do you find a bird and a butterfly in some of the same places? (Signal.) *Yes.* Name some of those places. (Call on individual students. Praise reasonable responses; for example, in the air, in trees, on the grass.)
    So, a bird and a butterfly are the same because you find them in some of the same places.

3. Can you point to a bird and a butterfly? (Signal.) *Yes.*
    So, name three ways a bird and a butterfly are the same. (Hold up one finger.) *They are objects.* (Hold up two fingers.) *They take up space.* (Hold up three fingers.) *You find them in some place.*

4. Do a bird and a butterfly **do** some of the same things? (Signal.) *Yes.* Name at least three of the things that they **do.** (Call on individual students. Praise reasonable responses; for example, fly, drink, see.)
    So, a bird and a butterfly are the same because they **do** some of the same things.

5. Do a bird and a butterfly have some of the same body parts? (Signal.) *Yes.* (Call on individual students. Praise reasonable responses; for example, wings, eyes, tail.)
    A bird and a butterfly are the same because they have some of the same body parts.

6. Are a bird and a butterfly in the same class? (Signal.) *Yes.* What class? (Signal.) *Animals.* So, how are they the same? (Signal.) *They are animals.*

7. Now, when I call on you, see how many ways you can name that a bird and a butterfly are the same. (Call on individual students. Each student should name at least seven ways birds and butterflies are the same.)

═══════ **EXERCISE 3** ═══════

DEDUCTIONS: With *some*

The next Thinking Operation is Deductions.

Task A

1. Listen to this rule. **Some** men are bald. Everybody, say that. (Signal.) *Some men are bald.*

2. That rule doesn't tell about **all** men. It tells about **some** men. How many men does it tell about? (Signal.) *Some.*

Task B

1. Listen. **Some** men are bald. Henry is a man. So, maybe Henry is bald. Is Henry bald? (Signal.) *Maybe.*
    To correct:
    a. Say **maybe.** The answer is **maybe.**
    b. (Repeat step 1.)

2. Listen. **Some** men are bald. Phil is a man. Is Phil bald? (Signal.) *Maybe.*
    Right. Maybe Phil is bald.
    (Repeat step 2 until firm.)

3. Listen. **Some** men are bald. John is a man. Is John bald? (Signal.) *Maybe.*
    Right. Maybe John is bald.

4. (Repeat steps 2 and 3 until firm.)

═══════ **EXERCISE 4** ═══════

DEDUCTIONS: With *all*

1. Listen to this rule. **All** weeks have seven days. Everybody, say that. (Signal.) *All weeks have seven days.*

2. March 3 to 9 is a week. What does the rule let you know about that week? (Signal.) *That week has seven days.* How do you know March 3 to 9 has seven days? (Signal.) *Because all weeks have seven days.*
    To correct students who say *Every week has seven days:*
    a. The rule is **all** weeks have seven days.
    b. Say the rule. (Signal.) *All weeks have seven days.*
    c. (Repeat step 2.)

3. Listen. **All** weeks have seven days. July 25 to July 31 is a week. What does the rule let you know about that week? (Signal.) *That week has seven days.* How do you know that July 25 to July 31 has seven days? (Signal.) *Because all weeks have seven days.*

4. Listen. **All** weeks have seven days. April 15 to 21 is a week. What does the rule let you know about that week? (Signal.) *That week has seven days.* How do you know that April 15 to 21 has seven days? (Signal.) *Because all weeks have seven days.*

5. (Repeat steps 2–4 until firm.)

━━━━━━━━━ **EXERCISE 5** ━━━━━━━━━

DEDUCTIONS: With *don't*

1. Listen to this rule. Chairs **don't** walk. Everybody, say that. (Signal.) *Chairs don't walk.*

2. Mary has two chairs. What does the rule let you know about those chairs? (Signal.) *Those chairs don't walk.* How do you know that those chairs **don't** walk? (Signal.) *Because chairs don't walk.*

3. Listen. Chairs **don't** walk. Jeff has five chairs. What does the rule let you know about those chairs? (Signal.) *Those chairs don't walk.* How do you know that those chairs **don't** walk? (Signal.) *Because chairs don't walk.*

4. (Repeat steps 2 and 3 until firm.)

━━━━━━━━━ **EXERCISE 6** ━━━━━━━━━

● **DEDUCTIONS: With *don't***

1. Listen to this rule. Snakes **don't** have wings. Everybody, say that. (Signal.) *Snakes don't have wings.* What don't snakes have? (Signal.) *Wings.* What don't have wings? (Signal.) *Snakes.*

2. What does the rule let you know about snakes? *(Signal.) Snakes don't have wings.* What does the rule let you know about fish? (Signal.) *Nothing.* What does the rule let you know about birds? (Signal.) *Nothing.* What does the rule let you know about snakes? (Signal.) *Snakes don't have wings.*

3. Listen to the rule again. Snakes **don't** have wings. Cobras are snakes. What does the rule let you know about cobras? (Signal.) *Cobras don't have wings.* How do you know that cobras don't have wings? (Signal.) *Because snakes don't have wings.*

4. Listen to the rule again. Snakes **don't** have wings. Trout are fish. What does the rule let you know about trout? (Signal.) *Nothing.* Yes, nothing. Because the rule tells only about snakes.

5. (Repeat steps 3 and 4 until firm.)

6. Listen to the rule again. Snakes **don't** have wings. Anacondas are snakes. What does the rule let you know about anacondas? (Signal.) *Anacondas don't have wings.* How do you know that anacondas don't have wings? (Signal.) *Because snakes don't have wings.*

7. Listen to the rule again. Snakes **don't** have wings. Swallows are birds. What does the rule let you know about swallows? (Signal.) *Nothing.* Yes, nothing. Because the rule tells only about (pause; signal) *snakes.*

8. (Repeat steps 6 and 7 until firm.)

━━━━━━━━━ **EXERCISE 7** ━━━━━━━━━

DESCRIPTION

The next Thinking Operation is **Description.**

1. I'm going to tell you about an object you know. But I'm going to call it a funny name. See if you can figure out what object I'm talking about.

2. (Hold up one finger.) A moffo is a vehicle. Say that. *A moffo is a vehicle.* (Hold up two fingers.) A moffo goes on tracks. Say that. *A moffo goes on tracks.* (Hold up three fingers.) A moffo has a caboose. Say that. *A moffo has a caboose.*

3. Everybody, say the three things you know about a moffo. (Hold up one finger.) *A moffo is a vehicle.* (Hold up two fingers.) *A moffo goes on tracks.* (Hold up three fingers.) *A moffo has a caboose.* (Repeat until the students say the statements in order.)

4. Everybody, tell me the thing I'm calling a moffo. (Signal.) *A train.* Yes, it's really a train.

EXERCISE 8

DEFINITIONS

The next Thinking Operation is **Definitions.**

1. **Descend** means **go down.**
2. What does **descend** mean? (Signal.) *Go down.*
   What word means **go down?** (Signal.) *Descend.*
   (Repeat step 2 until firm.)
3. Listen. The diver descended thirty meters. Say that. (Signal.) *The diver descended thirty meters.* (Repeat until firm.)
   Now say that sentence with different words for **descended.** (Pause.) Get ready. (Signal.) *The diver went down thirty meters.* (Repeat until firm.)
   (Repeat step 3 until firm.)
4. Listen. The miners went down the shaft. Say that. (Signal.) *The miners went down the shaft.* (Repeat until firm.)
   Now say that sentence with a different word for **went down.** (Pause.) Get ready. (Signal.) *The miners descended the shaft.* (Repeat until firm.)
   (Repeat step 4 until firm.)
5. Listen. He descended into that dark cave. Say that. (Signal.) *He descended into that dark cave.* (Repeat until firm.)
   Now say that sentence with different words for **descended.** (Pause.) Get ready. (Signal.) *He went down into that dark cave.* (Repeat until firm.)
   (Repeat step 5 until firm.)

EXERCISE 9

DEFINITIONS

1. **Lazy.** (Pause.) What's a synonym for **lazy?** (Signal.) *Indolent.*
   And what's a synonym for **indolent?** (Signal.) *Lazy.*
   (Repeat step 1 until firm.)
2. Listen. You can't be indolent and win the race. Say that. (Signal.) *You can't be indolent and win the race.* (Repeat until firm.)

Now say that sentence with a synonym for **indolent.** (Pause.) Get ready. (Signal.) *You can't be lazy and win the race.* (Repeat until firm.)
   (Repeat step 2 until firm.)
3. **Obtain.** (Pause.) What's a synonym for **obtain?** (Signal.) *Get.*
   And what's a synonym for **get?** (Signal.) *Obtain.*
   (Repeat step 3 until firm.)
4. Listen. It is hard to get water in the desert. Say that. (Signal.) *It is hard to get water in the desert.* (Repeat until firm.)
   Now say that sentence with a synonym for **get.** (Pause.) Get ready. (Signal.) *It is hard to obtain water in the desert.* (Repeat until firm.)
   (Repeat step 4 until firm.)
5. **Modify.** (Pause.) What's a synonym for **modify?** (Signal.) *Change.*
   And what's a synonym for **change?** (Signal.) *Modify.*
   (Repeat step 5 until firm.)
6. Listen. Actors can modify their voices. Say that. (Signal.) *Actors can modify their voices.* (Repeat until firm.)
   Now say that sentence with a synonym for **modify.** (Pause.) Get ready. (Signal.) *Actors can change their voices.* (Repeat until firm.)
   (Repeat step 6 until firm.)

EXERCISE 10

DEFINITIONS

1. **Amble.** What does **amble** mean? (Signal.) *Walk slowly.*
   Canine. What does **canine** mean? (Signal.) *Dog.* (Repeat step 1 until firm.)
2. Listen. I like to amble with my canine. Say that sentence. (Signal.) *I like to amble with my canine.* (Repeat until firm.)
   Now say that sentence with different words for **amble** and **canine.** (Pause.) Get ready. (Signal.) *I like to walk slowly with my dog.* (Repeat until firm. Repeat step 2 until firm.)
   To correct students who do not say the new sentence:
   a. (Say the sentence correctly.)
   b. (Have the students repeat the sentence.)
   c. (Repeat step 2.)

====== **EXERCISE 11** ======

STATEMENT INFERENCE

The next Thinking Operation is **Statement Inference.**

Task A

1. Listen. All fish have gills to get oxygen. Say that statement. (Signal.) *All fish have gills to get oxygen.* (Repeat until firm.)

> **Individual test**
> Call on a few individual students to say the statement.

2. Everybody, listen. All fish have gills to get oxygen. What have gills to get oxygen? (Signal.) *All fish.*
   How many fish have gills to get oxygen? (Signal.) *All.*
   What do all fish have to get oxygen? (Signal.) *Gills.*
   Why do all fish have gills? (Signal.) *To get oxygen.*
   What do all fish get with their gills? (Signal.) *Oxygen.*
   What do all fish have? (Signal.) *Gills.*
   (Repeat step 2 until firm.)

> **Individual test**
> Call on individual students to answer a question from step 2.

Task B

1. Listen. When Lou came home, the sky was getting light. Say that statement. (Signal.) *When Lou came home, the sky was getting light.* (Repeat until firm.)

> **Individual test**
> Call on a few individual students to say the statement.

2. Everybody, listen. When Lou came home, the sky was getting light. Who came home? (Signal.) *Lou.*
   What was happening when Lou came home? (Signal.) *The sky was getting light.*
   Where did Lou come when the sky was getting light? (Signal.) *Home.*
   How was the sky getting when Lou came home? (Signal.) *Light.*
   What was getting light when Lou came home? (Signal.) *The sky.*
   (Repeat step 2 until firm.)

> **Individual test**
> Call on individual students to answer a question from step 2.

Points

(Pass out the Workbooks.
Award points for Thinking Operations.)

WORKBOOK EXERCISES

We're going to do Workbooks now. Remember to follow my instructions carefully.

═══════ **EXERCISE 12** ═══════

DESCRIPTION

1. Everybody, touch part A in your Workbook. Figure out which object I describe. Listen. A yark is a container. You can easily pick up a yark. You put flowers or branches in a yark. **Put an A on** the object I'm calling a yark. (Wait.)

2. Listen. You find a smill in a living room. A smill uses electricity. You play CDs on a smill. **Put a B on** the object I'm calling a smill. (Wait.)

3. Listen. A gurp is clothing. It doesn't take much cloth to make a gurp. You wear a gurp in water. **Put a C on** the object I'm calling a gurp. (Wait.)

4. Everybody, get ready to check your work. Tell me the real name for the object that is a container, that you can easily pick up, and that you put flowers or branches in. Get ready. (Signal.) *A vase.* And how did you mark the vase? (Signal.) *Put an A on it.*

5. Tell me the real name for the object that uses electricity, that you find in the living room, and that you play CDs on. Get ready. (Signal.) *A CD player.* And how did you mark the CD player? (Signal.) *Put a B on it.*

6. Tell me the real name for the object that is clothing, that it doesn't take much cloth to make, and that you wear in water. Get ready. (Signal.) *A swimsuit.* And how did you mark the swimsuit? (Signal.) *Put a C on it.*

═══════ **EXERCISE 13** ═══════

TRUE—FALSE

1. Everybody, touch part B in your Workbook. I'll say statements that are true of one of the pictures. You write the letter of the right picture.

2. Item 1. **None** of the objects are furniture. Write the letter of the picture on line 1. (Wait.)

3. Item 2. **All** the objects are for sitting. Write the letter of the picture on line 2. (Wait.)

4. Item 3. **Only some** of the objects are for sitting. Write the letter of the picture on line 3. (Wait.)

5. Item 4. **Only some** of the objects are vehicles. Write the letter of the picture on line 4. (Wait.)

6. Let's check your answers. Mark any items you missed with an X. Tell me the letter of the right picture.

7. Item 1. **None** of the objects are furniture. (Signal.) *E.*

8. (Repeat step 7 for items 2–4.)

═══════ **EXERCISE 14** ═══════

DESCRIPTION

1. Everybody, touch part C in your Workbook. Figure out which man I describe.

2. Item 1. This man has very big ears. He does not have on a shirt. He does not have a beard. Listen again. (Repeat the description.) Write the letter for item 1.

3. Item 2. This man has very big ears. This man is fat. This man does not have on a shirt. Listen again. (Repeat the description.) Write the letter for item 2.

4. Item 3. This man has a shirt on. This man has small ears. This man has a beard. Listen again. (Repeat the description.) Write the letter for item 3.

5. Let's check your answers. Mark any items you missed with an X.

6. Item 1. This man has very big ears. He does not have on a shirt. He does not have a beard. Everybody, what letter? (Signal.) *C.*

7. (Repeat step 6 for items 2 and 3.)

EXERCISE 15

TRUE—FALSE

1. Everybody, touch part D in your Workbook. I'll say statements about the picture.
2. Get ready to circle **true, false,** or **maybe.** Item 1. A family of four lives in each house. Circle **true, false,** or **maybe.** (Wait.)
3. Item 2. **Only some** houses have broken windows. Circle **true, false,** or **maybe.** (Wait.)
4. Item 3. **All** the houses have trees in the yard. Circle **true, false,** or **maybe.** (Wait.)
5. Item 4. **Only some** of the houses have chimneys. Circle **true, false,** or **maybe.** (Wait.)
6. Let's check your answers. Mark any item you missed with an X. Everybody, tell me **true, false,** or **maybe.**
7. Item 1. A family of four lives in each house. (Signal.) *Maybe.*
8. (Repeat step 7 for items 2–4.)

Points
(Award points for Workbooks.)

INFORMATION

We're going to work on Information now.

EXERCISE 16

MEMORIZATION: Poem

1. Here's the poem we learned.
   A mechanic fixes cars,
   An astronomer looks at stars,
   A captain has two bars,
   And a boxer spars and spars.
2. Say it with me. (Signal. Say the poem with the students. Repeat until students are responding with you.)
3. All by yourselves. Say the poem. (Signal.) The students say the poem. (Repeat until firm.)

   To correct:
   a. (Stop the students as soon as you hear a mistake.)
   b. (Say the line they missed.)
   c. (Have them repeat the line they missed.)
   d. (Repeat step 3.)

> **Individual test**
> Call on individual students to say the whole poem.

EXERCISE 17

CALENDAR: Months in a Year

1. I'll name some months of the year. When I stop, you name the rest of the months.
2. My turn. January, February, March, April, May, June, July, August, September, October (pause; signal) *November, December.* (Repeat step 2 until firm.)
3. Here's another one. My turn. January, February, March, April, May (pause; signal) *June, July, August, September, October, November, December.* (Repeat step 3 until firm.)

EXERCISE 18

INFORMATION: Animals

1. You're learning about animals that have a backbone. How many classes of those animals are there? (Signal.) *Five.*
   You've learned facts about four of those classes. Which classes? (Signal.) *Mammals, reptiles, birds, and fish.* (Repeat until firm.)

2. The last class that you learned about was fish. Name a fish. (Call on individual students. The group is to name at least five fish.)
   You learned two facts about **all fish.** Everybody, tell me those two facts. (Hold up one finger.) First fact. *All fish have gills.* (Hold up two fingers.) Second fact. *All fish are cold-blooded.* (Repeat until the students say the facts in order.)

3. Name a mammal. (Call on individual students. The group is to name at least five mammals.)
   You learned two facts about **all mammals.** Everybody, tell me those two facts. (Hold up one finger.) First fact. *All mammals have hair.* (Hold up two fingers.) Second fact. *All mammals are warm-blooded.* (Repeat until the students say the facts in order.)

4. Name a reptile. (Call on individual students. The group is to name at least four reptiles.)
   You learned two facts about **all reptiles.** Everybody, tell me those two facts. (Hold up one finger.) First fact. *All reptiles are cold-blooded.* (Hold up two fingers.) Second fact. *All reptiles are born on land.* (Repeat until the students say the facts in order.)

5. Name a bird. (Call on individual students. The group is to name at least five birds.)
   You learned two facts about **all birds.**
   Everybody, tell me those two facts. (Hold up one finger.) First fact. *All birds have feathers.* (Hold up two fingers.) Second fact. *All birds are warm-blooded.* (Repeat until the students say the facts in order.)

6. Tell me what class **bears** are in. (Pause.) Get ready. (Signal.) *Mammals.*
   So, tell me the two facts you know about **bears.** (Hold up one finger.) First fact. *Bears have hair.* (Hold up two fingers.) Second fact. *Bears are warm-blooded.* (Repeat until the students say the facts in order.)

7. Tell me what class **sharks** are in. (Pause.) Get ready. (Signal.) *Fish.*
   So, tell me the two facts you know about **sharks.** (Hold up one finger.) First fact. *Sharks have gills.* (Hold up two fingers.) Second fact. *Sharks are cold-blooded.* (Repeat until the students say the facts in order.)

8. Tell me what class **cobras** are in. (Pause.) Get ready. (Signal.) *Reptiles.*
   So, tell me the two facts you know about **cobras.** (Hold up one finger.) First fact. *Cobras are cold-blooded.* (Hold up two fingers.) Second fact. *Cobras are born on land.* (Repeat until the students say the facts in order.)

9. Tell me what class **crows** are in. (Pause.) Get ready. (Signal.) *Birds.*
   So, tell me the two facts you know about **crows.** (Hold up one finger.) First fact. *Crows have feathers.* (Hold up two fingers.) Second fact. *Crows are warm-blooded.* (Repeat until the students say the facts in order.)

Points
(Award points for Information.
Have the students add up their daily total.)

END OF LESSON 16

THINKING OPERATIONS

━━━━ **EXERCISE 1** ━━━━

DESCRIPTION

The first Thinking Operation today is **Description.**

1. I'm going to tell you about an object you know. But I'm going to call it a funny name. See if you can figure out what object I'm talking about.

2. (Hold up one finger.) A pex is an animal. Say that. *A pex is an animal.* (Hold up two fingers.) A pex has four legs and a tail. Say that. *A pex has four legs and a tail.* (Hold up three fingers.) A pex barks. Say that. *A pex barks.*

3. Everybody, say the three things you know about a pex. (Hold up one finger.) *A pex is an animal.* (Hold up two fingers.) *A pex has four legs and a tail.* (Hold up three fingers.) *A pex barks.* (Repeat until the students say the statements in order.)

4. Everybody, tell me what thing I'm calling a pex. (Signal.) *A dog.* Yes, it's really a dog.

━━━━ **EXERCISE 2** ━━━━

SAME: Review

The next Thinking Operation is **Same.**

1. Let's name some ways that chairs and tables are the same. Can chairs and tables be made of the same material? (Signal.) *Yes.* Name a material. (Call on one student. Accept a reasonable response.)
   Everybody, so how are they the same? (Signal.) *They are made of* [material named].

2. Do you find chairs and tables in some of the same places? (Signal.) *Yes.* Name some of those places. (Call on individual students. Praise reasonable responses; for example, in houses, in restaurants, in school.)
   So, chairs and tables are the same because you find them in some of the same places.

3. Are chairs and tables in the same class? (Signal.) *Yes.* What class? (Signal.) *Furniture.* So, how are they the same? (Signal.) *They are furniture.*

4. Can you point to chairs and tables? (Signal.) *Yes.*
   So, name three ways chairs and tables are the same. (Hold up one finger.) *They are objects.* (Hold up two fingers.) *They take up space.* (Hold up three fingers.) *You find them in some place.*

5. Do you **do** some of the same things with chairs and tables? (Signal.) *Yes.* Name at least three of the same things you **do** with chairs and tables. (Call on individuals. Praise reasonable responses; for example, put them in a kitchen, move them around.)
   So, chairs and tables are the same because you **do** some of the same things with them.

6. Now, when I call on you, see how many ways you can name that chairs and tables are the same. (Call on individual students. Each student should name at least seven ways chairs and tables are the same.)

━━━━ **EXERCISE 3** ━━━━

BASIC EVIDENCE: Using Facts

The next Thinking Operation is **Basic Evidence.**

1. You're going to use two facts to explain things that happened. These are the only facts you can use. (Hold up one finger.) First fact. Some of the people owned cars. Say it. (Signal.) *Some of the people owned cars.* (Repeat until firm.)
   (Hold up two fingers.) Second fact. Some of the people owned horses. Say it. (Signal.) *Some of the people owned horses.* (Repeat until firm.)

2. Everybody, say those facts again. (Hold up one finger.) First fact. *Some of the people owned cars.* (Hold up two fingers.) Second fact. *Some of the people owned horses.* (Repeat until the students say the facts in order.)

3. Here's what happened. There were some gas stations in town. Tell me the fact that explains **why** there were some gas stations in town. (Pause.) Get ready. (Signal.) *Some of the people owned cars.*

4. Listen. (Hold up one finger.) First fact. Some of the people owned cars. (Hold up two fingers.) Second fact. Some of the people owned horses.

5. Here's what happened. It was hard to find a parking place. Tell me the fact that explains **why** it was hard to find a parking place. (Pause.) Get ready. (Signal.) *Some of the people owned cars.*

6. Here's what happened. Some people had barns. Tell me the fact that explains **why** some people had barns. (Pause.) Get ready. (Signal.) *Some of the people owned horses.*

7. Here's what happened. Some people had a garage. Tell me the fact that explains **why** some people had a garage. (Pause.) Get ready. (Signal.) *Some of the people owned cars.*

8. Here's what happened. Some of the people grew hay. Tell me the fact that explains **why** some of the people grew hay. (Pause.) Get ready. (Signal.) *Some of the people owned horses.*

9. (Repeat steps 5–8 until firm.)

EXERCISE 4

- **DEDUCTIONS: With *some***

The next Thinking Operation is **Deductions.**

1. Listen to this rule. **Some** girls are tall. Everybody, say that. (Signal.) *Some girls are tall.*

2. Mary is a girl. So, is Mary tall? (Signal.) *Maybe.* Yes, **maybe** Mary is tall. Again. **Some** girls are tall. Mary is a girl. So (pause; signal), *maybe Mary is tall.*

3. How do you know that maybe Mary is tall? (Signal.) *Because some girls are tall.* (Repeat step 3 until firm.)

4. Listen. **Some** girls are tall. Pat is a girl. So, is Pat tall? (Signal.) *Maybe.* Yes, maybe Pat is tall. Again. **Some** girls are tall. Pat is a girl. So (pause; signal), *maybe Pat is tall.* (Repeat step 4 until firm.)

5. How do you know that maybe Pat is tall? (Signal.) *Because some girls are tall.*

6. Listen. **Some** girls are tall. Karen is a girl. So (pause; signal), *maybe Karen is tall.*

7. How do you know that maybe Karen is tall? (Signal.) *Because some girls are tall.*

8. (Repeat steps 6 and 7 until firm.)

EXERCISE 5

DEDUCTIONS: With *no*

1. Listen to this rule. **No** man is a reptile. Everybody, say that. (Signal.) *No man is a reptile.*

2. Dr. Jackson is a man. What does the rule let you know about Dr. Jackson? (Signal.) *Dr. Jackson isn't a reptile.* How do you know that Dr. Jackson isn't a reptile? (Signal.) *Because no man is a reptile.*

3. Listen. **No** man is a reptile. Mr. Jones is a man. What does the rule let you know about Mr. Jones? (Signal.) *Mr. Jones isn't a reptile.* How do you know that Mr. Jones isn't a reptile? (Signal.) *Because no man is a reptile.*

4. Listen. **No** man is a reptile. Professor Dixon is a man. What does the rule let you know about Professor Dixon? (Signal.) *Professor Dixon isn't a reptile.* How do you know that Professor Dixon isn't a reptile? (Signal.) *Because no man is a reptile.*

5. (Repeat steps 2–4 until firm.)

EXERCISE 6

DEDUCTIONS: With *don't*

1. Listen to this rule. People **don't** have feathers. Everybody, say that. (Signal.) *People don't have feathers.*
   What don't people have? (Signal.) *Feathers.* What don't have feathers? (Signal.) *People.*

2. What does the rule let you know about vehicles? (Signal.) *Nothing.* What does the rule let you know about buildings? (Signal.) *Nothing.* What does the rule let you know about people? (Signal.) *People don't have feathers.*

3. Listen to the rule again. People **don't** have feathers. Houses are buildings. What does the rule let you know about houses? (Signal.) *Nothing.* Yes, nothing. Because the rule tells only about people.

4. Listen to the rule again. People **don't** have feathers. Babies are people. What does the rule let you know about babies? (Signal.) *Babies don't have feathers.* How do you know that babies don't have feathers? (Signal.) *Because people don't have feathers.*

5. (Repeat steps 3 and 4 until firm.)
6. Listen to the rule again. People **don't** have feathers. Men are people. What does the rule let you know about men? (Signal.) *Men don't have feathers.* How do you know that men don't have feathers? (Signal.) *Because people don't have feathers.*
7. Listen to the rule again. People **don't** have feathers. Trees are plants. What does the rule let you know about trees? (Signal.) *Nothing.* Yes, nothing. Because the rule tells only about (pause; signal) *people.*
8. Listen to the rule again. People **don't** have feathers. Motorcycles are vehicles. What does the rule let you know about motorcycles? (Signal.) *Nothing.* Yes, nothing. Because the rule tells only about (pause; signal) *people.*
9. (Repeat steps 6–8 until firm.)

═══════════ EXERCISE 7 ═══════════

● DEDUCTIONS: With *some*
1. Listen to this rule. Some spiders make webs. Everybody, say that. (Signal.) *Some spiders make webs.*
2. What does the rule tell you about some fish? (Signal.) *Nothing.* What does the rule tell you about some monkeys? (Signal.) *Nothing.* What does the rule tell you about? (Signal.) *Some spiders.* Yes, it doesn't tell about **all** spiders, only about **some** spiders.
3. Listen to the rule again. Some spiders make webs. Tarantulas are **spiders.** What does the rule let you know about tarantulas? (Signal.) *Maybe tarantulas make webs.* How do you know that maybe tarantulas make webs? (Signal.) *Because some spiders make webs.*
4. Listen to the rule again. Some spiders make webs. A monkey is a **mammal.** What does the rule let you know about a monkey? (Signal.) *Nothing.* Yes, nothing. Because the rule tells only about some spiders.
5. (Repeat steps 3 and 4 until firm.)
6. Listen to the rule again. Some spiders make webs. A black widow is a **spider.** What does the rule let you know about a black widow? (Signal.) *Maybe a black widow makes webs.* How do you know that maybe a black widow

makes webs? (Signal.) *Because some spiders make webs.*
7. Listen to the rule again. Some spiders make webs. A shark is a **fish.** What does the rule let you know about a shark? (Signal.) *Nothing.* Yes, nothing. Because the rule tells only about (pause; signal) *some spiders.*
8. (Repeat steps 6 and 7 until firm.)

═══════════ EXERCISE 8 ═══════════

DEFINITIONS
The next Thinking Operation is **Definitions.**
1. **Descend.** (Pause.) What does **descend** mean? (Signal.) *Go down.* What word means **go down?** (Signal.) *Descend.* (Repeat step 1 until firm.)
2. Listen. You descend quickly in that elevator. Say that. (Signal.) *You descend quickly in that elevator.* (Repeat until firm.) Now say that sentence with different words for **descend.** (Pause.) Get ready. (Signal.) *You go down quickly in that elevator.* (Repeat until firm.) (Repeat step 2 until firm.)
3. **Canine.** (Pause.) What's a synonym for **canine?** (Signal.) *Dog.* And what's a synonym for **dog?** (Signal.) *Canine.* (Repeat step 3 until firm.)
4. Listen. A beagle is a kind of canine. Say that. (Signal.) *A beagle is a kind of canine.* (Repeat until firm.) Now say that sentence with a synonym for **canine.** (Pause.) Get ready. (Signal.) *A beagle is a kind of dog.* (Repeat until firm.) (Repeat step 4 until firm.)
5. **Modify.** (Pause.) What's a synonym for **modify?** (Signal.) *Change.* And what's a synonym for **change?** (Signal.) *Modify.* (Repeat step 5 until firm.)
6. Listen. The trainer changed the tiger's behavior. Say that. (Signal.) *The trainer changed the tiger's behavior.* (Repeat until firm.) Now say that sentence with a synonym for **changed.** (Pause.) Get ready. (Signal.) *The trainer modified the tiger's behavior.* (Repeat until firm.) (Repeat step 6 until firm.)

EXERCISE 9

DEFINITIONS

1. **Complete.** What does **complete** mean?
   (Signal.) *Finish.*
   Obtain. What does **obtain** mean? (Signal.)
   Get.
   (Repeat step 1 until firm.)

2. Listen. Complete dinner and then obtain
   dessert. Say that sentence. (Signal.)
   Complete dinner and then obtain dessert.
   (Repeat until firm.)
   Now say that sentence with different words
   for **complete** and **obtain.** (Pause.) Get ready.
   (Signal.) *Finish dinner and then get dessert.*
   (Repeat until firm.)
   (Repeat step 2 until firm.)
   **To correct students who do not say the
   new sentence:**
   a. (Say the sentence correctly.)
   b. (Have the students repeat the sentence.)
   c. (Repeat step 2.)

EXERCISE 10

STATEMENT INFERENCE

The next Thinking Operation is **Statement
Inference.**

Task A

1. Listen. Bats come out when it gets dark. Say
   that statement. (Signal.) *Bats come out when
   it gets dark.* (Repeat until firm.)

> *Individual test*
> Call on a few individual students to say the
> statement.

2. Everybody, listen. Bats come out when it
   gets dark. When do bats come out? (Signal.)
   When it gets dark.
   What comes out when it gets dark? (Signal.)
   Bats.
   What do bats do when it gets dark? (Signal.)
   Come out.

What color are bats that come out when it
gets dark? (Signal.) *I don't know.*
What do bats do? (Signal.) *Come out when it
gets dark.*
What is it like when bats come out? (Signal.)
Dark.
(Repeat step 2 until firm.)

> *Individual test*
> Call on individual students to answer a
> question from step 2.

Task B

1. Listen. When he presses the button, the
   lights will flash. Say that statement. (Signal.)
   *When he presses the button, the lights will
   flash.* (Repeat until firm.)

> *Individual test*
> Call on a few individual students to say the
> statement.

2. Everybody, listen. When he presses the
   button, the lights will flash. What will happen
   if he presses the button? (Signal.) *The lights
   will flash.*
   When will the lights flash? (Signal.) *When he
   presses the button.*
   Who will press the button? (Signal.) *He will.*
   What will he do? (Signal.) *Press the button.*
   What will happen to the lights when he
   presses the button? (Signal.) *They will flash.*
   What kind of button will he press? (Signal.)
   I don't know.
   (Repeat step 2 until firm.)

> *Individual test*
> Call on individual students to answer a
> question from step 2.

Points

(Pass out the Workbooks.
Award points for Thinking Operations.)

WORKBOOK EXERCISES

We're going to do Workbooks now. Remember to follow my instructions carefully.

=== EXERCISE 11 ===

- **TRUE—FALSE**
1. Everybody, touch part A in your Workbook. ✔ I'll say statements about the picture.
2. Get ready to circle **true, false,** or **maybe.** Item 1. **All** the cups are **full.** Circle the answer. (Wait.)
3. Item 2. **Only one** cup is **empty.** Circle the answer. (Wait.)
4. Item 3. **All** the cups are **empty.** Circle the answer. (Wait.)
5. Item 4. **Only one** cup is **full.** Circle the answer. (Wait.)
6. Let's check your answers. Mark any item you missed with an X. Everybody, tell me **true, false,** or **maybe.**
7. Item 1. **All** the cups are **full.** (Signal.) *False.*
8. (Repeat step 7 for items 2–4.

Answer key 2. *True* 3. *False* 4. *False*

=== EXERCISE 12 ===

DESCRIPTION
1. Everybody, touch part B in your Workbook. ✔ Figure out which object I describe. Listen. You see a tok outside. A tok flies. A tok is an animal. **Make a 1 on** the object I'm calling a tok. (Wait.)
2. Listen. A wub is a tool. A wub is usually made of wood. A wub is used to play ball. **Make a 2 on** the object I'm calling a wub. (Wait.)
3. Listen. A lish is an appliance. A lish is usually found in a kitchen. A lish is used to cook food. **Make a 3 on** the object I'm calling a lish. (Wait.)
4. Everybody, get ready to check your work. Tell me the real name for the object that you see outside, that flies, and that is an animal. Get ready. (Signal.) *A bird.* And how did you mark the bird? (Signal.) *Made a 1 on it.*

5. Tell me the real name for the object that is a tool, that is made of wood, and that is used to play ball. Get ready. (Signal.) *A baseball bat.* And how did you mark the baseball bat? (Signal.) *Made a 2 on it.*
6. Tell me the real name for the object that is an appliance, that is usually found in a kitchen, and that is used to cook food. Get ready. (Signal.) *A stove.* And how did you mark the stove? (Signal.) *Made a 3 on it.*

=== EXERCISE 13 ===

TRUE—FALSE
1. Everybody, touch part C in your Workbook. ✔ I'll say statements that are true of one of the pictures. You write the letter of the right picture.
2. Item 1. **All** the objects are food. Write the letter of the picture on line 1. (Wait.)
3. Item 2. **None** of the objects are food. Write the letter of the picture on line 2. (Wait.)
4. Item 3. **Only some** of the objects are containers. Write the letter of the picture on line 3. (Wait.)
5. Item 4. **Only some** of the objects are food. Write the letter of the picture on line 4. (Wait.)
6. Let's check your answers. Mark any items you missed with an X. Tell me the letter of the right picture.
7. Item 1. **All** the objects are food. (Signal.) *N.*
8. (Repeat step 7 for items 2–4.)

Answer key 2. *O* 3. *M* 4. *M*

=== EXERCISE 14 ===

DESCRIPTION
1. Everybody, touch part D in your Workbook. ✔ Figure out which child I describe.
2. Item 1. This child has light hair. This child is not wearing glasses. This child is a boy. Listen again. (Repeat the description.) Write the letter for item 1.
3. Item 2. This child has dark hair. This child is a girl. This child is wearing glasses. Listen again. (Repeat the description.) Write the letter for item 2.

4. Item 3. This child is not wearing glasses. This child is a girl. This child has dark hair. Listen again. (Repeat the description.) Write the letter for item 3.
5. Let's check your answers. Mark any items you missed with an X.
6. Item 1. This child has light hair. This child is not wearing glasses. This child is a boy. Everybody, what letter? (Signal.) *A.*
7. (Repeat step 6 for items 2 and 3.)

Answer key   2. *C* **3.** *D*

Points
(Award points for Workbooks.)

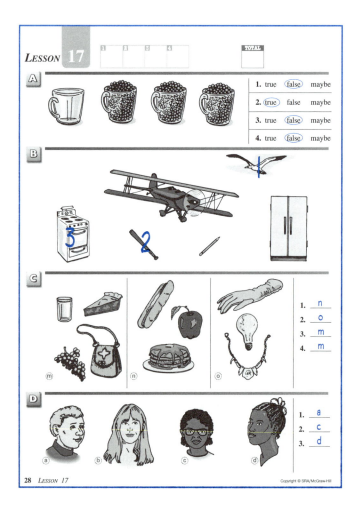

We're going to work on Information now.

━━━━━━━ **EXERCISE 15** ━━━━━━━

● **CALENDAR: Months, Seasons**

1. Everybody, tell me how many months are in a year. (Pause.) Get ready. (Signal.) *Twelve.*
2. Name the months in a year. (Signal.) *January, February, March, April, May, June, July, August, September, October, November, December.*
3. You told me the (pause; signal) *months in a year.*
4. Everybody, tell me how many seasons are in a year. (Pause.) Get ready. (Signal.) *Four.*
5. Name the seasons in a year. (Signal.) *Winter, spring, summer, fall.*
6. You told me the four (pause; signal) *seasons in a year.*

> ***Individual test***
> Call on individual students to name the months or seasons in a year.

━━━━━━━ **EXERCISE 16** ━━━━━━━

● **MEMORIZATION: Poem**

Say that poem we learned about the mechanic and the astronomer. Get ready. (Signal.)
> A mechanic fixes cars,
> An astronomer looks at stars,
> A captain has two bars,
> And a boxer spars and spars.
> (Repeat until firm.)

> ***Individual test***
> Call on individual students to say the whole poem.

EXERCISE 17

INFORMATION: Animals

Task A

1. See if you can figure out the class of animals I'm thinking of. I'm thinking of animals that are cold-blooded and are born on land. (Pause 3 seconds.) Everybody, what class of animals am I thinking of? (Signal.) *Reptiles.*

2. Yes, I told you: they are cold-blooded; they are born on land. Tell me the words I said that let you know I wasn't thinking of fish. (Pause 3 seconds.) Get ready. (Signal.) *They are born on land.*
(Repeat step 2 until firm.)

3. Name an animal in the class of reptiles. (Call on individual students. The group is to name at least four reptiles.)

4. Now I'm thinking of animals that are warm-blooded and have feathers. (Pause 3 seconds.) Everybody, what class of animals am I thinking of? (Signal.) *Birds.*

5. Yes, I told you: they are warm-blooded; they have feathers. Tell me the words I said that let you know I wasn't thinking of mammals. (Pause 3 seconds.) Get ready. (Signal.) *They have feathers.*
(Repeat step 5 until firm.)

6. Name an animal in the class of birds. (Call on individual students. The group is to name at least five birds.)

Task B

1. Now I'm thinking of an animal that is warm-blooded and has hair. Tell me if I could be thinking of a bass. (Pause 3 seconds.) Get ready. (Signal.) *No.* Right.

2. I told you: it is warm-blooded; it has hair. Tell me the words I said that let you know I wasn't thinking of a bass. (Pause 3 seconds.) Get ready. (Signal.) *It is warm-blooded. It has hair.* (Repeat step 2 until firm.)

3. Here are the facts again. The animal is warm-blooded and has hair. Tell me if I could be thinking of a mouse. (Pause.) Get ready. (Signal.) *Yes.*
Tell me what class mice are in. (Pause.) Get ready. (Signal.) *Mammals.*

4. Tell me the two facts you know about **all mammals.** (Hold up one finger.) First fact. *All mammals have hair.* (Hold up two fingers.) Second fact. *All mammals are warm-blooded.* (Repeat until the students say the facts in order.)
So, if I'm thinking of an animal that is warm-blooded and has hair, I could be thinking of a mouse.

5. Now I'm thinking of an animal that is cold-blooded and has gills. Tell me if I could be thinking of a perch. (Pause.) Get ready. (Signal.) *Yes.*
Tell me what class perch are in. (Pause.) Get ready. (Signal.) *Fish.*

6. Tell me the two facts you know about **all fish.** (Hold up one finger.) First fact. *All fish have gills.*
(Hold up two fingers.) Second fact. *All fish are cold-blooded.* (Repeat until the students say the facts in order.)
So, if I'm thinking of an animal that is cold-blooded and has gills, I could be thinking of a perch.

7. Here are the facts again. The animal is cold-blooded and has gills. Tell me if I could be thinking of a chicken. (Pause.) Get ready. (Signal.) *No.* Right.

8. I told you: it is cold-blooded; it has gills. Tell me the words I said that let you know I wasn't thinking of a chicken. (Pause.) Get ready. (Signal.) *It is cold-blooded. It has gills.*
(Repeat step 8 until firm.)

Points

(Award points for Information.
Have the students add up their daily total.)

END OF LESSON 17

THINKING OPERATIONS

EXERCISE 1

- **DEFINITIONS**

The first Thinking Operation is **Definitions.**

1. A synonym for **jump** is **leap.**
2. What's a synonym for **jump?** (Signal.) *Leap.* And what's a synonym for **leap?** (Signal.) *Jump.* (Repeat step 2 until firm.)
3. Listen. She can jump high in the air. Say that. (Signal.) *She can jump high in the air.* (Repeat until firm.)

   Now say that sentence with a synonym for **jump.** (Pause.) Get ready. (Signal.) *She can leap high in the air.* (Repeat until firm.) (Repeat step 3 until firm.)
4. Listen. The deer leaped over the log. Say that. (Signal.) *The deer leaped over the log.* (Repeat until firm.)

   Now say that sentence with a synonym for **leaped.** (Pause.) Get ready. (Signal.) *The deer jumped over the log.* (Repeat until firm.) (Repeat step 4 until firm.)

EXERCISE 2

DEFINITIONS

1. **Indolent.** (Pause.) What's a synonym for **indolent?** (Signal.) *Lazy.* And what's a synonym for **lazy?** (Signal.) *Indolent.* (Repeat step 1 until firm.)
2. Listen. The lazy lizard slept in the sun. Say that. (Signal.) *The lazy lizard slept in the sun.* (Repeat until firm.)

   Say that sentence with a synonym for **lazy.** (Pause.) Get ready. (Signal.) *The indolent lizard slept in the sun.* (Repeat until firm.) (Repeat step 2 until firm.)
3. **Masticate.** (Pause.) What's a synonym for **masticate?** (Signal.) *Chew.* And what's a synonym for **chew?** (Signal.) *Masticate.* (Repeat step 3 until firm.)
4. Listen. He chewed loudly. Say that. (Signal.) *He chewed loudly.* (Repeat until firm.)

   Now say that sentence with a synonym for **chewed.** (Pause.) Get ready. (Signal.) *He*

masticated loudly. (Repeat until firm.) (Repeat step 4 until firm.)
5. **Descend.** What does **descend** mean? (Signal.) *Go down.* What word means **go down?** (Signal.) *Descend.* (Repeat step 5 until firm.)
6. Listen. She went down the rope slowly. Say that. (Signal.) *She went down the rope slowly.* (Repeat until firm.)

   Now say that sentence with a different word for **went down.** (Pause.) Get ready. (Signal.) *She descended the rope slowly.* (Repeat until firm.) (Repeat step 6 until firm.)

EXERCISE 3

- **SAME: Review**

The next Thinking Operation is **Same.**

1. A knife and a saw are the same in a lot of ways.
2. They are in the same class. Name that same class. (Signal.) *Tools.* So, how are they the same? (Signal.) *They are tools.*
3. A knife and a saw are made of the same material. Name that same material. (Signal.) *Metal.* So, how are they the same? (Signal.) *They are made of metal.*
4. A knife and a saw have some of the same parts. Name some of those parts. (Call on individual students. Praise reasonable responses; for example, handle, blade, teeth.)
5. You can find a knife and a saw in some of the same places. Name some of those places. (Call on individual students. Praise reasonable responses; for example, tool box, drawer, kitchen.)
6. Everybody, you can point to a knife and a saw. So, name three ways that they are the same. (Hold up one finger.) *They are objects.* (Hold up two fingers.) *They take up space.* (Hold up three fingers.) *You find them in some place.*
7. You can **do** some of the same things with a knife and a saw. Name some of those things. (Call on individual students. Praise reasonable responses; for example, sharpen them, cut with them, hold them.)

═══════ **EXERCISE 4** ═══════

DEDUCTIONS: With *all*

The next Thinking Operation is Deductions.

1. Listen to this rule. **All years** have fifty-two weeks. Everybody, say that. (Signal.) *All years have fifty-two weeks.*

2. 1776 was a year. What does the rule let you know about that year? (Signal.) *That year had fifty-two weeks.* How do you know that 1776 had fifty-two weeks? (Signal.) *Because all years have fifty-two weeks.*

   To correct students who say *Every year has fifty-two weeks:*
   a. The rule is **all** years have fifty-two weeks.
   b. Say the rule. (Signal.) *All years have fifty-two weeks.*
   c. (Repeat step 2.)

3. Listen. 1492 was a year. What does the rule let you know about that year? (Signal.) *That year had fifty-two weeks.* How do you know that 1492 had fifty-two weeks? (Signal.) *Because all years have fifty-two weeks.*

4. Listen. 1066 was a year. What does the rule let you know about that year? (Signal.) *That year had fifty-two weeks.* How do you know that year had fifty-two weeks? (Signal.) *Because all years have fifty-two weeks.*

5. (Repeat steps 2–4 until firm.)

═══════ **EXERCISE 5** ═══════

DEDUCTIONS: With *all*

1. Listen to this rule.
   All oceans have salt water. Everybody, say that. (Signal.) *All oceans have salt water.* What do **all** oceans have? (Signal.) *Salt water.* What has salt water? (Signal.) *All oceans.*

   To correct students who don't say *All oceans:*
   a. **All** oceans. What has salt water? (Signal.) *All oceans.*
   b. (Repeat step 1.)

2. Say the rule again. (Signal.) *All oceans have salt water.* What does the rule let you know about **all** rivers? (Signal.) *Nothing.*

To correct students who don't say *Nothing:*
a. The answer is **nothing.**
b. The rule tells only about oceans. It tells **nothing** about rivers.
c. (Repeat step 2.)

What does the rule let you know about **all** lakes? (Signal.) *Nothing.* What does the rule let you know about **all** oceans? (Signal.) *They have salt water.*

3. Listen to the rule again. **All** oceans have salt water. The Pacific is an ocean. What does the rule let you know about the Pacific? (Signal.) *It has salt water.* How do you know that the Pacific has salt water? (Signal.) *Because all oceans have salt water.* (Repeat step 3 until firm.)

4. Listen to the rule again. **All** oceans have salt water. The Mississippi is a river. What does the rule let you know about the Mississippi? (Signal.) *Nothing.* Yes, nothing. Because the rule tells only about oceans. (Repeat step 4 until firm.)

5. Listen to the rule again. **All** oceans have salt water. The Atlantic is an ocean. What does the rule let you know about the Atlantic? (Signal.) *The Atlantic has salt water.* How do you know that the Atlantic has salt water? (Signal.) *Because all oceans have salt water.* (Repeat step 5 until firm.)

6. Listen to the rule again. **All** oceans have salt water. Tahoe is a lake. What does the rule let you know about Tahoe? (Signal.) *Nothing.* Yes, nothing. Because the rule tells only about (pause; signal) *oceans.*

7. Listen to the rule again. **All** oceans have salt water. The Columbia is a river. What does the rule let you know about the Columbia? (Signal.) *Nothing.* Yes, nothing. Because the rule tells only about (pause; signal) *oceans.*

8. (Repeat steps 6 and 7 until firm.)

═══════ **EXERCISE 6** ═══════

DEDUCTIONS: With *all* **and** *every*

1. I'll say rules with **all** and **every.** You say them the other way. What two words are we going to use? (Hold up one finger.) *All.* (Hold up two fingers.) *Every.*

2. Listen. **All** tires are made of rubber. Say that. (Signal.) *All tires are made of rubber.*
Now say it the other way. Get ready. (Signal.) *Every tire is made of rubber.*
(Repeat step 2 until firm.)

3. Here's a new rule. **Every** sock is made of cloth. Say that. (Signal.) *Every sock is made of cloth.*
Now say it the other way. Get ready. (Signal.) *All socks are made of cloth.*
(Repeat step 3 until firm.)

4. Here's a new rule. **All** snakes have skins. Say that. (Signal.) *All snakes have skins.*
Now say it the other way. Get ready. (Signal.) *Every snake has skin.* (Repeat step 4 until firm.)

5. Here's a new rule. **Every** frog jumps. Say that. (Signal.) *Every frog jumps.*
Now say it the other way. Get ready. (Signal.) *All frogs jump.*
(Repeat step 5 until firm.)

EXERCISE 7

BASIC EVIDENCE: Using Facts

The next Thinking Operation is **Basic Evidence.**

1. You're going to use two facts to explain things that happened. These are the only facts you can use. (Hold up one finger.) First fact. He plays the guitar. Say it. (Signal.) *He plays the guitar.* (Repeat until firm. Hold up two fingers.) Second fact. He plays the piano. Say it. (Signal.) *He plays the piano.* (Repeat until firm.)

2. Everybody, say those facts again. (Hold up one finger.) First fact. *He plays the guitar.* (Hold up two fingers.) Second fact. *He plays the piano.* (Repeat until the students say the facts in order.)

3. Here's what happened. He carried his instrument to the party. Tell me the fact that explains **why** he was able to carry his instrument. (Pause.) Get ready. (Signal.) *He plays the guitar.*

4. Listen. (Hold up one finger.) First fact. He plays the guitar. (Hold up two fingers.) Second fact. He plays the piano.

5. Here's what happened. His instrument had black and white keys. Tell me the fact that explains **why** his instrument had black and white keys. (Pause.) Get ready. (Signal.) *He plays the piano.*

6. Here's what happened. It took three people to move his instrument. Tell me the fact that explains **why** it took three people to move his instrument. (Pause.) Get ready. (Signal.) *He plays the piano.*

7. Here's what happened. His fingers plucked the metal strings. Tell me the fact that explains **why** his fingers plucked the metal strings. (Pause.) Get ready. (Signal.) *He plays the guitar.*

8. (Repeat steps 5–7 until firm.)

EXERCISE 8

STATEMENT INFERENCE

The next Thinking Operation is **Statement Inference.**

Task A

1. Listen. If a diver descends too far, he will die. Say that statement. (Signal.) *If a diver descends too far, he will die.* (Repeat until firm.)

> **Individual test**
> Call on individuals to say the statement.

2. Everybody, listen. If a diver descends too far, he will die. Who will die if he descends too far? (Signal.) *A diver.*
What will happen if a diver descends too far? (Signal.) *He will die.*
When will a diver die? (Signal.) *If he descends too far.*
If a diver goes down too far, will he die? (Signal.) *Yes.*
(Repeat step 2 until firm.)

> **Individual test**
> Call on individual students to answer a question from step 2.

Task B

1. Listen. When birds hatch from eggs, they cannot fly. Say that statement. (Signal.) *When birds hatch from eggs, they cannot fly.* (Repeat until firm.)

> **Individual test**
> Call on individuals to say the statement.

2. Everybody, listen. When birds hatch from eggs, they cannot fly. What can't birds do when they hatch from eggs? (Signal.) *Fly.* What cannot fly when they hatch from eggs? (Signal.) *Birds.* What happens when birds hatch from eggs? (Signal.) *They cannot fly.* When can birds not fly? (Signal.) *When they hatch from eggs.* (Repeat step 2 until firm.)

> **Individual test**
> Call on individual students to answer a question from step 2.

========= **EXERCISE 9** =========

DEDUCTIONS: With *some*

Now we're going to do some more Deductions.

1. Listen to this rule. Some tools have blades. Everybody, say that. (Signal.) *Some tools have blades.*

2. What does the rule tell you some tools have? (Signal.) *Blades.* What does the rule tell you about some **clothes?** (Signal.) *Nothing.* What does the rule tell you about some **plants?** (Signal.) *Nothing.* What does the rule tell you about? (Signal.) *Some tools.* Yes, it doesn't tell about **all** tools, only about **some** tools.

3. Listen to the rule again. Some tools have blades. Jim bought a **tool.** What does the rule let you know about that tool? (Signal.) *Maybe that tool has a blade.*

4. Listen to the rule again. Some tools have blades. Alan bought a **hat.** What does the rule tell you about that hat? (Signal.) *Nothing.* Yes, nothing. Because the rule tells only about some tools.

5. (Repeat steps 3 and 4 until firm.)

6. Listen to the rule again. Some tools have blades. Anne bought a **plant.** What does the rule let you know about that plant? (Signal.) *Nothing.* Yes, nothing. Because the rule tells only about (pause; signal) *some tools.*

7. Listen to the rule again. Some tools have blades. Susan bought a **tool.** What does the rule let you know about that tool? (Signal.) *Maybe that tool has a blade.*

8. Listen to the rule again. Some tools have blades. Harry bought a **coat.** What does the rule let you know about that coat? (Signal.) *Nothing.* Yes, nothing. Because the rule tells only about (pause; signal) *some tools.*

9. (Repeat steps 6–8 until firm.)

========= **EXERCISE 10** =========

DEDUCTIONS: With *some*

1. Listen to this rule. **Some** dogs are collies. Everybody, say that. (Signal.) *Some dogs are collies.*

2. Spot is a dog. So, is Spot a collie? (Signal.) *Maybe.* Yes, maybe Spot is a collie. Again. **Some** dogs are collies. Spot is a dog. So (pause; signal), *maybe Spot is a collie.*

3. How do you know that maybe Spot is a collie? (Signal.) *Because some dogs are collies.* (Repeat step 3 until firm.)

4. Listen. **Some** dogs are collies. Lulu is a dog. So, is Lulu a collie? (Signal.) *Maybe.* Yes, maybe Lulu is a collie. Again. **Some** dogs are collies. Lulu is a dog. So (pause; signal), *maybe Lulu is a collie.*

5. How do you know that maybe Lulu is a collie? (Signal.) *Because some dogs are collies.*

6. Listen. **Some** dogs are collies. Rover is a dog. So (pause; signal), *maybe Rover is a collie.*

7. How do you know that maybe Rover is a collie? (Signal.) *Because some dogs are collies.*

8. (Repeat steps 6 and 7 until firm.)

EXERCISE 11

DEDUCTIONS: With *no*

1. Listen to this rule. **No** month has thirty-three days. Everybody, say that. (Signal.) *No month has thirty-three days.*

2. July is a month. What does the rule let you know about July? (Signal.) *July doesn't have thirty-three days.* How do you know that July doesn't have thirty-three days? (Signal.) *Because no month has thirty-three days.*

3. Listen. **No** month has thirty-three days. February is a month. What does the rule let you know about February? (Signal.) *February doesn't have thirty-three days.* How do you know that February doesn't have thirty-three days? (Signal.) *Because no month has thirty-three days.*

4. Listen. **No** month has thirty-three days. March is a month. What does the rule let you know about March? (Signal.) *March doesn't have thirty-three days.* How do you know that March doesn't have thirty-three days? (Signal.) *Because no month has thirty-three days.*

5. (Repeat steps 2–4 until firm.)

EXERCISE 12

DESCRIPTION

The next Thinking Operation is **Description.**

1. I'm going to tell you about an object you know. But I'm going to call it a funny name. See if you can figure out what object I'm talking about.

2. (Hold up one finger.) A rog is a tool. Say that. *A rog is a tool.*
   (Hold up two fingers.) A rog is made of metal. Say that. *A rog is made of metal.*
   (Hold up three fingers.) You put screws in with a rog. Say that. *You put screws in with a rog.*

3. Everybody, say the three things you know about a rog. (Hold up one finger.) *A rog is a tool.* (Hold up two fingers.) *A rog is made of metal.* (Hold up three fingers.) *You put screws in with a rog.* (Repeat until the students say the statements in order.)

4. Everybody, tell me what thing I'm calling a rog. (Signal.) *A screwdriver.* Yes, it's really a screwdriver.

Points
(Pass out the Workbooks.
Award points for Thinking Operations.)

We're going to do Workbooks now. Remember to follow my instructions carefully.

EXERCISE 13

DESCRIPTION

1. Everybody, touch part A in your Workbook. Figure out which object I describe. Listen. Slok is food. Slok is yellow. Slok is good on pancakes, potatoes, and popcorn. **Make a 1 on** the object I'm calling slok. (Wait.)

2. Listen. A murn is an animal. A murn is very large. A murn lives in the water, and water spouts out of its head when it starts to breathe. **Circle** the object I'm calling a murn. (Wait.)

3. Listen. A gop is a vehicle. A gop has two wheels. A gop has a motor. **Make a 3 on** the object I'm calling a gop. (Wait.)

4. Everybody, get ready to check your work. Tell me the real name for the object that is food, that is yellow, and that is good on pancakes, potatoes, and popcorn. Get ready. (Signal.) *Butter.* And how did you mark the butter? (Signal.) *Made a 1 on it.*

5. Tell me the real name for the object that is an animal, that is very large, that lives in the water, and that has water spout out of its head when it starts to breathe. Get ready. (Signal.) *A whale.* And how did you mark the whale? (Signal.) *Circled it.*

6. Tell me the real name for the object that is a vehicle, that has two wheels, and that has a motor. Get ready. (Signal.) *A motorcycle.* And how did you mark the motorcycle? (Signal.) *Made a 3 on it.*

EXERCISE 14

TRUE—FALSE

1. Everybody, touch part B in your Workbook. I'll say statements about the picture.
2. Get ready to circle **true, false,** or **maybe.** Item 1. **All** the women are **eating.** Circle the answer. (Wait.)
3. Item 2. **Some** of the women are **eating.** Circle the answer. (Wait.)
4. Item 3. **All** the women are **twenty-five years old.** Circle the answer. (Wait.)
5. Item 4. **Some of** the women are **sleeping.** Circle the answer. (Wait.)
6. Let's check your answers. Mark any item you missed with an X. Everybody, tell me **true, false,** or **maybe.**
7. Item 1. **All** the women are **eating.** (Signal.) *False.*
8. (Repeat step 7 for items 2–4.)

EXERCISE 15

DESCRIPTION

1. Everybody, touch part C in your Workbook. Figure out which person I describe.
2. Item 1. This person is wearing a hat. This person is smiling. This person has long hair. Listen again. (Repeat the description.) Write the letter for item 1.
3. Item 2. This person is smiling. This person is a man. This person is not wearing a hat. Listen again. (Repeat the description.) Write the letter for item 2.
4. Item 3. This person is wearing glasses. This person has short hair. This person is not smiling. Listen again. (Repeat the description.) Write the letter for item 3.
5. Let's check your answers. Mark any items you missed with an X.
6. Item 1. This person is wearing a hat. This person is smiling. This person has long hair. Everybody, what letter? (Signal.) *A.*
7. (Repeat step 6 for items 2 and 3.)

EXERCISE 16

CLASSIFICATION

1. Everybody, touch the instructions for part D in your Workbook. I'll read the instructions. Don't write anything. Listen. Put an A on the vehicles. Put a B on the tools.
2. What are you going to do to every vehicle? (Signal.) *Put an A on it.*
3. What are you going to do to every tool? (Signal.) *Put a B on it.*
   Everybody, now put an A on the vehicles and put a B on the tools. (Wait.)
4. Get ready to mark your papers. Put an X by any object you got wrong.
5. What class is a **hammer** in? (Signal.) *Tools.* How did you mark the **hammer?** (Signal.) *Put a B on it.*
6. (Repeat step 5 for **pliers, cart, car, scissors, saw, jet plane,** and **rake.**)

Points
(Award points for Workbooks.)

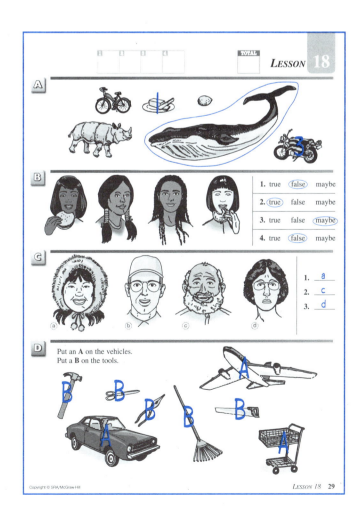

LESSON 18

INFORMATION

We're going to work on Information now.

EXERCISE 17

- **MEMORIZATION: Poem**

Task A

1. What does a beautician do? (Call on a student. Accept reasonable responses.) Yes, a beautician fixes people's hair.
2. What does a tailor do? (Call on a student. Accept reasonable responses.) Yes, a tailor makes clothes and fixes clothes.
3. Who knows what an exposition is? (Call on a student. Accept reasonable responses.) Yes, an exposition is a big fair.
4. Everybody, how many is a pair? (Signal.) *Two.* Right.

Task B

1. Here's a new poem that tells about the things we've talked about. Listen.
   A beautician fixes hair,
   A tailor can mend a tear,
   An exposition is a fair,
   And one plus one is a pair.
   Let's learn that poem.
2. A beautician fixes hair. Say it. (Signal.) *A beautician fixes hair.* (Repeat until firm.)
3. A tailor can mend a tear. Say it. *A tailor can mend a tear.* (Repeat until firm.)
4. A beautician fixes hair, a tailor can mend a tear. Say it with me. (Signal. Respond with the students.) *A beautician fixes hair, a tailor can mend a tear.* Your turn. (Signal.) *A beautician fixes hair, a tailor can mend a tear.* (Repeat until firm.)
5. An exposition is a fair. Say it. (Signal.) *An exposition is a fair.* (Repeat until firm.)
6. A beautician fixes hair, a tailor can mend a tear, an exposition is a fair. Say it with me. (Signal. Respond with the students.) *A beautician fixes hair, a tailor can mend a tear, an exposition is a fair.* (Repeat until students are responding with you.)

Your turn. (Signal.) *A beautician fixes hair, a tailor can mend a tear, an exposition is a fair.* (Repeat until firm.)
7. And one plus one is a pair. Say it. (Signal.) *And one plus one is a pair.* (Repeat until firm.)
8. Here's the whole poem.
   A beautician fixes hair,
   A tailor can mend a tear,
   An exposition is a fair,
   And one plus one is a pair.
   Say it with me. (Signal. Say the poem with the students. Repeat until students are responding with you.)
9. All by yourselves. Say the poem. (Signal.) The students say the poem. (Repeat until firm.)

EXERCISE 18

- **INFORMATION: Animals**

1. You're learning about animals that have a backbone. How many classes of those animals are there? (Signal.) *Five.* You've learned facts about four of those classes. Which classes? (Signal.) *Mammals, reptiles, birds, and fish.* (Repeat until firm.)
2. The next class you're going to learn about is amphibians. Which class? (Signal.) *Amphibians.* (Repeat until firm.)
   Frogs, toads, newts, and salamanders are amphibians. Here's the first fact about **all amphibians.** Listen. All amphibians are born in the water but grow up on land. Say that fact. (Signal.) *All amphibians are born in the water but grow up on land.* (Repeat until firm.)
3. Frogs, toads, newts, and salamanders are born from eggs. Those eggs are laid in the water. When baby amphibians get older, they move onto land. Amphibians grow up on land. But where do amphibians lay their eggs? (Signal.) *In the water.*
   And where do amphibians grow up? (Signal.) *On land.*
4. Here's the fact again. All amphibians are born in the water but grow up on land. Say that fact. (Signal.) *All amphibians are born in the water but grow up on land.*

Frogs are amphibians. So, frogs are born (pause; signal) *in the water.*
But frogs grow up (pause; signal) *on land.*

5. Here's that fact again. All amphibians are born in the water but grow up on land. Newts are amphibians. So, newts are born (pause; signal) *in the water.*
But newts grow up (pause; signal) *on land.*
(Repeat step 5 until firm.)

Individual test
(Call on individual students to do one of the following tasks:)
  a. Name five classes of animals that have a backbone.
  b. Name some amphibians.
  c. What's the first fact about all amphibians?

EXERCISE 19

CALENDAR: Months, Seasons

1. Everybody, tell me how many months are in a year. (Pause.) Get ready. (Signal.) *Twelve.*
2. Name the months in a year. (Signal.) *January, February, March, April, May, June, July, August, September, October, November, December.*
3. You told me the (pause; signal) *months in a year.*
4. Everybody, tell me how many seasons are in a year. (Pause.) Get ready. (Signal.) *Four.*
5. Name the seasons in a year. (Signal.) *Winter, spring, summer, fall.*
6. You told me the four (pause; signal) *seasons in a year.*

Individual test
Call on individual students to name the months or seasons in a year.

Points
(Award points for Information.
Have the students add up their daily total.)

END OF LESSON 18

LESSON 19

THINKING OPERATIONS

EXERCISE 1

DEFINITIONS

The first Thinking Operation today is **Definitions.**

1. **Leap.** (Pause.) What's a synonym for **leap?** (Signal.) *Jump.* And what's a synonym for **jump?** (Signal.) *Leap.*
   (Repeat step 1 until firm.)

2. Listen. Can you jump across that ditch? Say that. (Signal.) *Can you jump across that ditch?* (Repeat until firm.)
   Now say that sentence with a synonym for **jump.** (Pause.) Get ready. (Signal.) *Can you leap across that ditch?* (Repeat until firm.)
   (Repeat step 2 until firm.)

3. **Modify.** (Pause.) What's a synonym for **modify?** (Signal.) *Change.*
   And what's a synonym for **change?** (Signal.) *Modify.*
   (Repeat step 3 until firm.)

4. Listen. The racer changed part of the engine. Say that. (Signal.) *The racer changed part of the engine.* (Repeat until firm.)
   Now say that sentence with a different word for **changed.** (Pause.) Get ready. (Signal.) *The racer modified part of the engine.* (Repeat until firm.)
   (Repeat step 4 until firm.)

5. **Amble.** (Pause.) What does **amble** mean? (Signal.) *Walk slowly.*
   What word means **walk slowly?** (Signal.) *Amble.*
   (Repeat step 5 until firm.)

6. Listen. You will be late if you amble. Say that. (Signal.) *You will be late if you amble.* (Repeat until firm.)
   Now say that sentence with different words for **amble.** (Pause.) Get ready. (Signal.) *You will be late if you walk slowly.* (Repeat until firm.)
   (Repeat step 6 until firm.)

EXERCISE 2

DEFINITIONS

1. **Change.** What does **change** mean? (Signal.) *Modify.*
   Amble. What does **amble** mean? (Signal.) *Walk slowly.*
   (Repeat step 1 until firm.)

2. Listen. He had to change the way he ambled. Say that sentence. (Signal.) *He had to change the way he ambled. (Repeat until firm.)*
   Now say that sentence with different words for **change** and **ambled.** (Pause.) Get ready. (Signal.) *He had to modify the way he walked slowly. (Repeat until firm.)*
   (Repeat step 2 until firm.)

EXERCISE 3

BASIC EVIDENCE: Using Facts

The next Thinking Operation is **Basic Evidence.**

1. You're going to use two facts to explain things that happened. These are the only facts you can use. (Hold up one finger.) First fact. Linda was a champion swimmer. Say it. (Signal.) *Linda was a champion swimmer.* (Repeat until firm. Hold up two fingers.) Second fact. Susan was a champion runner. Say it. (Signal.) *Susan was a champion runner.* (Repeat until firm.)

2. Everybody, say those facts again. (Hold up one finger.) First fact. *Linda was a champion swimmer.* (Hold up two fingers.) Second fact. *Susan was a champion runner.* (Repeat until the students say the facts in order.)

3. Here's what happened. Her shoes were wearing out. Tell me the fact that explains **why** her shoes were wearing out. (Pause.) Get ready. (Signal.) *Susan was a champion runner.*

4. Listen. (Hold up one finger.) First fact. Linda was a champion swimmer. (Hold up two fingers.) Second fact. Susan was a champion runner.

5. Here's what happened. Her hair was always wet. Tell me the fact that explains **why** her hair was always wet. (Pause.) Get ready. (Signal.) *Linda was a champion swimmer.*

6. Here's what happened. She often had water in her ears. Tell me the fact that explains **why** she often had water in her ears. (Pause.) Get ready. (Signal.) *Linda was a champion swimmer.*

7. Here's what happened. She had a blister on her heel. Tell me the fact that explains **why** she had a blister on her heel. (Pause.) Get ready. (Signal.) *Susan was a champion runner.*

8. (Repeat steps 5–7 until firm.)

━━━━━━━━━ **EXERCISE 4** ━━━━━━━━━

DEDUCTIONS: With *don't*
The next Thinking Operation is **Deductions.**
1. Listen to this rule. Birds **don't** have hair. Everybody, say that. (Signal.) *Birds don't have hair.*

2. Canaries are birds. What does the rule let you know about canaries? (Signal.) *Canaries don't have hair.* How do you know that canaries don't have hair? (Signal.) *Because birds don't have hair.*

3. Listen. Birds **don't** have hair. Parrots are birds. What does the rule let you know about parrots? (Signal.) *Parrots don't have hair.* How do you know that parrots don't have hair? (Signal.) *Because birds don't have hair.*

4. Listen. Birds **don't** have hair. Sparrows are birds. What does the rule let you know about sparrows? (Signal.) *Sparrows don't have hair.* How do you know that sparrows don't have hair? (Signal.) *Because birds don't have hair.*

5. (Repeat steps 2–4 until firm.)

━━━━━━━━━ **EXERCISE 5** ━━━━━━━━━

DEDUCTIONS: With *no* **and** *don't*
1. I'll say rules with **no** or **don't.** You say them the other way. What two words are we going to use? (Hold up one finger.) *No.* (Hold up two fingers.) *Don't.*

2. Listen. **No** whale has gills. Say that. (Signal.) *No whale has gills.* Now say it the other way. Get ready. (Signal.) *Whales don't have gills.* (Repeat step 2 until firm.)

3. Here's a new rule. Flies **don't** talk. Say that. (Signal.) *Flies don't talk.* Now say it the other way. Get ready. (Signal.) *No flies talk.* (Repeat step 3 until firm.)

4. Here's a new rule. **No** chair grows. Say that. (Signal.) *No chair grows.* Now say it the other way. Get ready. (Signal.) *Chairs don't grow.* (Repeat step 4 until firm.)

5. Here's a new rule. Tables **don't** walk. Say that. (Signal.) *Tables don't walk.* Now say it the other way. Get ready. (Signal.) *No tables walk.* (Repeat step 5 until firm.)

━━━━━━━━━ **EXERCISE 6** ━━━━━━━━━

DEDUCTIONS: With *some*
1. Listen to this rule. **Some** rocks are diamonds. Everybody, say that. (Signal.) *Some rocks are diamonds.*

2. Ben has a rock. So, does Ben have a diamond? (Signal.) *Maybe.* Yes, maybe Ben has a diamond. Again. **Some** rocks are diamonds. Ben has a rock. So (pause; signal), *maybe Ben has a diamond.*

3. How do you know that maybe Ben has a diamond? (Signal.) *Because some rocks are diamonds.*

4. Listen. **Some** rocks are diamonds. Beth has a rock. So, does Beth have a diamond? (Signal.) *Maybe.* Yes, maybe Beth has a diamond. Again. Beth has a rock. So (pause; signal), *maybe Beth has a diamond.*

5. How do you know that maybe Beth has a diamond? (Signal.) *Because some rocks are diamonds.*

6. Listen. **Some** rocks are diamonds. Sarah has a rock. So (pause; signal), *maybe Sarah has a diamond.*

7. How do you know that maybe Sarah has a diamond? (Signal.) *Because some rocks are diamonds.*

8. (Repeat steps 6 and 7 until firm.)

EXERCISE 7

DEDUCTIONS: With *all*

1. Listen to this rule.
   All meat comes from animals. Everybody, say that. (Signal.) *All meat comes from animals.*
   Where does all meat come from? (Signal.) *Animals.* What comes from animals? (Signal.) *All meat.*

   To correct students who don't say *All meat*:
   a. **All** meat. What comes from animals? (Signal.) *All meat.*
   b. (Repeat step 1.)

2. Say the rule again. (Signal.) *All meat comes from animals.* What does the rule let you know about all vegetables? (Signal.) *Nothing.*

   To correct students who don't say *Nothing*:
   a. The answer is **nothing.**
   b. The rule tells only about meat. It tells **nothing** about vegetables.
   c. (Repeat step 2.)
   What does the rule let you know about all fruit? (Signal.) *Nothing.* What does the rule let you know about all meat? (Signal.) *It comes from animals.*

3. Listen to the rule again. **All** meat comes from animals. Carrots are vegetables. What does the rule let you know about carrots? (Signal.) *Nothing.* Yes, nothing. Because the rule tells only about all meat.
   (Repeat step 3 until firm.)

4. Listen to the rule again. **All** meat comes from animals. Beef is meat. What does the rule let you know about beef? (Signal.) *It comes from animals.* How do you know that beef comes from animals? (Signal.) *Because all meat comes from animals.*
   (Repeat step 4 until firm.)

5. Listen to the rule again. **All** meat comes from animals. Grapes are fruit. What does the rule let you know about grapes? (Signal.) *Nothing.* Yes, nothing. Because the rule tells only about (pause; signal) *meat.*
   (Repeat step 5 until firm.)

6. Listen to the rule again. **All** meat comes from animals. Hamburger is meat. What does the rule let you know about hamburger? (Signal.) *It comes from animals.* How do you know that hamburger comes from animals? (Signal.) *Because all meat comes from animals.*

7. Listen to the rule again. **All** meat comes from animals. Pork is meat. What does the rule let you know about pork? (Signal.) *It comes from animals.* How do you know that pork comes from animals? (Signal.) *Because all meat comes from animals.*

8. (Repeat steps 6 and 7 until firm.)

EXERCISE 8

SAME: Review

The next Thinking Operation is **Same.**

1. Green garbage cans and green boxes are the same in a lot of ways.

2. They are the same color. Name that same color. (Signal.) *Green.* So, how are they the same? (Signal.) *They are green.*

3. Everybody, you can point to green garbage cans and green boxes. So, name three ways green garbage cans and green boxes are the same. (Hold up one finger.) *They are objects.* (Hold up two fingers.) *They take up space.* (Hold up three fingers.) *You find them in some place.*

4. Green garbage cans and green boxes are in the same class. Name that class. (Signal.) *Containers.*
   So, how are they the same? (Signal.) *They are containers.*

5. You can **do** some of the same things with green garbage cans and green boxes. Name some of those things. (Call on individual students. Praise reasonable responses; for example, pick them up, drum on them, put things in them.)

6. Green garbage cans and green boxes have some of the same parts. Name some of those parts. (Call on individual students. Praise reasonable responses; for example, top, sides, bottom.)

7. You can find green garbage cans and green boxes in some of the same places. Name some of those places. (Call on individual students. Praise reasonable responses; for example, in backyards, in garages, in stores, on farms.)

━━━━━ **EXERCISE 9** ━━━━━

STATEMENT INFERENCE

The next Thinking Operation is **Statement Inference.**

1. Listen. Some spiders make webs to catch flies. Say that statement. (Signal.) *Some spiders make webs to catch flies.* (Repeat until firm.)

> **Individual test**
> Call on a few individual students to say the statement.

2. Everybody, listen. Some spiders make webs to catch flies. How many spiders make webs to catch flies? (Signal.) *Some.*
   What do some spiders do? (Signal.) *Make webs to catch flies.*
   Why do some spiders make webs? (Signal.) *To catch flies.*
   What do spiders make webs to catch? (Signal.) *Flies.*
   What do some spiders make to catch flies? (Signal.) *Webs.*
   What makes webs to catch flies? (Signal.) *Some spiders.*
   (Repeat step 2 until firm.)

> **Individual test**
> Call on individual students to answer a question from step 2.

━━━━━ **EXERCISE 10** ━━━━━

DESCRIPTION

The next Thinking Operation is **Description.**

1. I'm going to tell you about another object you know. But I'm going to call it a funny name. See if you can figure out what object I'm talking about.

2. (Hold up one finger.) A darz is food. Say that. *A darz is food.*
   (Hold up two fingers.) A darz is long. Say that. *A darz is long.*
   (Hold up three fingers.) A darz has a yellow peel. Say that. *A darz has a yellow peel.*

3. Everybody, say the three things you know about a darz. (Hold up one finger.) *A darz is food.* (Hold up two fingers.) *A darz is long.* (Hold up three fingers.) *A darz has a yellow peel.* (Repeat until the students say the statements in order.)

4. Everybody, tell me the thing I am calling a darz. (Signal.) *A banana.* Yes, it's really a banana.

━━━━━ **EXERCISE 11** ━━━━━

DESCRIPTION

1. Here's the rule. **Flam** is a funny word that we'll use for desk. What word are we using for desk? (Signal.) *Flam.*
   And what does **flam** mean? (Signal.) *Desk.*

2. Listen to this sentence. A flam can be made of cloth. Is that statement true or false? (Signal.) *False.*
   To correct:
   a. What does **flam** mean? (Signal.) *Desk.*
   b. A desk can be made of cloth. Is that statement true or false? (Signal.) *False.* Yes, it's false. So this statement is also false: A flam can be made of cloth.
   c. (Repeat step 2.)

3. Next sentence. A flam is furniture. Is that statement true or false? (Signal.) *True.*

4. Next sentence. Flams are found in school. Is that statement true or false? (Signal.) *True.*

5. Next sentence. You can do your work on a flam. Is that statement true or false? (Signal.) *True.*

6. Next sentence. You sleep in a flam. Is that statement true or false? (Signal.) *False.*

Points
(Pass out the Workbooks.
Award points for Thinking Operations.)

WORKBOOK EXERCISES

We're going to do Workbooks now. Remember to follow my instructions carefully.

━━━━━━━━ **EXERCISE 12** ━━━━━━━━

DESCRIPTION

1. Everybody, touch part A in your Workbook. Figure out which object I describe. Listen. A pilb is a tool. A pilb has a handle and a blade. A pilb is used for cutting wood. **Make a box around** the object I'm calling a pilb. (Wait.)

2. Listen. A zak can be made of leather or plastic. People keep things in their zaks. A zak is a container. **Underline** the object I'm calling a zak. (Wait.)

3. Listen. A herp is clothing. A herp is worn to keep you dry when it rains. A herp has sleeves and a collar. **Put a 3 on** the object I'm calling a herp.

4. Everybody, get ready to check your work. Tell me the real name for the object that is a tool, that has a handle and a blade, and that is used for cutting wood. Get ready. (Signal.) *A saw.* And how did you mark the saw? (Signal.) *Made a box around it.*

5. Tell me the real name for the object that can be made of leather or plastic, that people keep things in, and that is a container. Get ready. (Signal.) *A purse.* And how did you mark the purse? (Signal.) *Underlined it.*

6. Tell me the real name for the object that is clothing, that is worn to keep you dry when it rains, and that has sleeves and a collar. Get ready. (Signal.) *A raincoat.* And how did you mark the raincoat? (Signal.) *Put a 3 on it.*

━━━━━━━━ **EXERCISE 13** ━━━━━━━━

TRUE—FALSE

1. Everybody, touch part B in your Workbook. I'll say statements about the picture.

2. Get ready to circle **true, false,** or **maybe.** Item 1. **Only one** girl is **smiling.** Circle the answer. (Wait.)

3. Item 2. **None** of the girls are **smiling.** Circle the answer. (Wait.)

4. Item 3. **Some** of the girls are **thirsty.** Circle the answer. (Wait.)

5. Item 4. **Some** of the girls are **eating.** Circle the answer. (Wait.)

6. Let's check your answers. Mark any item you missed with an X. Everybody, tell me **true, false,** or **maybe.**

7. Item 1. **Only one** girl is **smiling.** (Signal.) *False.*

8. (Repeat step 7 for items 2–4.)

━━━━━━━━ **EXERCISE 14** ━━━━━━━━

DESCRIPTION

1. Everybody, touch part C in your Workbook. Figure out which cat I describe.

2. Item 1. This cat has a collar. This cat has a short tail. This cat is lying down. Listen again. (Repeat the description.) Write the letter for item 1.

3. Item 2. This cat has a long tail. This cat is black. This cat is running. Listen again. (Repeat the description.) Write the letter for item 2.

4. Item 3. This cat is black. This cat has a long tail. This cat has no collar. Listen again. (Repeat the description.) Write the letter for item 3.

5. Let's check your answers. Mark any items you missed with an X.

6. Item 1. This cat has a collar. This cat has a short tail. This cat is lying down. Everybody, what letter? (Signal.) *D.*

7. (Repeat step 6 for items 2 and 3.)

━━━━━━━━ **EXERCISE 15** ━━━━━━━━

TRUE—FALSE

1. Everybody, touch part D in your Workbook. I'll say statements that are true of one of the pictures. You write the letter of the right picture.

2. Item 1. **Only some** of the tools are used for cooking. Write the letter of the picture on line 1. (Wait.)

3. Item 2. **None** of the tools are used for cooking. Write the letter of the picture on line 2. (Wait.)

4. Item 3. **All** the tools are used for cooking. Write the letter of the picture on line 3. (Wait.)

5. Item 4. **All** the tools are used for repair work. Write the letter of the picture on line 4. (Wait.)

6. Let's check your answers. Mark any items you missed with an X. Tell me the letter of the right picture.

7. Item 1. **Only some** of the tools are used for cooking. (Signal.) *C.*

8. (Repeat step 7 for items 2–4.)

Points

(Award points for Workbooks.)

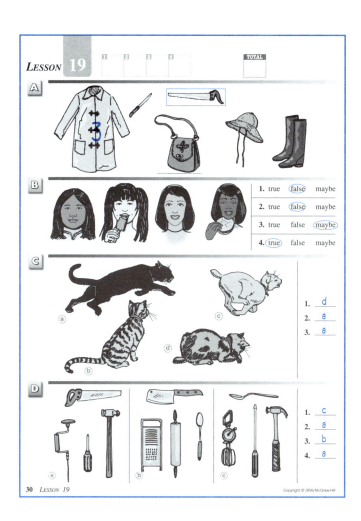

INFORMATION

We're going to work on Information now.

━━━ **EXERCISE 16** ━━━

● **MEMORIZATION: Poem**

1. Here's the poem we learned. Listen.
   A beautician fixes hair,
   A tailor can mend a tear,
   An exposition is a fair,
   And one plus one is a pair.

2. Say it with me. (Signal. Say the poem with the students. Repeat until students are responding with you.)

3. All by yourselves. (Signal.) The students say the poem. (Repeat until firm.)
   To correct:
   a. (Stop the students as soon as you hear a mistake.)
   b. (Say the line they missed.)
   c. (Have them repeat the line they missed.)
   d. (Repeat step 3.)
   (Repeat until firm.)

> *Individual test*
> Call on individual students to say the whole poem.

━━━ **EXERCISE 17** ━━━

● **INFORMATION: Animals**

Task A

1. You've learned about five classes of animals that have a backbone. Everybody, name those five classes. (Signal.) *Mammals, reptiles, birds, fish, and amphibians.* (Repeat until firm.)

2. Name a mammal. (Call on individual students.) The group is to name at least five mammals.
   You learned two facts about **all mammals.** Everybody, tell me those two facts. (Hold up one finger.) First fact. *All mammals have hair.*

(Hold up two fingers.) Second fact. *All mammals are warm-blooded.* (Repeat until the students say the facts in order.)

3. Name a reptile. (Call on individual students.) The group is to name at least four reptiles. You learned two facts about **all reptiles.** Everybody, tell me those two facts. (Hold up one finger.) First fact. *All reptiles are cold-blooded.* (Hold up two fingers.) Second fact. *All reptiles are born on land.* (Repeat until the students say the facts in order.)

4. Name a bird. (Call on individual students.) The group is to name at least five birds. You learned two facts about **all birds.** Everybody, tell me those two facts. (Hold up one finger.) First fact. *All birds have feathers.* (Hold up two fingers.) Second fact. *All birds are warm-blooded.* (Repeat until the students say the facts in order.)

5. Name a fish. (Call on individual students.) The group is to name at least five fish. You learned two facts about **all fish.** Everybody, tell me those two facts. (Hold up one finger.) First fact. *All fish have gills.* (Hold up two fingers.) Second fact. *All fish are cold-blooded.* (Repeat until the students say the facts in order.)

Task B

1. Name an amphibian. (Call on individual students. The group is to name at least three amphibians.) You learned one fact about **all amphibians.** Tell me that fact. (Signal.) *All amphibians are born in the water but grow up on land.* (Repeat until firm.)

2. Here's another fact about **all amphibians.** Listen. All amphibians are cold-blooded. Say that fact. (Signal.) *All amphibians are cold-blooded.* (Repeat until firm.)

3. Here are the two facts you've learned about **all amphibians.** (Hold up one finger.) First fact. *All amphibians are born in the water but grow up on land.* (Hold up two fingers.) Second fact. *All amphibians are cold-blooded.*

Everybody, tell me the two facts about **all amphibians.** (Hold up one finger.) First fact. *All amphibians are born in the water but grow up on land.* (Hold up two fingers.) Second fact. *All amphibians are cold-blooded.* (Repeat until the students say the facts in order.)

4. Tell me what class toads are in. (Pause.) Get ready. (Signal.) *Amphibians.* So, tell me the two facts you know about toads. (Hold up one finger.) First fact. *Toads are born in the water but grow up on land.* (Hold up two fingers.) Second fact. *Toads are cold-blooded.* (Repeat until the students say the facts in order.)

5. Tell me what class salamanders are in. (Pause.) Get ready. (Signal.) *Amphibians.* So, tell me the two facts you know about salamanders. (Hold up one finger.) First fact. *Salamanders are born in the water but grow up on land.* (Hold up two fingers.) Second fact. *Salamanders are cold-blooded.* (Repeat until the students say the facts in order.)

Individual test

(Call on individual students to do one of the following tasks:)

    a. Name three amphibians.
    b. What's the first fact about all amphibians?
    c. What's the second fact about all amphibians?

Points

(Award points for Information. Have the students add up their daily total.)

END OF LESSON 19

Introduction

Today we'll do a short lesson and then take a test. Since the lesson is short, you won't get points for it. However, you can earn as many as 25 points for the test. We'll go over those points just before the test.

EXERCISE 1

SAME: Review

The first Thinking Operation today is **Same.**

1. An orange and an apple are the same in a lot of ways.

2. An orange and an apple are the same shape. Name that same shape. (Signal.) *Round.* So, how are they the same? (Signal.) *They are round.*

3. An orange and an apple have some of the same parts. Name some of those parts. (Call on individual students. Praise reasonable responses; for example, skin, seeds, pulp, stem.)

4. Everybody, you can point to an orange and an apple. So, name three ways an orange and an apple are the same. (Hold up one finger.) *They are objects.* (Hold up two fingers.) *They take up space.* (Hold up three fingers.) *You find them in some place.*

5. You find an orange and an apple in some of the same places. Name some of those places. (Call on individual students. Praise reasonable responses; for example, trees, kitchens, stores.)

6. An orange and an apple are in the same class. Everybody, name that same class. (Signal.) *Food.* So, how are they the same? (Signal.) *They are food.*

7. You can **do** some of the same things with an orange and an apple. Name some of those things. (Call on individual students. Praise reasonable responses; for example, peel, pick, eat.)

EXERCISE 2

● **BASIC EVIDENCE: Using Facts**

The next Thinking Operation is **Basic Evidence.**

1. You're going to use two facts to explain things that happened. (Hold up one finger.) First fact. There was no rain that summer. Say it. (Signal.) *There was no rain that summer.* (Repeat until firm.)
(Hold up two fingers.) Second fact. The nights were very cold. Say it. (Signal.) *The nights were very cold.* (Repeat until firm.)

2. Everybody, say those facts again. (Hold up one finger.) First fact. *There was no rain that summer.*
(Hold up two fingers.) Second fact. *The nights were very cold.* (Repeat until the students say the facts in order.)

> **Individual test**
> Call on individual students to say the facts.

3. Here's what happened. Many gardens dried up. Tell me the fact that explains **why** that happened. (Pause.) Get ready. (Signal.) *There was no rain that summer.*

To correct students who give the wrong fact:

a. Does that fact explain **why** many gardens dried up? (Signal.) *No.*

b. So, tell me the fact that explains **why** many gardens dried up.

4. Listen. First fact. There was no rain that summer. Second fact. The nights were very cold.

5. Here's what happened. George wore a sweater and a coat. Tell me the fact that explains **why** that happened. (Pause.) Get ready. (Signal.) *The nights were very cold.*

6. Here's what happened. Everyone sat close to the fireplace. Tell me the fact that explains **why** that happened. (Pause.) Get ready. (Signal.) *The nights were very cold.*

7. Here's what happened. The lake was low. Tell me the fact that explains **why** that happened. (Pause.) Get ready. (Signal.) *There was no rain that summer.*

8. (Repeat steps 5–7 until firm.)

LESSON 20

=== EXERCISE 3 ===

• **DEDUCTIONS: With *some***
The next Thinking Operation is **Deductions.**
1. Listen. **Some** girls are tall. Karen is a girl. So (pause; signal), *maybe Karen is tall.* How do you know that maybe Karen is tall? (Signal.) *Because some girls are tall.* (Repeat step 1 until firm.)
2. Listen. **Some** girls are tall. Claudia is a girl. So (pause; signal), *maybe Claudia is tall.* How do you know that maybe Claudia is tall? (Signal.) *Because some girls are tall.* (Repeat step 2 until firm.)
3. Listen. **Some** girls are tall. Terry is a girl. So (pause; signal), *maybe Terry is tall.* How do you know that maybe Terry is tall? (Signal.) *Because some girls are tall.* (Repeat step 3 until firm.)

=== EXERCISE 4 ===

DEFINITIONS
The next Thinking Operation is **Definitions.**
1. **Ignore** means **pay no attention to.**
2. What does **ignore** mean? (Signal.) *Pay no attention to.*
   What word means **pay no attention to?** (Signal.) *Ignore.* (Repeat step 2 until firm.)
3. Listen. They paid no attention to the rain. Say that. (Signal.) *They paid no attention to the rain.* (Repeat until firm.)
   Now say that sentence with a different word for **paid no attention to.** (Pause.) Get ready. (Signal.) *They ignored the rain.* (Repeat until firm.)
   (Repeat step 3 until firm.)

4. Listen. She paid no attention to her brother. Say that. (Signal.) *She paid no attention to her brother.* (Repeat until firm.)
   Now say that sentence with a different word for **paid no attention to.** (Pause.) Get ready. (Signal.) *She ignored her brother.* (Repeat until firm.)
   (Repeat step 4 until firm.)
5. Listen. I ignored the loud noise. Say that. (Signal.) *I ignored the loud noise.* (Repeat until firm.)
   Now say that sentence with different words for **ignored.** (Pause.) Get ready. (Signal.) *I paid no attention to the loud noise.* (Repeat until firm.)
   (Repeat step 5 until firm.)

=== EXERCISE 5 ===

DEFINITIONS
1. **Masticate.** What does **masticate** mean? (Signal.) *Chew.*
   Indolent. What does **indolent** mean? (Signal.) *Lazy.* (Repeat step 1 until firm.)
2. Listen. I'm never too indolent to masticate gum. Say that sentence. (Signal.) *I'm never too indolent to masticate gum.* (Repeat until firm.)
   Now say that sentence with different words for **indolent** and **masticate.** (Pause.) Get ready. (Signal.) *I'm never too lazy to chew gum.* (Repeat until firm.)
   (Repeat step 2 until firm.)

Points
(Pass out the Workbooks.
Award no points for Thinking Operations.)

178 LESSON 20

WORKBOOK EXERCISES

We're going to do Workbooks now. Remember to follow my instructions carefully.

═══════ **EXERCISE 6** ═══════

● **TRUE—FALSE**

1. Everybody, touch part A in your Workbook. ✔ Don't write anything. I'll say statements about the picture. You say **true, false,** or **maybe.** What are you going to say? (Signal.) *True, false, or maybe.*

2. Listen. The deer is running. (Pause 4 seconds.) Get ready. (Signal.) *True.*
   Now I'll say that same thing another way. The deer is not standing still. (Pause 4 seconds.) Get ready. (Signal.) *True.*
   (Repeat step 2 until firm.)

3. New statement. The skunk is not running. (Pause 4 seconds.) Get ready. (Signal.) *True.*
   Now I'll say the same statement another way. The skunk is standing still. (Pause 4 seconds.) Get ready. (Signal.) *True.*
   (Repeat step 3 until firm.)

4. Let's do some more statements. Remember, if the statement is right, it is true. The deer is running. (Pause 4 seconds.) Get ready. (Signal.) *True.*
   The deer is not running. (Pause 4 seconds.) Get ready. (Signal.) *False.*
   The skunk is standing still. (Pause 4 seconds.) Get ready. (Signal.) *True.*
   The skunk is not standing still. (Pause 4 seconds.) Get ready. (Signal.) *False.*
   (Repeat step 4 until firm.)

5. Get ready to circle **true, false,** or **maybe** for each item. Item 1. The deer is running. Circle the answer for item 1. (Wait.)
   Item 2. The deer is not running. Circle the answer for item 2. (Wait.)
   Item 3. The skunk is standing still. Circle the answer for item 3. (Wait.)
   Item 4. The skunk is not standing still. Circle the answer for item 4. (Wait.)

6. Everybody, let's check your answers. Say **true, false,** or **maybe.**

7. Item 1. The deer is running. (Signal.) *True.*

8. (Repeat step 7 for items 2–4.)

Points
(Award no points for Workbooks.)

INFORMATION

We're going to work on Information now.

EXERCISE 7

MEMORIZATION: Poem

1. Here's the poem we learned. Listen.
   A beautician fixes hair,
   A tailor can mend a tear,
   An exposition is a fair,
   And one plus one is a pair.
2. Say it with me. (Signal. Say the poem with the students. Repeat until students are responding with you.)
3. All by yourselves. (Signal. The students say the poem. Repeat until firm.)
   To correct:
   a. (Stop the students as soon as you hear a mistake.)
   b. (Say the line they missed.)
   c. (Have them repeat the line they missed.)
   d. (Repeat step 3 until firm.)

> **Individual test**
> Call on individual students to say the whole poem.

EXERCISE 8

INFORMATION: Animals

1. I'm thinking of an animal that is warm-blooded and has feathers. Tell me if I could be thinking of a bluejay. (Pause.) Get ready. (Signal.) *Yes.*
   Tell me what class bluejays are in. (Pause.) Get ready. (Signal.) *Birds.*
2. Tell me the two facts you know about **all birds.** (Hold up one finger.) First fact. *All birds have feathers.* (Hold up two fingers.) Second fact. *All birds are warm-blooded.* (Repeat until the students say the facts in order.)
   So, if I'm thinking of an animal that is warm-blooded and has feathers, I could be thinking of a bluejay.

3. Here are the facts again. The animal is warm-blooded and has feathers. Tell me if I could be thinking of a trout. (Pause 3 seconds.) Get ready. (Signal.) *No.*
4. Right. I told you: it is warm-blooded; it has feathers. Tell me the words I said that let you know I wasn't thinking of a trout. (Pause 3 seconds.) Get ready. (Signal.) *It is warm-blooded. It has feathers.*
   (Repeat step 4 until firm.)

EXERCISE 9

MEMORIZATION: Poem

Say that poem we learned about the mechanic and the astronomer. Get ready. (Signal.)
   A mechanic fixes cars,
   An astronomer looks at stars,
   A captain has two bars,
   And a boxer spars and spars.
(Repeat until firm.)

> **Individual test**
> Call on individual students to say the whole poem.

Points

(Award no points for Information.)

Test Introduction

Now we're going to do the test. If you make zero errors or one error on the test, you will earn 25 points. If you make two or three errors, you will earn 14 points. If you make more than three errors, you fail the test and you earn 0 points. Some of the test items are on the next page in your Workbook. I will give you some other test items individually. We'll do the Workbook items first. Open your Workbook to Test 1.

═══ EXERCISE 10 ═══

IN-PROGRAM TEST 1

Task A

1. Everybody, touch part A on your test. Figure out which object I describe. Listen. A moop is an animal. A moop is warm-blooded. A moop flies. Circle the object I'm calling a moop. (Wait.)
2. Listen. A blarg is made of metal. A blarg is a vehicle. A blarg flies. Make a box around the object I'm calling a blarg. (Wait.)
3. Listen. A voom is found in the kitchen. A voom is a container. A voom has a handle. Cross out the object I'm calling a voom. (Wait.)

Task B

1. Everybody, touch part B on your test. I'll say statements that are true of one of the pictures. You write the letter of the right picture. Don't get fooled, because I might say statements about the same picture twice.
2. Item 1. All the plants are trees. Write the letter of the picture on line 1. (Wait.)
3. Item 2. All the plants are flowers. Write the letter of the picture on line 2. (Wait.)
4. None of the plants are flowers. Write the letter of the picture on line 3. (Wait.)
5. Only some of the plants are trees. Write the letter of the picture on line 4. (Wait.)

Task C

1. Everybody, touch part C on your test. Some of the objects in box 1 are made of the same material. **Make a line over** all the objects that are made of the same material. Do it. (Wait.)
2. Some of the objects in box 2 are in the same class. **Make an X under** all the objects that are usually in the same class. Do it. (Wait.)
3. Some of the objects in box 3 are usually the same color. **Make a box around** all the objects that are the same color. Do it. (Wait.)

Task D

1. Everybody, touch part D on your test. I'll say statements about the pictures.
2. Get ready to circle **true, false,** or **maybe.** Item 1. **None** of the objects are **vehicles.** Circle the answer. (Wait.)
3. Item 2. **All** the objects are **vehicles.** Circle the answer. (Wait.)
4. Item 3. **All** the objects cost over **$300.** Circle the answer. (Wait.)
5. Item 4. **All** the objects are usually found in a **living room.** Circle the answer. (Wait.)

Note: After presenting the Workbook test items, do Tasks E and F with each student where the other students cannot hear you. Circle *pass* or *fail* for each item on the student's test Workbook. The students must give specified responses to pass the items.

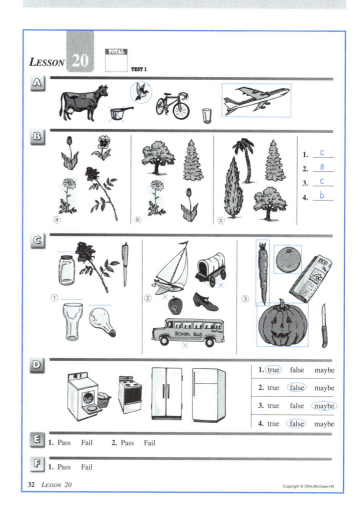

Copyright © SRA/McGraw-Hill

Task E

1. Tell me how many months are in a year. *Twelve.*

2. Name the months in a year. *January, February, March, April, May, June, July, August, September, October, November, December.* The students must name the months in order.

Task F

You learned two facts about all reptiles. Tell me those two facts.

(Hold up one finger.) *All reptiles are cold-blooded.*

(Hold up two fingers.) *All reptiles are born on land.* The students must say the facts in order.

> **Note:** After presenting the verbal items, check the students' written test items. Write the total number of errors for tasks A–F at the top of the test Workbook page.

Answer key   Task A: 1. *Bird, circled*   **2.** *Airplane, made a box around*   **3.** *Pot, crossed out*   **Task B: 1.** *C*   **2.** *A*   **3.** *C*   **4.** *B*   **Task C: 1.** *Jar, glass, light bulb; made a line over*   **2.** *Sailboat, wagon, bus; made an X under*   **3.** *Carrot, orange, pumpkin; made a box around*   **Task D: 1.** *True*   **2.** *False*   **3.** *Maybe*   **4.** *False*

Points for Test

Raise your hand if you made zero, one, two, or three mistakes on the test. If you made zero mistakes or one mistake, you earned 25 points. If you made two or three mistakes, you earned 14 points. If you made more than three mistakes, you didn't earn any points. Record your points for the test on your Point Chart.

(Check and correct.)

22-Lesson Point Summary

(Tell students to add the point totals for Lessons 16 through 20 on the Point Summary Chart and to write the totals for Block 4 and the Grade Period. Maximum for Grade Period 1 = 322 points.)

Remediation Procedures for Test 1

Students who failed the test (those who made more than three errors) must be firmed on items that were missed on the test. This must be done before you present Lesson 21.

1. Use the next class period to work with the group of students who failed the test.

2. Use the chart to determine which tasks to use for review. If any member of the group failed Task A, the review tasks indicated for Task A must be presented to the review group. If no member of the group failed Task A, do not present the review exercises for Task A.

3. For reviewing Workbook tasks (A–D) use the appropriate review pages near the back of the student Workbook.

4. After you have taught all review exercises to the group of students who failed the test, determine whether each student is firm by presenting all review tasks, individually, to him or her. A student is considered firm if he or she correctly responds to all tasks.

5. Students who passed the test should not be included in the review group. Assign them independent activities to do while you are working with the review group. The assignment should be reinforcing, such as a discussion about the types of homes that different animals make. Assign a leader for the group, rules for the discussion, and some reference material, such as illustrated books about animals.

Test Section	Orally Present These Review Tasks		Portion of Review Workbook
	Lesson	Exercise	
A	17	12	Part A
A	18	13	Part B
B	16	13	Part C
B	17	13	Part D
C	13	14	Part E
C	14	12	Part F
D	17	11	Part G
D	18	14	Part H
E	18	19	——
		Steps 1–3	
F	19	17	——
		Steps 1–3	

END OF LESSON 20

THINKING OPERATIONS

EXERCISE 1

● **ANALOGIES**

Task A

The first Thinking Operation today is **Analogies.**

1. We're going to make up an **analogy** that tells **how animals move.** What is the analogy going to tell? (Signal.) *How animals move.* (Repeat until firm.)
2. The animals we're going to use in the analogy are a hawk and a whale. Which animals? (Signal.) *A hawk and a whale.*
3. Name the first animal. (Signal.) *A hawk.* Yes, a hawk. How does that animal move? (Signal.) *It flies.* Yes, it flies.
4. So, here's the first part of the analogy. A hawk is to flying. What's the first part of the analogy? (Signal.) *A hawk is to flying.* Yes, a hawk is to flying. (Repeat until firm.)
5. The first part of the analogy told how an animal moves. So, the **next** part of the analogy must tell how another animal moves.
6. You told how a hawk moves. Now you're going to tell about a whale. What animal? (Signal.) *A whale.* How does that animal move? (Signal.) *It swims.* Yes, it swims.
7. So, here's the second part of the analogy. A whale is to swimming. What's the second part of the analogy? (Signal.) *A whale is to swimming.* Yes, a whale is to swimming.
8. (Repeat steps 2–7 until firm.)
9. Now we're going to say the whole analogy. First, we're going to tell how a **hawk** moves and then we're going to tell how a **whale** moves. Say the analogy with me. (Signal. Respond with the students.) A hawk is to flying as a whale is to swimming. (Repeat until the students are responding with you.)
10. All by yourselves. Say that analogy. (Signal.) *A hawk is to flying as a whale is to swimming.* (Repeat until firm.)
11. That analogy tells **how those animals move.** What does that analogy tell? (Signal.) *How those animals move.*
12. (Repeat steps 10 and 11 until firm.)

Individual test
Call on individual students to do step 10 or 11.

Task B

1. We're going to make up an **analogy** that tells **where you find animals.** What is the analogy going to tell? (Signal.) *Where you find animals.* (Repeat until firm.)
2. The animals we're going to use are a bird and a whale. Which animals? (Signal.) *A bird and a whale.*
3. Name the first animal. (Signal.) *A bird.* Yes, a bird. Where do you find that animal? (Signal.) *In the sky.* Yes, in the sky.
4. So, here's the first part of the analogy. A bird is to the sky. What's the first part of the analogy? (Signal.) *A bird is to the sky.* Yes, a bird is to the sky. (Repeat until firm.)
5. The first part of the analogy told where you find an animal. So, the **next** part of the analogy must tell where you find another animal.
6. You told where you find a bird. Now you're going to tell about a whale. What animal? (Signal.) *A whale.* Where do you find a whale? (Signal.) *In the ocean.* Yes, in the ocean.
7. So, here's the second part of the analogy. A whale is to the ocean. What's the second part of the analogy? (Signal.) *A whale is to the ocean.* Yes, a whale is to the ocean.
8. (Repeat steps 2–7 until firm.)
9. Now we're going to say the whole analogy. First, we're going to tell where you find a **bird** and then we're going to tell where you find a **whale.** Say the analogy with me. (Signal. Respond with the students.) *A bird is to the sky as a whale is to the ocean.* (Repeat until the students are responding with you.)

10. All by yourselves. Say that analogy. (Signal.) *A bird is to the sky as a whale is to the ocean.* (Repeat until firm.)
11. That analogy tells **where you find those animals.** What does that analogy tell? (Signal.) *Where you find those animals.*
12. (Repeat steps 10 and 11 until firm.)

> **Individual test**
> Call on individuals to do step 10 or 11.

═══════ **EXERCISE 2** ═══════

● **CLASSIFICATION**
The next Thinking Operation is **Classification.**
1. Here's the rule. If a class has more **kinds** of things, it is bigger. Listen again. If a class has more **kinds** of things, it is bigger. Everybody, say the rule. (Signal.) *If a class has more kinds of things, it is bigger.* (Repeat until firm.)

> **Individual test**
> Call on individual students to say the rule.

2. The class of vehicles has more **kinds** of things than the class of cars. So, tell me which class is bigger. (Pause.) Get ready. (Signal.) *Vehicles.*
3. How do you know that the class of vehicles is bigger? (Signal.) *Because it has more kinds of things.* (Repeat step 3 until firm.)
4. (Repeat steps 2 and 3 until firm.)
5. The class of vehicles has more **kinds** of things than the class of motorcycles. So, which class is bigger? (Signal.) *Vehicles.*
6. How do you know that the class of vehicles is bigger? (Signal.) *Because it has more kinds of things.* (Repeat step 6 until firm.)
7. The class of vehicles has more **kinds** of things than the class of trucks. So, which class is bigger? (Signal.) *Vehicles.* How do you know that the class of vehicles is bigger? (Signal.) *Because it has more kinds of things.* (Repeat step 7 until firm.)

═══════ **EXERCISE 3** ═══════

DEDUCTIONS: With *some*
The next Thinking Operation is **Deductions.**
1. Listen. **Some** boys have curly hair. Butch is a boy. So (pause; signal), *maybe Butch has curly hair.* How do you know that maybe Butch has curly hair? (Signal.) *Because some boys have curly hair.* (Repeat step 1 until firm.)
2. Listen. **Some** boys have curly hair. Fred is a boy. So (pause; signal), *maybe Fred has curly hair.* How do you know that maybe Fred has curly hair? (Signal.) *Because some boys have curly hair.* (Repeat step 2 until firm.)
3. Listen. **Some** boys have curly hair. Sam is a boy. So (pause; signal), *maybe Sam has curly hair.* How do you know that maybe Sam has curly hair? (Signal.) *Because some boys have curly hair.* (Repeat step 3 until firm.)

═══════ **EXERCISE 4** ═══════

STATEMENT INFERENCE
The next Thinking Operation is **Statement Inference.**
1. Listen. If snakes stay in the hot sun, they may die. Say that statement. (Signal.) *If snakes stay in the hot sun, they may die.* (Repeat until firm.)

> **Individual test**
> Call on individuals to say the statement.

2. Everybody, listen. If snakes stay in the hot sun, they may die. What will happen if snakes stay in the hot sun? *(Signal.) They may die.*
   What will die if they stay in the hot sun? (Signal.) *Snakes.* Snakes will die if they stay in what? (Signal.) *The hot sun.* How may snakes die? (Signal.) *If they stay in the hot sun.*
   (Repeat step 2 until firm.)

> **Individual test**
> Call on individual students to answer a question from step 2.

EXERCISE 5

DEFINITIONS

The next Thinking Operation is **Definitions.**

1. **Ignore** means **pay no attention to.**

2. What does **ignore** mean? (Signal.) *Pay no attention to.*
   What word means **pay no attention to?** (Signal.) *Ignore.*
   (Repeat step 2 until firm.)

3. Listen. Ignore them and they will go away. Say that. (Signal.) *Ignore them and they will go away.*
   Now say that sentence with different words for **ignore.** (Pause.) Get ready. (Signal.) *Pay no attention to them and they will go away.* (Repeat until firm.)
   (Repeat step 3 until firm.)

4. Listen. Some people can ignore candy. Say that. (Signal.) *Some people can ignore candy.* (Repeat until firm.)
   Now say that sentence with different words for **ignore.** (Pause.) Get ready. (Signal.) *Some people can pay no attention to candy.* (Repeat until firm.)
   (Repeat step 4 until firm.)

5. Listen. They paid no attention to all their plants. Say that. (Signal.) *They paid no attention to all their plants.* (Repeat until firm.) Now say that sentence with a different word for **paid no attention to.** (Pause.) Get ready. (Signal.) *They ignored all their plants.* (Repeat until firm.)
   (Repeat step 5 until firm.)

EXERCISE 6

DEFINITIONS

1. A synonym for **skinny** is **thin.**

2. What's a synonym for **skinny?** (Signal.) *Thin.* And what's a synonym for **thin?** (Signal.) *Skinny.*
   (Repeat step 2 until firm.)

3. Listen. The skinny dog wagged its tail. Say that. (Signal.) *The skinny dog wagged its tail.* (Repeat until firm.)
   Now say that sentence with a synonym for **skinny.** (Pause.) Get ready. (Signal.) *The thin dog wagged its tail.* (Repeat until firm.)
   (Repeat step 3 until firm.)

4. Listen. I like thin books. Say that. (Signal.) *I like thin books.* (Repeat until firm.)
   Now say that sentence with a synonym for **thin.** (Pause.) Get ~~...~~ *I like skinny*

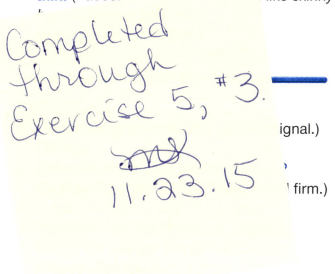

Completed through Exercise 5, #3. ~~...~~ 11.23.15

~~...~~ignal.)

~~...~~ firm.)

~~sen~~tence with different words for **modify** and **descends.** (Pause.) Get ready. (Signal.) *Change the way the elevator goes down.* (Repeat until firm.)
(Repeat step 2 until firm.)

EXERCISE 8

DESCRIPTION

The next Thinking Operation is **Description.**

1. I'm going to tell you about an object you know. But I'm going to call it a funny name. See if you can figure out what object I'm talking about.

2. (Hold up one finger.) A zork is a vehicle. Say that. (Signal.) *A zork is a vehicle.*
   (Hold up two fingers.) A zork goes in water. Say that. (Signal.) *A zork goes in water.*
   (Hold up three fingers.) You row a zork. Say that. (Signal.) *You row a zork.*

3. Everybody, say the three things you know about a zork. (Hold up one finger.) *A zork is a vehicle.* (Hold up two fingers.) *A zork goes in water.* (Hold up three fingers.) *You row a zork.* (Repeat until the students say the statements in order.)

4. Everybody, tell me the thing I am calling a zork. (Signal.) *A rowboat.* Yes, it's really a rowboat.

EXERCISE 9

BASIC EVIDENCE: Using Facts

The next Thinking Operation is **Basic Evidence.**

1. You're going to use two facts to explain things that happened. (Hold up one finger.) First fact. John hated to clean his room. Say it. (Signal.) *John hated to clean his room.* (Repeat until firm. Hold up two fingers.) Second fact. Fred was kind to his pets. Say it. (Signal.) *Fred was kind to his pets.* (Repeat until firm.)

2. Everybody, say those facts again. (Hold up one finger.) First fact. *John hated to clean his room.* (Hold up two fingers.) Second fact. *Fred was kind to his pets.* (Repeat until the students say the facts in order.)

> **Individual test**
> Call on individual students to say the facts.

3. Here's what happened: His mother was embarrassed when they had visitors. Tell me the fact that explains **why** that happened. (Pause.) Get ready. (Signal.) *John hated to clean his room.*

   To correct students who give the wrong fact:
   a. Does that fact explain **why** his mother was embarrassed when they had visitors? (Signal.) *No.*
   b. So, tell me the fact that explains **why** his mother was embarrassed when they had visitors.

4. Listen. First fact. John hated to clean his room. Second fact. Fred was kind to his pets.

5. Here's what happened. His dog followed him everywhere. Tell me the fact that explains **why** that happened. (Pause.) Get ready. (Signal.) *Fred was kind to his pets.*

6. Here's what happened. He spent part of his allowance for flea powder. Tell me the fact that explains **why** that happened. (Pause.) Get ready. (Signal.) *Fred was kind to his pets.*

7. Here's what happened. There was a pile of dusty CDs on his desk. Tell me the fact that explains **why** that happened. (Pause.) Get ready. (Signal.) *John hated to clean his room.*

8. (Repeat steps 5–7 until firm.)

EXERCISE 10

- **SAME: Review**

The next Thinking Operation is **Same.**

1. You're going to name at least twelve ways that a pen and a ruler are the same. Think about the **class** in which you find a pen and a ruler, what **material** they can be made of, and other ways a pen and a ruler are the same. (Pause 4 seconds.)

2. Name a way a pen and a ruler are the same. (Call on individual students. The students are not to repeat ways other students have named. For each new way named, make a tally mark on the board. Praise responses about object characteristics, parts, and so on.)

   To correct no response:
   a. Think of the class.
   b. Name a way they are the same.

   To correct general statements [*They are in the same class,*** for example]:**
   a. Yes, they are. But name that class. (Signal.) *Tools.*
   b. So, how are they the same? (Signal.) *They are tools.*

3. (After twelve ways have been named, say:) You named twelve ways. Does anybody know any more ways? (Call on individual students. Praise the group for naming more than twelve ways.)

Answer key   *They are tools, objects; take up space; are found in some place; can be made of plastic; can be blue; are found in drawers, desks, schools. You can hold them; and so on.*

Points

(Pass out the Workbooks.
Award points for Thinking Operations.)

WORKBOOK EXERCISES

We're going to do Workbooks now. Remember to follow my instructions carefully.

EXERCISE 11

TRUE—FALSE

1. Everybody, touch part A in your Workbook. ✔ Don't write anything. I'll say statements about the picture. You say **true, false,** or **maybe.** What are you going to say? (Signal.) *True, false, or maybe.*

2. Listen. The boat is in the water. (Pause 4 seconds.) Get ready. (Signal.) *True.*
   Now I'll say that same thing another way. The boat is not on the land. (Pause 4 seconds.) Get ready. (Signal.) *True.*
   (Repeat step 2 until firm.)

3. New statement. The person is not on the land. (Pause 4 seconds.) Get ready. (Signal.) *True.*
   Now I'll say that same thing another way. The person is in the boat. (Pause 4 seconds.) Get ready. (Signal.) *True.*
   (Repeat step 3 until firm.)

4. Let's do some more statements. Remember, if the statement is right, it is **true.** The boat is not on the shore. (Pause 4 seconds.) Get ready. (Signal.) *True.*
   The boat is not in the water. (Pause 4 seconds.) Get ready. (Signal.) *False.*
   The person is in the boat. (Pause 4 seconds.) Get ready. (Signal.) *True.*
   The person is not in the boat. (Pause 4 seconds.) Get ready. (Signal.) *False.*
   (Repeat step 4 until firm.)

5. Get ready to circle **true, false,** or **maybe** for each item. Item 1. The boat is not on the shore. Circle the answer for item 1. (Wait.)
   Item 2. The boat is not in the water. Circle the answer for item 2. (Wait.)
   Item 3. The person is in the boat. Circle the answer for item 3. (Wait.)
   Item 4. The person is not in the boat. Circle the answer for item 4. (Wait.)

6. Everybody, let's check your answers. Say **true, false,** or **maybe.**

7. Item 1. The boat is in the water. (Signal.) *True.*

8. (Repeat step 7 for items 2–4.)

Answer key 2. *False* 3. *True* 4. *False*

EXERCISE 12

DESCRIPTION

1. Everybody, touch part B in your Workbook. Figure out which chair I describe.

2. Item 1. This chair has arms. This chair has thick legs. This chair has a low back. Listen again. (Repeat the description.) Write the letter for item 1.

3. Item 2. This chair has thick legs. This chair has arms. This chair has a pillow on the seat. Listen again. (Repeat the description.) Write the letter for item 2.

4. Item 3. This chair has no arms. This chair has thin legs. This chair has a low back. Listen again. (Repeat the description.) Write the letter for item 3.

5. Let's check your answers. Mark any items you missed with an X.

6. Item 1. This chair has arms. This chair has thick legs. This chair has a low back. Everybody, what letter? (Signal.) *C.*

7. (Repeat step 6 for items 2 and 3.)

Answer key 2. *C* 3. *D*

EXERCISE 13

DESCRIPTION

1. Everybody, touch part C in your Workbook. Figure out which object I describe. Listen. A vilk is a tool. A vilk has a handle and bristles. A vilk is used to make hair look nice.
   Underline the object I'm calling a vilk. (Wait.)

2. Listen. Bidle is food. Bidle is part of a plant. Bidle is used mostly in salad.
   Circle the object I'm calling bidle. (Wait.)

3. Listen. A dib is furniture. A dib has four legs and a top. A dib is usually used to work on and to keep papers in.
   Cross out the object I'm calling a dib. (Wait.)

4. Everybody, get ready to check your work. Tell me the real name for the object that is a tool, that has a handle and bristles, and that is used to make hair look nice. Get ready. (Signal.) *Hairbrush.* And how did you mark the hairbrush? (Signal.) *Underlined it.*

5. Tell me the real name for the object that is food, that is part of a plant, and that is used mostly in salad. Get ready. (Signal.) *Lettuce.* And how did you mark the lettuce? (Signal.) *Circled it.*

6. Tell me the real name for the object that is furniture, that has four legs and a top, and that is usually used to work on and keep papers in. Get ready. (Signal.) *A desk.* And how did you mark the desk? (Signal.) *Crossed it out.*

EXERCISE 14

● **TRUE—FALSE**

1. Everybody, touch part D in your Workbook. I'll say statements about the picture.

2. Get ready to circle **true, false,** or **maybe.** Item 1. The dog is not looking at a cat. Circle the answer. (Wait.)

3. Item 2. The dog is not asleep. Circle the answer. (Wait.)

4. Item 3. The dog woke up when the cat meowed. Circle the answer. (Wait.)

5. Item 4. The dog is looking at the chair. Circle the answer. (Wait.)

6. Item 5. The dog is asleep. Circle the answer. (Wait.)

7. Item 6. The dog is listening to the cat purr. Circle the answer. (Wait.)

8. Everybody, let's check your answers. Say **true, false,** or **maybe.**

9. Item 1. The dog is not looking at the cat. (Signal.) *False.*

10. (Repeat step 9 for items 2–6.)

Points
(Award points for Workbooks.)

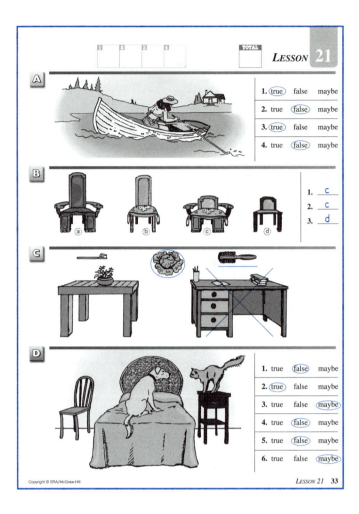

INFORMATION

We're going to work on Information now.

EXERCISE 15

● **MEMORIZATION: Concept Review**

1. Let's see if you remember some things from the poem you've learned.

2. Who spars and spars? (Signal.) *A boxer.*

3. What does a mechanic do? (Signal.) *Fixes cars.*

4. What does an astronomer do? (Signal.) *Looks at stars.*

5. Who has two bars on each shoulder? (Signal.) *A captain.*

6. Who looks at stars? (Signal.) *An astronomer.*

7. (Repeat steps 2–6 until firm.)

EXERCISE 16

● **INFORMATION: Animals**

Task A

1. You learned about five classes of animals that have a backbone. Everybody, name those five classes. (Signal.) *Mammals, reptiles, birds, fish, and amphibians.*

2. The last class that you learned about was amphibians. Name an amphibian. (Call on individual students. The group is to name at least three amphibians.)
   You learned two facts about **all amphibians.** Everybody, tell me those two facts. (Hold up one finger.) First fact. *All amphibians are born in the water but grow up on land.* (Hold up two fingers.) Second fact. *All amphibians are cold-blooded.* (Repeat until the students say the facts in order.)

3. Name a mammal. (Call on individual students.) The group is to name at least five mammals.
   You learned two facts about **all mammals.** Everybody, tell me those two facts. (Hold up one finger.) First fact. *All mammals have hair.* (Hold up two fingers.) Second fact. *All mammals are warm-blooded.* (Repeat until the students say the facts in order.)

4. Name a reptile. (Call on individual students. The group is to name at least four reptiles.)
   You learned two facts about **all reptiles.** Everybody, tell me those two facts. (Hold up one finger.) First fact. *All reptiles are cold-blooded.* (Hold up two fingers.) Second fact. *All reptiles are born on land.* (Repeat until the students say the facts in order.)

5. Name a bird. (Call on individual students. The group is to name at least five birds.)
   You learned two facts about **all birds.** Everybody, tell me those two facts. (Hold up one finger.) First fact. *All birds have feathers.* (Hold up two fingers.) Second fact. *All birds are warm-blooded.* (Repeat until the students say the facts in order.)

6. Name a fish. (Call on individual students. The group is to name at least five fish.)
   You learned two facts about **all fish.** Everybody, tell me those two facts.
   (Hold up one finger.) First fact. *All fish have gills.* (Hold up two fingers.) Second fact. *All fish are cold-blooded.* (Repeat until the students say the facts in order.)

Task B

1. Tell me what class **tortoises** are in. (Pause.) Get ready. (Signal.) *Reptiles.*
   So, tell me the two facts you know about **tortoises.** (Hold up one finger.) First fact. *Tortoises are cold-blooded.* (Hold up two fingers.) Second fact. *Tortoises are born on land.* (Repeat until the students say the facts in order.)

2. Tell me what class **newts** are in. (Pause.) Get ready. (Signal.) *Amphibians.*
   So, tell me the two facts you know about **newts.** (Hold up one finger.) First fact. *Newts are born in the water but grow up on land.* (Hold up two fingers.) Second fact. *Newts are cold-blooded.* (Repeat until the students say the facts in order.)

3. Tell me what class **ducks** are in. (Pause.) Get ready. (Signal.) *Birds.*
   So, tell me the two facts you know about **ducks.** (Hold up one finger.) First fact. *Ducks have feathers.* (Hold up two fingers.) Second fact. *Ducks are warm-blooded.* (Repeat until the students say the facts in order.)

4. Tell me what class **catfish** are in. (Pause.) Get ready. (Signal.) *Fish.*
   So, tell me the two facts you know about **catfish.** (Hold up one finger.) First fact. *Catfish have gills.* (Hold up two fingers.) Second fact. *Catfish are cold-blooded.* (Repeat until the students say the facts in order.)

5. Tell me what class **giraffes** are in. (Pause.) Get ready. (Signal.) *Mammals.*
   So, tell me the two facts you know about **giraffes.** (Hold up one finger.) First fact. *Giraffes have hair.* (Hold up two fingers.) Second fact. *Giraffes are warm-blooded.* (Repeat until the students say the facts in order.)

Individual test

Call on individual students to do one step from Task B.

═══════ **EXERCISE 17** ═══════

MEMORIZATION: Poem

1. Here's the poem we learned. Listen.

    A beautician fixes hair,
    A tailor can mend a tear,
    An exposition is a fair,
    And one plus one is a pair.

2. Say it with me. (Signal. Say the poem with the students. Repeat until the students are responding with you.)

3. All by yourselves. (Signal. The students say the poem. Repeat until firm.)

To correct:

a. (Stop the students as soon as you hear a mistake.)

b. (Say the line they missed.)

c. (Have them repeat the line they missed.)

d. (Repeat step 3.)

(Repeat until firm.)

Individual test

Call on individual students to say the whole poem.

Points

(Award points for Information.

Have the students add up their daily total.)

END OF LESSON 21

THINKING OPERATIONS

EXERCISE 1

DEFINITIONS

The first Thinking Operation today is **Definitions.**

1. **Feline** means **cat.**
2. What does **feline** mean? (Signal.) *Cat.*
   What word means **cat?** (Signal.) *Feline.*
   (Repeat step 2 until firm.)
3. Listen. Felines purr. Say that. (Signal.) *Felines purr.* (Repeat until firm.)
   Now say that sentence with a different word for **feline.** (Pause.) Get ready. (Signal.) *Cats purr.* (Repeat until firm.)
   (Repeat step 3 until firm.)
4. Listen. The cat is licking itself. Say that. (Signal.) *The cat is licking itself.* (Repeat until firm.)
   Now say that sentence with a different word for **cat.** (Pause.) Get ready. (Signal.) *The feline is licking itself.* (Repeat until firm.)
   (Repeat step 4 until firm.)
5. Listen. Felines like to eat fish. Say that. (Signal.) *Felines like to eat fish.* (Repeat until firm.)
   Now say that sentence with a different word for **felines.** (Pause.) Get ready. (Signal.) *Cats like to eat fish.* (Repeat until firm.)
   (Repeat step 5 until firm.)

EXERCISE 2

DEFINITIONS

1. **Ignore.** (Pause.) What does **ignore** mean? (Signal.) *Pay no attention to.*
   What word means **pay no attention to?** (Signal.) *Ignore.*
   (Repeat step 1 until firm.)
2. Listen. Ignore the television when it's on. Say that. (Signal.) *Ignore the television when it's on.* (Repeat until firm.)
   Now say that sentence with different words for **ignore.** (Pause.) Get ready. (Signal.) *Pay no attention to the television when it's on.* (Repeat until firm.)
   (Repeat step 2 until firm.)

3. **Skinny.** (Pause.) What's a synonym for **skinny?** (Signal.) *Thin.* And what's a synonym for **thin?** (Signal.) *Skinny.* (Repeat step 3 until firm.)
4. Listen. The skinny dog could run fast. Say that. (Signal.) *The skinny dog could run fast.* (Repeat until firm.)
   Now say that sentence with a synonym for **skinny.** (Pause.) Get ready. (Signal.) *The thin dog could run fast.* (Repeat until firm.)
   (Repeat step 4 until firm.)
5. **Modify.** (Pause.) What's a synonym for **modify?** (Signal.) *Change.*
   And what's a synonym for **change?** (Signal.) *Modify.*
   (Repeat step 5 until firm.)
6. Listen. We may learn how to change the weather. Say that. (Signal.) *We may learn how to change the weather.* (Repeat until firm.)
   Now say that sentence with a synonym for **change.** (Pause.) Get ready. (Signal.) *We may learn how to modify the weather.* (Repeat until firm.)
   (Repeat step 6 until firm.)

EXERCISE 3

ANALOGIES

The next Thinking Operation is **Analogies.**

Task A

1. We're going to make up an **analogy** that tells **what sounds animals make.** What is the analogy going to tell? (Signal.) *What sounds animals make.* (Repeat until firm.)
2. The animals we're going to use in the analogy are a cat and a dog. Which animals? (Signal.) *A cat and a dog.*
3. Name the first animal. (Signal.) *A cat.* Yes, a cat. What sound does that animal make? (Signal.) *It meows.* Yes, it meows.
4. So, here's the first part of the analogy. A cat is to meowing. What's the first part of the analogy? (Signal.) *A cat is to meowing.* Yes, a cat is to meowing. (Repeat until firm.)

5. The first part of the analogy told what sound an animal makes. So, the **next** part of the analogy must tell what sound another animal makes.

6. You told what sound a cat makes. Now you're going to tell about a dog. What animal? (Signal.) *A dog.* What sound does that animal make? (Signal.) *It barks.* Yes, it barks.

7. So, here's the second part of the analogy. A dog is to barking. What's the second part of the analogy? (Signal.) *A dog is to barking.* Yes, a dog is to barking.

8. (Repeat steps 2–7 until firm.)

9. Now we're going to say the whole analogy. First, we're going to tell what sound a **cat** makes and then we're going to tell what sound a **dog** makes. Say the analogy with me. (Signal. Respond with the students.) *A cat is to meowing as a dog is to barking.* (Repeat until the students are responding with you.)

10. All by yourselves. Say that analogy. (Signal.) *A cat is to meowing as a dog is to barking.* (Repeat until firm.)

11. That analogy tells **what sound those animals make.** What does that analogy tell? (Signal.) *What sound those animals make.*

12. (Repeat steps 10 and 11 until firm.)

Individual test
Call on individual students to do step 10 or 11.

Task B

1. We're going to make up an **analogy** that tells **what material objects are made of.** What is the analogy going to tell? (Signal.) *What material objects are made of.* (Repeat until firm.)

2. The objects we're going to use in the analogy are a shirt and a car. Which objects? (Signal.) *A shirt and a car.*

3. Name the first object. (Signal.) *A shirt.* Yes, a shirt. What material is that object made of? (Signal.) *Cloth.* Yes, cloth.

4. So, here's the first part of the analogy. A shirt is to cloth. What's the first part of the analogy? (Signal.) *A shirt is to cloth.* Yes, a shirt is to cloth. (Repeat until firm.)

5. The first part of the analogy told what material an object is made of. So, the **next** part of the analogy must tell what material another object is made of.

6. You told what material a shirt is made of. Now you're going to tell about a car. What object? (Signal.) *A car.*
What material is that object made of? (Signal.) *Metal.* Yes, metal.

7. So, here's the second part of the analogy. A car is to metal. What's the second part of the analogy? (Signal.) *A car is to metal.* Yes, a car is to metal.

8. (Repeat steps 2–7 until firm.)

9. Now we're going to say the whole analogy. First, we're going to tell what material a **shirt** is made of and then we're going to tell what material a **car** is made of. Say the analogy with me. (Signal. Respond with the students.) *A shirt is to cloth as a car is to metal.* (Repeat until the students are responding with you.)

10. All by yourselves. Say that analogy. (Signal.) *A shirt is to cloth as a car is to metal.* (Repeat until firm.)

11. That analogy tells **what material those objects are made of.** What does that analogy tell? (Signal.) *What material those objects are made of.*

12. (Repeat steps 10 and 11 until firm.)

Individual test
Call on individual students to do step 10 or 11.

Task C

1. We're going to make up an **analogy** that tells **where you find objects.** What is the analogy going to tell? (Signal.) *Where you find objects.* (Repeat until firm.)

2. The objects we're going to use are a couch and a bed. Which objects? (Signal.) *A couch and a bed.*

3. Name the first object. (Signal.) *A couch.* Yes, a couch. Where do you find that object? (Signal.) *In the living room.* Yes, in the living room.

4. So, here's the first part of our analogy. A couch is to the living room.
What's the first part of the analogy? (Signal.) *A couch is to the living room.* Yes, a couch is to the living room. (Repeat until firm.)

5. The first part of the analogy told where you find an object. So, the **next** part of the analogy must tell where you find another object.

6. You told where you find a couch. Now you're going to tell about a bed. Which object? (Signal.) *A bed.* Where do you find a bed? (Signal.) *In the bedroom.* Yes, in the bedroom.

7. So, here's the second part of the analogy. A bed is to the bedroom. What's the second part of the analogy? (Signal.) *A bed is to the bedroom.* Yes, a bed is to the bedroom.

8. (Repeat steps 2–7 until firm.)

9. Now we're going to say the whole analogy. First, we're going to tell where you find a couch and then we're going to tell where you find a bed. Say the analogy with me. (Signal. Respond with the students.) *A couch is to the living room as a bed is to the bedroom.* (Repeat until the students are responding with you.)

10. All by yourselves. Say that analogy. (Signal.) *A couch is to the living room as a bed is to the bedroom.* (Repeat until firm.)

11. That analogy tells **where you find those objects.** What does that analogy tell? (Signal.) *Where you find those objects.*

12. (Repeat steps 10 and 11 until firm.)

Individual test
Call on individual students to do step 10 or 11.

═══════ **EXERCISE 4** ═══════

CLASSIFICATION
The next Thinking Operation is **Classification.**

1. Here's the rule. If a class has more **kinds** of things, it is bigger. Listen again. If a class has more **kinds** of things, it is bigger. Everybody, say the rule.
(Signal.) *If a class has more kinds of things, it is bigger.* (Repeat until firm.)

Individual test
Call on individual students to say the rule.

---

2. The class of containers has more **kinds** of things than the class of cups. So, tell me which class is bigger. (Pause.) Get ready. (Signal.) *Containers.*

3. How do you know that the class of containers is bigger? (Signal.) *Because it has more kinds of things.*
(Repeat step 3 until firm.)

4. (Repeat steps 2 and 3 until firm.)

5. The class of containers has more **kinds** of things than the class of boxes. So, which class is bigger? (Signal.) *Containers.*

6. How do you know that the class of containers is bigger? (Signal.) *Because it has more kinds of things.*
(Repeat step 6 until firm.)

7. The class of containers has more **kinds** of things than the class of purses. So, which class is bigger? (Signal.) *Containers.* How do you know that the class of containers is bigger? (Signal.) *Because it has more kinds of things.*
(Repeat step 7 until firm.)

═══════ **EXERCISE 5** ═══════

● **DEDUCTIONS: With *every***
The next Thinking Operation is **Deductions.**

1. Listen to this rule. Every fish is cold-blooded. Say the rule. (Signal.) *Every fish is cold-blooded.*

2. A pike is a **fish.** What does the rule let you know about a pike? (Signal.) *A pike is cold-blooded.* How do you know that a pike is cold-blooded? (Signal.) *Because every fish is cold-blooded.*

3. Listen. Every fish is cold-blooded. A panther is a **cat.** What does the rule let you know about a panther? (Signal.) *Nothing.*

4. Listen. Every fish is cold-blooded. A collie is a **dog.** What does the rule let you know about a collie? (Signal.) *Nothing.*

5. Listen. Every fish is cold-blooded. A trout is a **fish.** What does the rule let you know about a trout? (Signal.) *A trout is cold-blooded.*

6. Listen. Every fish is cold-blooded. A starling is a **bird.** What does the rule let you know about a starling? (Signal.) *Nothing.*

7. Listen. Every fish is cold-blooded. A guppy is a **fish.** What does the rule let you know about a guppy? (Signal.) *A guppy is cold-blooded.* How do you know that a guppy is cold-blooded? (Signal.) *Because every fish is cold-blooded.*

8. (Repeat steps 2–7 until firm.)

━━━━━━━━━ **EXERCISE 6** ━━━━━━━━━

DESCRIPTION

The next Thinking Operation is **Description.**

1. I'm going to tell you about an object you know. But I'm going to call it a funny name. See if you can figure out what object I'm talking about.

2. (Hold up one finger.) Ling is a food. Say that. (Signal.) *Ling is a food.*
   (Hold up two fingers.) Ling is made from peanuts. Say that. (Signal.) *Ling is made from peanuts.*
   (Hold up three fingers.) You make sandwiches with ling. Say that. (Signal.) *You make sandwiches with ling.*

3. Everybody, say the three things you know about ling. (Hold up one finger.) *Ling is a food.* (Hold up two fingers.) *Ling is made from peanuts.* (Hold up three fingers.) *You make sandwiches with ling.* (Repeat until the students say the statements in order.)

4. Everybody, tell me the thing I am calling ling. (Signal.) *Peanut butter.* Yes, it's really peanut butter.

━━━━━━━━━ **EXERCISE 7** ━━━━━━━━━

BASIC EVIDENCE: Using Facts

The next Thinking Operation is **Basic Evidence.**

1. You're going to use two facts to explain things that happened. (Hold up one finger.) First fact. There were many chickens on the farm. Say it. (Signal.) *There were many chickens on the farm.* (Repeat until firm.) (Hold up two fingers.) Second fact. There were no trees on the farm. Say it. (Signal.) *There were no trees on the farm.* (Repeat until firm.)

2. Everybody, say those facts again. (Hold up one finger.) First fact. *There were many chickens on the farm.* (Hold up two fingers.) Second fact. *There were no trees on the farm.* (Repeat until the students say the facts in order.)

> **Individual test**
> Call on individual students to say the facts.

3. Here's what happened. They always had eggs for breakfast. Tell me the fact that explains **why** that happened. (Pause.) Get ready. (Signal.) *There were many chickens on the farm.*

   To correct students who give the wrong fact:
   a. Does that fact explain **why** they always had eggs for breakfast? (Signal.) *No.*
   b. So, tell me the fact that explains **why** they always had eggs for breakfast.

4. Listen. First fact. There were many chickens on the farm. Second fact. There were no trees on the farm.

5. Here's what happened. The farmer had to buy wood for the fireplace. Tell me the fact that explains **why** that happened. (Pause.) Get ready. (Signal.) *There were no trees on the farm.*

6. Here's what happened. Jim had a drumstick for lunch every day. Tell me the fact that explains **why** that happened. (Pause.) Get ready. (Signal.) *There were many chickens on the farm.*

7. Here's what happened. It was hard to find a shady place for a picnic. Tell me the fact that explains **why** that happened. (Pause.) Get ready. (Signal.) *There were no trees on the farm.*

8. (Repeat steps 5–7 until firm.)

═══════════ **EXERCISE 8** ═══════════

STATEMENT INFERENCE

The next Thinking Operation is **Statement Inference.**

1. Listen. If people were fish, they could breathe underwater. Say that statement. (Signal.) *If people were fish, they could breathe underwater.* (Repeat until firm.)

Individual test
Call on a few individual students to say the statement.

---

2. Everybody, listen. If people were fish, they could breathe underwater. Who could breathe underwater if they were fish? (Signal.) *People.*
What could people do if they were fish? (Signal.) *Breathe underwater.*
Where could people breathe if they were fish? (Signal.) *Underwater.*
What could people do underwater if they were fish? (Signal.) *Breathe.*
What would people have to be to breathe underwater? (Signal.) *Fish.*
(Repeat step 2 until firm.)

Individual test
Call on individual students to answer a question from step 2.

═══════════ **EXERCISE 9** ═══════════

SAME: Review

The next Thinking Operation is **Same.**

1. You're going to name at least twelve ways that a desk and a table are the same. Think about their **parts,** where you **find** a desk and a table, what **material** they can be made of, and other ways a desk and a table are the same. (Pause 4 seconds.)

2. Name a way a desk and a table are the same. (Call on individual students. The students are not to repeat ways other students have named. For each new way named, make a tally mark on the board. Praise responses about object characteristics, parts, and so on.)
   To correct no response:
   a. Think of the class.
   b. Name a way they are the same.
   To correct general statements [*They are in the same class,* **for example]:**
   a. Yes, they are. But name that class. (Signal.) *Furniture.*
   b. So, how are they the same? (Signal.) *They are furniture.*

3. (After twelve ways have been named, say:) You named twelve ways. Does anybody know any more ways? (Call on individual students. Praise the group for naming more than twelve ways.)

Answer key *They are furniture, objects; take up space; are found in some place; can be made of wood; can be brown; can be used to write at; can be used to eat at; can be used to sit on; are found in stores, houses, schools; have legs and a top; and so on.*

Points
(Pass out the Workbooks. Award points for Thinking Operations.)

WORKBOOK
EXERCISES

We're going to do Workbooks now. Remember to follow my instructions carefully.

EXERCISE 10

DESCRIPTION

1. Everybody, touch part A in your Workbook. ✔ Figure out which object I describe. Listen. A glip is made of cloth. You use a glip to keep warm. You wear a glip. **Put an A on** the object I'm calling a glip. (Wait.)

2. Listen. A zom is a vehicle. A zom holds many people. A zom travels in the air. **Put a B on** the object I'm calling a zom. (Wait.)

3. Listen. A siv is part of a vehicle. A siv is round. There are four sivs on a car. **Put a C on** the object I'm calling a siv. (Wait.)

4. Everybody, get ready to check your work. Tell me the real name of the object that is made of cloth, that you use to keep warm, and that you wear. Get ready. (Signal.) *A coat.* And how did you mark the coat? (Signal.) *Put an A on it.*

5. Tell me the real name of the object that is a vehicle, that holds many people, and that travels in the air. Get ready. (Signal.) *An airplane.* And how did you mark the airplane? (Signal.) *Put a B on it.*

6. Tell me the real name for the object that is part of a vehicle, that is round, and that there are four of on a car. Get ready. (Signal.) *A tire.* And how did you mark the tire? (Signal.) *Put a C on it.*

EXERCISE 11

TRUE—FALSE

Task A

1. Everybody, touch part B in your Workbook. ✔ I'll say statements about the picture.

2. Get ready to circle **true, false,** or **maybe.** Item 1. It is sunny. Circle the answer. (Wait.)

3. Item 2. It is not sunny. Circle the answer. (Wait.)

4. Item 3. The tree does not make a shadow. Circle the answer. (Wait.)

5. Item 4. The tree does make a shadow. Circle the answer. (Wait.)

6. Item 5. The tent is by the water. Circle the answer. (Wait.)

7. Item 6. There is a man inside the tent. Circle the answer. (Wait.)

8. Everybody, let's check your answers. Say **true, false,** or **maybe.**

9. Item 1. The sun is out. (Signal.) *True.*

10. (Repeat step 9 for items 2–6.)

Task B

1. Everybody, touch part C in your Workbook. ✔ I'll say statements about the picture.

2. Get ready to circle **true, false,** or **maybe.** Item 1. The man does not like to sweep. Circle the answer. (Wait.)

3. Item 2. The man is not sitting. Circle the answer. (Wait.)

4. Item 3. The man is sweeping. Circle the answer. (Wait.)

5. Item 4. The man is getting paid to sweep. Circle the answer. (Wait.)

6. Item 5. The man is sitting. Circle the answer. (Wait.)

7. Item 6. The man likes to watch TV. Circle the answer. (Wait.)

8. Item 7. The man is holding a tool. Circle the answer. (Wait.)

9. Everybody, let's check your answers. Say **true, false,** or **maybe.**

10. Item 1. The man does not like to sweep. (Signal.) *Maybe.*

11. (Repeat step 10 for items 2–7.)

EXERCISE 12

TRUE—FALSE

1. Everybody, touch part D in your Workbook. ✔ I'll say statements that are true of one of the pictures. You write the letter of the right picture.

2. Item 1. **All** the animals are mammals. Write the letter of the picture on line 1. (Wait.)

3. Item 2. **Only some** of the animals are reptiles. Write the letter of the picture on line 2. (Wait.)

4. Item 3. **None** of the animals are mammals. Write the letter of the picture on line 3. (Wait.)

5. Item 4. **All** the animals are reptiles. Write the letter of the picture on line 4. (Wait.)

6. Let's check your answers. Mark any items you missed with an X. Tell me the letter of the right picture.

7. Item 1. **All** the animals are mammals. (Signal.) *C.*

8. (Repeat step 7 for items 2–4.)

Points

(Award points for Workbooks.)

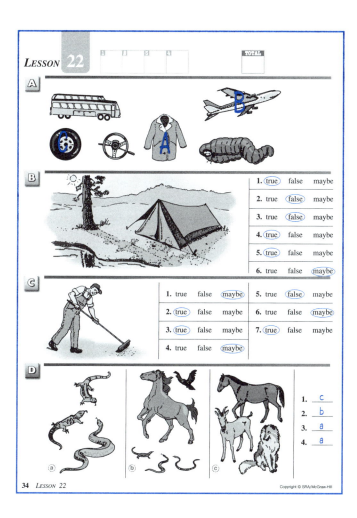

INFORMATION

EXERCISE 13

● **SPECIAL INFORMATION**

We're going to work on Information now.

1. What's a synonym for **cat?** (Signal.) *Feline.* Yes, all members of the cat family are called felines.

2. Lions are felines. Leopards are felines. Cougars and house cats are felines.

3. Your turn. See if you can name six felines. Name one feline. (Call on individual students. The students may name felines from step 2. The group is to name at least six felines.)

EXERCISE 14

CALENDAR: Months in a Year

1. I'll name some months of the year. When I stop, you name the rest of the months.

2. My turn. January, February, March, April (pause; signal), *May, June, July, August, September, October, November, December.* (Repeat step 2 until firm.)
Here's another one.

3. My turn. January, February, March, April, May, June, July (pause; signal), *August, September, October, November, December.* (Repeat step 3 until firm.)

Individual test

(Call on individual students to do one of the following tasks:)

   a. How many months are in a year?

   b. Name the months of the year.

   c. Name the rest of the months.
    (Repeat step 2 or step 3.)

EXERCISE 15

● **MEMORIZATION: Poem**

Say that poem we learned about the beautician and the tailor. Get ready. (Signal.)

> A beautician fixes hair,
> A tailor can mend a tear,
> An exposition is a fair,
> And one plus one is a pair.

(Repeat until firm.)

Individual test
Call on individuals to say the whole poem.

EXERCISE 16

INFORMATION: Animals

Task A

1. See if you can figure out the class of animals I'm thinking of. I'm thinking of animals that are warm-blooded and have hair. (Pause 3 seconds.) What class of animals am I thinking of? (Signal.) *Mammals.*

2. Yes, I told you: they are warm-blooded; they have hair. Tell me the words I said that let you know I wasn't thinking of birds. (Pause 3 seconds.) Get ready. (Signal.) *They have hair.* (Repeat step 2 until firm.)

3. Name an animal in the class of mammals. (Call on individual students.) The group is to name at least five mammals.

4. Now I'm thinking of animals that are cold-blooded and have gills. (Pause 3 seconds.) Everybody, what class of animals am I thinking of? (Signal.) *Fish.*

5. Yes, I told you: they are cold-blooded; they have gills. Tell me the words I said that let you know I wasn't thinking about reptiles. (Pause 3 seconds.) Get ready. (Signal.) *They have gills.* (Repeat step 5 until firm.)

6. Name an animal in the class of fish. (Call on individual students.) The group is to name at least five fish.

Task B

1. Now I'm thinking of an animal that is warm-blooded and has hair. Tell me if I could be thinking of an alligator. (Pause.) Get ready. (Signal.) *No.* Right.

2. I told you: it is warm-blooded; it has hair. Tell me the words I said that let you know I wasn't thinking of an alligator. (Pause 3 seconds.) Get ready. (Signal.) *It is warm-blooded. It has hair.* (Repeat step 2 until firm.)

3. Here are the facts again. The animal is warm-blooded and has hair. Tell me if I could be thinking of a beaver. (Pause.) Get ready. (Signal.) *Yes.* Tell me what class beavers are in. (Pause.) Get ready. (Signal.) *Mammals.*

4. Tell me the two facts you know about **all mammals.** (Hold up one finger.) First fact. *All mammals have hair.* (Hold up two fingers.) Second fact. *All mammals are warm-blooded.* (Repeat until the students say the facts in order.)
   So, if I'm thinking of an animal that is warm-blooded and has hair, I could be thinking of a beaver.

5. Now I'm thinking of an animal that is warm-blooded and has feathers. Tell me if I could be thinking of an eagle. (Pause.) Get ready. (Signal.) *Yes.* Tell me what class eagles are in. (Pause.) Get ready. (Signal.) *Birds.*

6. Tell me the two facts you know about **all birds.** (Hold up one finger.) First fact. *All birds have feathers.* (Hold up two fingers.) Second fact. *All birds are warm-blooded.* (Repeat until the students say the facts in order.)
   So, if I'm thinking of an animal that is warm-blooded and has feathers, I could be thinking of an eagle.

7. Here are the facts again. The animal is warm-blooded and has feathers. Tell me if I could be thinking of a frog. (Pause.) Get ready. (Signal.) *No.* Right.

8. I told you: it is warm-blooded; it has feathers. Tell me the words I said that let you know I wasn't thinking of a frog. (Pause 3 seconds.) Get ready. (Signal.) *It is warm-blooded. It has feathers.*
   (Repeat step 8 until firm.)

Points

(Award points for Information.
Have the students add up their daily total.)

END OF LESSON 22

THINKING OPERATIONS

EXERCISE 1

CLASSIFICATION

The first Thinking Operation today is **Classification.**

1. Here's the rule. If a class has more **kinds** of things, it is bigger. Listen again. If a class has more **kinds** of things, it is bigger. Everybody, say the rule. (Signal.) *If a class has more kinds of things, it is bigger.* (Repeat until firm.)

> **Individual test**
> Call on individual students to say the rule.

2. The class of buildings has more **kinds** of things than the class of houses. So, tell me which class is bigger. (Pause.) Get ready. (Signal.) *Buildings.*
3. How do you know that the class of buildings is bigger? (Signal.) *Because it has more kinds of things.* (Repeat step 3 until firm.)
4. (Repeat steps 2 and 3 until firm.)
5. The class of buildings has more **kinds** of things than the class of factories. So, which class is bigger? (Signal.) *Buildings.*
6. How do you know that the class of buildings is bigger? (Signal.) *Because it has more kinds of things.* (Repeat step 6 until firm.)
7. The class of buildings has more **kinds** of things than the class of schools. So, which class is bigger? (Signal.) *Buildings.* How do you know that the class of buildings is bigger? (Signal.) *Because it has more kinds of things.* (Repeat step 7 until firm.)

EXERCISE 2

STATEMENT INFERENCE

The next Thinking Operation is **Statement Inference.**

1. Listen. The feline ignored the screeching birds. Say that statement. (Signal.) *The feline ignored the screeching birds.* (Repeat until firm.)

> **Individual test**
> Call on individuals to say the statement.

2. Everybody, listen. The feline ignored the screeching birds. What kind of birds did the feline ignore? (Signal.) *Screeching.* What ignored the screeching birds? (Signal.) *The feline.* What kind of feline ignored the screeching birds? (Signal.) *I don't know.* What did the feline ignore? (Signal.) *The screeching birds.* (Repeat step 2 until firm.)

> **Individual test**
> Call on individual students to answer a question from step 2.

EXERCISE 3

DEDUCTIONS: With *all* and *every*

The next Thinking Operation is **Deductions.**

1. I'll say rules with **all** and **every.** You say them the other way. What two words are we going to use? (Hold up one finger.) *All.* (Hold up two fingers.) *Every.*
2. Listen. **All** axes are made to cut wood. Say that. (Signal.) *All axes are made to cut wood.* Now say it the other way. Get ready. (Signal.) *Every ax is made to cut wood.* (Repeat step 2 until firm.)
3. Here's a new rule. **Every** animal needs water. Say that. (Signal.) *Every animal needs water.* Now say it the other way. Get ready. (Signal.) *All animals need water.* (Repeat step 3 until firm.)
4. Here's a new rule. **All** fish are cold-blooded. Say that. (Signal.) *All fish are cold-blooded.* Now say it the other way. Get ready. (Signal.) *Every fish is cold-blooded.* (Repeat step 4 until firm.)
5. Here's a new rule. **Every** cat is a feline. Say that. (Signal.) *Every cat is a feline.* Now say it the other way. Get ready. (Signal.) *All cats are felines.* (Repeat step 5 until firm.)

LESSON 23

EXERCISE 4

- **DEDUCTIONS: With *all***

1. Listen to this rule. All insects have six legs. Say the rule. (Signal.) *All insects have six legs.*

2. An ant is an **insect.** What does the rule let you know about an ant? (Signal.) *An ant has six legs.* How do you know that an ant has six legs? (Signal.) *Because all insects have six legs.*

3. Listen. All insects have six legs. A rhinoceros is a **mammal.** What does the rule let you know about a rhinoceros? (Signal.) *Nothing.*

4. Listen. All insects have six legs. A wasp is an **insect.** What does the rule let you know about a wasp? (Signal.) *A wasp has six legs.* How do you know that a wasp has six legs? (Signal.) *Because all insects have six legs.*

5. Listen. All insects have six legs. A catfish is a **fish.** What does the rule let you know about a catfish? (Signal.) *Nothing.*

6. Listen. All insects have six legs. A bee is an **insect.** What does the rule let you know about a bee? (Signal.) *A bee has six legs.* How do you know that a bee has six legs? (Signal.) *Because all insects have six legs.*

7. Listen. All insects have six legs. A bush is a **plant.** What does the rule let you know about a bush? (Signal.) *Nothing.*

8. (Repeat steps 2–7 until firm.)

EXERCISE 5

DEFINITIONS

The next Thinking Operation is **Definitions.**

1. **Feline** means **cat.**

2. What does **feline** mean? (Signal.) *Cat.* What word means **cat?** (Signal.) *Feline.* (Repeat step 2 until firm.)

3. Listen. That cat is chasing a mouse. Say that. (Signal.) *That cat is chasing a mouse.* (Repeat until firm.)
   Now say that sentence with a different word for **cat.** (Pause.) Get ready. (Signal.) *That feline is chasing a mouse.* (Repeat until firm.)
   (Repeat step 3 until firm.)

4. Listen. My feline sleeps on my dad's chair. Say that. (Signal.) *My feline sleeps on my dad's chair.* (Repeat until firm.)
   Now say that sentence with a different word for **feline.** (Pause.) Get ready. (Signal.) *My cat sleeps on my dad's chair.* (Repeat until firm.)
   (Repeat step 4 until firm.)

5. Listen. She walks like a feline. Say that. (Signal.) *She walks like a feline.* (Repeat until firm.)
   Now say that sentence with a different word for **feline.** (Pause.) Get ready. (Signal.) *She walks like a cat.* (Repeat until firm.)
   (Repeat step 5 until firm.)

EXERCISE 6

DEFINITIONS

1. A synonym for **big** is **large.**

2. What's a synonym for **big?** (Signal.) *Large.* And what's a synonym for **large?** (Signal.) *Big.* (Repeat step 2 until firm.)

3. Listen. The building is large. Say that. (Signal.) *The building is large.* (Repeat until firm.)
   Now say that sentence with a synonym for **large.** (Pause.) Get ready. (Signal.) *The building is big.* (Repeat until firm.)
   (Repeat step 3 until firm.)

4. Listen. My class is big. Say that. (Signal.) *My class is big.* (Repeat until firm.)
   Now say that sentence with a synonym for **big.** (Pause.) Get ready. (Signal.) *My class is large.* (Repeat until firm.)
   (Repeat step 4 until firm.)

EXERCISE 7

DEFINITIONS

1. **Leap.** What does **leap** mean? (Signal.) *Jump.*
   Skinny. What does **skinny** mean? (Signal.) *Thin.*
   (Repeat step 1 until firm.)

2. Listen. The skinny horse leaped over the fence. Say that sentence. (Signal.) *The skinny horse leaped over the fence.* (Repeat until firm.)

Now say that sentence with different words for **skinny** and **leaped.** (Pause.) Get ready. (Signal.) *The thin horse jumped over the fence.* (Repeat until firm.)
(Repeat step 2 until firm.)

━━━━━━━━ **EXERCISE 8** ━━━━━━━━

● **CLASSIFICATION**

The next Thinking Operation is **Classification.**

Task A

1. What's the rule for figuring out which class of things is bigger? (Signal.) *If a class has more kinds of things, it is bigger.* (Repeat until firm.) Yes, the bigger class has more **kinds** of things in it.
2. Let's figure out whether the class of animals is bigger than the class of mammals. If you took all the mammals from the class of animals, tell me if there would be some kinds of animals left. (Pause 2 seconds.) Get ready. (Signal.) *Yes.*
3. (Call on individual students.) Name one **kind** of animal that would be left. (Praise correct responses; for example, fish, reptiles, birds.)
4. Everybody, if you took all the mammals from the class of animals, there would still be some kinds of animals left. But if you took all the **mammals** from the class of **mammals,** what would be left? (Signal.) *Nothing.* Yes, there would be nothing left.
5. So, which class has more **kinds** of things, the class of animals or the class of mammals? (Signal.) *The class of animals.* So, which class is bigger? (Signal.) *The class of animals.* How do you know that the class of animals is bigger? (Signal.) *Because it has more kinds of things.*
6. (Repeat steps 4 and 5 until firm.)

Task B

1. Let's figure out whether the class of animals is bigger than the class of reptiles. If you took all the reptiles from the class of animals, tell me if there would be some kinds of animals left. (Pause 2 seconds.) Get ready. (Signal.) *Yes.*

2. (Call on individual students). Name one kind of animal that would be left. (Praise correct responses; for example, mammals, birds, amphibians.)
3. Everybody, if you took all the reptiles from the class of animals, there would still be some kinds of animals left. But if you took all the **reptiles** from the class of **reptiles,** what would be left? (Signal.) *Nothing.* Yes, there would be nothing left.
4. So, which class has more **kinds** of things, the class of animals or the class of reptiles? (Signal.) *The class of animals.* So, which class is bigger? (Signal.) *The class of animals.* How do you know that the class of animals is bigger? (Signal.) *Because it has more kinds of things.*
5. (Repeat steps 3 and 4 until firm.)

Task C

1. Let's figure out whether the class of animals is bigger than the class of birds. If you took all the birds from the class of animals, tell me if there would be some kinds of animals left. (Pause 2 seconds.) Get ready. (Signal.) *Yes.*
2. (Call on individual students.) Name one kind of animal that would be left. (Praise correct responses; for example, fish, reptiles, mammals.)
3. Everybody, if you took all the birds from the class of animals, there would still be some kinds of animals left. But if you took all the **birds** from the class of **birds,** what would be left? (Signal.) *Nothing.* Yes, there would be nothing left.
4. So, which class has more **kinds** of things, the class of animals or the class of birds? (Signal.) *The class of animals.* So, which class is bigger? (Signal.) *The class of animals.* How do you know that the class of animals is bigger? (Signal.) *Because it has more kinds of things.*
5. (Repeat steps 3 and 4 until firm.)

EXERCISE 9

SAME: Review

The next Thinking Operation is **Same.**

1. You're going to name at least twelve ways that a moth and a parrot are the same. Think about what they **do,** their **class,** what **body parts** they have, and other ways a moth and a parrot are the same. (Pause 4 seconds.)

2. Name a way a moth and a parrot are the same. (Call on individual students. The students are not to repeat ways other students have named. For each new way named, make a tally mark on the board. Praise responses about object characteristics, parts, and so on.)

   To correct no response:
   a. Think of the class.
   b. Name a way they are the same.

   To correct general statements [*They are in the same class,* **for example]:**
   a. Yes, they are. But name that class. (Signal.) *Animals.*
   b. So, how are they the same? (Signal.) *They are animals.*

3. (After twelve ways have been named, say:) You named twelve ways. Does anybody know any more ways? (Call on individual students. Praise the group for naming more than twelve ways.)

Answer key   *They are animals; have wings, a head, legs. They fly; breathe; eat; are found in houses and in the air. They are objects; take up space; are found in some place; and so on.*

EXERCISE 10

BASIC EVIDENCE: Using Facts

The next Thinking Operation is **Basic Evidence.**

1. You're going to use two facts to explain things that happened. (Hold up one finger.) First fact. He couldn't shoot his bow and arrow very well. Say it. (Signal.) *He couldn't shoot his bow and arrow very well.* (Repeat until firm.)
   (Hold up two fingers.) Second fact. The train was never on time. Say it. (Signal.) *The train was never on time.* (Repeat until firm.)

2. Everybody, say those facts again. (Hold up one finger.) First fact. *He couldn't shoot his bow and arrow very well.* (Hold up two fingers.) Second fact. *The train was never on time.* (Repeat until the students say the facts in order.)

Individual test

Call on individual students to say the facts.

---

3. Here's what happened. He used his rifle for hunting. Tell me the fact that explains **why** that happened. (Pause.) Get ready. (Signal.) *He couldn't shoot his bow and arrow very well.*

4. Listen. First fact. He couldn't shoot his bow and arrow very well. Second fact. The train was never on time.

5. Here's what happened. People at the station were grouchy. Tell me the fact that explains **why** that happened. (Pause.) Get ready. (Signal.) *The train was never on time.*

6. Here's what happened. People took the bus. Tell me the fact that explains **why** that happened. (Pause.) Get ready. (Signal.) *The train was never on time.*

7. Here's what happened. He always missed the target. Tell me the fact that explains **why** that happened. (Pause.) Get ready. (Signal.) *He couldn't shoot his bow and arrow very well.*

8. (Repeat steps 5–7 until firm.)

EXERCISE 11

ANALOGIES

The next Thinking Operation is **Analogies.**

Task A

1. We're going to make up an **analogy** that tells **what color objects are.** What is the analogy going to tell? (Signal.) *What color objects are.* (Repeat until firm.)

2. The objects we're going to use are grass and sky. Which objects? (Signal.) *Grass and sky.*

3. Name the first object. (Signal.) *Grass. Yes,* grass. What color is grass? (Signal.) *Green.* Yes, green.

4. So, here's the first part of the analogy. Grass is to green. What's the first part of the analogy? (Signal.) *Grass is to green.* Yes, grass is to green. (Repeat until firm.)

5. The first part of the analogy told what color an object is. So, the **next** part of the analogy must tell what color another object is.

6. You told what color grass is. Now you're going to tell about sky. What object? (Signal.) *Sky.* What color is the sky? (Signal.) *Blue.* Yes, blue.

7. So, here's the second part of the analogy. Sky is to blue. What's the second part of the analogy? (Signal.) *Sky is to blue.* Yes, sky is to blue.

8. (Repeat steps 2–7 until firm.)

9. Now we're going to say the whole analogy. First, we're going to tell what color grass is and then we're going to tell what color sky is. Say the analogy with me. (Signal. Respond with the students.) *Grass is to green as sky is to blue.* (Repeat until the students are responding with you.)

10. All by yourselves. Say that analogy. (Signal.) *Grass is to green as sky is to blue.* (Repeat until firm.)

11. That analogy tells **what color those objects are.** What does that analogy tell? (Signal.) *What color those objects are.*

12. (Repeat steps 10 and 11 until firm.)

> **Individual test**
> Call on individual students to do step 10 or 11.

Task B

1. We're going to make up an **analogy** that tells **where you find objects.** What is the analogy going to tell? (Signal.) *Where you find objects.* (Repeat until firm.)

2. The objects we're going to use in the analogy are a toothbrush and a frying pan. Which objects? (Signal.) *A toothbrush and a frying pan.*

3. Name the first object. (Signal.) *A toothbrush.* Yes, a toothbrush. Where do you find a toothbrush? (Signal.) *In the bathroom.* Yes, in the bathroom.

4. So, here's the first part of the analogy. A toothbrush is to the bathroom. What's the first part of the analogy? (Signal.) *A toothbrush is to the bathroom.* Yes, a toothbrush is to the bathroom. (Repeat until firm.)

5. The first part of the analogy told where you find an object. So, the **next** part of the analogy must tell where you find another object.

6. You told where to find a toothbrush. Now you're going to tell about a frying pan. What object? (Signal.) *A frying pan.* Where do you find a frying pan? (Signal.) *In the kitchen.* Yes, in the kitchen.

7. So, here's the second part of the analogy. A frying pan is to the kitchen. What's the second part of the analogy? (Signal.) *A frying pan is to the kitchen.* Yes, a frying pan is to the kitchen.

8. (Repeat steps 2–7 until firm.)

9. Now we're going to say the whole analogy. First, we're going to tell where you find a toothbrush and then we're going to tell where you find a frying pan. Say the analogy with me. (Signal. Respond with the students.) *A toothbrush is to the bathroom as a frying pan is to the kitchen.* (Repeat until the students are responding with you.)

10. All by yourselves. Say that analogy. (Signal.) *A toothbrush is to the bathroom as a frying pan is to the kitchen.* (Repeat until firm.)

11. That analogy tells **where you find objects.** What does that analogy tell? (Signal.) *Where you find objects.*

12. (Repeat steps 10 and 11 until firm.)

> **Individual test**
> Call on individual students to do step 10 or 11.

EXERCISE 12

DESCRIPTION

The next Thinking Operation is **Description.**

1. I'm going to tell you about objects you know. But I'm going to call them a funny name. See if you can figure out what I'm talking about.
2. (Hold up one finger.) Gribs are clothing. Say that. (Signal.) *Gribs are clothing.*
   (Hold up two fingers.) Many gribs are made of leather. Say that. (Signal.) *Many gribs are made of leather.*
   (Hold up three fingers.) You wear gribs on your hands. Say that. (Signal.) *You wear gribs on your hands.*
3. Say the three things you know about gribs.
   (Hold up one finger.) *Gribs are clothing.*
   (Hold up two fingers.) *Many gribs are made of leather.*
   (Hold up three fingers.) *You wear gribs on your hands.* (Repeat until students say the statements in order.)
4. Everybody, tell me what I'm calling gribs. (Signal.) *Gloves.* Yes, gribs are really gloves.

Points

(Pass out the Workbooks.
Award points for Thinking Operations.)

WORKBOOK EXERCISES

We're going to do Workbooks now. Remember to follow my instructions carefully.

EXERCISE 13

TRUE—FALSE

Task A

1. Everybody, touch part A in your Workbook. ✔ I'll say statements about the picture.
2. Get ready to circle **true, false,** or **maybe.** Item 1. The building is not a school. Circle the answer. (Wait.)
3. Item 2. There is a vehicle in front of the building. Circle the answer. (Wait.)
4. Item 3. There are people in the building. Circle the answer. (Wait.)
5. Item 4. The car is not a station wagon. Circle the answer. (Wait.)
6. Item 5. The building is a library. Circle the answer. (Wait.)
7. Item 6. There is a camel in front of the building. Circle the answer. (Wait.)
8. Everybody, let's check your answers. Say **true, false,** or **maybe.**
9. Item 1. The building is not a school. (Signal.) *Maybe.*
10. (Repeat step 9 for items 2–6.)

EXERCISE 14

DESCRIPTION

1. Everybody, touch part B in your Workbook. ✔ Figure out which object I describe. Listen. A bamp is a vehicle. A bamp holds many people. A bamp does not travel on tracks. **Make a circle around** the object I'm calling a bamp. (Wait.)
2. Listen. A dom can be made of plastic. A dom is worn on a foot. A dom comes close to your knee. **Make a line over** the object I'm calling a dom. (Wait.)
3. Listen. A twif is an animal. A twif swims in the water. A twif is cold-blooded and has gills. **Make a line under** the object I'm calling a twif. (Wait.)
4. Everybody, get ready to check your work. Tell me the real name for the object that is a vehicle, that holds many people, and that does not travel on tracks. Get ready. (Signal.) *A bus.* And how did you mark the bus? (Signal.) *Made a circle around it.*
5. Tell me the real name for the object that can be made of plastic, that you wear on your foot, and that comes close to your knee. Get ready. (Signal.) *A boot.* And how did you mark the boot? (Signal.) *Made a line over it.*
6. Tell me the real name for the object that is an animal, that swims in the water, and that is cold-blooded and has gills. Get ready. (Signal.) *A fish.* And how did you mark the fish? (Signal.) *Made a line under it.*

EXERCISE 15

TRUE—FALSE

1. Everybody, touch part C in your Workbook. ✔ I'll say statements about the picture.
2. Get ready to circle **true, false,** or **maybe.** Item 1. The television is not off. Circle the answer. (Wait.)
3. Item 2. The appliance is a television. Circle the answer. (Wait.)
4. Item 3. The person watching TV is a girl. Circle the answer. (Wait.)
5. Item 4. The appliance is made by Zong TV. Circle the answer. (Wait.)
6. Item 5. The person watching TV is not a girl. Circle the answer. (Wait.)
7. Item 6. The television is off. Circle the answer. (Wait.)
8. Everybody, let's check your answers. Say **true, false,** or **maybe.**
9. Item 1. The television is not off. (Signal.) *True.*
10. (Repeat step 9 for items 2–6.)

EXERCISE 16

DESCRIPTION

1. Everybody, touch part D in your Workbook. Figure out which man I describe.
2. Item 1. This man is wearing a black suit. This man is wearing a hat. This man has a cane. Listen again. (Repeat the description.) Write the letter for item 1.
3. Item 2. This man is wearing a hat. This man has a cane. This man is wearing a white suit. Listen again. (Repeat the description.) Write the letter for item 2.
4. Item 3. This man is wearing a black suit. This man is wearing a hat. This man has his hands in his pockets. Listen again. (Repeat the description.) Write the letter for item 3.
5. Let's check your answers. Mark any items you missed with an X.
6. Item 1. This man is wearing a black suit. This man is wearing a hat. This man has a cane. Everybody, what letter? (Signal.) *C.*
7. (Repeat step 6 for items 2 and 3.)

Points

(Award points for Workbooks.)

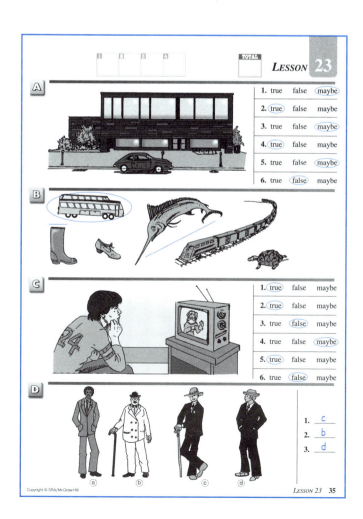

INFORMATION

● **SPECIAL INFORMATION**

We're going to work on Information now.

1. **Cat.** (Pause.) What's a synonym for **cat?** (Signal.) *Feline.*
2. **Dog.** (Pause.) What's a synonym for **dog?** (Signal.) *Canine.* Yes, all members of the dog family are called canines.
3. Foxes are canines. Jackals are canines. Wolves are canines. Retrievers and poodles are canines.
4. Your turn. See if you can name six canines. Name one canine. (Call on individual students. The students may name canines from step 3. The group is to name at least six canines.)
5. What are all members of the cat family called? (Signal.) *Felines.*
   What are all members of the dog family called? (Signal.) *Canines.*
   (Repeat step 5 until firm.)

MEMORIZATION: Poem

Say that poem we learned about the mechanic and the astronomer. Get ready. (Signal.)

> *A mechanic fixes cars,*
> *An astronomer looks at stars,*
> *A captain has two bars,*
> *And a boxer spars and spars.*

(Repeat until firm.)

> *Individual test*
> Call on individual students to say the whole poem.

INFORMATION: Animals

Task A

1. You learned about five classes of animals that have a backbone. Everybody, name those five classes. (Signal.) *Mammals, reptiles, birds, fish, and amphibians.*
2. The last class that you learned about was amphibians. Name an amphibian. (Call on individual students. The group is to name at least three amphibians.)
   You learned two facts about **all amphibians.** Everybody, tell me those two facts. (Hold up one finger.) First fact. *All amphibians are born in the water but grow up on land.* (Hold up two fingers.) Second fact. *All amphibians are cold-blooded.* (Repeat until the students say the facts in order.)
3. Name a mammal. (Call on individual students. The group is to name at least five mammals.)
   You learned two facts about **all mammals.** Everybody, tell me those two facts. (Hold up one finger.) First fact. *All mammals have hair.* (Hold up two fingers.) Second fact. *All mammals are warm-blooded.* (Repeat until the students say the facts in order.)
4. Name a reptile. (Call on individual students. The group is to name at least four reptiles.)
   You learned two facts about **all reptiles.** Everybody, tell me those two facts. (Hold up one finger.) First fact. *All reptiles are cold-blooded.* (Hold up two fingers.) Second fact. *All reptiles are born on land.* (Repeat until the students say the facts in order.)

5. Name a bird. (Call on individual students. The group is to name at least five birds.) You learned two facts about **all birds.** Everybody, tell me those two facts. (Hold up one finger.) First fact. *All birds have feathers.* (Hold up two fingers.) Second fact. *All birds are warm-blooded.* (Repeat until the students say the facts in order.)

6. Name a fish. (Call on individual students. The group is to name at least five fish.) You learned two facts about **all fish.** Everybody, tell me those two facts. (Hold up one finger.) First fact. *All fish have gills.* (Hold up two fingers.) Second fact. *All fish are cold-blooded.* (Repeat until the students say the facts in order.)

Task B

1. Tell me what class **guppies** are in. (Pause.) Get ready. (Signal.) *Fish.* So, tell me the two facts you know about **guppies.** (Hold up one finger.) First fact. *Guppies have gills.* (Hold up two fingers.) Second fact. *Guppies are cold-blooded.* (Repeat until the students say the facts in order.)

2. Tell me what class **geese** are in. (Pause.) Get ready. (Signal.) *Birds.* So, tell me the two facts you know about **geese.** (Hold up one finger.) First fact. *Geese have feathers.* (Hold up two fingers.) Second fact. *Geese are warm-blooded.* (Repeat until the students say the facts in order.)

3. Tell me what class **salamanders** are in. (Pause.) Get ready. (Signal.) *Amphibians.* So, tell me the two facts you know about **salamanders.** (Hold up one finger.) First fact. *Salamanders are born in the water but grow up on land.* (Hold up two fingers.) Second fact. *Salamanders are cold-blooded.* (Repeat until the students say the facts in order.)

4. Tell me what class **chipmunks** are in. (Pause.) Get ready. (Signal.) *Mammals.* So, tell me the two facts you know about **chipmunks.** (Hold up one finger.) First fact. *Chipmunks have hair.* (Hold up two fingers.) Second fact. *Chipmunks are warm-blooded.* (Repeat until the students say the facts in order.)

5. Tell me what class **pythons** are in. (Pause.) Get ready. (Signal.) *Reptiles.* So, tell me the two facts you know about **pythons.** (Hold up one finger.) First fact. *Pythons are cold-blooded.* (Hold up two fingers.) Second fact. *Pythons are born on land.* (Repeat until the students say the facts in order.)

Individual test
Call on individual students to do one step from Task B.

EXERCISE 20

MEMORIZATION: Poem
Say that poem we learned about the beautician and the tailor. Get ready. (Signal.)
> *A beautician fixes hair,*
> *A tailor can mend a tear,*
> *An exposition is a fair,*
> *And one plus one is a pair.*
(Repeat until firm.)

Individual test
Call on individual students to say the whole poem.

Points
(Award points for Information.
Have the students add up their daily total.)

END OF LESSON 23

THINKING OPERATIONS

EXERCISE 1

SAME: Review

The first Thinking Operation today is **Same.**

1. A wooden wagon and a wooden canoe are the same in a lot of ways.
2. They are in the same class. Name that same class. (Signal.) *Vehicles.* So, how are they the same? (Signal.) *They are vehicles.*
3. A wooden wagon and a wooden canoe are made of the same material. Name that same material. (Signal.) *Wood.*
   So, how are they the same? (Signal.) *They are made of wood.*
4. You can point to a wooden wagon and a wooden canoe. So, name three ways a wooden wagon and a wooden canoe are the same. (Hold up one finger.) *They are objects.*
   (Hold up two fingers.) *They take up space.*
   (Hold up three fingers.) *You find them in some place.*
5. You **do** some of the same things with a wooden wagon and a wooden canoe. Name some of those things. (Call on individual students. Praise reasonable responses; for example, steer, turn, stop, make them move.)

EXERCISE 2

● **SAME: Living Things**

Task A

1. Plants are alive. Animals are alive. If things are alive, they are the same in four ways.
   (Hold up one finger.) They grow.
   (Hold up two fingers.) They need food.
   (Hold up three fingers.) They can reproduce.
   (Hold up four fingers.) They die.
2. Let's say those four ways that living things are the same. (Respond with the students.)
   (Hold up one finger.) *They grow.*
   (Hold up two fingers.) *They need food.*
   (Hold up three fingers.) *They can reproduce.*
   (Hold up four fingers.) *They die.* (Repeat until students are responding with you.)

3. All by yourselves. Say the four ways that living things are the same. (Hold up one finger.) *They grow.*
   (Hold up two fingers.) *They need food.*
   (Hold up three fingers.) *They can reproduce.*
   (Hold up four fingers.) *They die.* (Repeat until firm.)

Individual test

Call on individual students to do step 3.

Task B

1. Let's name some ways that trees and frogs are the same.
2. Are trees and frogs alive? (Signal.) *Yes.*
   So, name four ways that trees and frogs are the same. (Hold up one finger.) *They grow.*
   (Hold up two fingers.) *They need food.*
   (Hold up three fingers.) *They can reproduce.*
   (Hold up four fingers.) *They die.* (Repeat until firm.)
3. Can you point to trees and frogs? (Signal.) *Yes.* So, name three ways that trees and frogs are the same. (Hold up one finger.) *They are objects.*
   (Hold up two fingers.) *They take up space.*
   (Hold up three fingers.) *You find them in some place.*
4. (Repeat steps 2 and 3 until firm.)
5. Now, when I call on you, see how many ways you can name that trees and frogs are the same. (Call on individual students. Praise all reasonable responses.)

EXERCISE 3

● **ANALOGIES**

The next Thinking Operation is **Analogies.**

Task A

1. We're going to make up an **analogy** that tells **what sounds animals make.** What is the analogy going to tell? (Signal.) *What sounds animals make.*
2. The animals you're going to use in the analogy are a frog and a cow. Which animals? (Signal.) *A frog and a cow.*

3. What sound does a frog make? (Call on individual students. Accept all reasonable answers.)
Let's say our frog croaks.
4. What sound does a cow make? (Signal.) *Moo.*
5. A frog croaks and a cow moos. Say the whole analogy about a frog and a cow. (Pause.) Get ready. (Signal.) *A frog is to croaking as a cow is to mooing.* (Repeat until firm.)
6. You made up an analogy that tells **what sounds those animals make.** What does that analogy tell about those animals? (Signal.) *What sounds those animals make.*

Task B
1. We're going to make up an **analogy** that tells **what material objects are made of.** What is the analogy going to tell? (Signal.) *What material objects are made of.*
2. The objects you're going to use in the analogy are a comb and a tire. Which objects? (Signal.) *A comb and a tire.*
3. What is a comb made of? (Call on individual students. Accept all reasonable answers.)
Let's say our comb is made of plastic.
4. What is a tire made of? (Signal.) *Rubber.*
5. A comb is made of plastic and a tire is made of rubber. Say the whole analogy about a comb and a tire. (Pause.) Get ready. (Signal.) *A comb is to plastic as a tire is to rubber.* (Repeat until firm.)
6. You made up an analogy about what **material those objects are made of.** What does that analogy tell about those objects? (Signal.) *What material those objects are made of.*

Task C
1. We're going to make up an **analogy** that tells **what shape objects are.** What is the analogy going to tell? (Signal.) *What shape objects are.*
2. The objects you're going to use in the analogy are a sheet of paper and an orange. Which objects? (Signal.) *A sheet of paper and an orange.*
3. What shape is a sheet of paper? (Call on individual students. Accept all reasonable answers.) Let's say our sheet of paper is rectangular.
4. What shape is an orange? (Signal.) *Round.*
5. A sheet of paper is rectangular and an orange is round. Say the whole analogy about a sheet of paper and an orange. (Pause.) Get ready. (Signal.) *A sheet of paper is to rectangular as an orange is to round.* (Repeat until firm.)
6. You made up an analogy that tells **what shape those objects are.** What does that analogy tell about those objects? (Signal.) *What shape those objects are.*

━━━━━━━━━━ **EXERCISE 4** ━━━━━━━━━━

BASIC EVIDENCE: Using Facts
The next Thinking Operation is **Basic Evidence.**
1. You're going to use two facts to explain things that happened. (Hold up one finger.) First fact. All vehicles move. Say it. (Signal.) *All vehicles move.* (Repeat until firm.) (Hold up two fingers.) Second fact. All felines eat meat. Say it. (Signal.) *All felines eat meat.* (Repeat until firm.)
2. Everybody, say those facts again. (Hold up one finger.) First fact. *All vehicles move.* (Hold up two fingers.) Second fact. *All felines eat meat.* (Repeat until the students say the facts in order.)

> *Individual test*
> Call on individual students to say the facts.

3. Here's what happened. The train traveled on the tracks. Tell me the fact that explains **why** that happened. (Pause.) Get ready. (Signal.) *All vehicles move.*

4. Listen. First fact. All vehicles move. Second fact. All felines eat meat.

5. Here's what happened. A lion ate a zebra. Tell me the fact that explains **why** that happened. (Pause.) Get ready. (Signal.) *All felines eat meat.*

6. Here's what happened. A wagon rolled down a steep hill. Tell me the fact that explains **why** that happened. (Pause.) Get ready. (Signal.) *All vehicles move.*

7. Here's what happened. Two kittens chewed on a piece of liver. Tell me the fact that explains **why** that happened. (Pause.) Get ready. (Signal.) *All felines eat meat.*

8. (Repeat steps 5–7 until firm.)

EXERCISE 5

STATEMENT INFERENCE

The next Thinking Operation is **Statement Inference.**

1. Listen. Their hats were caught by a stiff wind. Say that statement. (Signal.) *Their hats were caught by a stiff wind.* (Repeat until firm.)

> **Individual test**
> Call on a few individual students to say the statement.

2. Listen. What was caught by a stiff wind? (Signal.) *Their hats.*
   What caught their hats? (Signal.) *A stiff wind.*
   What kind of wind caught their hats? (Signal.) *Stiff.*
   What did a stiff wind do? (Signal.) *Caught their hats.*
   How many hats were caught by a stiff wind? (Signal.) *I don't know.*
   (Repeat step 2 until firm.)

> **Individual test**
> Call on individual students to answer a question from step 2.

EXERCISE 6

DEFINITIONS

The next Thinking Operation is **Definitions.**

1. **Instruct** means **teach.**

2. What does **instruct** mean? (Signal.) *Teach.* What word means **teach?** (Signal.) *Instruct.* (Repeat step 2 until firm.)

3. Listen. Jack instructs a swimming class. Say that. (Signal.) *Jack instructs a swimming class.* (Repeat until firm.)
   Now say that sentence with a different word for **instructs.** (Pause.) Get ready. (Signal.) *Jack teaches a swimming class.* (Repeat until firm.)
   (Repeat step 3 until firm.)

4. Listen. If you want to drive, I will teach you. Say that. (Signal.) *If you want to drive, I will teach you.* (Repeat until firm.)
   Now say that sentence with a different word for **teach.** (Pause.) Get ready. (Signal.) *If you want to drive, I will instruct you.* (Repeat until firm.)
   (Repeat step 4 until firm.)

5. Listen. She instructed them in water skiing. Say that. (Signal.) *She instructed them in water skiing.* (Repeat until firm.)
   Now say that sentence with a different word for **instructed.** (Pause.) Get ready. (Signal.) *She taught them in water skiing.* (Repeat until firm.)
   (Repeat step 5 until firm.)

===== **EXERCISE 7** =====

DEFINITIONS

1. **Feline.** (Pause.) What's a synonym for **feline?** (Signal.) *Cat.* And what's a synonym for **cat?** (Signal.) *Feline.*
   (Repeat step 1 until firm.)

2. Listen. The feline watched from a tree. Say that. (Signal.) *The feline watched from a tree.* (Repeat until firm.)
   Now say that sentence with a synonym for **feline.** (Pause.) Get ready. (Signal.) *The cat watched from a tree.* (Repeat until firm.)
   (Repeat step 2 until firm.)

3. **Big.** (Pause.) What's a synonym for **big?** (Signal.) *Large.* And what's a synonym for **large?** (Signal.) *Big.*
   (Repeat step 3 until firm.)

4. Listen. She ate a very large piece of pie. Say that. (Signal.) *She ate a very large piece of pie.* (Repeat until firm.)
   Now say that sentence with a synonym for **large.** (Pause.) Get ready. (Signal.) *She ate a very big piece of pie.* (Repeat until firm.)
   (Repeat step 4 until firm.)

5. **Ignore.** What does **ignore** mean? (Signal.) *Pay no attention to.* What word means **pay no attention to?** (Signal.) *Ignore.*
   (Repeat step 5 until firm.)

6. Listen. He ignored the fly on his nose. Say that. (Signal.) *He ignored the fly on his nose.* (Repeat until firm.)
   Now say that sentence with different words for **ignored.** (Pause.) Get ready. (Signal.) *He paid no attention to the fly on his nose.* (Repeat until firm.)
   (Repeat step 6 until firm.)

===== **EXERCISE 8** =====

DEDUCTIONS: With *no* and *don't*

1. I'll say rules with **no** or **don't.** You say them the other way. What two words are we going to use? (Hold up one finger.) *No.* (Hold up two fingers.) *Don't.*

2. Listen. Amphibians **don't** lay eggs on land. Say that. (Signal.) *Amphibians don't lay eggs on land.*

   Now say it the other way. Get ready. *No amphibian lays eggs on land.* (Repeat step 2 until firm.)

3. Here's a new rule. **No** mammal has scales. Say that. (Signal.) *No mammal has scales.* Now say it the other way. Get ready. (Signal.) *Mammals don't have scales.* (Repeat step 3 until firm.)

4. Here's a new rule. Canines **don't** have gills. Say that. (Signal.) *Canines don't have gills.* Now say it the other way. Get ready. (Signal.) *No canine has gills.* (Repeat step 4 until firm.)

5. Here's a new rule. **No** container masticates. Say that. (Signal.) *No container masticates.* Now say it the other way. Get ready. (Signal.) *Containers don't masticate.* (Repeat step 5 until firm.)

===== **EXERCISE 9** =====

• **DEDUCTIONS: With *don't***

The next Thinking Operation is **Deductions.**

1. Listen to this rule. Tools don't talk. Say the rule. (Signal.) *Tools don't talk.*

2. An apple is a **food.** What does the rule let you know about an apple? (Signal.) *Nothing.*

3. Listen. Tools don't talk. A shovel is a **tool.** What does the rule let you know about a shovel? (Signal.) *A shovel doesn't talk.* How do you know that a shovel doesn't talk? (Signal.) *Because tools don't talk.*

4. Listen. Tools don't talk. A dog is an **animal.** What does the rule let you know about a dog? (Signal.) *Nothing.*

5. Listen. Tools don't talk. A hammer is a **tool.** What does the rule let you know about a hammer? (Signal.) *A hammer doesn't talk.* How do you know that a hammer doesn't talk? (Signal.) *Because tools don't talk.*

6. Listen. Tools don't talk. A table is **furniture.** What does the rule let you know about a table? (Signal.) *Nothing.*

7. Listen. Tools don't talk. A pencil is a **tool.** What does the rule let you know about a pencil? (Signal.) *A pencil doesn't talk.* How do you know that a pencil doesn't talk? (Signal.) *Because tools don't talk.*

8. (Repeat steps 2–7 until firm.)

━━━━━ **EXERCISE 10** ━━━━━

CLASSIFICATION

The next Thinking Operation is **Classification.**

Task A

1. What's the rule for figuring out which class of things is bigger? (Signal.) *If a class has more kinds of things, it is bigger.* (Repeat until firm.)
   Yes, the bigger class has more **kinds** of things in it.
2. Let's figure out whether the class of tools is bigger than the class of hammers. If you took all the hammers from the class of tools, tell me if there would be some kinds of tools left. (Pause 2 seconds.) Get ready. (Signal.) *Yes.*
3. (Call on individual students.) Name one **kind** of tool that would be left. (Praise correct responses; for example, pliers, screwdrivers, saws.)
4. Everybody, if you took all the hammers from the class of tools, there would still be some kinds of tools left. But if you took all the **hammers** from the class of **hammers,** what would be left? (Signal.) *Nothing.* Yes, there would be nothing left.
5. So, which class has more **kinds** of things, the class of tools or the class of hammers? (Signal.) *The class of tools.*
   So, which class is bigger? (Signal.) *The class of tools.* How do you know that the class of tools is bigger? (Signal.) *Because it has more kinds of things.*
6. (Repeat steps 4 and 5 until firm.)

Task B

1. Let's figure out whether the class of tools is bigger than the class of toothbrushes. If you took all the toothbrushes from the class of tools, tell me if there would be some kinds of tools left. (Pause 2 seconds.) Get ready. (Signal.) *Yes.*
2. (Call on individual students.) Name one kind of tool that would be left. (Praise correct responses; for example, spoons, hairbrushes, combs.)

3. Everybody, if you took all the toothbrushes from the class of tools, there would still be some kinds of tools left. But if you took all the **toothbrushes** from the class of **toothbrushes,** what would be left? (Signal.) *Nothing.* Yes, there would be nothing left.
4. So, which class has more **kinds** of things, the class of tools or the class of toothbrushes? (Signal.) *The class of tools.* So, which class is bigger? (Signal.) *The class of tools.* How do you know that the class of tools is bigger? (Signal.) *Because it has more kinds of things.*

Task C

1. Let's figure out whether the class of tools is bigger than the class of rulers. If you took all the rulers from the class of tools, tell me if there would be some kinds of tools left. (Pause 2 seconds.) Get ready. (Signal.) *Yes.*
2. (Call on individual students.) Name one kind of tool that would be left. (Praise correct responses; for example, hammers, toothbrushes, forks.)
3. Everybody, if you took all rulers from the class of tools, there would still be some kinds of tools left. But if you took all the **rulers** from the class of **rulers,** what would be left? (Signal.) *Nothing.* Yes, there would be nothing left.
4. So, which class has more **kinds** of things, the class of tools or the class of rulers? (Signal.) *The class of tools.*
   So, which class is bigger? (Signal.) *The class of tools.* How do you know that the class of tools is bigger? (Signal.) *Because it has more kinds of things.*
5. (Repeat steps 3 and 4 until firm.)

Points

(Pass out the Workbooks.
Award points for Thinking Operations.)

WORKBOOK EXERCISES

We're going to do Workbooks now. Remember to follow my instructions carefully.

EXERCISE 11

• **ANALOGIES**

1. Everybody, get ready to complete each analogy when I signal. The first analogy tells where you find animals. Listen. A bird is to sky as a fish is to (pause; signal) *water.* (Repeat until firm.)
   The next analogy tells where vehicles go. Listen. A car is to a road as a train is to a (pause; signal) *track.* (Repeat until firm.)

2. Touch part A-1 in your Workbook. ✔ That box shows one of the analogies we just said. Touch the right pictures and say the analogy. Get ready. (Signal.) *A bird is to sky as a fish is to water.* (Repeat until firm.)
   Everybody, which picture completes the analogy? (Signal.) *Water.* Circle the picture of water. ✔

3. Everybody, touch part A-2 of your Workbook. That box shows the other analogy we just said. Touch the right pictures and say the analogy. Get ready. (Signal.) *A car is to a road as a train is to a track.* (Repeat until firm.)
   Everybody, which picture completes the analogy? (Signal.) *Track.* Circle the picture of the track. ✔

EXERCISE 12

TRUE—FALSE

Task A

1. Everybody, touch part B in your Workbook. ✔ I'll say statements about the picture.

2. Get ready to circle **true, false,** or **maybe.** Item 1. The man is not playing a piano. Circle the answer. (Wait.)

3. Item 2. The man knows how to play the piano. Circle the answer. (Wait.)

4. Item 3. The man is playing a banjo. Circle the answer. (Wait.)

5. Item 4. The man can see well without his glasses. Circle the answer. (Wait.)

6. Item 5. The man is playing a violin. Circle the answer. (Wait.)

7. Item 6. The man does not have short hair. Circle the answer. (Wait.)

8. Item 7. The man has short hair. Circle the answer. (Wait.)

9. Everybody, let's check your answers. Say **true, false,** or **maybe.**

10. Item 1. The man is not playing a piano. (Signal.) *True.*

11. (Repeat step 10 for items 2–7.)

Answer key   2. *Maybe*   **3.** *True*   **4.** *Maybe*   **5.** *False*
6. *False*   **7.** *True*

EXERCISE 13

DESCRIPTION

1. Everybody, touch part C in your Workbook. ✔ Figure out which bottle I describe.

2. Item 1. This bottle is tall and has a label. This bottle is not cracked. Listen again. (Repeat the description.) Write the letter for item 1.

3. Item 2. This bottle has a label and no lid. This bottle is cracked. Listen again. (Repeat the description.) Write the letter for item 2.

4. Item 3. This bottle is cracked and is short. This bottle has a lid. Listen again. (Repeat the description.) Write the letter for item 3.

5. Let's check your answers. Mark any items you missed with an X.

6. Item 1. This bottle is tall and has a label. This bottle is not cracked. Everybody, what letter? (Signal.) *D.*

7. (Repeat step 6 for items 2 and 3.)

Answer key   2. *A*   **3.** *B*

EXERCISE 14

TRUE—FALSE

1. Everybody, touch part D in your Workbook. ✔ I'll say statements about the picture.

2. Get ready to circle **true, false,** or **maybe.** Item 1. The person is not a man. Circle the answer. (Wait.)

3. Item 2. The lamp is turned off. Circle the answer. (Wait.)

4. Item 3. The person is a woman. Circle the answer. (Wait.)

5. Item 4. The woman is not running. Circle the answer. (Wait.)

6. Item 5. The woman is a doctor. Circle the answer. (Wait.)

7. Item 6. The lamp is not on the floor. Circle the answer. (Wait.)

8. Item 7. The lamp is turned on. Circle the answer. (Wait.)

9. Everybody, let's check your answers. Say **true, false,** or **maybe.**

10. Item 1. The person is not a man. (Signal.) *True.*

11. (Repeat step 9 for items 2–7.)

Points
(Award points for Workbooks.)

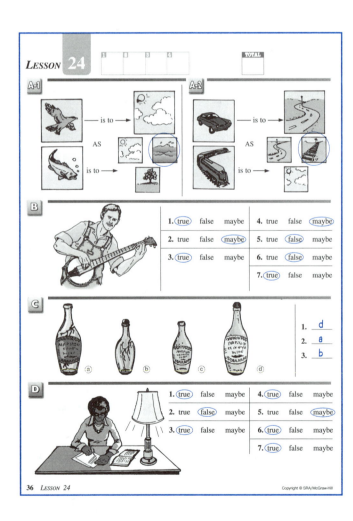

INFORMATION

We're going to work on Information now.

━━━━━ **EXERCISE 15** ━━━━━

● **SPECIAL INFORMATION**

1. What are all members of the cat family called? (Signal.) *Felines.* Name some felines. (Call on individual students. Praise reasonable responses; for example, cougars, leopards, house cats, lions. The group is to name at least six felines.)

2. What are all members of the dog family called? (Signal.) *Canines.* Name some canines. (Call on individual students. Praise reasonable responses; for example, wolf, hyena, poodle, boxer, fox. The group is to name at least six canines.)

━━━━━ **EXERCISE 16** ━━━━━

CALENDAR: Months, Seasons

1. Everybody, tell me how many months are in a year. (Pause.) Get ready. (Signal.) *Twelve.*

2. Name the months in a year. (Signal.) *January, February, March, April, May, June, July, August, September, October, November, December.*

3. You told me the (pause; signal) *months in a year.*

4. Everybody, tell me how many seasons are in a year. (Pause.) Get ready. (Signal.) *Four.*

5. Name the seasons in a year. (Signal.) *Winter, spring, summer, fall.*

6. You told me the four (pause; signal) *seasons in a year.*

> **Individual test**
> Call on individual students to name the
> months or seasons in a year.

EXERCISE 17

MEMORIZATION: Poem

Say that poem we learned about the beautician and the tailor. Get ready. (Signal.)

> *A beautician fixes hair,*
> *A tailor can mend a tear,*
> *An exposition is a fair,*
> *And one plus one is a pair.*

(Repeat until firm.)

> **Individual test**
> Call on individual students to say the whole poem.

EXERCISE 18

INFORMATION: Animals

Task A

1. See if you can figure out the class of animals I'm thinking of. I'm thinking of animals that are warm-blooded and have feathers. (Pause 3 seconds.)
   What class of animals am I thinking of? (Signal.) *Birds.*

2. Yes, I told you: they are warm-blooded; they have feathers. Tell me the words I said that let you know I wasn't thinking of reptiles. (Pause 3 seconds.) Get ready. (Signal.) *They are warm-blooded. They have feathers.* (Repeat step 2 until firm.)

3. Name an animal in the class of birds. (Call on individual students.) The group is to name at least five birds.

4. Now I'm thinking of animals that are born on land and are cold-blooded. (Pause 3 seconds.) Everybody, what class of animals am I thinking of? (Signal.) *Reptiles.*

5. Yes, I told you: they are born on land; they are cold-blooded. Tell me the words I said that let you know I wasn't thinking of fish. (Pause 3 seconds.) Get ready. (Signal.) *They are born on land.*
   (Repeat step 5 until firm.)

6. Name an animal in the class of reptiles. (Call on individual students.) The group is to name at least four reptiles.

Task B

1. Now I'm thinking of an animal that is cold-blooded and has gills. Tell me if I could be thinking of a salmon. (Pause.) Get ready. (Signal.) *Yes.*
   Tell me what class salmon are in. (Pause.) Get ready. (Signal.) *Fish.*

2. Tell me the two facts you know about **all fish.** (Hold up one finger.) First fact. *All fish have gills.*
   (Hold up two fingers.) Second fact. *All fish are cold-blooded.* (Repeat until the students say the facts in order.)
   So, if I'm thinking of an animal that is cold-blooded and has gills, I could be thinking of a salmon.

3. Here are the facts again. The animal is cold-blooded and has gills.
   Tell me if I could be thinking of a horse. (Pause.) Get ready. (Signal.) *No.* Right.

4. I told you: it is cold-blooded; it has gills. Tell me the words I said that let you know I wasn't thinking of a horse. (Pause 3 seconds.) Get ready. (Signal.) *It is cold-blooded. It has gills.*
   (Repeat step 4 until firm.)

5. Now I'm thinking of an animal that is cold-blooded and is born on land. Tell me if I could be thinking of a toad. (Pause.) Get ready. (Signal.) *No.* Right.

6. I told you: it is cold-blooded; it is born on land. Tell me the words I said that let you know I wasn't thinking of a toad. (Pause 3 seconds.) Get ready. (Signal.) *It is born on land.*
   (Repeat step 6 until firm.)

7. Here are the facts again. The animal is cold-blooded and is born on land. Tell me if I could be thinking of a cobra. (Pause.) Get ready. (Signal.) *Yes.*
   Tell me what class cobras are in. (Pause.) Get ready. (Signal.) *Reptiles.*

8. Tell me the two facts you know about **all reptiles.** (Hold up one finger.) First fact. *All reptiles are cold-blooded.*
   (Hold up two fingers.) Second fact. *All reptiles are born on land.* (Repeat until the students say the facts in order.)
   So, if I'm thinking of an animal that is cold-blooded and is born on land, I could be thinking of a cobra.

━━━━━━━━━━━ **EXERCISE 19** ━━━━━━━━━━━

MEMORIZATION: Concept Review

1. Let's see if you remember some things from the poems you've learned.
2. What does a beautician do? (Signal.) *Fixes hair.*
3. How many are in a pair? (Signal.) *Two.*
4. Who looks at stars? (Signal.) *An astronomer.*
5. Who spars and spars? (Signal.) *A boxer.*
6. What does a captain have on each shoulder? (Signal.) *Two bars.*
7. What does a tailor do? (Signal.) *Mends [or makes] clothes.*
8. What is an exposition? (Signal.) *A fair.*
9. Who fixes cars? (Signal.) *A mechanic.*
10. (Repeat steps 2–9 until firm.)

Points
(Award points for Information.
Have the students add up their daily total.)

END OF LESSON 24

THINKING
OPERATIONS

3. It has a tail and stripes and it likes to eat zebras. Everybody, name the animal I am talking about. (Signal.) *A tiger.*

EXERCISE 1

• **DEDUCTIONS: With *no***

The first Thinking Operation today is **Deductions.**

1. Listen to this rule. No cows fly. Say the rule. (Signal.) *No cows fly.*
2. A Hereford is a **cow.** What does the rule let you know about a Hereford? (Signal.) *A Hereford doesn't fly.* How do you know that a Hereford doesn't fly? (Signal.) *Because no cows fly.*
3. Listen. No cows fly. Randy rode a **horse.** What does the rule let you know about that horse? (Signal.) *Nothing.*
4. Listen. No cows fly. Terry milked a **cow.** What does the rule let you know about that cow? (Signal.) *That cow doesn't fly.* How do you know that cow doesn't fly? (Signal.) *Because no cows fly.*
5. Listen. No cows fly. The **sheep** jumped over a fence. What does the rule let you know about those sheep? (Signal.) *Nothing.*
6. Listen. No cows fly. One **robin** built a nest. What does the rule let you know about that robin? (Signal.) *Nothing.*
7. Listen. No cows fly. The **horse** galloped across the field. What does the rule let you know about that horse? (Signal.) *Nothing.*
8. (Repeat steps 2–7 until firm.)

EXERCISE 2

• **DESCRIPTION**

The next Thinking Operation is **Description.**

1. Listen. See if you can figure out what I'm talking about. It has a tail. Name three animals I could be talking about. (Call on individual students. Accept all reasonable responses; for example, dog, cat, horse, lion, cow.)
2. It has a tail and stripes. Name two animals I could be talking about. (Call on individual students. Accept all reasonable responses; for example, zebras, tigers, skunks.)

EXERCISE 3

STATEMENT INFERENCE

The next Thinking Operation is **Statement Inference.**

1. Listen. The lion's cousin is the jaguar. Say that statement. (Signal.) *The lion's cousin is the jaguar.* (Repeat until firm.)

> **Individual test**
> Call on individual students to say the statement.

2. Everybody, listen. The lion's cousin is the jaguar. Whose cousin is the jaguar? (Signal.) *The lion's.*
   Whose cousin is the lion? (Signal.) *The jaguar's.*
   What is the jaguar? (Signal.) *The lion's cousin.*
   Where does the lion live? (Signal.) *I don't know.*
   How big is the jaguar? (Signal.) *I don't know.* (Repeat step 2 until firm.)

> **Individual test**
> Call on individual students to answer a question from step 2.

EXERCISE 4

CLASSIFICATION

The next Thinking Operation is **Classification**

Task A

1. What's the rule for figuring out which class of things is bigger? (Signal.) *If a class has more kinds of things, it is bigger.* (Repeat until firm.)
   Yes, the bigger class has more **kinds** of things in it.
2. Let's figure out whether the class of food is bigger than the class of meat. If you took all the meat from the class of food, tell me if there would be some kinds of food left. (Pause 2 seconds.) Get ready. (Signal.) *Yes.*

3. (Call on individual students.) Name one **kind** of food that would be left. (Praise correct responses; for example, fruit, vegetables.)

4. Everybody, if you took all the meat from the class of food, there would still be some kinds of food left. But if you took all the **meat** from the class of **meat,** what would be left? (Signal.) *Nothing.* Yes, there would be nothing left.

5. So, which class has more **kinds** of things, the class of food or the class of meat? (Signal.) *The class of food.*
So, which class is bigger? (Signal.) *The class of food.* How do you know that the class of food is bigger? (Signal.) *Because it has more kinds of things.*

6. (Repeat steps 4 and 5 until firm.)

Task B

1. Let's figure out whether the class of food is bigger than the class of vegetables. If you took all the vegetables from the class of food, tell me if there would be some kinds of food left. (Pause 2 seconds.) Get ready. (Signal.) *Yes.*

2. (Call on individual students.) Name one kind of food that would be left. (Praise correct responses; for example, meat, fruit.)

3. Everybody, if you took all the vegetables from the class of food, there would still be some kinds of food left. But if you took all the **vegetables** from the class of **vegetables,** what would be left? (Signal.) *Nothing.* Yes, there would be nothing left.

4. So, which class has more **kinds** of things, the class of food or the class of vegetables? (Signal.) *The class of food.*
So, which class is bigger? (Signal.) *The class of food.* How do you know that the class of food is bigger? (Signal.) *Because it has more kinds of things.*

5. (Repeat steps 3 and 4 until firm.)

Task C

1. Let's figure out whether the class of food is bigger than the class of fruit. If you took all the fruit from the class of food, tell me if there would be some kinds of food left. (Pause 2 seconds.) Get ready. (Signal.) *Yes.*

2. (Call on individual students.) Name one kind of food that would be left. (Praise correct responses; for example, meat, vegetables.)

3. Everybody, if you took all the fruit from the class of food, there would still be some kinds of food left. But if you took all the **fruit** from the class of **fruit,** what would be left? (Signal.) *Nothing.* Yes, there would be nothing left.

4. So, which class has more **kinds** of things, the class of food or the class of fruit? (Signal.) *The class of food.*
So, which class is bigger? (Signal.) *The class of food.* How do you know that the class of food is bigger? (Signal.) *Because it has more kinds of things.*

5. (Repeat steps 3 and 4 until firm.)

===== **EXERCISE 5** =====

BASIC EVIDENCE: Using Facts
The next Thinking Operation is **Basic Evidence.**

1. You're going to use two facts to explain things that happened. (Hold up one finger.) First fact. Amphibians are born in water. Say it. (Signal.) *Amphibians are born in water.* (Repeat until firm.)
(Hold up two fingers.) Second fact. Reptiles are born on land. Say it. (Signal.) *Reptiles are born on land.* (Repeat until firm.)

2. Everybody, say those facts again. (Hold up one finger.) First fact. *Amphibians are born in water.*
(Hold up two fingers.) Second fact. *Reptiles are born on land.* (Repeat until the students say the facts in order.)

> **Individual test**
> Call on individual students to say the facts.

3. Here's what happened. The snake dug a hole in the sand for its eggs. Tell me the fact that explains **why** that happened. (Pause.) Get ready. (Signal.) *Reptiles are born on land.*

4. Listen. First fact. Amphibians are born in water. Second fact. Reptiles are born on land.

5. Here's what happened. There were many tadpoles in the pond. Tell me the fact that explains **why** that happened. (Pause.) Get ready. (Signal.) *Amphibians are born in water.*

6. Here's what happened. The baby newt hid from the big fish. Tell me the fact that explains **why** that happened. (Pause.) Get ready. (Signal.) *Amphibians are born in water.*

7. Here's what happened. The alligator's eggs were under the bush. Tell me the fact that explains **why** that happened. (Pause.) Get ready. (Signal.) *Reptiles are born on land.*

8. (Repeat steps 5–7 until firm.)

========= **EXERCISE 6** =========

DEFINITIONS

The next Thinking Operation is **Definitions.**

1. **Instruct** means **teach.**

2. What does **instruct** mean? (Signal.) *Teach.* What word means **teach?** (Signal.) *Instruct.* (Repeat step 2 until firm.)

3. Listen. I would like to instruct a class in cooking. Say that. (Signal.) *I would like to instruct a class in cooking.* (Repeat until firm.)
   Now say that sentence with a different word for **instruct.** (Pause.) Get ready. (Signal.) *I would like to teach a class in cooking.* (Repeat until firm.)
   (Repeat step 3 until firm.)

4. Listen. He teaches riding classes. Say that. (Signal.) *He teaches riding classes.* (Repeat until firm.)
   Now say that sentence with a different word for **teaches.** (Pause.) Get ready. (Signal.) *He instructs riding classes.* (Repeat until firm.)
   (Repeat step 4 until firm.)

5. Listen. She taught him in the library. Say that. (Signal.) *She taught him in the library.* (Repeat until firm.)
   Now say that sentence with a different word for **taught.** (Pause.) Get ready. (Signal.) *She instructed him in the library.* (Repeat until firm.)
   (Repeat step 5 until firm.)

========= **EXERCISE 7** =========

DEFINITIONS

1. A synonym for **healthy** is **well.**

2. What's a synonym for **healthy?** (Signal.) *Well.*
   And what's a synonym for **well?** (Signal.) *Healthy.*
   (Repeat step 2 until firm.)

3. Listen. The teacher is well. Say that. (Signal.) *The teacher is well.* (Repeat until firm.)
   Now say that sentence with a synonym for **well.** (Pause.) Get ready. (Signal.) *The teacher is healthy.* (Repeat until firm.)
   (Repeat step 3 until firm.)

4. Listen. You look very healthy. Say that. (Signal.) *You look very healthy.* (Repeat until firm.)
   Now say that sentence with a synonym for **healthy.** (Pause.) Get ready. (Signal.) *You look very well.* (Repeat until firm.)
   (Repeat step 4 until firm.)

========= **EXERCISE 8** =========

DEFINITIONS

1. **Cat.** What does **cat** mean? (Signal.) *Feline.*
   Obtain. What does **obtain** mean? (Signal.) *Get.*
   (Repeat step 1 until firm.)

2. Listen. The cat jumped on the table to obtain food. Say that sentence. (Signal.) *The cat jumped on the table to obtain food.* (Repeat until firm.)
   Now say that sentence with different words for **cat** and **obtain.** (Pause.) Get ready. (Signal.) *The feline jumped on the table to get food.* (Repeat until firm.)
   (Repeat step 2 until firm.)

EXERCISE 9

SAME: Review

The next Thinking Operation is **Same.**

1. You're going to name at least twelve ways that a jacket and a belt are the same. Think about what **material** they can be made of, what you **do** with them, where you **find** them, and other ways a jacket and a belt are the same. (Pause 4 seconds.)

2. Name a way a jacket and a belt are the same. (Call on individual students. The students are not to repeat ways other students have named. For each new way named, make a tally mark on the board. Praise responses about object characteristics, parts, and so on.)

3. (After twelve ways have been named, say:) You named twelve ways. Does anybody know any more ways? (Call on individual students. Praise the group for naming more than twelve ways.)

Answer key   *They are clothing, objects; take up space; are found in some place; can be made of leather or plastic. You can wear them; buy them; clean them. They are found in closets and stores; and so on.*

EXERCISE 10

SAME: Living Things

Task A

1. Plants are alive. Animals are alive. If things are alive, they are the same in four ways. (Hold up one finger.) They grow. (Hold up two fingers.) They need food. (Hold up three fingers.) They can re[p] (Hold up four fingers.) They die.

2. Let's say those four ways that living thing are the same. (Respond with the students. Hold up one finger.) *They grow.* (Hold up two fingers.) *They need food.* (Hold up three fingers.) *They can reproduce.* (Hold up four fingers.) *They die.* (Repeat until students are responding with you.)

3. All by yourselves. Say the four ways that living things are the same. (Hold up one finger.) *They grow.* (Hold up two fingers.) *They need food.* (Hold up three fingers.) *They can reproduce.* (Hold up four fingers.) *They die.* (Repeat until firm.)

> *Individual test*
> Call on individual students to do step 3.

Task B

1. Let's name some ways that poodles and flowers are the same.

2. Are poodles and flowers alive? (Signal.) *Yes.* So, name four ways that poodles and flowers are the same. (Hold up one finger.) *They grow.*
   (Hold up two fingers.) *They need food.*
   (Hold up three fingers.) *They can reproduce.*
   (Hold up four fingers.) *They die.* (Repeat until firm.)

3. Can you point to poodles and flowers? (Signal.) *Yes.* So, name three ways that poodles and flowers are the same. (Hold up one finger.) *They are objects.*
   (Hold up two fingers.) *They take up space.*
   (Hold up three fingers.) *You find them in some place.*

4. (Repeat steps 2 and 3 until firm.)

5. Now, when I call on you, see how many ways you can name that poodles and flowers are the same. (Call on individual students. Praise all reasonable responses.)

EXERCISE 11

ANALOGIES

The next Thinking Operation is **Analogies.**

Task A

1. We're going to make up an **analogy** that tells **what material objects are made of.** What is the analogy going to tell? (Signal.) *What material objects are made of.*

2. The objects you're going to use in the analogy are a pencil and a spoon. Which objects? (Signal.) *A pencil and a spoon.*

3. What material is a pencil made of? (Signal.) *Wood.*

4. What material is a spoon made of? (Signal.) *Metal.*

5. A pencil is made of wood and a spoon is made of metal. Say the whole analogy about a pencil and a spoon. (Pause.) Get ready. (Signal.) *A pencil is to wood as a spoon is to metal.* (Repeat until firm.)

6. You made up an analogy that tells **what materal those objects are made of.** What does that analogy tell about those objects? (Signal.) *What material those objects are made of.*

Task B

1. We're going to make up an **analogy** that tells **where you find objects.** What is the analogy going to tell? (Signal.) *Where you find objects.*
2. The objects you're going to use in the analogy are a ship and a barn. Which objects? (Signal.) *A ship and a barn.*
3. Where do you find a ship? (Call on individual students. Accept all reasonable answers.) Let's say you find our ship on the ocean.
4. Where do you find a barn? (Signal.) *On a farm.*
5. You find a ship on the ocean and a barn on a farm. Say the whole analogy about a ship and a barn. (Pause.) Get ready. (Signal.) *A ship is to ocean as a barn is to farm.* (Repeat until firm.)
6. You made up an analogy that tells **where you find those objects.** What does that analogy tell about those objects? (Signal.) *Where you find those objects.*

Task C

1. We're going to make up an **analogy** that tells **what you do with tools.** What is the analogy going to tell? (Signal.) *What you do with tools.*
2. The tools you're going to use in the analogy are a saw and a hammer. Which tools? (Signal.) *A saw and a hammer.*
3. What do you do with a saw? (Call on individual students. Accept all reasonable answers.) Let's say you cut wood with a saw.
4. What do you do with a hammer? (Signal.) *Pound nails.*
5. You cut wood with a saw and pound nails with a hammer. Say the whole analogy about a saw and a hammer. (Pause.) Get ready. (Signal.) *A saw is to cutting wood as a hammer is to pounding nails.* (Repeat until firm.)

6. You made up an analogy that tells **what you do with those tools.** What does that analogy tell about those tools? (Signal.) *What you do with those tools.*

Points

(Pass out the Workbooks.
Award points for Thinking Operations.)

We're going to do Workbooks now. Remember to follow my instructions carefully.

=========== **EXERCISE 12** ===========

1. Everybody, get ready to complete each analogy when I signal. The first analogy tells what parts objects have. Listen. A tree is to a branch as a person is to an (pause; signal) *arm.* (Repeat until firm.) The next analogy tells what parts animals have. Listen. A bird is to a wing as a horse is to a (pause; signal) *leg.* (Repeat until firm.)
2. Touch part A-1 in your Workbook. That box shows one of the analogies we just said. Touch the right pictures and say the analogy. Get ready. (Signal.) *A tree is to a branch as a person is to an arm.* (Repeat until firm.) Everybody, which picture completes the analogy? (Signal.) *Arm.* Circle the picture of an arm. ✔
3. Everybody, touch part A-2 in your Workbook. That box shows the other analogy we just said. Touch the right pictures and say the analogy. Get ready. (Signal.) *A bird is to a wing as a horse is to a leg.* (Repeat until firm.) Everybody, which picture completes the analogy? (Signal.) *A leg.* Circle the picture of a leg. ✔

EXERCISE 13

DESCRIPTION

1. Everybody, touch part B in you Workbook. Figure out which object I describe.
2. Item 1. This car is black and has a top. This car is little. Listen again. (Repeat the description.) Write the letter for item 1.
3. Item 2. This car is little. This car has a person in it. This car is white. Listen again. (Repeat the description.) Write the letter for item 2.
4. Item 3. This car is big. This car has a top. This car is white. Listen again. (Repeat the description.) Write the letter for item 3.
5. Let's check your answers. Mark any items you missed with an X.
6. Item 1. This car is black and has a top. This car is little. Everybody, what letter? (Signal.) *D.*
7. (Repeat step 6 for items 2 and 3.)

Answer key   2. *B*   **3.** *C*

EXERCISE 14

TRUE—FALSE

1. Everybody, touch part C in your Workbook. ✔ I'll say statements about the picture.
2. Get ready to circle **true, false,** or **maybe.** Item 1. The horse will not stop near the tree. Circle the answer. (Wait.)
3. Item 2. The boy is riding on a galloping horse. Circle the answer. (Wait.)
4. Item 3. The boy is not standing still. Circle the answer. (Wait.)
5. Item 4. The horse will stop near the tree. Circle the answer. (Wait.)
6. Item 5. The horse is eating hay. Circle the answer. (Wait.)

7. Item 6. The tree is in front of the horse. Circle the answer. (Wait.)
8. Everybody, let's check your answers. Say **true, false,** or **maybe**.
9. Item 1. The horse will not stop near the tree. (Signal.) *Maybe.*
10. (Repeat step 9 for items 2–6.)

Answer key   2. *True*   **3.** *True*   **4.** *Maybe*   **5.** *False*   **6.** *True*

EXERCISE 15

● CLASSIFICATION

Task A

1. Everybody, touch part D. ✔ You're going to work on classification. One of these boxes shows the class of striped cars. One of these boxes shows the class of cars. One of these boxes shows the class of vehicles.
2. You're going to tell me which box shows the class of **striped cars**, box A, box B, or box C. (Pause 3 seconds.) Get ready. (Signal.) *Box B.*
3. Now you're going to tell me which box shows the class of **cars.** (Pause 3 seconds.) Get ready. (Signal.) *Box A.*
4. You're ging to tell me which box shows the class of **vehicles.** (Pause 3 seconds.) Get ready. (Signal.) *Box C.*
5. Now let's figure out which of these classes is the biggest. What's the rule about the bigger class? (Signal.) *If a class has more kinds of things, it is bigger.* (Repeat until firm.)
6. Box C shows the class of vehicles. That means that **all kinds** of vehicles would be in box C. So, would all cars be in box C? (Signal.) *Yes.*

   To correct students who say *No:*
   a. All cars are vehicles. Box C shows the class of vehicles; so **all** cars **would be** in box C.
   b. (Repeat step 6.)

   Would all striped cars be in box C? (Signal.) *Yes.* Would vehicles that are not cars be in box C? (Signal.) *Yes.*
   (Repeat step 6 until firm.)

Individual test

(Call on three different students. Have each student do steps a, b, and c.)

Note: The students may name a vehicle **not** illustrated.

a. Name a vehicle that is **not** a car. (Praise correct responses; for example, boat, train, bike.)

b. Would that vehicle be in box C? (Signal.) *Yes.*

c. Would that vehicle be in any of the other boxes? (Signal.) *No.*

7. Everybody, box C has more **kinds** of things in it. So, which box shows the biggest class? (Signal.) *Box C*
Tell me the class **name** for the things in box C. (Pause 3 seconds.) Get ready. (Signal.) *Vehicles.*
How do you know that the class of vehicles is bigger than the other classes? (Signal.) *Because it has more kinds of things.*

Task B

1. Now look at box A and box B and figure out which box has more **kinds** of things. (Pause 4 seconds.) Get ready. (Signal.) *Box A. And* tell me the class **name** for the things in box A. (Pause 3 seconds.) Get ready. (Signal.) *Cars.*

2. I can name some things in the class of cars that **wouldn't** be in the class of striped cars. Some of these would be dotted cars, plain cars, and checkered cars. Everybody, how do you know that the class of cars is bigger than the class of striped cars? (Signal.) *Because it has more kinds of things.*

3. Everybody, look at all the boxes and tell me which box shows the smallest class. (Pause.) Get ready. (Signal.) *Box B.* Tell me the class **name** for the things in box B. (Pause.) Get ready. (Signal.) *Striped cars.*

4. You know that striped cars is the smallest class because it has only one kind of thing in it. What kind of thing? (Signal.) *Striped cars.* How do you know that striped cars is the smallest class? (Signal.) *Because it has only one kind of thing.*

━━━━━ EXERCISE 16 ━━━━━

CLASSIFICATION

Task A

1. Everybody, touch part E. ✔ You're going to work on classification. One of these boxes shows the class of small **tables.** One of these boxes shows the class of **tables.** One of these boxes shows the class of **furniture.**

2. You're going to tell me which box shows the class of **small tables,** box A, box B, or box C. (Pause 3 seconds.) Get ready. (Signal.) *Box A.*

3. Now you're going to tell me which box shows the class of **tables.** (Pause 3 seconds.) Get ready. (Signal.) *Box C.*

4. Now you're going to tell me which box shows the class of **furniture.** (Pause 3 seconds.) Get ready. (Signal.) *Box B.*

5. Now let's figure out which of these classes is the biggest. What's the rule about the bigger class? (Signal.) *If a class has more kinds of things, it is bigger.* (Repeat until firm.)

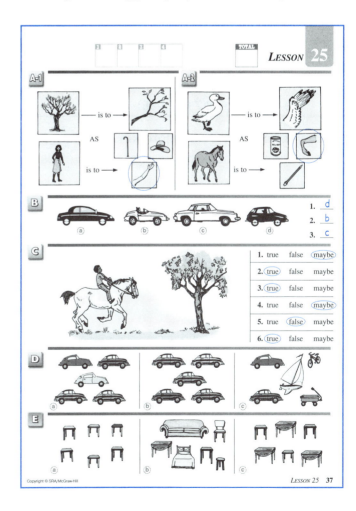

LESSON 25 37

6. Box B shows the class of furniture. That means that **all kinds** of furniture would be in box B. So, would all tables be in box B? (Signal.) *Yes.*

To correct students who say *No:*
a. All tables are furniture. Box B shows the class of furniture; so all tables **would be** in box B.
b. (Repeat step 6.)
Would all small tables be in box B? (Signal.) *Yes.*
Would all furniture that is not tables be in box B? (Signal.) *Yes.*
(Repeat step 6 until firm.)

Individual test
(Call on three different students. Have each student do steps a, b, and c.)

Note: The students may name a piece of furniture **not** illustrated.
a. Name a piece of furniture that is **not** a table. (Praise correct responses; for example, chair, couch, bookcase.)
b. Would that piece of furniture be in box B? (Signal.) *Yes.*
c. Would that piece of furniture be in any of the other boxes? (Signal.) *No.*

---

7. Everybody, box B has more **kinds** of things in it. So, which box shows the biggest class? (Signal.) *Box B.*
Tell me the class **name** for the things in box B. (Pause 3 seconds.) Get ready. (Signal.) *Furniture.* How do you know that the class of furniture is bigger than the other classes? (Signal.) *Because it has more kinds of things.*

Task B
1. Now look at boxes A and C and figure out which box has more **kinds** of things. (Pause 4 seconds.) Get ready. (Signal.) *Box C.*
And tell me the class **name** for the things in box C. (Pause 3 seconds.) Get ready. (Signal.) *Tables.*

2. I can name some things in the class of tables that **wouldn't** be in the class of small tables. Some of these would be long tables, wide tables, and big tables. Everybody, how do you know that the class of tables is bigger than the class of small tables? (Signal.) *Because it has more kinds of things.*

3. Everybody, look at all the boxes and tell me which box shows the smallest class. (Pause.) Get ready. (Signal.) *Box A.*
Tell me the class **name** for the things in box A. (Pause.) Get ready. (Signal.) *Small tables.*

4. You know that small tables is the smallest class because it has only one kind of thing in it. What kind of thing? (Signal.) *Small tables.*
How do you know that small tables is the smallest class? (Signal.) *Because it has only one kind of thing.*

Points
(Award points for Workbooks.)

INFORMATION

We're going to work on Information now.

━━━━━━━━ **EXERCISE 13** ━━━━━━━━

● **MEMORIZATION: Poem**

1. There are many different tribes of Indians. Today you're going to learn a poem about some Indian tribes that lived in the southeastern part of the United States. Some of their names are hard.

2. Listen. Creek. Say that. (Signal.) *Creek.* Choctaw. Say that. (Signal.) *Choctaw.* Cherokee. Say that. (Signal.) *Cherokee.* Seminole. Say that. (Signal.) *Seminole.* Chickasaw. Say that. (Signal.) *Chickasaw.*

   To correct mispronunciations [*Chickasaw,* for example]:
   a. Listen. Chick. Say that. (Signal.) *Chick.*
   b. Listen. Chick-a-saw. Say that. (Signal.) *Chick-a-saw.*
   c. Listen. Chickasaw. Say that. (Signal.) *Chickasaw.*
   (Repeat step 2 until firm.)

3. Here's the first line of the poem. Listen. American Indians were what they saw. Say that with me. (Signal. Respond with the students.) *American Indians were what they saw.* Say that by yourselves. (Signal.) *American Indians were what they saw.* (Repeat until firm.)

4. Here's the second line of the poem. Listen. Some were Creek and some Choctaw. Say that with me. (Signal. Respond with the students.) *Some were Creek and some Choctaw.* Say that by yourselves. (Signal.) *Some were Creek and some Choctaw.* (Repeat until firm.)

5. Here are the first two lines. Listen. American Indians were what they saw. Some were Creek and some Choctaw. Say that with me. (Signal. Respond with the students.) *American Indians were what they saw. Some were Creek and some Choctaw.* (Repeat until the students are responding with you.) Say that by yourselves. (Signal.) *American Indians were what they saw. Some were Creek and some Choctaw.* (Repeat until firm.)

6. Here's the last line of the poem. Listen. Cherokee, Seminole, and Chickasaw. Say that with me. (Signal. Respond with the students.) *Cherokee, Seminole, and Chickasaw. Say that by yourselves.* (Signal.) *Cherokee, Seminole, and Chickasaw.* (Repeat until firm.)

7. Here's the whole poem from the beginning. American Indians were what they saw. Some were Creek and some Choctaw. American Indians were what they saw. Cherokee, Seminole, and Chickasaw.

8. Say it with me. (Signal. Respond with the students.) *American Indians were what they saw. Some were Creek and some Choctaw. American Indians were what they saw. Cherokee, Seminole, and Chickasaw.* (Repeat until students are responding with you.)

━━━━━━━━ **EXERCISE 14** ━━━━━━━━

● **CALENDAR: Months, Seasons**

1. Everybody, tell me how many seasons are in a year. (Pause.) Get ready. (Signal.) *Four.*

2. Name the seasons in a year. (Signal.) *Winter, spring, summer, fall.*

3. You told me the four (pause; signal) *seasons in a year.*

4. Everybody, tell me how many months are in a year. (Pause.) Get ready. (Signal.) *Twelve.*

5. Name the months in a year. (Signal.) *January, February, March, April, May, June, July, August, September, October, November, December.*

6. You told me the (pause; signal) *months in a year.*

┌─────────────────────────────────────┐
Individual test
Call on individual students to name the months or seasons in a year.
└─────────────────────────────────────┘

===== **EXERCISE 15** =====

INFORMATION: Animals

Task A

1. You learned about five classes of animals that have a backbone. Everybody, name those five classes. (Signal.) *Mammals, reptiles, birds, fish, and amphibians.*

2. The last class that you learned about was amphibians. Name an amphibian. (Call on individual students. The group is to name at least three amphibians.)
   You learned two facts about **all amphibians.** Everybody, tell me those two facts. (Hold up one finger.) First fact. *All amphibians are born in water but grow up on land.* (Hold up two fingers.) Second fact. *All amphibians are cold-blooded.* (Repeat until the students say the facts in order.)

3. Name a mammal. (Call on individual students. The group is to name at least five mammals.)
   You learned two facts about **all mammals.** Everybody, tell me those two facts. (Hold up one finger.) First fact. *All mammals have hair.* (Hold up two fingers.) Second fact. *All mammals are warm-blooded.* (Repeat until the students say the facts in order.)

4. Name a reptile. (Call on individual students. The group is to name at least four reptiles.)
   You learned two facts about **all reptiles.** Everybody, tell me those two facts. (Hold up one finger.) First fact. *All reptiles are cold-blooded.* (Hold up two fingers.) Second fact. *All reptiles are born on land.* (Repeat until the students say the facts in order.)

5. Name a bird. (Call on individual students. The group is to name at least five birds.)
   You learned two facts about **all birds.** Everybody, tell me those two facts. (Hold up one finger.) First fact. *All birds have feathers.* (Hold up two fingers.) Second fact. *All birds are warm-blooded.* (Repeat until the students say the facts in order.)

6. Name a fish. (Call on individual students. The group is to name at least five fish.)
   You learned two facts about **all fish.** Everybody, tell me those two facts. (Hold up one finger.) First fact. *All fish have gills.* (Hold up two fingers.) Second fact. *All fish are cold-blooded.* (Repeat until the students say the facts in order.)

Task B

1. Tell me what class **deer** are in. (Pause.) Get ready. (Signal.) *Mammals.*
   So, tell me the two facts you know about **deer.** (Hold up one finger.) First fact. *Deer have hair.*
   (Hold up two fingers.) Second fact. *Deer are warm-blooded.* (Repeat until the students say the facts in order.)

2. Tell me what class **lizards** are in. (Pause.) Get ready. (Signal.) *Reptiles.*
   So, tell me the two facts you know about **lizards.** (Hold up one finger.) First fact. *Lizards are cold-blooded.*
   (Hold up two fingers.) Second fact. *Lizards are born on land.* (Repeat until the students say the facts in order.)

3. Tell me what class **perch** are in. (Pause.) Get ready. (Signal.) *Fish.*
   So, tell me the two facts you know about **perch.** (Hold up one finger.) First fact. *Perch have gills.*
   (Hold up two fingers.) Second fact. *Perch are cold-blooded.* (Repeat until the students say the facts in order.)

4. Tell me what class **ostriches** are in. (Pause.) Get ready. (Signal.) *Birds.*
   So, tell me the two facts you know about **ostriches.** (Hold up one finger.) First fact. *Ostriches have feathers.*
   (Hold up two fingers.) Second fact. *Ostriches are warm-blooded.* (Repeat until the students say the facts in order.)

5. Tell me what class **frogs** are in. (Pause.) Get ready. (Signal.) *Amphibians.*
So, tell me the two facts you know about **frogs.** (Hold up one finger.) First fact. *Frogs are born in water but grow up on land.* (Hold up two fingers.) Second fact. *Frogs are cold-blooded.* (Repeat until the students say the facts in order.)

> **Individual test**
> Call on individual students to do one step from Task B.

Points

(Award points for Information.
Have the students add up their daily total.)

> **Note:** Before beginning Lesson 26, present Fact Game Lesson 4, which appears at the end of this book.

END OF LESSON 25

THINKING OPERATIONS

═══════════ **EXERCISE 1** ═══════════

● **ANALOGIES**

The first Thinking Operation today is **Analogies.**

Task A

1. We're going to make up an **analogy** that tells **how people move.** What is the analogy going to tell? (Signal.) *How people move.*
2. The people we're going to use in the analogy are a woman and a baby. Which people? (Signal.) *A woman and a baby.*
3. How does a woman move? (Call on individual students. Accept all reasonable answers.) Let's say our woman walks.
4. How does a baby move? (Signal.) *It crawls.*
5. A woman walks and a baby crawls. Say the whole analogy about a woman and a baby. (Pause.) Get ready. (Signal.) *A woman is to walking as a baby is to crawling.* (Repeat until firm.)
6. The analogy tells something about those people. (Pause.) What does that analogy tell about those people? (Signal.) *How those people move.*
7. (Repeat steps 5 and 6 until firm.)

Task B

1. We're going to make up an **analogy** that tells **what material objects are made of.** What is the analogy going to tell? (Signal.) *What material objects are made of.*
2. The objects you're going to use in the analogy are a table and a fork. Which objects? (Signal.) *A table and a fork.*
3. What material is a table made of? (Call on individual students. Accept all reasonable answers.) Let's say our table is made of wood.
4. What material is a fork made of? (Signal.) *Metal.*
5. A table is made of wood and a fork is made of metal. Say the whole analogy about a table and a fork. (Pause.) Get ready. (Signal.) *A table is to wood as a fork is to metal.*

6. The analogy tells something about those objects. (Pause.) What does that analogy tell about those objects? (Signal.) *What material those objects are made of.*
7. (Repeat steps 5 and 6 until firm.)

Task C

1. We're going to make up an **analogy** that tells **what you do with tools.** What is the analogy going to tell? (Signal.) *What you do with tools.*
2. The tools you're going to use in the analogy are a spoon and a pencil. Which tools? (Signal.) *A spoon and a pencil.*
3. What do you do with a spoon? (Call on individual students. Accept all reasonable answers.)
   Let's say you eat with a spoon.
4. What do you do with a pencil? (Signal.) *Write.*
5. You eat with a spoon and write with a pencil. Say the whole analogy about a spoon and a pencil. (Pause.) Get ready. (Signal.) *A spoon is to eating as a pencil is to writing.* (Repeat until firm.)
6. The analogy tells something about those tools. What does that analogy tell about those tools? (Signal.) *What you do with those tools.*
7. (Repeat steps 5 and 6 until firm.)

═══════════ **EXERCISE 2** ═══════════

● **DEDUCTIONS: With *some***

The next Thinking Operation is **Deductions.**

1. Listen to this rule. **Some** bears live in a zoo. Everybody, say that. (Signal.) *Some bears live in a zoo.* Yes, only **some** bears live in a zoo. Do **all** bears live in a zoo? (Signal.) *No.* How many bears live in a zoo? (Signal.) *Some.*
2. **Some** bears live in a zoo. A grizzly bear ate a **fish.** What does the rule let you know about that bear? (Signal.) *Maybe that bear lives in a zoo.*

To correct students who say *That bear lives in a zoo:*

a. Listen. Only **some** bears live in a zoo; so **maybe** that bear lives in a zoo.

b. (Repeat step 2 until firm.)
How do you know that maybe that bear lives in a zoo? (Signal.) *Because some bears live in a zoo.*

3. Listen. **Some** bears live in a zoo. **Sid** slipped on a banana. What does the rule let you know about Sid? (Signal.) *Nothing.*

4. Listen. **Some** bears live in a zoo. A whale is a **mammal.** What does the rule let you know about a whale? (Signal.) *Nothing.*

5. Listen. **Some** bears live in a zoo. A big bear stubbed its toe. What does the rule let you know about that bear? (Signal.) *Maybe that bear lives in a zoo.* How do you know that maybe that bear lives in a zoo? (Signal.) *Because some bears live in a zoo.*

EXERCISE 3

DESCRIPTION

The next Thinking Operation is **Description.**

1. I'm going to tell you about an object you know. But I'm going to call it a funny name. See if you can figure out what object I'm talking about.

2. (Hold up one finger.) A glap is a tool. Say that. (Signal.) *A glap is a tool.*
(Hold up two fingers.) A glap has a handle. Say that. (Signal.) *A glap has a handle.*
(Hold up three fingers.) You dig holes with a glap. Say that. (Signal.) *You dig holes with a glap.*

3. Everybody, say the three things you know about a glap. (Hold up one finger.) *A glap is a tool.*
(Hold up two fingers.) *A glap has a handle.*
(Hold up three fingers.) *You dig holes with a glap.* (Repeat until the students say the statements in order.)

4. Everybody, tell me the thing I am calling a glap. (Signal.) *A shovel.* Yes, it's really a shovel.

EXERCISE 4

DESCRIPTION

1. Listen. See if you can figure out what I'm talking about. You can work with it. Name three tools I could be talking about. (Call on individual students. Accept all reasonable responses; for example, hammer, wrench, saw.)

2. You can work with it and you can write with it. Name two tools I could be talking about. (Call on individual students. Accept all reasonable responses; for example, pen, crayon, pencil.)

3. You can work with it, write with it, and it is made of wood. Everybody, name the tool I am talking about. (Signal.) *A pencil.*

EXERCISE 5

SAME: Review

The next Thinking Operation is **Same.**

1. An ant and a snake are the same in many ways.

2. You can point to an ant and a snake. So, name three ways they are the same. (Hold up one finger.) *They are objects.* (Hold up two fingers.) *They take up space.* (Hold up three fingers.) *You find them in some place.*

3. An ant and a snake **do** some of the same things. Name some of those things. (Call on individual students. Praise reasonable responses; for example, eat, sleep, breathe.)

4. Everybody, an ant and a snake are alive. So, name four ways that they are the same. (Hold up one finger.) *They grow.* (Hold up two fingers.) *They need food.* (Hold up three fingers.) *They can reproduce.* (Hold up four fingers.) *They die.*

5. You find an ant and a snake in some of the same places. Name some of those places. (Call on individual students. Praise reasonable responses; for example, on the ground, under a rock, in a tree.)

6. An ant and a snake are in the same class. Everybody, name that same class. (Signal.) *Animals.* So, how are they the same? (Signal.) *They are animals.*

7. An ant and a snake have some of the same body parts. Name some of those body parts. (Call on individual students. Praise reasonable responses; for example, head, eyes, mouth.)

8. An ant and a snake can be the same color. Name a color they can be. (Call on one student. Accept a reasonable response.) Everybody, so how are they the same? (Signal.) *They can be* [color named].

=========== EXERCISE 6 ===========

DEFINITIONS

The next Thinking Operation is **Definitions.**

1. **Duplicate** means **copy.**

2. What does **duplicate** mean? (Signal.) *Copy.* What word means **copy?** (Signal.) *Duplicate.* (Repeat step 2 until firm.)

3. Listen. Can you duplicate his action? Say that. (Signal.) *Can you duplicate his action?* (Repeat until firm.)
   Now say that sentence with a different word for **duplicate.** (Pause.) Get ready. (Signal.) *Can you copy his action?* (Repeat until firm.)
   (Repeat step 3 until firm.)

4. Listen. That machine is used to duplicate letters. Say that. (Signal.) *That machine is used to duplicate letters.* (Repeat until firm.)
   Now say that sentence with a different word for **duplicate.** (Pause.) Get ready. (Signal.) *That machine is used to copy letters.* (Repeat until firm.)
   (Repeat step 4 until firm.)

5. Listen. It is against the law to copy money. Say that. (Signal.) *It is against the law to copy money.* (Repeat until firm.)
   Now say that sentence with a different word for **copy.** (Pause.) Get ready. (Signal.) *It is against the law to duplicate money.* (Repeat until firm.)
   (Repeat step 5 until firm.)

=========== EXERCISE 7 ===========

DEFINITIONS

1. **Instruct.** (Pause.) What's a synonym for **instruct?** (Signal.) *Teach.* And what's a synonym for **teach?** (Signal.) *Instruct.* (Repeat until firm.)

2. Listen. If you don't know how, I will instruct you. Say that. (Signal.) *If you don't know how, I will instruct you.* (Repeat until firm.)
   Now say that sentence with a synonym for **instruct.** (Pause.) Get ready. (Signal.) *If you don't know how, I will teach you.* (Repeat until firm.)
   (Repeat step 2 until firm.)

3. **Descend.** (Pause.) What does **descend** mean? (Signal.) *Go down.* And what word means **go down?** (Signal.) *Descend.* (Repeat step 3 until firm.)

4. Listen. The kite went down into a cornfield. Say that. (Signal.) *The kite went down into a cornfield.* (Repeat until firm.)
   Now say that sentence with a different word for **went down.** (Pause.) Get ready. (Signal.) *The kite descended into a cornfield.* (Repeat until firm.)
   (Repeat step 4 until firm.)

5. **Well.** (Pause.) What's a synonym for **well?** (Signal.) *Healthy.*
   And what's a synonym for **healthy?** (Signal.) *Well.*
   (Repeat step 5 until firm.)

6. Listen. You look very well today. Say that. (Signal.) *You look very well today.* (Repeat until firm.)
   Now say that sentence with a synonym for **well.** (Pause.) Get ready. (Signal.) *You look very healthy today.)*
   (Repeat until firm.)
   (Repeat step 6 until firm.)

EXERCISE 8

DEFINITIONS

1. **Pay no attention to.** What does **pay no attention to** mean? (Signal.) *Ignore.*
   Big. What does **big** mean? (Signal.) *Large.*
   (Repeat step 1 until firm.)
2. Listen. We paid no attention to the big, howling dog. Say that sentence. (Signal.) *We paid no attention to the big, howling dog.* (Repeat until firm.)
   Now say that sentence with different words for **paid no attention to** and **big.** (Pause.) Get ready. (Signal.) *We ignored the large, howling dog.* (Repeat until firm.)
   (Repeat step 2 until firm.)

EXERCISE 9

STATEMENT INFERENCE

The next Thinking Operation is **Statement Inference.**

1. Listen. The hunter's python ate only once a week. Say that statement. (Signal.) *The hunter's python ate only once a week.* (Repeat until firm.)

> **Individual test**
> Call on individuals to say the statement.

2. Everybody, listen. The hunter's python ate only once a week. When did the hunter's python eat? (Signal.) *Only once a week.*
   Whose python ate only once a week? (Signal.) *The hunter's.*
   What did the hunter's python do only once a week? (Signal.) *Ate.*
   What ate only once a week? (Signal.) *The hunter's python.*
   What did the hunter have that ate only once a week? (Signal.) *A python.*
   How much did the python eat? (Signal.) *I don't know.*
   (Repeat step 2 until firm.)

> **Individual test**
> Call on individual students to answer a question from step 2.

EXERCISE 10

BASIC EVIDENCE: Using Facts

The next Thinking Operation is **Basic Evidence.**

1. You're going to use two facts to explain things that happened. (Hold up one finger.) First fact. Dry plants burn easily. Say it. (Signal.) *Dry plants burn easily.* (Repeat until firm.)
   (Hold up two fingers.) Second fact. Water wears down rocks. Say it. (Signal.) *Water wears down rocks.* (Repeat until firm.)
2. Everybody, say those facts again. (Hold up one finger.) First fact. *Dry plants burn easily.* (Hold up two fingers.) Second fact. *Water wears down rocks.* (Repeat until the students say the facts in order.)

> **Individual test**
> Call on individual students to say the facts.

3. Here's what happened. There were many forest fires in the summer. Tell me the fact that explains **why** that happened. (Pause.) Get ready. (Signal.) *Dry plants burn easily.*
4. Listen. First fact. Dry plants burn easily. Second fact. Water wears down rocks.
5. Here's what happened. The river made a valley. Tell me the fact that explains **why** that happened. (Pause.) Get ready. (Signal.) *Water wears down rocks.*
6. Here's what happened. There were caves along the seashore. Tell me the fact that explains **why** that happened. (Pause.) Get ready. (Signal.) *Water wears down rocks.*
7. Here's what happened. The farmer did not allow smoking in the cornfield. Tell me the fact that explains **why** that happened. (Pause.) Get ready. (Signal.) *Dry plants burn easily.*
8. (Repeat steps 5–7 until firm.)

Points
(Pass out the Workbooks.
Award points for Thinking Operations.)

LESSON 26

WORKBOOK EXERCISES

We're going to do Workbooks now. Remember to follow my instructions carefully.

EXERCISE 11

- **ANALOGIES**

1. Everybody, touch part A-1 in your Workbook. ✔
   This analogy shows where vehicles go. What does the analogy show? (Signal.) *Where vehicles go.*
   Look at the pictures and name the vehicles that are in the analogy. (Pause.) Get ready. (Signal.) *A boat and a plane.*
   Remember, the analogy shows where those vehicles go. Circle the picture that completes the analogy. (Wait.)

2. Everybody, touch the right pictures and say the whole analogy. Get ready. (Signal.) *A boat is to water as a plane is to sky.* (Repeat until firm.)
   If you didn't circle the picture of sky, make an X next to the picture you circled.

3. Everybody, touch part A-2 in your Workbook. This analogy shows what body parts clothing is for. What does this analogy show? (Signal.) *What body parts clothing is for.*
   Look at the pictures and name the clothing in the analogy. (Pause.) Get ready. (Signal.) *A glove and a hat.*
   Remember, the analogy shows what body parts clothing is for. Circle the picture that completes the analogy. (Wait.)

4. Everybody, touch the right pictures and say the whole analogy. Get ready. (Signal.) *A glove is to hand as a hat is to head.* (Repeat until firm.)
   If you didn't circle the picture of a head, make an X next to the picture you circled.

Individual test
(Call on individual students to do one of the following:)
   a. Say the analogy shown in part A-1.
   b. What does that analogy show about those vehicles?
   c. Say the analogy shown in part A-2.
   d. What does that analogy show about clothing?

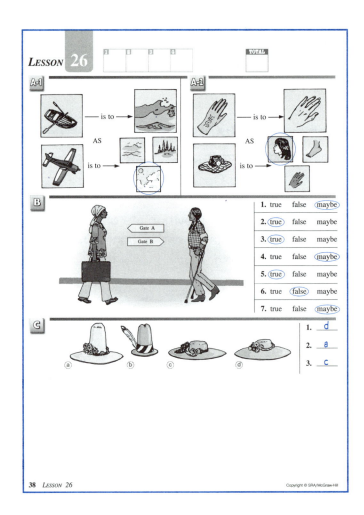

═══════ **EXERCISE 12** ═══════

TRUE—FALSE

1. Everybody, touch part B in your Workbook. ✔ I'll say statements about the picture.
2. Get ready to circle **true, false,** or **maybe.** Item 1. The woman is coming home from a trip. Circle the answer. (Wait.)
3. Item 2. The man is not carrying a suitcase. Circle the answer. (Wait.)
4. Item 3. The woman is carrying a suitcase. Circle the answer. (Wait.)
5. Item 4. The suitcase is not heavy. Circle the answer. (Wait.)
6. Item 5. The person carrying the suitcase is not a man. Circle the answer. (Wait.)
7. Item 6. The person walking and carrying the suitcase is a man. Circle the answer. (Wait.)
8. Item 7. The suitcase is heavy. Circle the answer. (Wait.)
9. Everybody, let's check your answers. Say **true, false,** or **maybe.**
10. Item 1. The woman is coming home from a trip. (Signal.) *Maybe.*
11. (Repeat step 10 for items 2–7.)

═══════ **EXERCISE 13** ═══════

DESCRIPTION

1. Everybody, touch part C in your Workbook. ✔ Figure out which hat I describe.
2. Item 1. This hat has a wide brim and flowers. This hat is short. Listen again. (Repeat the description.) Write the letter for item 1.
3. Item 2. This hat has a black band. This hat is tall and wide. Listen again. (Repeat the description.) Write the letter for item 2.
4. Item 3. This hat is wide and short. This hat has fruit on it. Listen again. (Repeat the description.)
5. Let's check your answers. Mark any items you missed with an X.
6. Item 1. This hat has a wide brim and flowers. This hat is short. Everybody, what letter? (Signal.) *D.*
7. (Repeat step 6 for items 2 and 3.)

═══════ **EXERCISE 14** ═══════

TRUE—FALSE

1. Everybody, touch part D in your Workbook. ✔ I'll say statements that are true of one of the pictures. You write the letter of the right picture.
2. Item 1. **Only some** of the animals are cold-blooded. Write the letter of the picture on line 1. (Wait.)
3. Item 2. **None** of the animals are cold-blooded. Write the letter of the picture on line 2. (Wait.)
4. Item 3. **All** the animals are cold-blooded. Write the letter of the picture on line 3. (Wait.)
5. Item 4. **Only some** of the animals are warm-blooded. Write the letter of the picture on line 4. (Wait.)
6. Let's check your answers. Mark any items you missed with an X. Tell me the letter of the right picture.
7. Item 1. **Only some** of the animals are cold-blooded. (Signal.) *B.*
8. (Repeat step 7 for items 2–4.)

LESSON 26 **39**

LESSON 26 **233**

EXERCISE 15

CLASSIFICATION

1. Everybody, touch part E in your Workbook. ✔ You're going to work on classification. One of these boxes shows the class of reptiles. One of these boxes shows the class of animals. One of these boxes shows the class of objects.

2. You're going to tell me which box shows the class of **reptiles,** box A, box B, or box C. (Pause 3 seconds.) Get ready. (Signal.) *Box B.*

3. Now you're going to tell me which box shows the class of **animals.** (Pause 3 seconds.) Get ready. (Signal.) *Box A.*

4. You're going to tell me which box shows the class of **objects.** (Pause 3 seconds.) Get ready. (Signal.) *Box C.*

5. Now let's figure out which of these classes is the biggest. What's the rule about the bigger class? (Signal.) *If a class has more kinds of things, it is bigger.* (Repeat until firm.)

6. Box C shows the class of objects. That means that **all kinds** of objects would be in box C. So, would all animals be in box C? (Signal.) *Yes.*

   To correct students who say *No:*

   a. All animals are objects. Box C shows the class of objects; so **all** animals **would be** in box C.

   b. (Repeat step 6.)

   Would all reptiles be in box C? (Signal.) *Yes.* Would objects that are not animals be in box C? (Signal.) *Yes.* (Repeat step 6 until firm.)

   Individual test

   (Call on three different students. Have each student do the following tasks.)

   Note: The students may name objects **not** illustrated.

   a. Name an object that is **not** an animal. (Praise correct responses; for example, desk, person, chair, food.)

   b. Would that object be in box C? (Signal.) *Yes.*

   c. Would that object be in any of the other boxes? (Signal.) *No.*
   ---

7. Everybody, box C has more **kinds** of things in it. So, which box shows the biggest class? (Signal.) *Box C.*
   Tell me the class **name** for the things in box C. (Pause 3 seconds.) Get ready. (Signal.) *Objects.* How do you know that the class of objects is bigger than the other classes? (Signal.) *Because it has more kinds of things.*

EXERCISE 16

- **CLASSIFICATION**

1. Everybody, touch part F in your Workbook. ✔ You're going to work on classification. One of these boxes shows the class of tools. One of these boxes shows the class of saws. One shows the class of power saws.

2. You're going to tell me which box shows the class of **power saws,** box A, box B, or box C. (Pause 3 seconds.) Get ready. (Signal.) *Box A.*

3. Which box shows the class of saws? (Pause 3 seconds.) Get ready. (Signal.) *Box B.*

4. Which box shows the class of tools? (Pause 3 seconds.) Get ready. (Signal.) *Box C.*

5. Now let's figure out which of these classes is the biggest. What's the rule about the bigger class? (Signal.) *If a class has more kinds of things, it is bigger.* (Repeat until firm.)

6. Look at box A, box B, and box C and figure out which box has more **kinds** of things than the others. (Pause 4 seconds.) Which box? (Signal.) *Box C.*

   To correct:

   a. Box C has more kinds of things than the other boxes. It has a hammer, a saw, and a broom.

   b. (Repeat step 6.)

   Tell me the class **name** for box C. (Pause 3 seconds.) Get ready. (Signal.) *Tools.* How do you know that the class of tools is bigger than the other classes? (Signal.) *Because it has more kinds of things.* (Repeat step 6 until firm.)

7. Now look at boxes A and B and figure out which box has more **kinds** of things. (Pause.) Get ready. (Signal.) *Box B.* Tell me the class **name** for the things in box B. (Pause.) Get ready. (Signal.) *Saws.*

How do you know that the class of saws is bigger than the class shown in box A? (Signal.) *Because it has more kinds of things.* (Repeat step 7 until firm.)

8. Which box shows the smallest class? (Signal.) *Box A.* And what's the class **name** for the things in box A? (Signal.) *Power saws.* How do you know that power saws is the smallest class? (Call on one student.) *Because it has only one kind of thing.* (Repeat step 8 until firm.)

Points

(Award points for Workbooks.)

We're going to work on Information now.

EXERCISE 17

● **MEMORIZATION: Poem**

1. You're learning a poem about American Indians. Let's name those Indians.
2. Creek. Say it. (Signal.) *Creek.* Choctaw. Say it. (Signal.) *Choctaw.* Cherokee. Say it. (Signal.) *Cherokee.* Seminole. Say it. (Signal.) *Seminole.* Chickasaw. Say it. (Signal.) *Chickasaw.* (Repeat step 2 until firm.)
3. I'll say the whole poem about American Indians. American Indians were what they saw. Some were Creek and some Choctaw. American Indians were what they saw. Cherokee, Seminole, and Chickasaw.
4. Say it with me. (Signal. Say the poem with the students.) (Repeat until students are responding with you.)

> *Individual test*
>
> (Call on individual students.)
>
> Say as much of the poem as you can.
>
> (Praise students who correctly say at least two lines.)

EXERCISE 18

● **CALENDAR: Holidays**

1. I'm going to tell you facts about holidays. Holidays are special days. Here's the first fact. Christmas and New Year's Day are winter holidays. What are two winter holidays? (Signal.) *Christmas and New Year's Day.*
2. Christmas is in December. What month is Christmas in? (Signal.) *December.*
3. New Year's Day comes exactly one week after Christmas. New Year's Day is always the first day of a new year. So, New Year's Day is always January first. What **date** is New Year's Day? (Signal.) *January first.*
4. Tell me the holiday that is in December. (Pause 2 seconds.) Get ready. (Signal.) *Christmas.*
   Tell me the **holiday** that comes exactly one week after Christmas. (Pause 2 seconds.) Get ready. (Signal.) *New Year's Day.* Is New Year's Day in December? (Signal.) *No.* Tell me what **month** New Year's Day is in. (Pause 2 seconds.) Get ready. (Signal.) *January.* Tell me the **date** of New Year's Day. (Pause 2 seconds.) Get ready. (Signal.) *January first.* (Repeat step 4 until firm.)

> *Individual test*
>
> Call on individuals to do part of step 4.

EXERCISE 19

MEMORIZATION: Poem

Say that poem we learned about the mechanic and the astronomer. Get ready. (Signal.)
A mechanic fixes cars, An astronomer looks at stars, A captain has two bars, And a boxer spars and spars.

> *Individual test*
>
> Call on individuals to say the whole poem.

Points

(Award points for Information.
Have the students add up their daily total.)

END OF LESSON 26

THINKING OPERATIONS

EXERCISE 1

● **AND/OR**

The first Thinking Operation Today is **And/Or.**

1. Listen. I'm going to pat my head **or** pat my knee. What am I going to do? (Signal.) *Pat your head or pat your knee.* (Repeat until firm.)

2. Am I going to pat my head? (Signal.) *Maybe.*
   To correct students who say *Yes:*
   a. You don't know.
   b. Maybe I'm going to pat my head. Maybe I'm going to pat my knee.
   c. (Repeat steps 1 and 2.)
   Am I going to pat my knee? (Signal.) *Maybe.*

3. Here I go. (Pat your knee.)
   Did I pat my head? (Signal.) *No.*
   Did I pat my knee? (Signal.) *Yes.*

4. (Repeat steps 1–3 until firm.)

5. New problem. I'm going to pat my head **and** pat my knee. What am I going to do? (Signal.) *Pat your head and pat your knee.* (Repeat until firm.)

6. Am I going to pat my head? (Signal.) *Yes.*
   To correct students who say *Maybe:*
   a. I am going to pat my head.
   b. (Repeat steps 5 and 6.)
   Am I going to pat my knee? (Signal.) *Yes.*

7. Here I go. (Pat your head and pat your knee at the same time.)
   Did I pat my head? (Signal.) *Yes.*
   Did I pat my knee? (Signal.) *Yes.*

8. (Repeat steps 5–7 until firm.)

EXERCISE 2

STATEMENT INFERENCE

The next Thinking Operation is **Statement Inference.**

Task A

1. Listen. They said that the doctor's son was always healthy. Say that statement. (Signal.) *They said that the doctor's son was always healthy.* (Repeat until firm.)

> **Individual test**
> Call on individual students to say the statement.

2. Everybody, listen. They said that the doctor's son was always healthy. Who said that the doctor's son was always healthy? (Signal.) *They.*
   What did they say? (Signal.) *That the doctor's son was always healthy.*
   When was the doctor's son healthy? (Signal.) *Always.*
   Who did they say was always healthy? (Signal.) *The doctor's son.*
   Why was the doctor's son always healthy? (Signal.) *I don't know.*
   Whose son did they say was always healthy? (Signal.) *The doctor's.*
   How did they say the doctor's son was always? (Signal.) *Healthy.*
   (Repeat step 2 until firm.)

> **Individual test**
> Call on individual students to answer a question from step 2.

Task B

1. Listen. The beavers near the creek completed their dam. Say that statement. (Signal.) *The beavers near the creek completed their dam.* (Repeat until firm.)

> **Individual test**
> Call on individual students to say the statement.

2. Everybody, listen. The beavers near the creek completed their dam. What did the beavers near the creek do? (Signal.) *Completed their dam.*
   What did the beavers near the creek complete? (Signal.) *Their dam.*
   Which beavers completed their dam? (Signal.) *The ones near the creek.*
   When did the beavers near the creek complete their dam? (Signal.) *I don't know.*
   Did the beavers near the creek finish their dam? (Signal.) *Yes.*

What completed their dam? (Signal.) *The beavers.*

Where were the beavers that completed their dam? (Signal.) *Near the creek.*

Whose dam did the beavers near the creek complete? (Signal.) *Theirs.*

(Repeat step 2 until firm.)

Individual test

Call on individual students to answer a question from step 2.

═══════ **EXERCISE 3** ═══════

ANALOGIES

The next Thinking Operation is **Analogies.**

Task A

1. We're going to make up an **analogy** that tells **how animals move.** What is the analogy going to tell? (Signal.) *How animals move.*

2. The animals you're going to use in the analogy are a kangaroo and a sparrow. Which animals? (Signal.) *A kangaroo and a sparrow.*

3. How does a kangaroo move? (Call on individual students. Accept all reasonable answers.) Let's say our kangaroo hops.

4. How does a sparrow move? (Signal.) *It flies.*

5. A kangaroo hops and a sparrow flies. Say the whole analogy about a kangaroo and a sparrow. (Pause.) Get ready. (Signal.) *A kangaroo is to hopping as a sparrow is to flying.* (Repeat until firm.)

6. The analogy tells something about those animals. (Pause.) What does that analogy tell about those animals? (Signal.) *How those animals move.*

7. (Repeat steps 5 and 6 until firm.)

Task B

1. We're going to make up an **analogy** that tells **what color objects are.** What is the analogy going to tell? (Signal.) *What color objects are.*

2. The objects you're going to use in the analogy are a stoplight and butter. Which objects? (Signal.) *A stoplight and butter.*

3. What color is a stoplight? (Signal.) *Red.*

4. What color is butter? (Signal.) *Yellow.*

5. A stoplight is red and butter is yellow. Say the whole analogy about a stoplight and butter. (Pause.) Get ready. (Signal.) *A stoplight is to red as butter is to yellow.* (Repeat until firm.)

6. The analogy tells something about those objects. (Pause.) What does that analogy tell about those objects? (Signal.) *What color those objects are.*

7. (Repeat steps 5 and 6 until firm.)

Task C

1. We're going to make up an **analogy** that tells **where you find objects.** What is the analogy going to tell? (Signal.) *Where you find objects.*

2. The objects you're going to use in the analogy are a bed and a stove. Which objects? (Signal.) *A bed and a stove.*

3. Where do you find a bed? (Signal.) *In the bedroom.*

4. Where do you find a stove? (Signal.) *In the kitchen.*

5. You find a bed in the bedroom and a stove in the kitchen. Say the whole analogy about a bed and a stove. (Pause.) Get ready. (Signal.) *A bed is to a bedroom as a stove is to a kitchen.* (Repeat until firm.)

6. The analogy tells something about those objects. (Pause.) What does that analogy tell about those objects? (Signal.) *Where you find those objects.*

7. (Repeat steps 5 and 6 until firm.)

═══════ **EXERCISE 4** ═══════

SAME: Review

The next Thinking Operation is **Same.**

1. You're going to name at least twelve ways that a tree and an elephant are the same. Think about where you **find** them, what **parts** they have, what they **do,** and other ways a tree and an elephant are the same. (Pause 4 seconds.)

2. Name a way a tree and an elephant are the same. (Call on individuals. The students are not to repeat ways others have named. For each new way, make a tally mark on the

board. Praise responses about characteristics, parts, and so on.)

3. (After twelve ways have been named, say:) You named twelve ways. Does anybody know any more ways? (Call on individuals. Praise the group for naming more than twelve ways.)

Answer key *They are alive; grow; need food; can reproduce; die. They are objects; take up space; are found in some place; are found in a jungle and in a zoo; have trunks. You can climb them. They move; and so on.*

═══════════ **EXERCISE 5** ═══════════

DESCRIPTION

The next Thinking Operation is **Description.**

1. I'm going to tell you about an object you know. But I'm going to call it a funny name. See if you can figure out what object I'm talking about.

2. (Hold up one finger.) A blarg is a container. Say that. (Signal.) *A blarg is a container.* (Hold up two fingers.) A blarg is made of glass. Say that. (Signal.) *A blarg is made of glass.* (Hold up three fingers.) Soda pop is often in blargs. Say that. (Signal.) *Soda pop is often in blargs.*

3. Everybody, say the three things you know about blargs. (Hold up one finger.) *A blarg is a container.* (Hold up two fingers.) *A blarg is made of glass.* (Hold up three fingers.) *Soda pop is often in blargs.* (Repeat until the students say the statements in order.)

4. Everybody, tell me the thing I'm calling a blarg. (Signal.) *A bottle.* Yes, it's really a bottle.

═══════════ **EXERCISE 6** ═══════════

DESCRIPTION

1. Listen. See if you can figure out what I'm talking about. It has walls and a roof. Name three buildings I could be talking about. (Call on individuals. Accept reasonable responses; for example, school, house, store.)

2. It has walls and a roof, and people work there. Name two buildings I could be talking about. (Call on individual students. Accept all reasonable responses; for example, school, skyscraper, store.)

3. It has walls and a roof, people work there, and you go there to buy gas. Everybody, name the building I am talking about. (Signal.) *A gas station.*

═══════════ **EXERCISE 7** ═══════════

DEDUCTIONS: With *some*

The next Thinking Operation is **Deductions.**

1. Listen to this rule. **Some** books have pictures. Everybody, say that. (Signal.) *Some books have pictures.* Yes, only **some** books have pictures. Do **all** books have pictures? (Signal.) *No.* How many books have pictures? (Signal.) *Some.*

2. **Some** books have pictures. Owen will read a book. What does the rule let you know about that book? (Signal.) *Maybe that book has pictures.*

   To correct students who say *That book has pictures:*
   a. Listen. Only **some** books have pictures; so **maybe** that book has pictures.
   b. (Repeat step 2 until firm.)
   How do you know that maybe that book has pictures? (Signal.) *Because some books have pictures.*

3. Listen. **Some** books have pictures. The **hippopotamus** snored. What does the rule let you know about the hippopotamus? (Signal.) *Nothing.*

4. Listen. **Some** books have pictures. Mr. Carroll wrote a **book.** What does the rule let you know about that book? (Signal.) *Maybe that book has pictures.* How do you know that maybe that book has pictures? (Signal.) *Because some books have pictures.*

5. Listen. **Some** books have pictures. Joe read a **newspaper.** What does the rule let you know about that newspaper? (Signal.) *Nothing.*

═══ EXERCISE 8 ═══

BASIC EVIDENCE: Using Facts

The next Thinking Operation is **Basic Evidence.**

1. You're going to use two facts to explain things that happened. (Hold up one finger.) First fact. There was no electricity at the house. Say it. (Signal.) *There was no electricity at the house.* (Repeat until firm.) (Hold up two fingers.) Second fact. Most people enjoy eating. Say it. (Signal.) *Most people enjoy eating.* (Repeat until firm.)

2. Everybody, say those facts again. (Hold up one finger.) First fact. *There was no electricity at the house.* (Hold up two fingers.) Second fact. *Most people enjoy eating.* (Repeat until the students say the facts in order.)

Individual test
Call on individual students to say the facts.
---

3. Here's what happened. Many restaurants made lots of money. Tell me the fact that explains **why** that happened. (Pause.) Get ready. (Signal.) *Most people enjoy eating.*

4. Here's what happened. They were reading by candlelight. Tell me the fact that explains **why** that happened. (Pause.) Get ready. (Signal.) *There was no electricity at the house.*

5. Here's what happened. The television would not work. Tell me the fact that explains **why** that happened. (Pause.) Get ready. (Signal.) *There was no electricity at the house.*

6. Here's what happened. There was lots of food at the party. Tell me the fact that explains **why** that happened. (Pause.) Get ready. (Signal.) *Most people enjoy eating.*

7. (Repeat steps 4–6 until firm.)

═══ EXERCISE 9 ═══

DEFINITIONS

The next Thinking Operation is **Definitions.**

1. **Duplicate** means **copy.**

2. What does **duplicate** mean? (Signal.) *Copy.* What word means **copy?** (Signal.) *Duplicate.* (Repeat step 2 until firm.)

3. Listen. Nobody could copy your pies. Say that. (Signal.) *Nobody could copy your pies.* (Repeat until firm.) Now say that sentence with a different word for **copy.** (Pause.) Get ready. (Signal.) *Nobody could duplicate your pies.* (Repeat until firm.) (Repeat step 3 until firm.)

4. Listen. The artist didn't want anyone to copy her pictures. Say that. (Signal.) *The artist didn't want anyone to copy her pictures.* (Repeat until firm.) Now say that sentence with a different word for **copy.** (Pause.) Get ready. (Signal.) *The artist didn't want anyone to duplicate her pictures.* (Repeat until firm.) (Repeat step 4 until firm.)

5. Listen. Can you duplicate that trick? Say that. (Signal.) *Can you duplicate that trick?* (Repeat until firm.) Now say that sentence with a different word for **duplicate.** (Pause.) Get ready. (Signal.) *Can you copy that trick?* (Repeat until firm.) (Repeat step 5 until firm.)

═══ EXERCISE 10 ═══

DEFINITIONS

1. A synonym for **small** is **little.**

2. What's a synonym for **small?** (Signal.) *Little.* And what's a synonym for **little?** (Signal.) *Small.* (Repeat step 2 until firm.)

3. Listen. His bicycle is too small. Say that. (Signal.) *His bicycle is too small.* (Repeat until firm.) Now say that sentence with a synonym for **small.** (Pause.) Get ready. (Signal.) *His bicycle is too little.* (Repeat until firm.) (Repeat step 2 until firm.)

4. Listen. The container was little. Say that. (Signal.) *The container was little.* Now say that sentence with a synonym for **little.** (Pause.) Get ready. (Signal.) *The container was small.* (Repeat until firm.) (Repeat step 4 until firm.)

EXERCISE 11

DEFINITIONS

1. **Leap.** (Pause.) What's a synonym for **leap?**
   (Signal.) *Jump.*
   And what's a synonym for **jump?** (Signal.)
   Leap.
   (Repeat step 1 until firm.)

2. Listen. They had to jump from the burning
   building. Say that. (Signal.) *They had to jump*
   from the burning building. (Repeat until firm.)
   Now say that sentence with a synonym for
   jump. (Pause.) Get ready. (Signal.) *They had*
   to leap from the burning building. (Repeat
   until firm.)
   (Repeat step 2 until firm.)

3. **Instruct.** (Pause.) What's a synonym for
   instruct? (Signal.) *Teach.* And what's a
   synonym for **teach?** (Signal.) *Instruct.*
   (Repeat step 3 until firm.)

4. Listen. He taught us for three days. Say that.
   (Signal.) *He taught us for three days.*
   Now say the sentence with a synonym for
   taught. (Pause.) Get ready. (Signal.) *He*
   instructed us for three days. (Repeat until
   firm.)
   (Repeat step 4 until firm.)

5. **Modify.** (Pause.) What's a synonym for
   modify? (Signal.) *Change.*
   And what's a synonym for **change?** (Signal.)
   Modify.
   (Repeat step 5 until firm.)

6. Listen. A beautician's job is to modify how
   you look. Say that. (Signal.) *A beautician's*
   job is to modify how you look. (Repeat until
   firm.)
   Now say that sentence with a synonym for
   modify. (Pause.) Get ready. (Signal.) *A*
   beautician's job is to change how you look.
   (Repeat until firm.)
   (Repeat step 6 until firm.)

Points

(Pass out the Workbooks.
Award points for Thinking Operations.)

WORKBOOK EXERCISES

We're going to do Workbooks now. Remember
to follow my instructions carefully.

EXERCISE 12

TRUE—FALSE

1. Everybody, touch part A in your Workbook. ✔
   I'll say statements about the picture.

2. Get ready to circle **true, false,** or **maybe.**
   Item 1. There are two mammals in the
   picture. Circle the answer. (Wait.)

3. Item 2. Both animals are warm-blooded.
   Circle the answer. (Wait.)

4. Item 3. There is a reptile behind the tree.
   Circle the answer. (Wait.)

5. Item 4. All the things in the picture are
   objects. Circle the answer. (Wait.)

6. Item 5. There are no reptiles shown in the
   picture. Circle the answer. (Wait.)

7. Item 6. One animal in the picture is cold-
   blooded. Circle the answer. (Wait.)

8. Everybody, let's check your answers. Say
   true, false, or **maybe.**

9. Item 1. There are two mammals in the
   picture. (Signal.) *True.*

10. (Repeat step 9 for items 2–6.)

EXERCISE 13

DESCRIPTION

1. Everybody, touch part B in your Workbook.
   Figure out which object I describe. Listen. A
   clor is a container. You can put clothes in a
   clor. You take a clor when you go on a trip.
   Underline the object I'm calling a clor.
   (Wait.)

2. Listen. A snib is a food. A snib is yellow. A
   snib is not sour. **Circle** the object I'm calling
   a snib. (Wait.)

3. Listen. A lin is a container. A lin has a
   handle. You drink from a lin. **Make a box**
   around the object I'm calling a lin. (Wait.)

4. Everybody, get ready to check your work.
   Tell me the real name for the object that is a

container, that you can put clothes in, and that you take on a trip. Get ready. (Signal.) *A suitcase.* And how did you mark the suitcase? (Signal.) *Underlined it.*
5. Tell me the real name for the object that is a food, that is yellow, and that is not sour. Get ready. (Signal.) *A banana.* And how did you mark the banana? (Signal.) *Circled it.*
6. Tell me the real name for the object that is a container, that has a handle, and that you drink from. Get ready. (Signal.) *A cup.* And how did you mark the cup? (Signal.) *Made a box around it.*

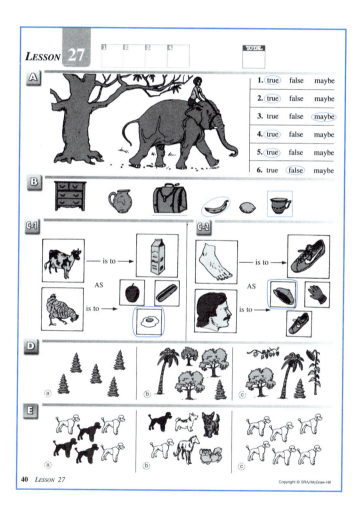

EXERCISE 14

ANALOGIES

1. Everybody, touch part C-1. ✔ This analogy shows what food comes from animals. What does the analogy show? (Signal.) *What food comes from animals.*
   Look at the pictures and name the animals that are in the analogy. (Pause.) Get ready. (Signal.) *A cow and a chicken.*
   Remember, the analogy shows what food comes from those animals. Circle the picture that completes the analogy. (Wait.)
2. Everybody, touch the right pictures and say the whole analogy. Get ready. (Signal.) *A cow is to milk as a chicken is to an egg.* (Repeat until firm.)
   If you didn't circle the picture of the egg, make an X next to the picture you circled.
3. Everybody, touch part C-2 in your Workbook. This analogy shows what body parts clothing is for. What does the analogy show? (Signal.) *What body parts clothing is for.*
   Look at the pictures and name the body parts in the analogy. (Pause.) Get ready. (Signal.) *A foot and a head.*
   Remember, the analogy shows what body parts clothing is for. Circle the picture that completes the analogy. (Wait.)
4. Everybody, touch the right pictures and say the whole analogy. Get ready. (Signal.) *A foot is to a shoe as a head is to a hat.* (Repeat until firm.)
   If you didn't circle the picture of a hat, make an X next to the picture you circled.

Individual test
(Call on individual students to do one of the following:)
  a. Say the analogy shown in part C-1.
  b. What does that analogy show about those animals?
  c. Say the analogy shown in part C-2.
  d. What does that analogy show about clothing?

EXERCISE 15

CLASSIFICATION

1. Everybody, touch part D. ✔ You're going to work on classification. One of these boxes shows the class of Christmas trees. One of these boxes shows the class of trees. One of these boxes shows the class of plants.

2. You're going to tell me which box shows the class of **Christmas trees,** box A, box B, or box C. (Pause 3 seconds.) Get ready. (Signal.) *Box A.*

3. You're going to tell me which box shows the class of **trees.** (Pause 3 seconds.) Get ready. (Signal.) *Box B.*

4. You're going to tell me which class shows the class of **plants.** (Pause 3 seconds.) Get ready. (Signal.) *Box C.*

5. Now let's figure out which of these classes is the biggest. What's the rule about the bigger class? (Signal.) *If a class has more kinds of things, it is bigger.* (Repeat until firm.)

6. Box C shows the class of plants. That means that **all kinds** of plants would be in box C. So, would all trees be in box C? (Signal.) *Yes.*

To correct students who say *No:*

a. All trees are plants. Box C shows the class of plants; so **all** trees **would be** in box C.

b. (Repeat step 6.)

Would all Christmas trees be in box C? (Signal.) *Yes.* Would plants that are not trees be in box C? (Signal.) *Yes.* (Repeat step 6 until firm.)

Individual test

(Call on three different students. Have each student do the following tasks:)

Note: The students may name plants **not** illustrated.

a. Name a plant that is **not** a tree. (Praise correct responses; for example, flower, grass, bush.)

b. Would that plant be in box C? (Signal.) *Yes.*

c. Would that plant be in any of the other boxes? (Signal.) *No.*

---

7. Everybody, box C has more **kinds** of things in it. So, which box shows the biggest class? (Signal.) *Box C.*
Tell me the class **name** for the things in box C. (Pause 3 seconds.) Get ready. (Signal.) *Plants.* How do you know that the class of plants is bigger than the other classes? (Signal.) *Because it has more kinds of things.*

EXERCISE 16

CLASSIFICATION

1. Everybody, touch part E. ✔ You're going to work on classification. One of these boxes shows the class of dogs. One of these boxes shows the class of poodles. One of these boxes shows the class of white poodles.

2. You're going to tell me which box shows the class of **white poodles,** box A, box B, or box C. (Pause 3 seconds.) Get ready. (Signal.) *Box C.*

3. Now tell me which box shows the class of **poodles.** (Pause 3 seconds.) Get ready. (Signal.) *Box A.*

4. Tell me which box shows the class of **dogs.** (Pause 3 seconds.) Get ready. (Signal.) *Box B.*

5. Now let's figure out which of these classes is the biggest. What's the rule about the bigger class? (Signal.) *If a class has more kinds of things, it is bigger.* (Repeat until firm.)

6. Look at box A, box B, and box C and figure out which box has more **kinds** of things than the others. (Pause 4 seconds.) Which box? (Signal.) *Box B.*

To correct:

a. Box B has more kinds of things than the other boxes. It has a setter, a cocker spaniel, and a beagle.

b. (Repeat step 6.)

Tell me the class **name** for box B. (Pause 3 seconds.) Get ready. (Signal.) *Dogs.* How do you know that the class of dogs is bigger than the other classes? (Signal.) *Because it has more kinds of things.*
(Repeat step 6 until firm.)

7. Now look at box A and box C and figure out which box has more **kinds** of things. (Pause 4 seconds.) Get ready. (Signal.) *Box A.*
   And tell me the class **name** for the things in box A. (Pause 3 seconds.) Get ready. (Signal.) *Poodles.* How do you know that the class of poodles is bigger than the class shown in box C? (Signal.) *Because it has more kinds of things.*
   (Repeat step 7 until firm.)

8. Which box shows the smallest class? (Signal.) *Box C.*
   And what's the class **name** for the things in box C? (Signal.) *White poodles.* How do you know that white poodles is the smallest class? (Call on one student.) *Because it has only one kind of thing.*
   (Repeat step 8 until firm.)

Points
(Award points for Workbooks.)

INFORMATION

We're going to work on Information now.

══════════ **EXERCISE 17** ══════════

MEMORIZATION: Poem

1. You're learning a poem about American Indians. Let's name those Indians.
2. Creek. Say it. (Signal.) *Creek.*
   Choctaw. Say it. (Signal.) *Choctaw.*
   Cherokee. Say it. (Signal.) *Cherokee.*
   Seminole. Say it. (Signal.) *Seminole.*
   Chickasaw. Say it. (Signal.) *Chickasaw.*
   (Repeat step 2 until firm.)
3. I'll say the whole poem about American Indians. American Indians were what they saw.
   Some were Creek and some Choctaw.
   American Indians were what they saw.
   Cherokee, Seminole, and Chickasaw.
4. Say it with me. (Signal. Respond with the students.) *American Indians were what they saw. Some were Creek and some Choctaw. American Indians were what they saw. Cherokee, Seminole, and Chickasaw.*
   (Repeat until the students are responding with you.)

Individual test
(Call on individual students.)
Say as much of the poem as you can.
(Praise students who correctly say at least two lines.)

EXERCISE 18

● **CALENDAR: Holidays**

1. Get ready to answer some questions about holidays.
2. Tell me two winter holidays. (Pause.) Get ready. (Signal.) *Christmas and New Year's Day.*
   Tell me which holiday comes in December. (Pause 2 seconds.) Get ready. (Signal.) *Christmas.* Tell me which holiday is always on January first. (Pause 2 seconds.) Get ready. (Signal.) *New Year's Day.*
   Tell me which holiday comes exactly one week **before** New Year's Day. (Pause 2 seconds.) Get ready. (Signal.) *Christmas.*
   (Repeat step 2 until firm.)
3. Here's a new fact. Christmas is always on December twenty-fifth. Say that fact. (Signal.) *Christmas is always on December twenty-fifth.* (Repeat until firm.)
4. Tell me the **date** of New Year's Day. (Pause 2 seconds.) Get ready. (Signal.) *January first.*
   Tell me the **date** of Christmas. (Pause 2 seconds.) Get ready. (Signal.) *December twenty-fifth.*
   Tell me what **season** both of those holidays are in. (Pause 2 seconds.) Get ready. (Signal.) *Winter.*
   (Repeat step 4 until firm.)

> **Individual test**
> Call on individual students to do part of step 4.

EXERCISE 19

MEMORIZATION: Poem

Say that poem we learned about the beautician and the tailor. Get ready. (Signal.)

> *A beautician fixes hair,*
> *A tailor can mend a tear,*
> *An exposition is a fair,*
> *And one plus one is a pair.*

(Repeat until firm.)

> **Individual test**
> Call on individual students to say the whole poem.

Points

(Award points for Information.
Have the students add up their daily total.)

END OF LESSON 27

THINKING OPERATIONS

EXERCISE 1

● **SAME: Review**

The first Thinking Operation today is **Same.**

1. I'll name some things. When I call on you, name ways that those things are the same.
2. A boat and a truck. (Call on one student.) Name eight ways they are the same. (Praise the student if he or she names eight ways.)
3. A bird and an airplane. (Call on one student.) Name eight ways they are the same. (Praise the student if he or she names eight ways.)
4. A fish and a goat. (Call on one student.) Name eight ways they are the same. (Praise the student if he or she names eight ways.)
5. A store and a school. (Call on one student.) Name eight ways they are the same. (Praise the student if he or she names eight ways.)

EXERCISE 2

And/Or

The next Thinking Operation is **And/Or.**

1. Listen. I'm going to touch my nose **and** touch my ear. What am I going to do? (Signal.) *Touch your nose and touch your ear.* (Repeat until firm.)
2. Am I going to touch my nose? (Signal.) *Yes.* Am I going to touch my ear? (Signal.) *Yes.*
3. Here I go. (Touch your nose and touch your ear at the same time.) Did I touch my nose? (Signal.) *Yes.* Did I touch my ear? (Signal.) *Yes.*
4. (Repeat steps 1–3 until firm.)
5. New problem. I'm going to touch my nose **or** touch my ear. What am I going to do? (Signal.) *Touch your nose or touch your ear.* (Repeat until firm.)
6. Am I going to touch my nose? (Signal.) *Maybe.* Am I going to touch my ear? (Signal.) *Maybe.*
7. Here I go. (Touch your ear.) Did I touch my nose? (Signal.) *No.* Did I touch my ear? (Signal.) *Yes.*
8. (Repeat steps 5–7 until firm.)

EXERCISE 3

DEDUCTIONS: With *some*

The next Thinking Operation is **Deductions.**

1. Listen to this rule. **Some** dogs are retrievers. Everybody, say that. (Signal.) *Some dogs are retrievers.* Yes, only **some** dogs are retrievers. Are **all** dogs retrievers? (Signal.) *No.*
   How many dogs are retrievers? (Signal.) *Some.*
2. **Some** dogs are retrievers. The dog looked for cats. What does the rule tell you about that dog? (Signal.) *Maybe that dog is a retriever.*
   To correct students who say *That dog is a retriever:*
   a. Listen. Only **some** dogs are retrievers; so **maybe** that dog is a retriever.
   b. (Repeat step 2 until firm.)
   How do you know that maybe that dog is a retriever? (Signal.) *Because some dogs are retrievers.*
3. Listen. **Some** dogs are retrievers. The **cat** climbed the tree. What does the rule let you know about the cat? (Signal.) *Nothing.*
4. Listen. **Some** dogs are retrievers. **Zonker** is a lazy dog. What does the rule let you know about Zonker? (Signal.) *Maybe Zonker is a retriever.* How do you know that maybe Zonker is a retriever? (Signal.) *Because some dogs are retrievers.*
5. Listen. **Some** dogs are retrievers. The **bear** scratched its stomach. What does the rule let you know about the bear? (Signal.) *Nothing.*

EXERCISE 4

DESCRIPTION

The next Thinking Operation is **Description.**

1. Listen. See if you can figure out what I'm talking about. It can fly. Name three animals I could be talking about. (Call on individual students. Accept all reasonable responses; for example, bird, bee, fly.)
2. It can fly and it makes a noise. Name two animals I could be talking about. (Call on individual students. Accept all reasonable responses; for example, bird, bee, parakeet.)

LESSON 28

3. It can fly, it makes noise, and it makes honey. Everybody, name the animal I'm talking about. (Signal.) *A bee.*

═══════════════ EXERCISE 5 ═══════════════

ANALOGIES

The next Thinking Operation is **Analogies.**

Task A

1. We're going to make up an **analogy** that tells **what sounds animals make.** What is the analogy going to tell? (Signal.) *What sounds animals make.*
2. The animals you're going to use in the analogy are a pig and a sheep. Which animals? (Signal.) *A pig and a sheep.*
3. What sound does a pig make? (Signal.) *Oink.*
4. What sound does a sheep make? (Call on individual students. Accept all reasonable answers.)
   Let's say our sheep bleats.
5. A pig oinks and a sheep bleats. Say the whole analogy about a sheep and a pig. (Pause.) Get ready. (Signal.) *A pig is to oinking as a sheep is to bleating.* (Repeat until firm.)
6. The analogy tells something about those animals. (Pause.) What does that analogy tell about those animals? (Signal.) *What sounds those animals make.*
7. (Repeat steps 5 and 6 until firm.)

Task B

1. We're going to make up an **analogy** that tells **where you find objects.** What is the analogy going to tell? (Signal.) *Where you find objects.*
2. The objects you're going to use in the analogy are a refrigerator and a bathtub. Which objects? (Signal.) *A refrigerator and a bathtub.*
3. Where do you find a refrigerator? (Signal.) *In the kitchen.*
4. Where do you find a bathtub? (Signal.) *In the bathroom.*
5. You find a refrigerator in the kitchen and a bathtub in the bathroom. Say the whole analogy about a refrigerator and a bathtub. (Pause.) Get ready. (Signal.) *A refrigerator is*

to kitchen as a bathtub is to bathroom. (Repeat until firm.)
6. The analogy tells something about those objects. (Pause.) What does that analogy tell about those objects? (Signal.) *Where you find those objects.*
7. (Repeat steps 5 and 6 until firm.)

Task C

1. We're going to make up an **analogy** that tells **how you move vehicles.** What is the analogy going to tell? (Signal.) *How you move vehicles.*
2. The vehicles you're going to use in the analogy are a bicycle and a canoe. Which vehicles? (Signal.) *A bicycle and a canoe.*
3. How do you move a bicycle? (Signal.) *You pedal it.*
4. How do you move a canoe? (Signal.) *You paddle it.*
5. You pedal a bicycle and you paddle a canoe. Say the whole analogy about a bicycle and a canoe. (Pause.) Get ready. (Signal.) *A bicycle is to pedaling as a canoe is to paddling.* (Repeat until firm.)
6. The analogy tells something about those vehicles. (Pause.) What does the analogy tell about those vehicles? (Signal.) *How you move those vehicles.*
7. (Repeat steps 5 and 6 until firm.)

═══════════════ EXERCISE 6 ═══════════════

BASIC EVIDENCE: Using Facts

The next Thinking Operation is **Basic Evidence.**

1. You're going to use two facts to explain things that happened. (Hold up one finger.) First fact. Soap and hot water kill germs. Say it. (Signal.) *Soap and hot water kill germs.* (Repeat until firm.)
   (Hold up two fingers.) Second fact. Wet streets are slippery. Say it. (Signal.) *Wet streets are slippery.* (Repeat until firm.)
2. Everybody, say those facts again. (Hold up one finger.) First fact. *Soap and hot water kill germs.* (Hold up two fingers.) Second fact. *Wet streets are slippery.* (Repeat until the students say the facts in order.)

Individual test
Call on individual students to say the facts.

---

3. Here's what happened. He fell down in the crosswalk. Tell me the fact that explains **why** that happened. (Pause.) Get ready. (Signal.) *Wet streets are slippery.*
4. Listen. First fact. Soap and hot water kill germs. Second fact. Wet streets are slippery.
5. Here's what happened. The doctors scrubbed their hands before the operation. Tell me the fact that explains **why** that happened. (Pause.) Get ready. (Signal.) *Soap and hot water kill germs.*
6. Here's what happened. The car slowed down when the rain started. Tell me the fact that explains **why** that happened. (Pause.) Get ready. (Signal.) *Wet streets are slippery.*
7. Here's what happened. He washed his cut. Tell me the fact that explains **why** that happened. (Pause.) Get ready. (Signal.) *Soap and hot water kill germs.*
8. (Repeat steps 5–7 until firm.)

EXERCISE 7

STATEMENT INFERENCE

The next Thinking Operation is **Statement Inference.**

1. Listen. If you pay three dollars, you can go to the exposition. Say that statement. (Signal.) *If you pay three dollars, you can go to the exposition.* (Repeat until firm.)

Individual test
Call on individual students to say the statement.

---

2. Everybody, listen. If you pay three dollars, you can go to the exposition. How much do you pay to go to the exposition? (Signal.) *Three dollars.*
   If you pay three dollars, where can you go? (Signal.) *To the exposition.*
   If you pay three dollars, what can you do? (Signal.) *Go to the exposition.*
   What can you do at the exposition? (Signal.) *I don't know.*

What do you have to do to go to the exposition? (Signal.) *Pay three dollars.*
How many dollars do you have to pay to go to the exposition? (Signal.) *Three.*
(Repeat step 2 until firm.)

Individual test
Call on individual students to answer a question from step 2.

EXERCISE 8

DEFINITIONS

The next Thinking Operation is **Definitions.**

1. **Destroy** means **wreck.**
2. What does **destroy** mean? (Signal.) *Wreck.*
   What word means **wreck?** (Signal.) *Destroy.*
   (Repeat step 2 until firm.)
3. Listen. The tornado destroyed the town. Say that. (Signal.) *The tornado destroyed the town.* (Repeat until firm.)
   Now say that sentence with a different word for **destroyed.** (Pause.) Get ready. (Signal.) *The tornado wrecked the town.* (Repeat until firm.)
   (Repeat step 3 until firm.)
4. Listen. The bear wrecked the garden. Say that. (Signal.) *The bear wrecked the garden.* (Repeat until firm.)
   Now say that sentence with a different word for **wrecked.** (Pause.) Get ready. (Signal.) *The bear destroyed the garden.* (Repeat until firm.)
   (Repeat step 4 until firm.)
5. Listen. The fire almost destroyed the house. Say that. (Signal.) *The fire almost destroyed the house.* (Repeat until firm.)
   Now say that sentence with a different word for **destroyed.** (Pause.) Get ready. (Signal.) *The fire almost wrecked the house.* (Repeat until firm.)
   (Repeat step 5 until firm.)

LESSON 28

EXERCISE 9

DEFINITIONS

1. **Small.** (Pause.) What's a synonym for **small?** (Signal.) *Little.*
   And what's a synonym for **little?** (Signal.) *Small.* (Repeat step 1 until firm.)

2. Listen. These shoes are too small. Say that. (Signal.) *These shoes are too small.* (Repeat until firm.)
   Now say that sentence with a synonym for **small.** (Pause.) Get ready. (Signal.) *These shoes are too little.* (Repeat until firm.)
   (Repeat step 2 until firm.)

3. **Obtain.** (Pause.) What's a synonym for **obtain?** (Signal.) *Get.* And what's a synonym for **get?** (Signal.) *Obtain.* (Repeat until firm.)

4. Listen. The children got a lot of candy on Halloween. Say that. (Signal.) *The children got a lot of candy on Halloween.* (Repeat until firm.)
   Now say that sentence with a synonym for **got.** (Pause.) Get ready. (Signal.) *The children obtained a lot of candy on Halloween.* (Repeat until firm.)
   (Repeat step 4 until firm.)

5. **Amble.** (Pause.) What does **amble** mean? (Signal.) *Walk slowly.*
   What word means **walk slowly?** (Signal.) *Amble.* (Repeat step 5 until firm.)

6. Listen. The bear ambled through our camp. Say that. (Signal.) *The bear ambled through our camp.* (Repeat until firm.)
   Now say that sentence with different words for **ambled.** (Pause.) Get ready. (Signal.) *The bear walked slowly through our camp.* (Repeat until firm.)
   (Repeat step 6 until firm.)

EXERCISE 10

DEFINITIONS

1. **Well.** What does **well** mean? (Signal.) *Healthy.*
   Instruct. What does **instruct** mean? (Signal.) *Teach.* (Repeat step 1 until firm.)

2. Listen. She will instruct us about staying well. Say that sentence. (Signal.) *She will instruct us about staying well.* (Repeat until firm.)
   Now say that sentence with different words for **well** and **instruct.** (Pause.) Get ready. (Signal.) *She will teach us about staying healthy.* (Repeat until firm.)
   (Repeat step 2 until firm.)

Points

(Pass out the Workbooks.
Award points for Thinking Operations.)

WORKBOOK EXERCISES

We're going to do Workbooks now. Remember to follow my instructions carefully.

EXERCISE 11

TRUE—FALSE

1. Everybody, touch part A in your Workbook. ✔ I'll say statements about the picture.
2. Get ready to circle **true, false,** or **maybe.** Item 1. The man will eat all the food. Circle the answer. (Wait.)
3. Item 2. None of the food comes from plants. Circle the answer. (Wait.)
4. Item 3. All the food comes from animals. Circle the answer. (Wait.)
5. Item 4. The man is sitting. Circle the answer. (Wait.)
6. Item 5. The man is eating. Circle the answer. (Wait.)
7. Item 6. The man will drink. Circle the answer. (Wait.)
8. Item 7. The man is eating part of an animal. Circle the answer. (Wait.)
9. Everybody, let's check your answers. Say **true, false,** or **maybe.**
10. Item 1. The man will eat all the food. (Signal.) *Maybe.*
11. (Repeat step 10 for items 2–7.)

EXERCISE 12

TRUE—FALSE

1. Everybody, touch part B in your Workbook. ✔ I'll say statements that are true of one of the pictures. You write the letter of the right picture.
2. Item 1. **All** the objects are vehicles. Write the letter of the picture on line 1. (Wait.)
3. Item 2. **Only some** of the objects are vehicles. Write the letter of the picture on line 2. (Wait.)
4. Item 3. **None** of the objects are vehicles. Write the letter of the picture on line 3. (Wait.)

5. Item 4. **Only some** of the vehicles go in water. Write the letter of the picture on line 4. (Wait.)
6. Let's check your answers. Mark any items you missed with an X. Tell me the letter of the right picture.
7. Item 1. **All** the objects are vehicles. (Signal.) *A.*
8. (Repeat step 7 for items 2–4.)

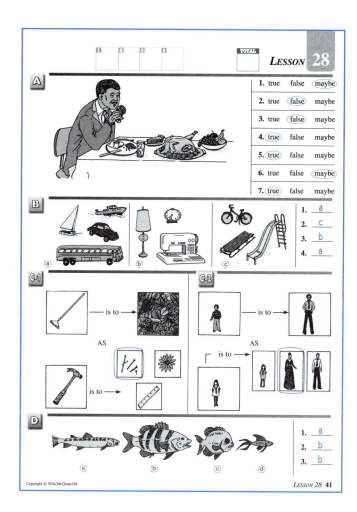

EXERCISE 13

ANALOGIES

1. Everybody, touch part C-1. ✔ This analogy shows what goes with tools. What does the analogy show? (Signal.) *What goes with tools.*
   Look at the pictures and name the tools that are in the analogy. (Pause.) Get ready. (Signal.) *A rake and a hammer.*
   Remember, the analogy shows what goes with those tools. Circle the picture that completes the analogy. (Wait.)

2. Everybody, touch the right pictures and say the whole analogy. Get ready. (Signal.) *A rake is to leaves as a hammer is to nails.* (Repeat until firm.)
   If you didn't circle the picture of nails, make an X next to the picture you circled.

3. Everybody, touch part C-2 in your Workbook. This analogy shows what people grow into. What does the analogy show? (Signal.) *What people grow into.*
   Look at the pictures and name the people in the analogy. (Pause.) Get ready. (Signal.) *A boy and a girl.*
   Remember, the analogy shows what people grow into. Circle the picture that completes the analogy. (Wait.)

4. Everybody, touch the right pictures and say the whole analogy. Get ready. (Signal.) *A boy is to a man as a girl is to a woman.* (Repeat until firm.)
   If you didn't circle the picture of a woman, make an X next to the picture you circled.

Individual test
(Call on individual students to do one of the following:)
   a. Say the analogy shown in part C-1.
   b. What does that analogy show about those tools?
   c. Say the analogy shown in part C-2.
   d. What does that analogy show about people?

EXERCISE 14

DESCRIPTION

1. Everybody, touch part D. ✔ Figure out which fish I describe.
2. Item 1. This fish has little eyes. This fish is long and thin. Listen again. (Repeat the description.) Write the letter for item 1.
3. Item 2. This fish is fat. This fish has little eyes and stripes. Listen again. (Repeat the description.) Write the letter for item 2.
4. Item 3. This fish is long and fat. This fish is striped. Listen again. (Repeat the description.) Write the letter for item 3.
5. Let's check your answers. Mark any items you missed with an X.
6. Item 1. This fish has little eyes. This fish is long and thin. Everybody, what letter? (Signal.) *A.*
7. (Repeat step 6 for items 2 and 3.)

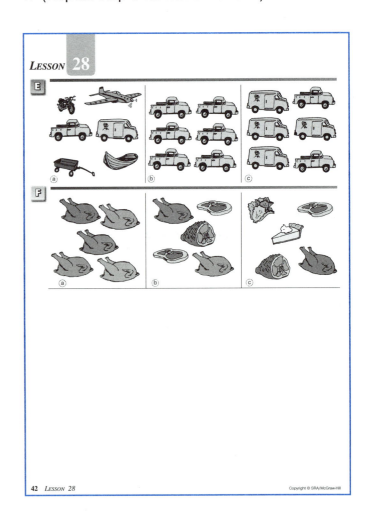

LESSON **28**

42 LESSON 28   Copyright © SRA/McGraw-Hill

EXERCISE 15

CLASSIFICATION

Task A

1. Everybody, touch part E. ✔ You're going to work on classification. One of these boxes shows the class of vehicles. One of these boxes shows the class of trucks. One of these boxes shows the class of pickup trucks.

2. You're going to tell me which box shows the class of **pickup trucks,** box A, box B, or box C. (Pause 3 seconds.) Get ready. (Signal.) *Box B.*

3. Now tell me which box shows the class of **trucks.** (Pause 3 seconds.) Get ready. (Signal.) *Box C.*

4. Tell me which box shows the class of **vehicles.** (Pause 3 seconds.) Get ready. (Signal.) *Box A.*

5. Now let's figure out which of these classes is the biggest. What's the rule about the bigger class? (Signal.) *If a class has more kinds of things, it is bigger.* (Repeat until firm.)

6. Look at box A, box B, and box C and figure out which box has more **kinds** of things than the others. (Pause 4 seconds.) Which box? (Signal.) *Box A.*

   To correct:
   a. Box A has more **kinds** of things than the other boxes. It has a rowboat, a wagon, and an airplane.
   b. (Repeat step 6.)
   Tell the class **name** for box A. (Pause 3 seconds.) Get ready. (Signal.) *Vehicles.* How do you know that the class of vehicles is bigger than the other classes? (Signal.) *Because it has more kinds of things.* (Repeat step 6 until firm.)

7. Now look at box B and box C and figure out which box has more **kinds** of things. (Pause 4 seconds.) Get ready. (Signal.) *Box C.* And tell me the class **name** for the things in box C. (Pause 3 seconds.) Get ready. (Signal.) *Trucks.* How do you know that the class of trucks is bigger than the class shown in box B? (Signal.) *Because it has more kinds of things.* (Repeat step 7 until firm.)

8. Which box shows the smallest class? (Signal.) *Box B.* And what's the class **name** for the things in box B? (Signal.) *Pickup trucks.* How do you know that pickup trucks is the smallest class? (Call on one student.) *Because it has only one kind of thing.* (Repeat step 8 until firm.)

Task B

1. Everybody, touch part F. ✔ You're going to work on classification. One of these boxes shows the class of food.
   One of these boxes shows the class of meat. One of these boxes shows the class of turkey.

2. You're going to tell me which box shows the class of **turkey,** box A, box B, or box C. (Pause 3 seconds.) Get ready. (Signal.) *Box A.*

3. Now tell me which box shows the class of **meat.** (Pause 3 seconds.) Get ready. (Signal.) *Box B.*

4. Tell me which box shows the class of **food.** (Pause 3 seconds.) Get ready. (Signal.) *Box C.*

5. Now let's figure out which of these classes is the biggest. What's the rule about the bigger class? (Signal.) *If a class has more kinds of things, it is bigger.* (Repeat until firm.)

6. Look at box A, box B, and box C and figure out which box has more **kinds** of things than the others. (Pause 4 seconds.) Which box? (Signal.) *Box C.* Tell me the class **name** for box C. (Pause 3 seconds.) Get ready. (Signal.) *Food.* How do you know that the class of food is bigger than the other classes? (Signal.) *Because it has more kinds of things.*
   (Repeat step 6 until firm.)

7. Now look at box A and box B and figure out which box has more **kinds** of things. (Pause 4 seconds.) Get ready. (Signal.) *Box B.*
And tell me the class **name** for the things in box B. (Pause 3 seconds.) Get ready. (Signal.) *Meat.* How do you know that the class of meat is bigger than the class shown in box A? (Signal.) *Because it has more kinds of things.*
(Repeat step 7 until firm.)

8. Which box shows the smallest class? (Signal.) *Box A.*
And what's the class **name** for the things in box A? (Signal.) *Turkey.* How do you know that turkey is the smallest class? (Call on one student.) *Because it has only one kind of thing.*
(Repeat step 8 until firm.)

Points
(Award points for Workbooks.)

INFORMATION

We're going to work on Information now.

======= **EXERCISE 16** =======

- **CALENDAR: Holidays**

1. Get ready to answer some questions about holidays.

2. Tell me two winter holidays. (Pause.) Get ready. (Signal.) *Christmas and New Year's Day.*
Tell me which holiday comes in December. (Pause 2 seconds.) Get ready. (Signal.) *Christmas.* Tell me which holiday is always on January first. (Pause 2 seconds.) Get ready. (Signal.) *New Year's Day.*
Tell me which holiday comes exactly one week **before** New Year's Day. (Pause 2 seconds.) Get ready. (Signal.) *Christmas.*
(Repeat step 2 until firm.)

3. Tell me the **date** of New Year's Day. (Pause 2 seconds.) Get ready. (Signal.) *January first.*
Tell me the **date** of Christmas. (Pause 2 seconds.) Get ready. (Signal.) *December twenty-fifth.*
Tell me what **season** both of those holidays are in. (Pause 2 seconds.) Get ready. (Signal.) *Winter.* (Repeat step 3 until firm.)

Individual test
Call on individual students to do part of step 3.

EXERCISE 17

● **MEMORIZATION: Poem**

1. You're learning a poem about American Indians. Let's name those Indians.
2. Creek. Say it. (Signal.) *Creek.*
   Choctaw. Say it. (Signal.) *Choctaw.*
   Cherokee. Say it. (Signal.) *Cherokee.*
   Seminole. Say it. (Signal.) *Seminole.*
   Chickasaw. Say it. (Signal.) *Chickasaw.*
   (Repeat step 2 until firm.)
3. I'll say the whole poem about American Indians. American Indians were what they saw. Some were Creek and some Choctaw. American Indians were what they saw. Cherokee, Seminole, and Chickasaw.
4. Say it with me. (Signal. Respond with the students.) *American Indians were what they saw. Some were Creek and some Choctaw. American Indians were what they saw. Cherokee, Seminole, and Chickasaw.* (Repeat until students are responding with you.)
5. All by yourselves. (Signal.) *American Indians were what they saw. Some were Creek and some Choctaw. American Indians were what they saw. Cherokee, Seminole, and Chickasaw.* (Repeat until firm.)

   To correct:
   a. (Stop the students as soon as you hear a mistake.)
   b. (Say the line they missed.)
   c. (Have them repeat the line they missed.)
   d. (Repeat step 5.)

Individual test
Call on individual students to say the whole poem. Praise students who make no errors.

EXERCISE 18

CALENDAR: Months in a Year

1. I'll name some months of the year. When I stop, you name the rest of the months.
2. My turn. January, February (pause; signal) *March, April, May, June, July, August, September, October, November, December.* (Repeat step 2 until firm.)
   Here's another one.
3. My turn. January, February, March, April, May, June, July, August, September (pause; signal) *October, November, December.* (Repeat step 3 until firm.)

Individual test
(Call on individual students to do one of the following tasks:)
   a. How many months in a year?
   b. Name the months of the year.
   c. Name the rest of the months. (Repeat step 2 or step 3.)

Points
(Award points for Information.
Have the students add up their daily total.)

END OF LESSON 28

THINKING OPERATIONS

EXERCISE 1

- **ANALOGIES**

The first Thinking Operation is **Analogies.**

Task A

1. We're going to make up an **analogy.** Everybody, what class are a horse and a frog in? (Signal.) *Animals.* Yes, animals.
2. We're going to make up an analogy that tells how those animals move. What's the analogy going to tell about those animals? (Signal.) *How those animals move.* Remember that.
3. What are some ways that a horse moves? (Call on individual students. Accept all reasonable answers.)
Let's say our horse gallops.
4. What are some ways that a frog moves? (Call on individual students. Accept all reasonable answers.) Let's say our frog hops.
5. A horse gallops and a frog hops. Everybody, say the whole analogy. (Pause.) Get ready. (Signal.) *A horse is to galloping as a frog is to hopping.* (Repeat until firm.)
6. The analogy tells something about those animals. (Pause.) What does the analogy tell about those animals? (Signal.) *How those animals move.* (Repeat until firm.)
7. Everybody, say the analogy one more time. (Signal.) *A horse is to galloping as a frog is to hopping.*
8. (Repeat steps 6 and 7 until firm.)

Task B

1. We're going to make up an **analogy.** Everybody, what class are a rooster and a lion in? (Signal.) *Animals.* Yes, animals.
2. We're going to make up an analogy that tells where you find those animals. What's the analogy going to tell about those animals? (Signal.) *Where you find those animals.* Remember that.
3. Where are some places you find a rooster? (Call on individual students. Accept all reasonable answers.)
Let's say you find our rooster on a farm.

4. Where are some places you find a lion? (Call on individual students. Accept all reasonable answers.) Let's say you find our lion in a zoo.
5. You find a rooster on a farm and a lion in a zoo. Everybody, say the whole analogy. (Pause.) Get ready. (Signal.) *A rooster is to farm as a lion is to zoo.* (Repeat until firm.)
6. The analogy tells something about those animals. (Pause.) What does that analogy tell about those animals? (Signal.) *Where you find those animals.* (Repeat until firm.)
7. Everybody, say the analogy one more time. (Signal.) *A rooster is to farm as a lion is to zoo.*
8. (Repeat steps 6 and 7 until firm.)

EXERCISE 2

DEFINITIONS

The next Thinking Operation is **Definitions.**

1. **Destroy** means **wreck.**
2. What does **destroy** mean? (Signal.) *Wreck.* What word means **wreck?** (Signal.) *Destroy.* (Repeat step 2 until firm.)
3. Listen. The baby wrecked the toy. Say that. (Signal.) *The baby wrecked the toy.* (Repeat until firm.)
Now say that sentence with a different word for **wrecked.** (Pause.) Get ready. (Signal.) *The baby destroyed the toy.* (Repeat until firm.)
(Repeat step 3 until firm.)
4. Listen. His car was wrecked in the accident. Say that. (Signal.) *His car was wrecked in the accident.* (Repeat until firm.)
Now say that sentence with a different word for **wrecked.** (Pause.) Get ready. (Signal.) *His car was destroyed in the accident.* (Repeat until firm.)
(Repeat step 4 until firm.)
5. Listen. The storm destroyed the field. Say that. (Signal.) *The storm destroyed the field.* (Repeat until firm.)
Now say that sentence with a different word for **destroyed.** (Pause.) Get ready. (Signal.) *The storm wrecked the field.* (Repeat until firm.)
(Repeat step 5 until firm.)

═══════ **EXERCISE 3** ═══════

DEFINITIONS

1. A synonym for **fast** is **quick.**
2. What's a synonym for **fast?** (Signal.) *Quick.* And what's a synonym for **quick?** (Signal.) *Fast.*
   (Repeat step 2 until firm.)
3. Listen. His motorcycle is very fast. Say that. (Signal.) *His motorcycle is very fast.* (Repeat until firm.)
   Now say that sentence with a synonym for **fast.** (Pause.) Get ready. (Signal.) *His motorcycle is very quick.* (Repeat until firm.)
   (Repeat step 3 until firm.)
4. Listen. The horse was not quick. Say that. (Signal.) *The horse was not quick.* (Repeat until firm.)
   Now say that sentence with a synonym for **quick.** (Pause.) Get ready. (Signal.) *The horse was not fast.* (Repeat until firm.)
   (Repeat step 4 until firm.)

═══════ **EXERCISE 4** ═══════

DEFINITIONS

1. **Big.** (Pause.) What's a synonym for **big?** (Signal.) *Large.*
   And what's a synonym for **large?** (Signal.) *Big.*
   (Repeat step 1 until firm.)
2. Listen. The moon looks very big tonight. Say that. (Signal.) *The moon looks very big tonight.* (Repeat until firm.)
   Now say that sentence with a synonym for **big.** (Pause.) Get ready. (Signal.) *The moon looks very large tonight.* (Repeat until firm.)
   (Repeat step 2 until firm.)
3. **Duplicate.** (Pause.) What's a synonym for **duplicate?** (Signal.) *Copy.* And what's a synonym for **copy?** (Signal.) *Duplicate.*
   (Repeat step 3 until firm.)
4. Listen. I can copy her writing. Say that. (Signal.) *I can copy her writing.* (Repeat until firm.)
   Now say that sentence with a synonym for **copy.** (Pause.) Get ready. (Signal.) *I can duplicate her writing.* (Repeat until firm.)
   (Repeat step 4 until firm.)

5. **Indolent.** (Pause.) What's a synonym for **indolent?** (Signal.) *Lazy.* And what's a synonym for **lazy?** (Signal.) *Indolent.*
   (Repeat step 5 until firm.)
6. Listen. I feel lazy after eating a lot. Say that. (Signal.) *I feel lazy after eating a lot.* (Repeat until firm.)
   Now say that sentence with a synonym for **lazy.** (Pause.) Get ready. (Signal.) *I feel indolent after eating a lot.* (Repeat until firm.)
   (Repeat step 6 until firm.)

═══════ **EXERCISE 5** ═══════

STATEMENT INFERENCE

The next Thinking Operation is **Statement Inference.**

1. Listen. The hawk descended to catch a small amphibian. Say that statement. (Signal.) *The hawk descended to catch a small amphibian.* (Repeat until firm.)

Individual test
Call on individual students to say the statement.
---

2. Everybody, listen. The hawk descended to catch a small amphibian. What kind of amphibian did the hawk descend to catch? (Signal.) *Small.*
   What descended to catch a small amphibian? (Signal.) *The hawk.*
   What did the hawk do to catch the small amphibian? (Signal.) *Descended.*
   What did the hawk do? (Signal.) *Descended to catch the small amphibian.*
   Why did the hawk descend? (Signal.) *To catch the small amphibian.*
   (Repeat step 2 until firm.)

Individual test
Call on individual students to answer a question from step 2.

EXERCISE 6

BASIC EVIDENCE: Using Facts

The next Thinking Operation is **Basic Evidence.**

1. You're going to use two facts to explain things that happened. (Hold up one finger.) First fact. Most animals breathe air. Say it. (Signal.) *Most animals breathe air.* (Repeat until firm.)
   (Hold up two fingers.) Second fact. Sweets cause cavities. Say it. (Signal.) *Sweets cause cavities.* (Repeat until firm.)
2. Everybody, say those facts again. (Hold up one finger.) First fact. *Most animals breathe air.* (Hold up two fingers.) Second fact. *Sweets cause cavities.* (Repeat until the students say the facts in order.)

Individual test
Call on students to say the facts in order.

---

3. Here's what happened. The whale swam to the surface of the water. Tell me the fact that explains **why** that happened. (Pause.) Get ready. (Signal.) *Most animals breathe air.*
4. Listen. First fact. Most animals breathe air. Second fact. Sweets cause cavities.
5. Here's what happened. George would not eat candy. Tell me the fact that explains **why** that happened. (Pause.) Get ready. (Signal.) *Sweets cause cavities.*
6. Here's what happened. The dentist did not want her patients to chew gum. Tell me the fact that explains **why** that happened. (Pause.) Get ready. (Signal.) *Sweets cause cavities.*
7. Here's what happened. The fly died in the covered jar. Tell me the fact that explains **why** that happened. (Pause.) Get ready. (Signal.) *Most animals breathe air.*
8. (Repeat steps 5–7 until firm.)

EXERCISE 7

DESCRIPTION

The next Thinking Operation is **Description.**

1. Listen. See if you can figure out what I'm talking about. It has a handle. Name three tools I could be talking about. (Call on individual students. Accept all reasonable responses; for example, hammer, rake, broom.)
2. It has a handle and it has bristles. Name two tools I could be talking about. (Call on individual students. Accept all reasonable responses; for example, broom, toothbrush.)
3. It has a handle, it has bristles, and you sweep with it. Everybody, name the tool I'm talking about. (Signal.) *A broom.*

EXERCISE 8

DEDUCTIONS: With *all* and *every*

The next Thinking Operation is **Deductions.**

1. I'll say rules with **all** or **every.** You say them the other way. What two words are we going to use? (Hold up one finger.) *All.* (Hold up two fingers.) *Every.*
2. Listen. **Every** bird is warm-blooded. Say that. (Signal.) *Every bird is warm-blooded.*
   Now say it the other way. Get ready. (Signal.) *All birds are warm-blooded.*
   (Repeat step 2 until firm.)
3. Here's a new rule. **All** purses are containers. Say that. (Signal.) *All purses are containers.*
   Now say it the other way. Get ready. *Every purse is a container.*
   (Repeat step 3 until firm.)
4. Here's a new rule. **All** canines are dogs. Say that. (Signal.) *All canines are dogs.*
   Now say it the other way. Get ready. (Signal.) *Every canine is a dog.*
   (Repeat step 4 until firm.)
5. Here's a new rule. **Every** human being is a mammal. Say that. (Signal.) *Every human being is a mammal.*
   Now say it the other way. Get ready. (Signal.) *All human beings are mammals.*
   (Repeat step 5 until firm.)

EXERCISE 9

DEDUCTIONS: With *every*

1. Listen to this rule. Every bird has bones. Say the rule. (Signal.) *Every bird has bones.*
2. Listen. A Bengal tiger is a **feline.** What does the rule let you know about a Bengal tiger? (Signal.) *Nothing.*
3. Listen. Every bird has bones. A salmon is a **fish.** What does the rule let you know about a salmon? (Signal.) *Nothing.*
4. Listen. Every bird has bones. A rooster is a **bird.** What does the rule let you know about a rooster? (Signal.) *A rooster has bones.* How do you know that a rooster has bones? (Signal.) *Because every bird has bones.*
5. Listen. Every bird has bones. A pheasant is a **bird.** What does the rule let you know about a pheasant? (Signal.) *A pheasant has bones.* How do you know that a pheasant has bones? (Signal.) *Because every bird has bones.*
6. (Repeat steps 2–5 until firm.)

EXERCISE 10

AND/OR

The next Thinking Operation is **And/Or.**

1. Listen. I'm going to touch my ear **or** touch my eye. What am I going to do? (Signal.) *Touch your ear or touch your eye.* (Repeat until firm.)
2. Am I going to touch my ear? (Signal.) *Maybe.* Am I going to touch my eye? (Signal.) *Maybe.*
3. Here I go. (Touch your ear.) Did I touch my eye? (Signal.) *No.* Did I touch my ear? (Signal.) *Yes.*
4. (Repeat steps 1–3 until firm.)
5. New problem. I'm going to touch my ear **and** touch my eye. What am I going to do? (Signal.) *Touch your ear and touch your eye.* (Repeat until firm.)

6. Am I going to touch my ear? (Signal.) *Yes.* Am I going to touch my eye? (Signal.) *Yes.*
7. Here I go. (Touch your ear and touch your eye at the same time.) Did I touch my ear? (Signal.) *Yes.* Did I touch my eye? (Signal.) *Yes.*
8. (Repeat steps 5–7 until firm.)

EXERCISE 11

SAME: Review

The next Thinking Operation is **Same.**

1. I'll name some things. When I call on you, name ways that those things are the same.
2. A hairbrush and a broom. (Call on one student.) Name eight ways they are the same. (Praise the student if he or she names eight ways.)
3. A bicycle and a ship. (Call on one student.) Name eight ways they are the same. (Praise the student if he or she names eight ways.)
4. A banana and a lemon. (Call on one student.) Name eight ways they are the same. (Praise the student if he or she names eight ways.)
5. An oak tree and a pig. (Call on one student.) Name eight ways they are the same. (Praise the student if he or she names eight ways.)

Points

(Pass out the Workbooks. Award points for Thinking Operations.)

WORKBOOK EXERCISES

We're going to do Workbooks now. Remember to follow my instructions carefully.

=== **EXERCISE 12** ===

DESCRIPTION

1. Everybody, touch part A in your Workbook. Figure out which cake I describe.
2. Item 1. This cake is a dark cake that is square. This cake has two layers. Listen again. (Repeat the description.) Write the letter for item 1.
3. Item 2. This cake is a round cake that has three layers. This cake is light. Listen again. (Repeat the description.) Write the letter for item 2.
4. Item 3. This cake is square and dark. This cake has a cherry on top. Listen again. (Repeat the description.) Write the letter for item 3.
5. Let's check your answers. Mark any items you missed with an X.
6. Item 1. This cake is a dark cake that is square. This cake has two layers. Everybody, what letter? (Signal.) *B.*
7. (Repeat step 6 for items 2 and 3.)

Answer key   **2.** *D*   **3.** *A*

=== **EXERCISE 13** ===

ANALOGIES

1. Everybody, touch part B-1 in your Workbook. This analogy shows what appliances clean. What does the analogy show? (Signal.) *What appliances clean.*
   Look at the pictures and name the appliances that are in the analogy. (Pause.) Get ready. (Signal.) *A vacuum cleaner and a washing machine.*
   Remember, the analogy shows what those appliances clean. Circle the picture that completes the analogy. (Wait.)

2. Everybody, touch the right pictures and say the whole analogy. Get ready. (Signal.) *A vacuum cleaner is to a rug as a washing machine is to a shirt.* (Repeat until firm.)
   If you didn't circle the picture of a shirt, make an X next to the picture you circled.
3. Everybody, touch part B-2 in your Workbook. This analogy shows what parts objects have. What does the analogy show? (Signal.) *What parts objects have.*
   Look at the pictures and name the objects in the analogy. (Pause.) Get ready. (Signal.) *A tree and a car.*
   Remember, the analogy shows what parts those objects have. Circle the picture that completes the analogy. (Wait.)
4. Everybody, touch the right pictures and say the whole analogy. Get ready. (Signal.) *A tree is to a leaf as a car is to a tire.* (Repeat until firm.)
   If you didn't circle the picture of a tire, make an X next to the picture you circled.

Individual test
(Call on individual students to do one of the following:)
  a. Say the analogy shown in part B-1.
  b. What does that analogy show about those appliances?
  c. Say the analogy shown in part B-2.
  d. What does that analogy show about those objects?

=== **EXERCISE 14** ===

TRUE—FALSE

1. Everybody, touch part C in your Workbook. I'll say statements about the picture.
2. Get ready to circle **true, false,** or **maybe.** Item 1. There is a mammal in the picture. Circle the answer. (Wait.)
3. Item 2. The frog will jump on the horse. Circle the answer. (Wait.)
4. Item 3. There are no reptiles in the picture. Circle the answer. (Wait.)
5. Item 4. The mammal was born in water. Circle the answer. (Wait.)

6. Item 5. The frog was born in water. Circle the answer. (Wait.)

7. Item 6. Both of the animals are cold-blooded. Circle the answer. (Wait.)

8. Everybody, let's check your answers. Say **true, false,** or **maybe.**

9. Item 1. There is a mammal in the picture. (Signal.) *True.*

10. (Repeat step 9 for items 2–6.)

═══ **EXERCISE 15** ═══

● **CLASSIFICATION**

1. Everybody, touch part D in your Workbook. These boxes show 3 classes. Touch box B. All the things in that box are chairs. Tell me what kind of chairs they are. (Pause 3 seconds.) Get ready. (Signal.) *Rocking chairs.*
   So, box B shows the class of rocking chairs.

2. Touch box A. Not all the things in that box are rocking chairs. Tell me the class name for the things in box A. (Pause 3 seconds.) Get ready. (Signal.) *Chairs.*

3. Touch box C. Not all the things in that box are chairs or rocking chairs. Tell me the class name for the things in box C. (Pause 3 seconds.) Get ready. (Signal.) *Furniture.*

4. Now let's figure out which of these classes is the biggest. Tell me the rule about the bigger class. (Signal.) *If a class has more kinds of things, it's bigger.* Look at box A, box B, and box C and figure out which box has more kinds of things than the others. (Pause 4 seconds.)
   Which box? (Signal.) *Box C.*
   Tell me the class name for the things in box C. (Pause.) Get ready. (Signal.) *Furniture.*

Points
(Award points for Workbooks.)

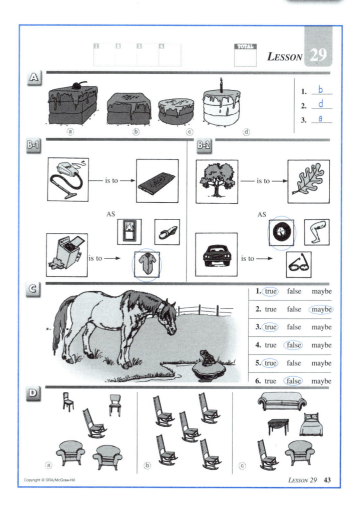

INFORMATION

We're going to work on Information now.

━━━━━━ **EXERCISE 16** ━━━━━━

● **CALENDAR: Holidays**

1. Here's a fact about another winter holiday. Valentine's Day is always in February. Say that fact. (Signal.) *Valentine's Day is always in February.* (Repeat until firm.)

2. Tell me three holidays that are in winter. (Pause 2 seconds.) Get ready. (Signal.) *Christmas, New Year's Day, and Valentine's Day.*
   Tell me the holiday that is in February. (Pause 2 seconds.) Get ready. (Signal.) *Valentine's Day.*
   Tell me the holiday that is in December. (Pause 2 seconds.) Get ready. (Signal.) *Christmas.*
   Tell me the **date** of Christmas. (Pause 2 seconds.) Get ready. (Signal.) *December twenty-fifth.*
   (Repeat step 2 until firm.)

3. Tell me the holiday that is in January. (Pause 2 seconds.) Get ready. (Signal.) *New Year's Day.*
   Tell me the **date** of New Year's Day. (Pause 2 seconds.) Get ready. (Signal.) *January first.*
   Tell me the holiday that is in February. (Pause 2 seconds.) Get ready. (Signal.) *Valentine's Day.*
   Tell me the **season** that all those holidays are in. (Pause 2 seconds.) Get ready. (Signal.) *Winter.*
   (Repeat step 3 until firm.)

4. (Repeat steps 2 and 3 until firm.)

Individual test
(Call on individual students to answer one of the following questions:)
   a. What season is Christmas in?
   b. What's the date of Christmas?
   c. What season is New Year's Day in?
   d. What's the date of New Year's Day?
   e. What season is Valentine's Day in?
   f. What month is Valentine's Day in?

━━━━━━ **EXERCISE 17** ━━━━━━

MEMORIZATION: Poem

1. You're learning a poem about American Indians. Let's name those Indians.

2. Creek. Say it. (Signal.) *Creek.*
   Choctaw. Say it. (Signal.) *Choctaw.*
   Cherokee. Say it. (Signal.) *Cherokee.*
   Seminole. Say it. (Signal.) *Seminole.*
   Chickasaw. Say it. (Signal.) *Chickasaw.*
   (Repeat step 2 until firm.)

3. I'll say the whole poem about American Indians. American Indians were what they saw. Some were Creek and some Choctaw. American Indians were what they saw. Cherokee, Seminole, and Chickasaw.

4. Say it with me. (Signal. Respond with the students.) *American Indians were what they saw. Some were Creek and some Choctaw. American Indians were what they saw. Cherokee, Seminole, and Chickasaw.* (Repeat until students are responding with you.)

5. All by yourselves. (Signal.) *American Indians were what they saw. Some were Creek and some Choctaw. American Indians were what they saw. Cherokee, Seminole, and Chickasaw.* (Repeat until firm.)

   To correct:
   a. (Stop the students as soon as you hear a mistake.)
   b. (Say the line they missed.)
   c. (Have them repeat the line they missed.)
   d. (Repeat step 5.)

Individual test
Call on individual students to say the whole poem. Praise students who make no errors.

EXERCISE 18

CALENDAR: Months, Seasons

1. Everybody, tell me how many months are in a year. (Pause.) Get ready. (Signal.) *Twelve.*
2. Name the months in a year. (Signal.) *January, February, March, April, May, June, July, August, September, October, November, December.*
3. You told me the (pause; signal) *months in a year.*
4. Everybody, tell me how many seasons are in a year. (Pause.) Get ready. (Signal.) *Four.*
5. Name the seasons in a year. (Signal.) *Winter, spring, summer, fall.*
6. You told me the four (pause; signal) *seasons in a year.*

> ***Individual test***
> Call on individual students to name the months or seasons in a year.

EXERCISE 19

MEMORIZATION: Poem

Say that poem we learned about the mechanic and the astronomer. Get ready. (Signal.)

> *A mechanic fixes cars,*
> *An astronomer looks at stars,*
> *A captain has two bars,*
> *And a boxer spars and spars.*

(Repeat until firm.)

> ***Individual test***
> Call on individual students to say the whole poem.

Points

(Award points for Information.
Have the students add up their daily total.)

END OF LESSON 29

Introduction

Today we'll do a short lesson and then do the test. Since the lesson is short, you won't get points for it. However, you can earn as many as 25 points for the test. We'll go over those points just before the test.

EXERCISE 1

● **ANALOGIES: Synonyms**

The first Thinking Operation today is **Analogies.**

1. Get ready to do some **synonyms.**
2. **Leap.** (Pause.) What's a synonym for **leap?** (Signal.) *Jump.*
   Skinny. (Pause.) What's a synonym for **skinny?** (Signal.) *Thin.*
   (Repeat step 2 until firm.)
3. Now complete this analogy. **Leap** is to **jump** as **skinny** is to. . . (Pause 2 seconds.) Get ready. (Signal.) *Thin.*
   Everybody, say that analogy. (Signal.) *Leap is to jump as skinny is to thin.* (Repeat until firm.)
4. **Leap** and **skinny** are words. The analogy tells what synonyms those words have. What does the analogy tell? (Signal.) *What synonyms those words have.* (Repeat until firm.)
5. Here's the analogy again.
   Leap is to **jump** as **skinny** is to **thin.**
6. Say the analogy. (Signal.) *Leap is to jump as skinny is to thin.*
7. That analogy tells something about those words. (Pause.) What does that analogy tell about those words? (Signal.) *What synonyms those words have.*
8. (Repeat steps 6 and 7 until firm.)

EXERCISE 2

DEDUCTIONS: With *no* and *don't*

The next Thinking Operation is **Deductions.**

1. I'll say rules with **no** and **don't.** You say them the other way. What two words are we going to use? (Hold up one finger.) *No.* (Hold up two fingers.) *Don't.*

2. Listen. **No** amphibians have warm blood. Say that. (Signal.) *No amphibians have warm blood.*
   Now say it the other way. Get ready. (Signal.) *Amphibians don't have warm blood.*
   (Repeat step 2 until firm.)
3. Here's a new rule. Fish **don't** have feathers. Say that. (Signal.) *Fish don't have feathers.*
   Now say it the other way. Get ready. (Signal.) *No fish have feathers.*
   (Repeat step 3 until firm.)
4. Here's a new rule. **No** felines bark. Say that. (Signal.) *No felines bark.*
   Now say it the other way. Get ready. (Signal.) *Felines don't bark.*
   (Repeat step 4 until firm.)
5. Here's a new rule. Vehicles **don't** think. Say that. (Signal.) *Vehicles don't think.*
   Now say it the other way. Get ready. (Signal.) *No vehicles think.*
   (Repeat step 5 until firm.)

EXERCISE 3

● **DEDUCTIONS: With *some***

1. Listen to this rule. **Some** people work in a factory. Everybody, say that. (Signal.) *Some people work in a factory.*
2. **Some** people work in a factory. **Ms. Allen** is a person. What does the rule let you know about Ms. Allen? (Signal.) *Maybe Ms. Allen works in a factory.*

   To correct students who say *Ms. Allen works in a factory:*
   a. Listen. Only some people work in a factory; so **maybe** Ms. Allen works in a factory.
   b. (Repeat step 2.)
   How do you know that maybe Ms. Allen works in a factory? (Signal.) *Because some people work in a factory.*
3. Listen. **Some** people work in a factory. The **seal** likes to eat fish. What does the rule let you know about that seal? (Signal.) *Nothing.*
4. Listen. **Some** people work in a factory. That **sweater** is made of wool. What does the rule let you know about that sweater? (Signal.) *Nothing.*

5. Listen. **Some** people work in a factory. Six **people** are eating lunch. What does the rule let you know about those six people? (Signal.) *Maybe those six people work in a factory.* How do you know that maybe those six people work in a factory? (Signal.) *Because some people work in a factory.*
6. (Repeat steps 2–5 until firm.)

═══════════ EXERCISE 4 ═══════════

DEFINITIONS

The next Thinking Operation is **Definitions.**

1. **Destroy.** (Pause.) What's a synonym for **destroy?** (Signal.) *Wreck.* And what's a synonym for **wreck?** (Signal.) *Destroy.* (Repeat step 1 until firm.)
2. Listen. The monster wrecked the city. Say that. (Signal.) *The monster wrecked the city.* (Repeat until firm.)
   Now say that sentence with a synonym for **wrecked.** (Pause.) Get ready. (Signal.) *The monster destroyed the city.* (Repeat until firm.)
   (Repeat step 2 until firm.)
3. **Descend.** (Pause.) What does **descend** mean? (Signal.) *Go down.*
   What word means **go down?** (Signal.) *Descend.* (Repeat step 3 until firm.)
4. Listen. The helicopter descended to the roof. Say that. (Signal.) *The helicopter descended to the roof.* (Repeat until firm.)
   Now say that sentence with different words for **descended.** (Pause.) Get ready. (Signal.) *The helicopter went down to the roof.* (Repeat until firm.)
   (Repeat step 4 until firm.)

5. **Complete.** (Pause.) What's a synonym for **complete?** (Signal.) *Finish.* And what's a synonym for **finish?** (Signal.) *Complete.* (Repeat step 5 until firm.)
6. Listen. It takes a long time to complete this job. Say that. (Signal.) *It takes a long time to complete this job.* (Repeat until firm.)
   Now say that sentence with a synonym for **complete.** (Pause.) Get ready. (Signal.) *It takes a long time to finish this job.* (Repeat until firm.)
   (Repeat step 6 until firm.)

═══════════ EXERCISE 5 ═══════════

DEFINITIONS

1. **Copy.** What does **copy** mean? (Signal.) *Duplicate.*
   Small. What does **small** mean? (Signal.) *Little.* (Repeat step 1 until firm.)
2. Listen. It was hard to copy the small painting. Say that sentence. (Signal.) *It was hard to copy the small painting.* (Repeat until firm.)
   Now say that sentence with different words for **copy** and **small.** (Pause.) Get ready. (Signal.) *It was hard to duplicate the little painting.* (Repeat until firm.)
   (Repeat step 2 until firm.)

Points

(Pass out the Workbooks.
Award no points for Thinking Operations.)

WORKBOOK EXERCISES

We're going to do Workbooks now. Remember to follow my instructions carefully.

EXERCISE 6

CLASSIFICATION

1. Everybody, touch part A in your Workbook. ✔ These boxes show three classes. Touch box A. All the things in that box are mammals. Tell me what kind of mammals they are. (Pause 3 seconds.) Get ready. (Signal.) *Cows.*
   So, box A shows the class of cows.

2. Touch box C. Not all the things in that box are cows. Tell me the class name for the things in box C. (Pause 3 seconds.) Get ready. (Signal.) *Mammals.*

3. Touch box B. Not all the things in that box are cows or mammals. Tell me the class name for the things in box B. (Pause 3 seconds.) Get ready. (Signal.) *Animals.*

4. Now let's figure out which of these classes is the biggest. Tell me the rule about the bigger class. (Signal.) *If a class has more kinds of things, it is bigger.* Look at box A, box B, and box C and figure out which box has more kinds of things than the others. (Pause 4 seconds.)
   Which box? (Signal.) *Box B.*
   Tell me the class name for the things in box B. (Pause.) Get ready. (Signal.) *Animals.*

Points

(Award no points for Workbooks.)

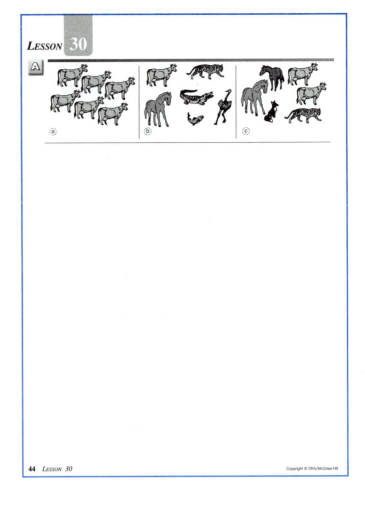

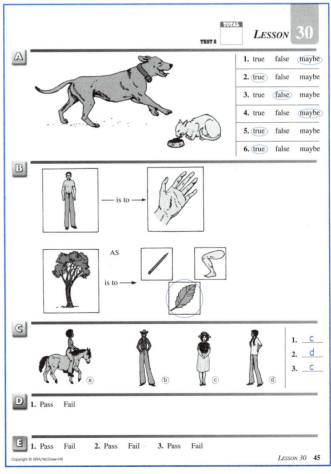

INFORMATION

We're going to work on Information now.

EXERCISE 7

● **CALENDAR: Holidays**

1. Tell me three holidays that are in winter.
(Pause 2 seconds.) Get ready. (Signal.)
Christmas, New Year's Day, and Valentine's Day.
Tell me the holiday that is in February.
(Pause 2 seconds.) Get ready. (Signal.)
Valentine's Day.
Tell me the holiday that is in December.
(Pause 2 seconds.) Get ready. (Signal.)
Christmas.
Tell me the **date** of Christmas. (Pause
2 seconds.) Get ready. (Signal.) *December twenty-fifth.*
(Repeat step 1 until firm.)

2. Tell me the holiday that is in January. (Pause
2 seconds.) Get ready. (Signal.) *New Year's Day.*
Tell me the **date** of New Year's Day. (Pause
2 seconds.) Get ready. (Signal.) *January first.*
Tell me the holiday that is in February.
(Pause 2 seconds.) Get ready. (Signal.)
Valentine's Day.
Tell me the **season** that all those holidays are in. (Pause 2 seconds.) Get ready. (Signal.)
Winter.
(Repeat step 2 until firm.)

3. (Repeat steps 1 and 2 until firm.)

Individual test
(Call on individual students to answer one of the following questions:)
a. What season is Christmas in?
b. What's the date of Christmas?
c. What season is New Year's Day in?
d. What's the date of New Year's Day?
e. What season is Valentine's Day in?
f. What month is Valentine's Day in?

EXERCISE 8

MEMORIZATION: Poem

1. You're learning a poem about American Indians. Let's name those Indians.

2. Creek. Say it. (Signal.) *Creek.*
Choctaw. Say it. (Signal.) *Choctaw.*
Cherokee. Say it. (Signal.) *Cherokee.*
Seminole. Say it. (Signal.) *Seminole.*
Chickasaw. Say it. (Signal.) *Chickasaw.*
(Repeat step 2 until firm.)

3. I'll say the whole poem about American Indians. American Indians were what they saw. Some were Creek and some Choctaw. American Indians were what they saw. Cherokee, Seminole, and Chickasaw.

4. Say it with me. (Signal. Respond with the students.) *American Indians were what they saw. Some were Creek and some Choctaw. American Indians were what they saw. Cherokee, Seminole, and Chickasaw.* (Repeat until students are responding with you.)

5. All by yourselves. (Signal.) *American Indians were what they saw. Some were Creek and some Choctaw. American Indians were what they saw. Cherokee, Seminole, and Chickasaw.* (Repeat until firm.)

To correct:
a. (Stop the students as soon as you hear a mistake.)
b. (Say the line they missed.)
c. (Have them repeat the line they missed.)
d. (Repeat step 5.)

Individual test
Call on individual students to say the whole poem.
Praise students who make no errors.

Points

Award no points for Information.

Test Introduction

Now we're going to do the test. If you make zero errors or one error on the test, you will earn 25 points. If you make two or three errors, you will earn 14 points. If you make more than three errors, you fail the test and you earn 0 points. Some of the test items are on the next page in your Workbook. I will give you some other test items individually. We'll do the Workbook items first. Open your Workbook to Test 2.

=======EXERCISE 9=======

IN-PROGRAM TEST 2

Task A

1. Everybody, touch part A on your test. I'll say statements about the picture.
2. Get ready to circle **true, false,** or **maybe.** Item 1. The pets belong to a boy. Circle the answer. (Wait.)
3. Item 2. The cat is not running. Circle the answer. (Wait.)
4. Item 3. The dog is not running. Circle the answer. (Wait.)
5. Item 4. The dog likes the cat. Circle the answer. (Wait.)
6. Item 5. The cat is eating. Circle the answer. (Wait.)
7. Item 6. The dog is running. Circle the answer. (Wait.)

Task B

Everybody, touch part B on your test. This analogy shows what parts those objects have. What does the analogy show? (Signal.) *What parts those objects have.* Look at the pictures and name the objects that are in the analogy. (Pause.) Get ready. (Signal.) *A man and a tree.* Remember, the analogy shows what parts those objects have. Circle the picture that completes the analogy. (Wait.)

Task C

1. Everybody, touch part C on your test. Figure out which object I describe.
2. Item 1. This woman is wearing a hat. This woman is standing. This woman is wearing a skirt. Listen again. (Repeat the description.) Write the letter for item 1.
3. Item 2. This woman is not wearing a hat. This woman is wearing pants. This woman is standing. Listen again. (Repeat the description.) Write the letter for item 2.
4. Item 3. This woman is not riding a horse. This woman is wearing a hat and a skirt. Listen again. (Repeat the description.) Write the letter for item 3.

Note: After presenting the Workbook test items, do these tasks with each student where the other students cannot hear you. Circle *pass* or *fail* for each item on the student's test Workbook. The students must give specified responses to pass the items.

Task D

Say that poem you learned about the mechanic and the astronomer. Get ready.

> *A mechanic fixes cars,*
> *An astronomer looks at stars,*
> *A captain has two bars,*
> *And a boxer spars and spars.*

Task E

1. Get ready to do some definitions. **Ignore.** (Pause.) What does **ignore** mean? *Pay no attention to.*
2. **Instruct.** (Pause.) What's a synonym for **instruct?** *Teach.*
3. **Duplicate.** (Pause.) What's a synonym for **duplicate?** *Copy.*

Note: After presenting the verbal items, check the student's written test items. Write the total number of errors for tasks A-E at the top of the test Workbook.

Answer key   Task A: 1. *Maybe*   2. *True*   3. *False* 4. *Maybe*   5. *True*   6. *True*   Task B: *Leaf*   Task C: 1. *C* 2. *D*   3. *C*

Points for Test

Raise your hand if you made zero, one, two, or three mistakes on the test. If you made zero mistakes or one mistake, you earned 25 points. If you made two or three mistakes, you earned 14 points. If you made more than three mistakes, you didn't earn any points. Record your points for the test on your Point Chart. ✔

Five-Lesson Point Summary

(Tell students to add the point totals for Lessons 26 through 30 on the Point Summary Chart and to write the total.

Remediation Procedures for Test 2

Students who failed the test (those who made more than three errors) must be firmed on items that were missed on the test. This must be done before you present Lesson 31.

1. Use the next class period to work with the group of students who failed the test.
2. Use the chart to determine which tasks to use for review. If any member of the group failed Task A, the review tasks indicated for Task A must be presented to the review group. If no member of the group failed Task A, do not present the review exercises for Task A.
3. For reviewing Workbook tasks (A–C), use the appropriate review pages near the back of the student Workbook.
4. After you have taught all review exercises to the group of students who failed the test, determine whether each student is firm by presenting all review tasks, individually, to the student. A student is considered firm if he or she correctly responds to all tasks.
5. Students who passed the test should not be included in the review group. Assign them independent activities to do while you are working with the review group. The assignment should be reinforcing, such as a discussion

about the types of homes that different animals make. Assign a leader for the group, rules for the discussion, and some reference material, such as illustrated books about animals.

Portion of Test Section	Orally Present These Review Tasks		Review Workbook
	Lesson	Exercise	
A	27	12	Part A
A	28	11	Part B
B	27	14	Part C
B	28	13	Part D
C	26	13	Part E
C	28	14	Part F
D	26	19	——
E	22	2 step 1	——
E	26	7 step 1	——
E	29	4 step 3	——

END OF LESSON 30

FACT GAME
LESSON 2

After Lesson 5

> **Note:** Before beginning Lesson 6, present this Fact Game lesson. For the Fact Game, students are paired. Each pair has an A member and a B member. Assign partners and indicate whether each member is an A or a B. You will need one die for the game, and each student will need a pencil and Workbook.

FACT GAME

━━━━━━━ EXERCISE 1 ━━━━━━━

1. Everybody, exchange Workbooks with your partner. (Wait.) Now open the Workbook to page 94. These are items for a fact game. You'll work in pairs. All A members, raise your hand. ✔ All B members, raise your hand. ✔

2. Everybody, touch the scoreboard at the top of the page. ✔ Every time you get an item right, your partner will make a check on your scorecard. Each check mark stands for one point. So, if you get seven items right, you'll earn seven points.

3. For the first item, A members will tell the answer to B members. B members will make a check mark if the item is right. Here we go. (Hand the die to the first student.)
   Roll the die and tell us how many dots are on top. (Wait.) I'll read the item for that number. Follow along and don't say the answer.
   (Read the item that corresponds to the number.) A members, raise your hand. ✔ Whisper the answer to your partner. (Wait.) B members, raise your hand. ✔ The correct answer to that item is_____. Raise your hand again if your partner got it right. ✔ If your partner got it right, make a check mark in Box 1 of your partner's scorecard. Box 1. (Check and correct.)

4. Now we'll switch. B members will whisper the answer. A members will mark their partner's scorecard. (Pass the die to the next student.) Roll the die and say the number. (After the student says the number:) I'll read the item for that number. Follow along, but don't say the answer. (Read the item.)
   B members, whisper the answer to your partner. (Wait.)
   The correct answer is_____. A members, raise your hand if your partner got it right. ✔ A members who raised your hand, make a check mark in Box 1 of your partner's scorecard. (Check and correct.)

5. Now the die goes to the next student. (Pass the die to the next student.) Roll the die and say the number. (Wait.)
   I'll read the item for that number. Follow along. (Read the item.) A members, whisper the answer to your partner. (Wait.)
   The correct answer is_____. B members, raise your hand if your partner got it right. ✔ B members who raised your hand, make a check mark in Box 2 if you already made a check mark in Box 1. Make a check mark in Box 1 if you haven't made a check mark. (Check and correct.)

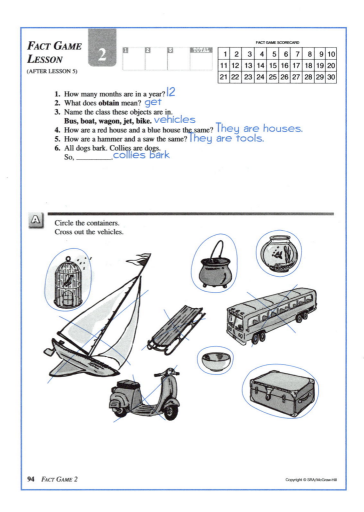

FACT GAME LESSON **2** (AFTER LESSON 5)

FACT GAME SCORECARD									
1	2	3	4	5	6	7	8	9	10
11	12	13	14	15	16	17	18	19	20
21	22	23	24	25	26	27	28	29	30

1. How many months are in a year? 12
2. What does **obtain** mean? get
3. Name the class these objects are in.
   Bus, boat, wagon, jet, bike. vehicles
4. How are a red house and a blue house the same? They are houses.
5. How are a hammer and a saw the same? They are tools.
6. All dogs bark. Collies are dogs.
   So, _____. collies bark

Ⓐ Circle the containers.
Cross out the vehicles.

94 *FACT GAME 2*

6. (Pass the die to the next student.)
   Roll the die and say the number. (Wait.)
   I'll read the item for that number. Follow
   along. (Read the item.) B members, whisper
   the answer to your partner. (Wait.)
   The correct answer is_____. A members,
   raise your hand if your partner got it right. ✔
   A members who raised your hand, make a
   check mark in Box 2 if you already made a
   check mark in Box 1. Make a check mark in
   Box 1 if you haven't made a check mark.
   (Check and correct.)

7. (Pass the die to the next student.)
   Roll the die and say the number. (Wait.)
   I'll read the item for that number. Follow
   along. (Read the item.) A members, whisper
   the answer. (Wait.)
   The correct answer is_____. B members,
   raise your hand if your partner got it right.
   Then make a check mark in the next box.
   (Check and correct.)

8. (Play the game for 15 minutes more,
   following the procedure in step 7. Alternate
   turns for B members and A members.)

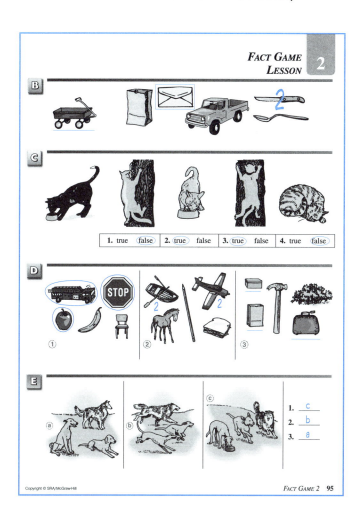

Points for Fact Game

1. At the end of the game: Raise your hand if
   you earned 8 or more points. If you earned 8
   or more points, you get 5 bonus points.

2. Everybody, write your game points in Box 1
   on your point chart. Write your bonus points
   in Box 3. (Check and correct.)

WORKBOOK
EXERCISES

We are going to do Workbook pages now.

═══════════ EXERCISE 2 ═══════════

CLASSIFICATION

1. Pencils down. Don't write anything yet.
   Everybody, touch the instructions for part A
   in your Workbook. ✔ I'll read the first
   instruction. Listen. Circle the containers.

2. What are you going to do to every container
   in the picture? (Signal.) *Circle it.*

3. I'll read the next instruction. Cross out the
   vehicles. What are you going to do to every
   vehicle? (Signal.) *Cross it out.*
   Everybody, do it. Circle the containers and
   cross out the vehicles. (Wait.)

4. Get ready to mark your papers. Put an X by
   any object you got wrong.

5. What class is a bowl in? (Signal.) *Containers.*
   How did you mark the bowl? (Signal.)
   Circled it.

6. (Repeat step 5 for **sailboat, cage, kettle,
   bus, fishbowl, motor scooter, sled,** and
   footlocker.)

═══════════ EXERCISE 3 ═══════════

DESCRIPTION

1. Everybody, touch part B in your Workbook. ✔
   Figure out which object I describe. Listen. A
   reep is made of metal. You cut things with a
   reep. A reep has a handle and a blade. **Make
   a 2 on** the object I'm calling a reep. (Wait.)

2. Listen. A blim is a vehicle. A blim has four
   wheels. You pull a blim. **Underline** the object
   I'm calling a blim. (Wait.)

3. Listen. An urk is made of paper. You put
   things in an urk. You put an urk in a mailbox.
   Make a box around the object I'm calling
   an urk.

FACT GAME
LESSON 2

4. Everybody, get ready to check your work. Tell me the real name for the object that is made of metal, that you cut things with, and that has a handle and a blade. Get ready. (Signal.) *A knife.* And how did you mark the knife? (Signal.) *Made a 2 on it.*
5. Tell me the real name for the object that is a vehicle, that has four wheels, and that you pull. Get ready. (Signal.) *A wagon.* And how did you mark the wagon? (Signal.) *Underlined it.*
6. Tell me the real name for the object that is made of paper, that you put things in, and that you put in a mailbox. Get ready. (Signal.) *An envelope.* And how did you mark the envelope? (Signal.) *Made a box around it.*

EXERCISE 4

TRUE—FALSE

1. Everybody, touch part C in your Workbook. ✔ I'll say statements about the picture. Some of these statements are true and some are false.
2. Item 1. Listen. **Some** of the cats are **running.** Circle **true** or **false** for item 1. (Wait.)
3. Item 2. Listen. **Some** of the cats are **eating.** Circle **true** or **false** for item 2. (Wait.)
4. Item 3. Listen. **Some** of the cats are **climbing.** Circle **true** or **false** for item 3. (Wait.)
5. Item 4. Listen. **Some** of the cats are **sitting.** Circle **true** or **false** for item 4. (Wait.)
6. Let's check your answers. Mark any item you miss with an X. Everybody, tell me **true** or **false.**
7. Item 1. **Some** of the cats are **running.** (Signal.) *False.*
   Item 2. **Some** of the cats are **eating.** (Signal.) *True.*
   Item 3. **Some** of the cats are **climbing.** (Signal.) *True.*
   Item 4. **Some** of the cats are **sitting.** (Signal.) *False.*

EXERCISE 5

SAME

1. Everybody, touch part D in your Workbook. ✔ Some of the objects in box 1 are usually the same color. **Circle** the objects that are usually the same color. Do it. (Wait.)
2. Some of the objects in box 2 are in the same class. **Make a 2 under** the objects that are in the same class. Do it. (Wait.)
3. Some of the objects in box 3 are in the same class. **Make a line under** the objects that are in the same class. Do it. (Wait.)
4. Everybody, get ready to check part D. Name the color of the objects you marked in box 1. (Pause.) Get ready. (Signal.) *Red.*
   Name the class of the objects you marked in box 2. (Pause.) Get ready. (Signal.) *Vehicles.*
   Name the class of the objects you marked in box 3. (Pause.) Get ready. (Signal.) *Containers.*
5. Which objects did you mark in box 1? (Call on a student.) *Fire engine, apple, stop sign.* What is the same about those objects? (Call on a student.) *They are red.* How did you mark each of those objects? (Call on a student.) *Circled them.*
6. (Repeat step 5 for boxes 2 and 3.)

Answer key **2.** *Airplane, boat; they are vehicles; made a 2 under them.* **3.** *Bag, box, suitcase; they are containers; made a line under them.*

═══════ **EXERCISE 6** ═══════

TRUE—FALSE

1. Everybody, touch part E in your Workbook. ✔
I'll say statements that are true of one of the pictures.

2. Listen: **Only some** of the dogs are running. Touch the right picture. (Signal.)
(Repeat step 2 until firm.)

3. Listen: **All** the dogs are running. Touch the right picture. (Signal. Repeat step 3 until firm.)

4. Listen: **None** of the dogs are running. Touch the right picture. (Signal.)
(Repeat step 4 until firm.)

5. (Repeat steps 2–4 until firm.)

6. Let's do it again. This time you'll write the letter of each picture I describe.
Here's item 1: **Only some** of the dogs are running. Touch the right picture. (Signal.)
What letter is under that picture? (Signal.) *C.*
Write the letter **C** on line 1. (Wait.)

7. Here's item 2: **All** the dogs are running. Touch the right picture. (Signal.) What letter is under that picture? (Signal.) *B.*
Write the letter **B** on line 2. (Wait.)

8. Here's item 3: **None** of the dogs are running. Touch the right picture. (Signal.)
Write the letter of that picture on line 3. (Wait.)

9. Let's check your answer. Item 3. **None** of the dogs are running. What's the letter of that picture? (Signal.) *A.* Yes, the answer to item 3 is **A.**

Points
(Award up to 5 points for Workbooks. Have students record their points in Box 2 and add up their daily total.)

Point Summary Chart
(Tell students to write their point total in the box labeled FG2 on the Point Summary Chart.)

Six-Lesson Point Summary
(Tell students to add the point totals for Lessons 1 through 5 and FG2 on the Point Summary Chart and to write the total for Block 1.)

PRESENT LESSON 6 NEXT

FACT GAME
LESSON 3

After Lesson 15

EXERCISE 1

1. Everybody, exchange Workbooks with your partner. (Wait.) Now open the Workbook to page 96. This is a new Fact Game. A members will go first. Then B members will have a turn, and so forth. A members, raise your hand. ✔ B members, raise your hand. ✔

2. (Hand the die to the first student.) Roll the die and say the number. (Wait.) I'll read the item for that number. Follow along, but don't say the answer. (Read the item.) A members, whisper the answer to your partner. (Wait.)

3. The correct answer is _____. B members, raise your hand if your partner got it right. ✔ B members who raised your hand, make a check mark in Box 1 of your partner's scorecard. ✔

4. For remaining turns: (Pass the die to the next student.) Roll the die and say the number. (Wait.) I'll read the item. Follow along. (Read the item.) _____ members, whisper the answer. (Wait. Tell the correct answer.) _____ members, make a check mark if your partner got it right. ✔ (Play the game for 15 minutes more, alternating turns for A members and B members.)

Points for Fact Game

1. (At the end of the game:) Raise you hand if you earned 8 or more points. If you earned 8 or more points, you get 5 bonus points.

2. Everybody, write your game points in Box 1 on your Point Chart. Write your bonus points in Box 3. (Check and correct.)

EXERCISE 2

TRUE-FALSE

1. Everybody, touch part A in your Workbook. ✔ I'll say statement about the picture.

2. Get ready to circle **true, false,** or **maybe.** Item 1. **All** of the dogs are **sitting.** Circle **true, false,** or **maybe** for item 1. (Wait.)

3. Item 2. **Only one** of the dogs **has a collar.** Circle **true, false,** or **maybe.** (Wait.)

4. Item 3. **Some** of the dogs **have a collar.** Circle **true, false,** or **maybe.** (Wait.)

5. Item 4. **None** of the dogs **have a collar.** Circle **true, false,** or **maybe.** (Wait.)

6. Item 5. **All** of the dogs **have a long tail.** Circle **true, false,** or **maybe.** (Wait.)

7. Let's check your answers. Mark any item you missed with an X. Everybody, tell me **true, false,** or **maybe.**

8. Item 1. **All** of the dogs are **sitting.** (Signal.) *Maybe.*

9. (Repeat step 8 for items 2–5.)

═══ EXERCISE 3 ═══

CLASSIFICATION

1. Everybody, touch the instructions for part B in your Workbook. ✔ I'll read the instructions. Listen. Circle the tools. Cross out the buildings.
2. What are you going to do to every tool? (Signal.) *Circle it.*
   What are you going to do to every building? (Signal.) *Cross it out.*
3. Everybody, do it. Circle the tools and cross out the buildings. (Wait.)
4. Get ready to mark your papers. Put an X by any object you got wrong.
5. What class is a school in? (Signal.) *Buildings.* How did you mark the school? (Signal.) *Crossed it out.*
6. (Repeat step 5 for **scissors, wrench, church, house, screwdriver, gas station, shovel,** and **pliers.**)

Point Summary Chart
(Tell students to write their point total in the box labeled FG3 on the Point Summary Chart.)

Six-Lesson Point Summary
(Tell students to add the point totals for Lesson 11 through 15 and FG3 on the Point Summary Chart and to write the total for Block 3.)

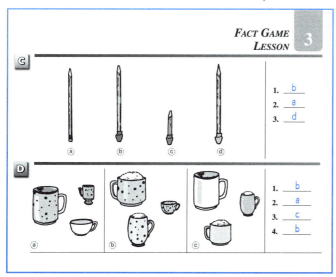

═══ EXERCISE 4 ═══

DESCRIPTION

1. Everybody, touch part C in your Workbook. ✔ Figure out which pencil I describe.
2. Item 1. This pencil is long. This pencil has a big eraser. This pencil does not have a point. Listen again. (Repeat the description.)
   Write the letter for item 1.
3. Item 2. This pencil is long. This pencil does not have a point. This pencil has a small eraser. Listen again. (Repeat description.)
   Write the letter for item 2.
4. Item 3. This pencil has a big eraser. This pencil is long. This pencil has a point. Listen again. (Repeat the description.)
   Write the letter for item 3.
5. Let's check your answers.
   Mark any items you missed with an X.
6. Item 1. This pencil is long. This pencil has a big eraser. This pencil does not have a point. Everybody, what letter? (Signal.) *B.*
7. (Repeat step 6 for items 2 and 3.)

═══ EXERCISE 5 ═══

TRUE-FALSE

1. Everybody, touch part D in your Workbook. ✔ I'll say statements that are true of one of the pictures. You write the letter of the right picture.
2. Item 1. **All** the cups have spots. Write the letter of the picture on line 1. (Wait.)
3. Item 2. **Only some** of the cups have spots. Write the letter of the picture on line 2. (Wait.)
4. Item 3. **None** of the cups have spots. Write the letter of the picture on line 3. (Wait.)
5. Item 4. **None** of the cups are white. Write the letter of the picture on line 4. (Wait.)
6. Let's check your answers. Mark any items you missed with an X. Tell me the letter of the right picture.
7. Item 1. **All** the cups have spots. (Signal.) *B.*
8. (Repeat step 7 for items 2–4.)

Points
(Award up to 5 points for Workbooks. Have students record their points in Box 2 and add up their daily total.)

FACT GAME
LESSON 4

After Lesson 25

Note: You will need two dice for this Fact Game.

FACT GAME

EXERCISE 1

1. Everybody, exchange Workbooks with your partner. (Wait.) Now open the Workbook to page 98. This is a new Fact Game. Today's game is played with two dice. When you say the number, you have to count up the dots that are on both dice. A members will go first. Then B members will have a turn, and so forth. A members, raise your hand. ✔ B members, raise your hand. ✔

2. (Hand the dice to the first student.) Roll the dice and say the number. (Wait.)
I'll read the item for that number. Follow along, but don't say the answer. (Read the item.) A members, whisper the answer to your partner. (Wait.)

3. The correct answer is ____. B members, raise your hand if your partner got it right. ✔ B members who raised your hand, make a check mark in Box 1 of your partner's scorecard. ✔

4. For remaining turns:
(Pass the dice to the next student.)
Roll the dice and say the number. (Wait.)
I'll read the item. Follow along. (Read the item.) ____ members, whisper the answer. (Wait.)
(Tell the correct answer.) ____ members, make a check mark if your partner got it right. ✔ (Play the game for 20 minutes more, alternating turns for A members and B members.)

Points for Fact Game

1. (At the end of the game:) Raise your hand if you earned 12 or more points. If you earned 12 or more points, you get 5 bonus points.

2. Everybody, write your game points in Box 1 on your Point Chart. Write your bonus points in Box 3. (Check and correct.)

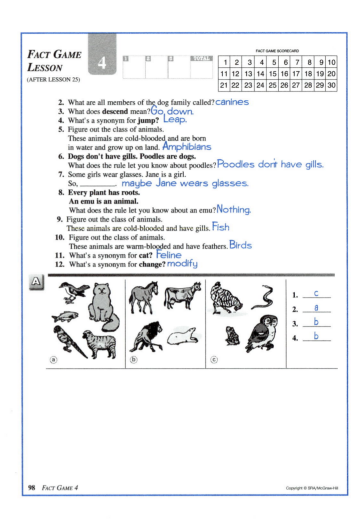

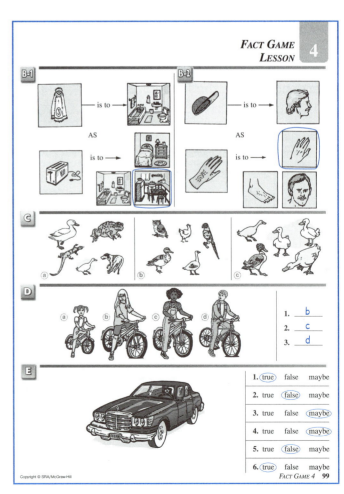

WORKBOOK EXERCISES

==== **EXERCISE 2** ====

TRUE–FALSE

1. Everybody, touch part A in your Workbook. ✔ I'll say statements that are true of one of the pictures. You write the letter of the right picture.

2. Item 1. **None** of the animals are mammals. Write the letter of the picture on line 1. (Wait.) Item 2. **Only some** of the animals are mammals. Write the letter of the picture on line 2. (Wait.)

4. Item 3. **All** of the animals are mammals. Write the letter of the picture on line 3. (Wait.)

5. Item 4. **None** of the animals are birds. Write the letter of the picture on line 4. (Wait.)

6. Let's check your answers. Mark any items you missed with an X. Tell me the letter of the right picture.

7. Item 1. **None** of the animals are mammals. (Signal.) *C.*

8. (Repeat step 7 for items 2–4.)

==== **EXERCISE 3** ====

ANALOGIES

1. Everybody, get ready to complete each analogy when I signal. The first analogy tells where you find objects. Listen. A towel is to a bathroom as a toaster is to a (pause; signal) *kitchen.* (Repeat until firm.)
The next analogy tells what body parts clothing is for. Listen. A hat is to a head as a glove is to a (pause; signal) *hand.* (Repeat until firm.)

2. Touch part B-1 in your Workbook. ✔ That box shows one of the analogies we just said. Touch the right pictures and say the analogy. Get ready. (Signal.) *A towel is to a bathroom as a toaster is to a kitchen.* (Repeat until firm.)
Everybody, which picture completes the analogy? (Signal.) *Kitchen.* Circle the picture of the kitchen. ✔

3. Everybody, touch part B-2 of your Workbook. That box shows the other analogy we just said. Touch the right pictures and say the analogy. Get ready. (Signal.) *A hat is to a head as a glove is to a hand.* (Repeat until firm.)
Everybody, which picture completes the analogy? (Signal.) *Hand.* Circle the picture of the hand. ✔

==== **EXERCISE 4** ====

CLASSIFICATION

Task A

1. Everybody, touch part C in your Workbook. ✔ You're going to work on classification. One of these boxes shows the class of ducks. One of these boxes shows the class of birds. One of these boxes shows the class of animals.

2. You're going to tell me which box shows the class of **ducks:** box A, box B, or box C. (Pause 3 seconds.) Get ready. (Signal.) *Box C.*

3. Now you're going to tell me which box shows the class of **birds.** (Pause 3 seconds.) Get ready. (Signal.) *Box B.*

4. You're going to tell me which box shows the class of **animals.** (Pause 3 seconds.) Get ready. (Signal.) *Box A.*

5. Now let's figure out which of these classes is the biggest. What's the rule about the bigger class? (Signal.) *If a class has more kinds of things, it is bigger.* (Repeat until firm.)

6. Box A shows the class of animals. That means that **all kinds** of animals would be in box A. So, would all birds be in box A? (Signal.) *Yes.*
   To correct students who say *No:*
   a. All birds are animals. Box A shows the class of animals; so all birds **would be** in box A.
   b. (Repeat step 6.)
   Would all ducks be in box A? (Signal.) *Yes.*
   Would animals that are not ducks be in box A? (Signal.) *Yes.*
   (Repeat step 6 until firm.)

Individual test

(Call on three different students. Have each student do steps a, b, and c.)

Note: The students may name animals **not** illustrated.
   a. Name an animal that is **not** a bird. (Praise correct responses; for example, elephant, snake, dog.)
   b. Would that animal be in box A? (Signal.) *Yes.*
   c. Would that animal be in any of the other boxes? (Signal.) *No.*

---

7. Everybody, box A has more **kinds** of things in it. So, which box shows the biggest class? (Signal.) *Box A.*
   Tell me the class **name** for the things in box A. (Pause 3 seconds.) Get ready. (Signal.) *Animals.*
   How do you know that the class of animals is bigger than the other classes? (Signal.) *Because it has more kinds of things.*

Task B

1. Now look at box B and box C and figure out which box has more **kinds** of things. (Pause 4 seconds.) *Box B.*
   And tell me the class **name** for the things in box B. (Pause 3 seconds.) Get ready. (Signal.) *Birds.*

2. I can name some things in the class of birds that **wouldn't** be in the class of ducks. Some of these would be robins, bluejays, and chickens. Everybody, how do you know that the class of birds is bigger than the class of ducks? (Signal.) *Because it has more kinds of things.*

3. Everybody, look at all the boxes and tell me which Box shows the **smallest** class. (Pause.) Get ready. (Signal.) *Box C.*
   Tell me the class **name** for the things in box C. (Pause.) Get ready. (Signal.) *Ducks.*

4. You know that ducks is the smallest class because it has only one kind of thing in it. What kind of thing? (Signal.) *Ducks.* How do you know that ducks is the smallest class? (Signal.) *Because it has only one kind of thing.*

EXERCISE 5

DESCRIPTION

1. Everybody, touch part D in your Workbook. ✔ Figure out which bicycle I describe.
2. Item 1. This bicycle is big. This bicycle has a flat tire. This bicycle has a girl on it. Listen again. (Repeat the description.)
Write the letter for item 1.
3. Item 2. This bicycle is big. This bicycle has a girl on it. This bicycle does not have a flat tire. Listen again. (Repeat the description.)
Write the letter for item 2.
4. Item 3. This bicycle is big. This bicycle has a flat tire. This bicycle does not have a girl on it. Listen again. (Repeat the description.)
Write the letter for item 3.
5. Let's check your answers. Mark any items you missed with an X.
6. Item 1. This bicycle is big. This bicycle has a flat tire. This bicycle has a girl on it. Everybody, what letter? (Signal.) *B.*
7. (Repeat step 6 for items 2 and 3.)

Answer key   2. *C* **3.** *D*

EXERCISE 6

TRUE–FALSE

1. Everybody, touch part E in your Workbook. ✔ I'll say statements about the picture.
2. Get ready to circle **true, false,** or **maybe.** Item 1. The woman is wearing sunglasses. Circle the answer. (Wait.)
3. Item 2. The woman is not driving a car. Circle the answer. (Wait.)
4. Item 3. The woman is going to the store. Circle the answer. (Wait.)
5. Item 4. The woman is not listening to the radio. Circle the answer. (Wait.)
6. Item 5. The woman is not wearing sunglasses. Circle the answer. (Wait.)
7. Item 6. The woman is sitting. Circle the answer. (Wait.)
8. Everybody, let's check your answers. Say **true, false,** or **maybe.**
9. Item 1. The woman is wearing sunglasses. (Signal.) *True.*
10. (Repeat step 9 for items 2–6.)

Answer key   2. *False* **3.** *Maybe* **4.** *Maybe* **5.** *False* **6.** *True*

Points
(Award up to 5 points for Workbooks. Have students record their points in Box 2 and add up their daily total.)

Point Summary Chart
(Tell students to write their point total in the box labeled FG4 on the Point Summary Chart.)

Six-Lesson Point Summary
(Tell students to add the point totals for Lesson 21 through 25 and FG4 on the Point Summary Chart and to write the total for Block 4.)

REMEDIATION AND REVIEW

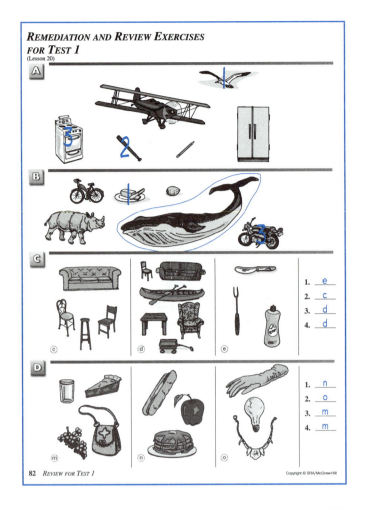

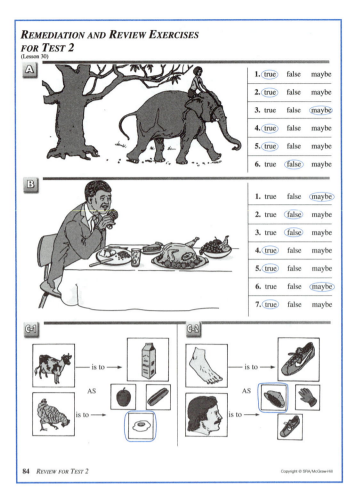

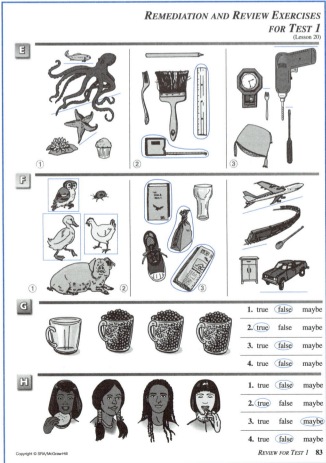

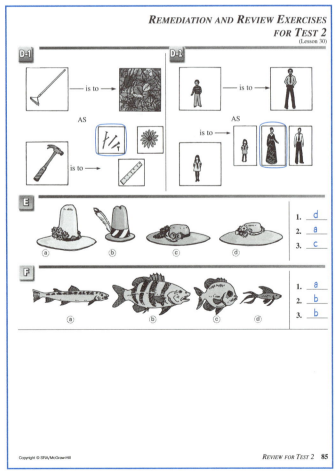